Write Your Way Into Animation and Games

Write Your Way Into Animation and Games

Create a Writing Career in Animation and Games

Christy Marx

Routledge
Taylor & Francis Group

LONDON AND NEW YORK

First published 2010

This edition published 2015 by Focal Press

Published 2017 by Routledge
2 Park Square, Milton Park, Abingdon, Oxon OX14 4RN
711 Third Avenue, New York, NY 10017, USA

First issued in hardback 2017

Routledge is an imprint of the Taylor and Francis Group, an informa business

Notices
Practitioners and researchers must always rely on their own experience and knowledge in evaluating and using any information, methods, compounds, or experiments described herein. In using such information or methods they should be mindful of their own safety and the safety of others, including parties for whom they have a professional responsibility.

Product or corporate names may be trademarks or registered trademarks, and are used only for identification and explanation without intent to infringe.

Library of Congress Cataloging-in-Publication Data
Marx, Christy.
  Write your way into animation and games : create a writing career in animation and games / Christy Marx.
     p. cm.
  Includes bibliographical references and index.
  ISBN 978-0-240-81343-1 (pbk. : alk. paper) 1. Animated films--Authorship. 2. Video games--Authorship I. Title.
  PN1996.M444 2010
  808.2'3--dc22   2009049947

 British Library Cataloguing-in-Publication Data
A catalogue record for this book is available from the British Library.

ISBN 13: 978-1-138-40316-1 (hbk)
ISBN 13: 978-0-240-81343-1 (pbk)

Contents

CONTENTS

vi

The multimedia components for this book can be found by visiting the companion Web site: www.focalpress.com/9780240813431

PART 1
Writing for Animation

INTRODUCTION

Audiovisual storytelling has a long, well-developed history. As far back as the earliest known prehistoric times, human beings have communicated the essence of story through the use of pictures and sound: whether it's cave paintings of the hunt, a poet proclaiming the epic adventures of Odysseus, Greek actors performing tragedy or comedy in an open amphitheatre, or through modern times where this primal form of storytelling is expressed on a digital "stage" through television, film, computers and other gadgets.

To write for the fields of animation and games, we must master the craft of using words to create images and sounds in the mind of the reader. It's a form of storytelling that is both entirely new and essentially ancient. The words we write when working in animation or games aren't intended for the final audience but are interpreted and expressed through the talents of many contributors: concept artists, animators, actors, directors, programmers, game designers, world designers, composers, and others. If you thrive on this sort of collaborative creative effort, you'll enjoy working in animation or games.

First, you must learn your craft and be prepared for whatever opportunities come your way, and that's what this book is designed to do. The authors in this book will present you with a variety of information, experience, and viewpoints. If you like what you read of their contributing chapters, you can seek out their complete books to expand your knowledge and expertise.

In the first half of the book, we'll cover writing for animation. Today, animation is thriving as never before. Television series come in a variety of flavors and styles, ranging from comedy to action, with material for kids and for adults. Increasing numbers of animated features are being released theatrically or as direct-to-video DVDs. There's an international movement for independent animation production that is rich and varied, representing many cultures. Finally, there is the no-holds-barred frontier of the Internet where (for better or worse) anyone can create and post a work of animated storytelling. There are many paths available for the writer who loves the animation medium.

In this half of the book, we'll cover topics such as these:
- Terminology
- Script formats
- Television series
- Features
- Developing characters
- Creating pitch bibles
- Writing comedy
- Making a pitch
- How to find work
- Agents and networking

Two authors share their many years of experience in developing, producing, and writing animation.

Christy Marx, *Writing for Animation, Comics and Games* (ISBN-13: 978-0-240-80582-5)

Christy Marx has spent nearly 30 years developing, story editing, and writing animation series and features. Her experience spans working on 65 half-hour shows for syndication through to network television. She created the cult favorite animation series *Jem and the Holograms*, along with developing, story editing, or writing dozens of animation series such as *Zorro: Generation Z*, *Conan*, *X-Men: Evolution*, *Beast Wars*, *G.I. Joe*, *ReBoot*, *War Planets (Shadow Raiders)*, *Spider-Man*, *He-Man*, *Bucky O'Hare*, and *Teenage Mutant Ninja Turtles*. She was awarded the WGA/Animation Writers Caucus Award for making outstanding contributions to the profession of the animation writer. She contributed Chapters 1, 2, and 8 to this book.

You can learn more about Christy Marx by going to www.christymarx.com.

Jean Ann Wright, *Animation Writing and Development: From Script Development to Pitch* (ISBN-13: 978-0-240-80549-8)

Jean Ann Wright started professionally in the entertainment industry when she was in the fourth grade. Her college degrees are in acting from the Pasadena Playhouse and art from California State University Northridge. Her first job in the animation industry was at Hanna-Barbera as an artist trainee. She worked there for eight years before moving on to work as a freelance animation writer.

Most recently she's had her own business as an animation preproduction consultant, giving advice on developing animated series and films (including character and background design, writing, and recording). She has taught at schools and conferences in the Hollywood area and in Brazil. She's written two books for Focal Press: *Animation Writing and Development* and most recently, with M.J. Lallo, *Voice-Over for Animation*. She did the writing, and Lallo produced a CD to go with the book. Wright is a member of Women in Animation (where she takes part in a voice-over group and serves on the Los Angeles Chapter Steering Committee), the Writer's Guild Animation Caucus, and the Academy of Television Arts and Sciences. She contributed Chapters 3, 4, 5, 6, 7, and 9 to this book.

SECTION 1
The First Things You Need to Know

CHAPTER 1
Animation Terminology

Christy Marx

Most of the scriptwriting terms employed in animation scripts are the same as those employed in live-action scripts, with perhaps a few exceptions. Here are the terms you want to know before we move ahead to discuss script format.

They are followed by a further glossary of animation-related terms that will be useful to you.

SCRIPT TERMS

ACTION

The ACTION, or description, paragraph occurs immediately below the SLUGLINE and is just what you think it is—a line or paragraph that serves any number of functions: to describe a setting or location, to describe what actions the character in the shot is taking, to set mood or tone, to indicate sounds, to give certain specific camera-movement directions, or whatever else is required to convey what the reader needs to know about that shot or for establishing a scene.

ANGLE ON, ANGLE -

A more generic way to call out an individual shot that indicates to the storyboard artist what to concentrate on for this shot, or simply who is in the shot.

DOI: 10.1016/B978-0-240-81343-1.00001-7

```
ANGLE   ON JACK

ANGLE ON JACK, DICK, AND JANE

ANGLE ON CORNER OF WEATHERED BUILDING

ANGLE - JACK

ANGLE - JACK, DICK, AND JANE

ANGLE - BARBARIAN HORDE
```

B.G. (BACKGROUND)

Used to indicate that some part of the action, an object, a character is to be set in the background of the shot. Or you could just be describing something that's in the b.g.

BEAT, A BEAT

This term, set inside parentheses, is used to indicate that you want the character to pause briefly between pieces of dialogue. It can convey hesitation, a moment of thought, a point of emphasis, or a moment of silence (where the character might be listening to someone on the other end of a phone conversation, but we don't hear the other side). (See other uses of the word "beat" under Other Animation Terms at the end of this chapter.)

```
ANGLE ON JACK AND JANE

She glares at him.

                    JANE
          You want me to leave? Fine,
          I'll leave.
             (a beat)
          When I'm good and ready!

ANGLE ON JANE

who answers the phone.

                    JANE
          Hello?
             (beat)
```

```
He did what?
    (beat)
Of all the stupid tricks. Where
are you now?
    (beat)
Stay put. I'm on my way.
```

CLOSE-UP, CLOSE ON

Used in a SLUGLINE to indicate to the storyboard artist that in this shot you want the camera to be very close on a person or thing, as indicated. You should have a solid reason for using a close-up rather than calling for it at random. Good reasons include wanting to emphasize a reaction, to call special attention to an important object, or to make sure the camera is close enough to clearly convey a significant piece of action.

```
CLOSE-UP ON JACK'S EYES

He squints against the painful glare of the sun that
blinds him.

CLOSE ON JACK'S HAND

as he secretly passes a flash drive to Jane.
```

9

CONT'D (CONTINUED)

CONT'D is used in three ways:

1. At the bottom of a page on a shooting script, to indicate that the script continues.
2. When a long chunk of dialogue is broken up across two pages, to indicate there is more dialogue on the following page. In this usage, it's centered in the middle of the dialogue column at the bottom of the page where the dialogue breaks.
3. After a character's name and placed parentheses, to indicate the character is continuing a speech that was begun in another piece of dialogue, but was interrupted by a piece of action. Ellipses are used to further indicate that the dialogue is being broken up and continued.

```
ANGLE FAVORING JACK
                        JACK
              I told you...

Jane reacts with surprise to his anger.

                    JACK (CONT'D)
              ...I don't need your help!
```

CUT TO:

This is a TRANSITION that is used to indicate that this scene is ended and we are cutting to an entirely different scene in a different location. Visually, it means that the image on the screen is instantly gone and instantly replaced by the next image, with no time lag in between the two images. CUT TO: is a general, all-purpose transition, though it's better to use a DISSOLVE TO: to convey a significant passage of time between scenes.

In a script, a transition is positioned along the right margin and is followed by a colon.

DIALOGUE

The DIALOGUE portion of a script consists of the character name and what the character says. There can be a parenthetical below the character name or within the body of the dialogue. There can be special instructions to the right of the character name, such as V.O., O.S., or CONT'D.

The reason for indenting and setting out the dialogue in this way is old and simple: to make it easy for actors to flip through a script and see what their lines are.

In animation, it also makes it easy to count the number of lines, as is sometimes required. NOTE: each individual "chunk" of dialogue is considered to be a "line" of dialogue. In the sample shown below, this would count as two lines of dialogue for Jack, one line of dialogue for Dick, one line of dialogue for Jane (even though all she has for a "line" is a burst of laughter), and one line for Jack's Dog—for a total of five lines. Jane's "line" and the Dog's whine still have to be recorded, and still take up time in the audio track, hence being counted as dialogue.

```
                      JACK
                (annoyed - to Jane)
          Give me one good reason why I
          shouldn't drop-kick you from here
          to tomorrow? Well?
```

```
                    JACK'S DOG
                 (worried whine)

                      JANE
                 (burst of laughter)

                      JACK
        What's that supposed to mean?

                      DICK
        It means you're asking for a
        broken leg, Jack.
                      (a beat)
        Trust me, you want to stay on her
        good side.
```

DISSOLVE TO:

This is a TRANSITION that is used to indicate that this scene is ended and we are cutting to another scene with some amount of time passing between the two scenes. Visually, it indicates that the image on the screen will slowly dissolve, to be replaced by a new image. The time difference between the two scenes could be minutes, hours, days, years, past, or future. A DISSOLVE TO: is more about changing time than changing location. You might dissolve from Jack collapsing in bed in the morning to Jack waking up on the bed at night—same place, different time. It's a gradual transition on the screen rather than the instantaneous transition of a CUT TO:

On occasion, a writer might also use RAPID DISSOLVE TO: (just a faster-than-usual dissolve to indicate a very short passage of time).

In a script, a transition is positioned along the right margin and is followed by a colon.

DURING:

This is a handy word to use to indicate that you want a piece of dialogue to occur while a certain piece of action takes place, without breaking away from the continuous movement of that shot or cutting it down into smaller shots. However, be careful not to use DURING: at times when you *should* break out those actions.

```
ANGLE ON JACK AND DICK

who enter the stairwell and work their way down the
stairs, tense, alert, weapons ready. DURING:

                    JACK
          They could be anywhere around
          here, kid. Don't get careless.
          And don't get nervous. And don't
          get in my way.
```

ECU, EXTREME CLOSE-UP

Just what it sounds like – going very, very close on someone or something in a shot. It can be used in a slugline or used in a shot.

```
ECU ON JANE'S EYES

which brim with tears.

ON JACK'S EYES

Go to ECU to show that Jack is also at the point of
tears.
```

ENTERS FRAME, EXITS FRAME

A command used in the action paragraph when you want to have one or more characters enter or leave the shot after you've established it.

```
INT. BUNGALOW - JACK AND DICK

look over the stolen documents. Jane ENTERS FRAME to
join them. Jack barely glances up at Jane.

                    JACK
          Good, you're here. Get me a glass
          of water.

Fuming, Jane EXITS FRAME. Dick grins and shakes his
head.

                    DICK
          That was a baaaad idea.

Jane ENTERS FRAME and dumps a glass of water on Jack's
head.
```

EST., ESTABLISHING

Used in a SLUGLINE or ACTION PARAGRAPH when you're establishing where a scene is taking place before jumping into the interior action. This works best when the location has already been seen, and only a quick establishing shot is needed to alert the audience that the action is going back to that place. It's like seeing a quick establishing shot of a spaceship before jumping to the bridge or some other room inside the spaceship. Or an exterior shot to establish a well-known city, such as Los Angeles or New York, before jumping to another shot that is then assumed to be somewhere in that city. An establishing shot is usually a wide or long shot.

```
EXT. ESTABLISH OCEAN LINER - DAY

It plies a calm ocean.


EXT. HOLLYWOOD SIGN

just long enough TO ESTABLISH.


EXT. SPACESHIP - DEEP SPACE

Establishing shot.
```

EXT. (EXTERIOR)

EXT. is used at the beginning of a SLUGLINE to establish that this scene or shot is in an exterior location. Because you're establishing a scene, it's also vital to indicate whether it's DAY or NIGHT for the exterior location (with a couple of exceptions, such as space or the bottom of the ocean or someplace where day and night are irrelevant).

```
EXT. AIRPORT CONTROL TOWER - NIGHT

EXT. MEDICAL BUILDING - DAY

EXT. SPACESHIP - DEEP SPACE
```

FADE IN:, FADE OUT

FADE IN: is used to start the script and start each act; FADE OUT is used to end each act and end the script. Most commonly, FADE IN: is on the left margin, FADE OUT is on the right margin. For whatever mysterious reason, FADE IN: is followed by a colon; FADE OUT isn't. FADE IN: should lead directly into the first SLUGLINE. Other information, such as TEASER or ACT ONE, comes before the FADE IN:. FADE OUT comes immediately after the final shot of that act or the script, followed by END OF TEASER, END OF ACT ONE, THE END, and so on.

FAVORING

One way to call out an individual shot in a script once the location or setting is established. This would be the start of a SLUGLINE, followed by the character, object, or whatever it is that you want the storyboard artist to emphasize in that shot. If there are a number of characters in the shot, FAVORING would most commonly be used to indicate that you want emphasis given to a particular character (or to more than one).

```
FAVORING JACK'S HAND

as he reaches out for the crystal skull.

ANGLE FAVORING THE SKULL

Which reflects Jack's reaching hand. The glint of
the ring on Jack's hand creates the illusion of a
glint in the skull's eye.
```

F.G. (FOREGROUND)

Used to indicate that some part of the action, an object, a character is to be set in the foreground of the shot.

INT. (INTERIOR)

INT. is used at the beginning of a SLUGLINE to establish that this scene is in an interior location or set. Generally, you don't need to worry about establishing whether it's a DAY or NIGHT location for interiors unless you haven't established that information previously (such as going from an exterior shot of the same location to an interior shot), and there's some reason that you need to (an airport control tower, for example, where it would be important to indicate what can be seen from the windows).

```
INT. AIRPORT CONTROL TOWER - NIGHT

INT. SUBWAY STATION

INT. SPACESHIP COCKPIT
```

INTERCUT TO, INTERCUTTING TO

Another term that can be used when doing quick cuts back and forth between two ongoing lines of action, or a larger piece of action (such as a battle)—where there might be multiple fronts to deal with or multiple characters to follow, and where everything is happening more or less at the same time. Best used when it doesn't involve dialogue (see also QUICK CUT), but it can also be used when cutting back and forth between people engaged in a phone conversation.

```
INTERCUT TO:

JACK hits the ground and readies his gun.

JANE takes cover behind a metal container, her gun
in hand.

DICK drops from the roof and takes up position
outside a window, a gun in one hand and smoke bomb
in the other.
```

MATCH DISSOLVE TO:

This is a nice visual trick when called for, but don't overuse it. In a MATCH DISSOLVE TO: some element in the scene that is ending will match up to an opening element in the next scene. Obviously, there should be a good thematic or story reason to tie the two elements together.

```
ANGLE ON JACK

who holds up the crystal skull to study it. MOVE IN
on the skull until it fills the screen.

                          MATCH DISSOLVE TO:

CLOSE-UP ON CRYSTAL SKULL

Except that this one is in a display case at the
city museum, labelled "Peruvian Quartz Skull".
```

MOVE IN

This tells the storyboard artist that you want a camera movement that moves in closer to something on the screen. Use in the ACTION (description) paragraph rather than in a SLUGLINE.

```
ANGLE ON WEATHERED BUILDING

A door <BANGS> crazily in the storm wind. MOVE IN on
the door as a hand suddenly grabs the door's edge.
```

(OC), (O.C.)

OFF CAMERA. Same as OFFSTAGE. See below.

(OS), (O.S.)

OFFSTAGE. It's used to the right of the character's name in dialogue to indicate that someone is speaking who is in the scene, but is not seen in that shot.

```
ANGLE FAVORING JACK

who stands by himself, staring moodily out a window.

                        JACK
              Guess I'm on my own.

                       JANE (O.S.)
              Not yet, you old grouch.

Jane ENTERS FRAME to stand next to him.
```

OTS

OVER THE SHOULDER. This tells the storyboard artist to draw the view of the scene as though the camera were seeing it over the shoulder of a particular character.

```
OTS ON JACK

facing Dick and Jane, who wait for him to speak.
```

PAN

Refers to a horizontal camera movement—either from right to left, or from left to right. It's used in the action paragraph and is especially useful when establishing a new location where you want to show more of it or

linger over it for a few seconds more than you would with a quick establishing shot.

```
EXT. SURFACE OF THE MOON - SUNLIT SIDE

PAN ACROSS the stark beauty of sharp-edged craters
until we come to the moon base, a lonely haven on
the airless surface.
```

PARENTHETICALS

A PARENTHETICAL is extra information about the character who is speaking
or making a sound. It's placed inside parentheses below the character's name
in the dialogue. Parentheticals have three basic uses:

1. Indicating a specific tone, emotion, or inflection for the voice actor. This
   is discouraged in live-action scripts, but voice actors often receive only
   their own lines, and record their lines without interacting with the other
   voice actors. Consequently, parentheticals are more commonly used in
   animation scripts to clue in the voice actors to a tone or emotion they
   might otherwise miss.
2. Indicating that the voice needs special filtering or modification in editing (as in a voice coming through a communications device).
3. Describing a sound you want the voice actor to make, especially in the
   case of a nonspeaking character or creature. Even if you want a character
   only to laugh or scream, you need to cover it as a piece of dialogue by
   using a parenthetical. You would also use the parenthetical to indicate a
   whisper or low voice (sotto voce).

```
ANGLE FAVORING JACK
                    JACK
              (sarcastic)
         Oh, that's just great.

                 JACK'S DOG
            (scolding barks)

                    JACK
              (with a snort)
         Everybody's got an opinion around
         here.
                 (laughter)
```

17

POV

POINT OF VIEW. In this type of shot, you're asking the storyboard artist to draw the scene from a specific character's point of view, to see the scene the way the character is seeing it.

```
JACK'S POV - THROUGH WINDOW

The thick glass distorts what he sees so that all
he can make out is the dark, indistinct shape of an
unknown person.


JANE'S POV - THROUGH SCOPE

The crosshairs in the scope focus on an enemy
vehicle. The scope's laser indicator LIGHTS UP.
```

PULL BACK, PULL BACK TO REVEAL

As with MOVE IN, this tells the storyboard artist that you want a camera movement that pulls the camera farther away from the shot or from something in the shot. See also WIDEN.

```
CLOSE ON CRYSTAL SKULL

held in a man's hand, but we PULL BACK TO REVEAL
it's held by Dick instead of Jack.
```

QUICK CUT

This is a method of intercutting (cutting back and forth) between quickly paced shots that may or may not be in the same location, but are occurring more or less instantaneously or in very quick sequence. It's especially useful in an action sequence, such as a battle, where you've already established where the characters are and basically what's going on, but you need to jump around a lot. It saves having to use space-eating CUT TO: transitions where they aren't really needed.

```
ANGLE ON JACK

settled into position. Satisfied everything's ready,
he talks into his commlink.
                        JACK
                  (into commlink)
              This is it. Countdown!

QUICK CUT - JANE
                        JANE
                  (into commlink)
              Three!

QUICK CUT - DICK
                        DICK
                  (into commlink)
              Two!

QUICK CUT BACK TO JACK
                        JACK
                  (into commlink)
              One! Hit it!

He charges forward!
```

19

SCENE HEADING (SEE SLUGLINE)

(SFX:)

SOUND EFFECTS. This method of specifically notating a sound effect using (SFX:) was more prevalent in animation scripts earlier than it is now. What has become common is to call attention to a specific sound by putting the sound in CAPS. Depending on the preferences of the story editor, some scripts will make the sound effects in **bold**, in capital letters, or will add carets around the sound: <CAPS>. Adding the carets helps draw attention to the sound.

The original intent of using (SFX:) was to make it easier for a sound editor to find the sounds he or she needed to know about. I've dropped the use of (SFX:) in favor of the other two methods. Here are examples of three ways to indicate sound effects:

```
WIDE SHOT ON ENEMY TANK

It's hit by Jane's laser beam and <EXPLODES MASSIVELY>!
```

or

```
WIDE SHOT ON ENEMY TANK

It's hit by Jane's laser beam and EXPLODES MASSIVELY!
```

or

```
WIDE SHOT ON ENEMY TANK

As it is hit by Jane's laser beam and explodes!(SFX:
massive metallic explosion)
```

SLUGLINE

A slugline is always typed in CAPS. The slugline immediately informs the reader that this is a new scene or a new shot. In animation, every individual shot needs to be set up with a slugline. A slugline should never be more than a few words, only the bare minimum necessary to establish who, what, or where. Anytime a script transitions to a different scene or location, the slugline needs to begin with an EXT. or INT. In some current scriptwriting software, SLUGLINE is instead called SCENE HEADING.

SOTTO VOCE

Latin for "low voice." Nowadays, many writers simply write "low voice" or "under his breath" instead. It means just what it says, that the character should speak in a low-volume voice as though not wanting to be overheard—which is different from speaking in a whisper. This falls into the category of being a parenthetical, which is voice direction for the actor.

```
                         JACK
                      (low voice)
                 Do you think she heard us?
```

TRACK WITH

This is used in the action paragraph when you want to have a shot that follows a particular character, vehicle, or object while in motion.

```
INSIDE MEDICAL LAB - JACK

enters stealthily. TRACK WITH HIM as he moves
silently across the lab to a table of virus samples.
```

TRANSITIONS

Transitions are a way of telling the reader and the editor—and ultimately, the viewer—that the story is shifting from one time or place to another. The three most common transitions are CUT TO:, DISSOLVE TO:, and WIPE TO:. A show can have specialized transitions. *X-Men: Evolution* had an X-WIPE TO:. Why? Just for fun, really. There are endless variations on transitions—such as DISSOLVE THRU TO: (as in moving through a wall to see what's inside), RIPPLE DISSOLVE: (in which a ripple effect is used), RAPID DISSOLVE TO: (just a faster-than-usual dissolve to indicate a very short passage of time), FLASH CUT TO:, INTERCUT TO:, and on occasion, I've seen a writer invent weird and meaningless transitions simply to mess with the artists' heads. I prefer to keep it simple. CUT, DISSOLVE, and WIPE work fine 99 percent of the time.

Over the years, I've seen a trend in animation scripts toward doing away with transitions almost completely. The main reason for this is to save the three lines that would be used for a transition so that those lines are available for the other parts of the script. In other words, it's a space-saving cheat. I don't recommend using this cheat for spec scripts or when first breaking in, but I also don't recommend going overboard with excessive transitions. Use them only when really needed for a major scene or location shift.

In a script, transitions are positioned along the right margin and are followed by a colon.

21

TWO-SHOT, 2SHOT, 2S

Used in a SLUGLINE to indicate a medium shot, meaning the camera moves in close enough to frame two characters fairly tightly. It's more commonly used in live-action scripts than in animation. I include it mainly in case you run across it somewhere.

(VO), (V.O.)

VOICE-OVER. This is placed to the right of the character's name in dialogue to indicate that the voice being heard is coming from some other location, and that the character is not present in the scene or the shot—such as a voice coming over a phone or communications device. One exception to the rule of the character not being in the scene would be narration where you want to hear the character narrating a piece of the story rather than speaking in dialogue. The narration could be done with the character relating the story as a flashback, or it might be done with the viewer hearing the character's thoughts.

```
EXT. CITY STREET - NIGHT

Rain drenches the desolate street. Jack comes into
view under a streetlamp, a long figure hunched
inside a dripping wet coat. He looks thoroughly
miserable.

                    JACK (V.O.)
                  (narrating)
              It began on one of the most
              miserable nights of my life.

A cell phone <BEEPS> in his pocket. With no great
enthusiasm, he pulls it out and answers.

                    JACK
                  (into phone)
              Yeah?

                    JANE (V.O.)
                  (via phone)
              If this is Jack, I have an offer
              for you.
```

WALLA

An old script term to indicate general crowd or background voice noise. Typical walla would be the murmur of a crowd before the concert begins, the angry noises of a mob, background chatter at a party. It's never used for individual dialogue. It's written as a parenthetical.

```
                    MOB
                  (angry walla)

                    CONCERT AUDIENCE
                  (walla)
```

WIDE SHOT

Used in a SLUGLINE. Pretty much self-explanatory. Use it when the shot requires seeing a wider view of what's going on.

```
WIDE SHOT - A LINE OF ENEMY TANKS

<RUMBLES> toward the camera.
```

WIDEN, WIDEN TO INCLUDE

This is used in the action paragraph to indicate to the storyboard artist a camera move to widen the frame of the shot to include something else. It's similar to a PULL BACK, but usually indicates widening the frame to include something to the left or right, rather than overall.

```
ANGLE ON JACK

who kneels to examine prints on the dusty floor.
WIDEN TO INCLUDE JANE as she kneels down beside him.
```

WIPE TO:

A transition that is used to convey a change in location, but not time. Use a WIPE TO: when the new scene could be taking place concurrently with the scene that just ended, or immediately after it. The visual swiping effect of a WIPE TO: suggests immediacy, rather than a passage of time between scenes. It says to the eye that "we've whipped from here to there." In a script, a transition is positioned along the right margin and is followed by a colon.

23

OTHER ANIMATION TERMS
2D, 3D (CG)

2D = two-dimensional—traditional cel animation that is drawn or painted. 3D = three-dimensional, also called CGI (computer-generated images), or CG for short. This is animation created using computer software in which the characters and sets are created as 3D models, allowing the camera to move freely around them from any angle. Besides the fully 3D look, CG can be modified to superficially look like 2D cel animation, while retaining the capability of making 3D movements.

ACT BREAK

The point in a television script where you end the act to provide for commercials.

BACKGROUNDS

In 2D, the background is a drawing or painting that is used behind the animated characters as the shot requires. It's important to understand that a background is different from a location. For example, let's say that in the script, you've asked for a location that is the interior of a bus terminal. In your mind, you might think *INT. BUS TERMINAL = one background*. That depends on what action you've written for that bus terminal. If your character enters, walks past a wall lined with seats, buys a ticket at the ticket window, then looks out a window while waiting for the bus to pull up, you've created at least four backgrounds: (1) entrance to terminal, (2) wall of seats, (3) ticket window, and (4) window to the outside. The number of backgrounds that need to be designed and created affects both schedule and cost.

In 3D, the bus terminal is constructed in the computer, but the CG artist might construct only whatever part of it is necessary. If a full 3D effect is wanted (as in being able to move around the room in any direction), then the entire location will be constructed, which again affects the schedule and the cost.

BACKSTORY

A term for the story that takes place before the time your script or series begins. It could be an origin story, a series of events leading up to the opening of the series, an epic history, a personal biography—whatever leads up to the current moment of the story you're telling. The backstory may or may not ever be related within the series or the movie, but you need to know the backstories of your world, your characters, and your current story in order to have the richness and depth a good story requires.

BEATS

A "beat" within a script relates specifically to a pause in dialogue, but there are many other uses of a beat or beats in the writing process; especially during the outline stage, where you're establishing the structure of the story. If you imagine that you're working out the structure of your story on 3 × 5 inch index cards, then each card would have a notation for a key scene to cover your major plot points, your major action moments, your important emotional moments, and so forth. Each index card is a beat, and the sequential beats are the structure of your story. I will often work out the beats of my story using pen and paper, simply because that method somehow feels more comfortable. Then I go to the computer to put the flesh on the bones until I have an outline.

BIBLE

The show bible—or series bible, or just "the bible"—refers to the development document that was written before the show went into production. A bible contains all the information about the concept, character biographies, character relationships, setting, vehicles, weapons, what a story editor does or doesn't want to have pitched, or any other details that a writer needs to know in order to write for the show. Ideally, a bible is added to, and updated throughout, the course of a series. For details on creating a bible, see Chapter 8 *Breaking and Entering.*

BUMPERS

These are very short pieces of animation, only a few seconds long, which are inserted at the end of acts and at the beginning of acts to create a distinct transition between the show and the commercials. Their purpose, supposedly, is to make it obvious to the kids that the show is stopping at this point and starting at this other point, and that whatever comes in between isn't part of the show. At one time, there were advocacy groups complaining that kids had trouble discerning the difference between the show and the commercials, hence the bumpers.

You as the writer do not have to be concerned about bumpers or include indications for them in your scripts. It's strictly a production element.

CEL

Short for cellulose acetate. Each cel is a clear plastic sheet of acetate (an average size being 12 ½ inches × 10 ½ inches) on which the characters or objects to be animated are painted. The cel is then laid over a background and photographed to complete a single frame of film. One cel = one frame. In full animation, twenty-four frames = one second of animation. Sadly, the new digital methods of creating animation are making this traditional method of cel animation obsolete and original cels will become rare collector items.

CHARACTER ARC

This is a common term used when talking about how a character will begin, develop, and change over the course of time. That time could be one episode, one movie, or an entire series. It's easier to create a strong character arc for a character in a feature, which runs longer and is usually self-contained (unless it's a trilogy or series). It's trickier to come up with good character arcs over the course of a continuing, episodic series. If your character never changes at all, never has insights or losses or gains, you have a boring character. But a character who reaches the end of his or her arc before a series ends can cause you all sorts of other problems. If his or her arc is resolved, where do you take the character next? Is there a new arc? Is the character played out and no longer useful to the series?

Obviously, this isn't much of an issue for comedy shows. You don't really expect Bart Simpson to have a character arc. He is what he is, and his inherent nature drives the gags. Character arc applies to shows that rely on some level of continuity in the stories.

EXAMPLE

Jack begins as a loner, unwilling to make friends. During the course of the series, he is forced to ally himself with Dick and Jane in order to achieve his goals. He is indifferent toward them at first, but as they face danger and adventures together, Jack comes to realize the importance of friendship. At the climax, Jack is willing to put his own life on the line to save his friends.

HIGH CONCEPT

This term is commonly used throughout the film and television industry. It means that the underlying concept that is being pitched is strong enough, or quirky enough, or has a good enough, hook that it can be summed up in one sentence that sells the idea. Here are some examples of high concept:

- A man trapped in a high-rise office building, unarmed and barefoot, must single-handedly defeat a group of terrorists to save his wife.
- A little boy who can see dead people gets help from a doctor who doesn't realize that he himself is a ghost.
- An ogre becomes human to win back the princess he loves, only to find that she prefers the ogre.

LIMITED ANIMATION

Animation produced using fewer than twenty-four frames per second, or other production shortcuts. See "SHOT ON THREES," "SHOT ON TWOS" for more details.

MODELS ("ON MODEL")

Refers to the drawings that are done of the characters, locations, or major props to pin down exactly how they should look consistently from show to show. If a character that should be short is suddenly tall, the character is no longer "on model."

"SHOT ON THREES," "SHOT ON TWOS"

The standard frame rate for anything that is shot on film is twenty-four frames per second (fps) because this is the rate that tricks the eye into seeing twenty-four still shots as being in fluid motion when run at the proper rate of speed. In digital, the higher-calibre videocameras emulate twenty-four fps. In 2D animation, the only way to achieve truly comparable, fluid motion is to use twenty-four fps, but this is expensive and time-consuming because one has to create twenty-four unique cels of animation for each second of the show. To cut budget and production time, lesser-quality animation may use twelve fps or only eight fps. This is achieved by using the same cel for two frames instead of one, or using the same cel for three frames instead of one. It can go even higher than that, but the quality of the animation suffers drastically. Anime is commonly shot on threes.

SIDES

"Sides" is a term that refers to sample dialogue (a hefty paragraph's worth) for characters that need to be cast. The dialogue should capture the personality and speech patterns of the characters. Sides are then given to the actors who are auditioning for those roles.

SPEC SCRIPT

This is a script written on speculation, not for money or on an assignment. For more details on spec scripts, see Chapter 8 *Breaking and Entering*.

STORY ARC

Story arc is another way of laying out the beginning, middle, and end of your story, but in episodic television, it can apply to the overall story thread that runs through a group of episodes. Arcs can encompass anything from a single episode to any number of seasons. It's difficult to lay in a big story arc for a kids' animated series because the general preference in this field is to have "stand-alone" stories that don't have to be aired in any particular sequence. This makes it easier to strip the show for syndication (meaning the episodes air each day of the week at the same time, a "strip" of syndication).

STORYBOARDS

An artist's rendering in pencil or pen (usually black-and-white, rarely in color) onto a series of panels to approximate what the composition, angle, and movement within the frame will be for each shot of animation. The storyboard shows what the visual sequence of the entire episode or movie will be. Dialogue and sound effects from the script are placed beneath the shots where the dialogue and sound should occur. The storyboard is used as the guide for all further artwork and production in creating that piece of animation, as well as providing an early indication of whether the script is too long or too short.

TAG

A short scene that is used to wrap up the end of a TV episode. It occurs after the final set of commercials and before the closing credits.

TEASER

A short scene that opens a TV episode in some exciting way that snags the viewers' attention so they'll return to watch the rest of the show after the opening credits and first set of commercials.

CHAPTER 2
The Basics

Christy Marx

This section covers the fundamentals of how animation is created; the format of a premise, an outline, and an animation script for television; and information about feature-film animation writing. After that, we get into "Beyond the Basics," where I give additional tips, tricks, and advice.

THE ANIMATION PROCESS

Many books have been written that cover the animation process from beginning to end. Unless you work up to a position of producer, most of these steps don't have much effect on writing the script. To be thorough, here is a brief description of the process by which animation is created for television:

- DEVELOPMENT: The concept is born, whether it's an idea pitched by someone from the inside, developed by a producer on the inside, or adapted from an acquired property (such as a comic or game). Someone is hired to write the bible and a pilot episode. For details on writing an animation bible, see Chapter 8. Development can go on for a long time until the concept is either approved and moved into production, or killed.
- SCRIPT: A story editor is hired (unless the producer fills this role), who in turn hires writers and has scripts written.
- VOICE RECORDING: The scripts are sent to a voice director, and the dialogue is recorded. The storyboards and animation must be matched to these dialogue audio tracks.
- STORYBOARDS: The final, approved scripts are given to storyboard artists to break into storyboards, which become the primary template for

DOI: 10.1016/B978-0-240-81343-1.00002-9

the rest of the animation process. Directors time the storyboards to arrive at an estimate of running time.

- BACKGROUNDS AND CHARACTER DESIGN: Usually at the same time as storyboards are being done, a production designer or art director will be designing the look of the show, the major backgrounds, and the major characters, creating model sheets to be used as the template by all other artists and animators. Additional model sheets will be created for new characters, creatures, props, specialized effects, or what have you for the individual shows. Something called a Special Pose is a model sheet for an established character wearing an outfit that hasn't been seen on that character before.
- ANIMATIC: An animatic is a very roughly animated storyboard (sometimes also called a leica reel or a pencil test), edited with the vocal track, which is used to judge the timing and length of a show. It's also a good place to catch errors that need fixing before the animatic and other art is shipped overseas to complete the animation.
- ANIMATION PRODUCTION: For a 2D show, this is the process of painting the backgrounds, inking the cels of the moving elements, painting the cels, and shooting the cels to create the moving animation. Virtually all 2D animation for the United States is sent to studios in Canada, Japan, Korea, Australia, India, France, and elsewhere. For a 3D show, it goes to the CG studio, where the background and all the elements are created on computers using 3D software. Much of the CG work is being done in Canada, Hong Kong, and India.
- POSTPRODUCTION: The completed animation comes back so that the producer and directors can check for errors, do color correction, fix pacing or timing problems, and send problems or errors back to the animators for retakes (fixing the errors). Once the retakes are done, the dialogue, sound effects, music, titles, and other elements are edited together to create the completed show.

As you can see from this, there is only one step of the process where the writer is involved, and that's early on. You might, on occasion, get a chance to look at storyboards if you ask for them. Most production companies won't think of sending storyboards to writers, but anytime I've asked for them, the company has been willing to send them. By studying storyboards of your own scripts, you may be able to pick up on areas where you can improve your storytelling or writing skills.

THE SCRIPT PROCESS

The script process I'm covering here is for television. Feature-animation development happens on a longer schedule, and the process will vary from studio to studio (see section on feature scripts – The Animated Feature Film – later in this chapter).

With a few rare exceptions, it all begins with the script. An animation script is usually created in a series of stages:

- Springboard (not as common)
- Premise
- Outline
- First draft
- Second draft
- Polish

I'm going to use as an example a produced half-hour script from *X-Men: Evolution*, cowritten with my partner, Randy Littlejohn. The episode was titled "Spykecam," and featured the skateboarding character Spyke.

The Springboard

A springboard should be no more than a few sentences with just a very basic concept for a story idea. If we had written a springboard for "Spykecam," it would have been something like this: "Spyke is given a class assignment to make a documentary about his family . . . just as Sabretooth decides to attack the X-Men."

When there are a lot of stories already pitched to a series, a story editor may ask for springboards. This keeps the writers from having to do too much development when the odds are high that an idea may have already been done. If the story editor sees something interesting that hasn't been done, he or she can then have the writer work it into a premise.

Note that all scriptwriting—including springboards, premises, and outlines—is written in present tense.

The Premise

A premise must contain the beginning, middle, and end of the story in concise form, but with enough detail to sell the idea. There are two different methods of developing premises: outside pitches or internal development.

OUTSIDE PITCHES: The first step, of course, is being invited to pitch. Story editors will not accept unsolicited pitches. On most shows, you'll receive the show bible and other material to work from. If it's a brand-new show, you should also get the pilot script. If the show's been on for a while, try to get a synopsis list of all the episodes approved or produced so far. This will save you from pitching something that has already been approved or done. Be very familiar with an established show before pitching for it.

Unless told otherwise, you should come up with three to six premises to submit. Try to keep it within that range. Fewer than three doesn't make much of an impression, but more than six is getting to be too much.

Submit the written pitches as quickly as you can (these days, usually by email), because you're in competition with other writers, and inevitably more than one writer will submit similar or the same ideas. Being the first one to submit an idea gives you an edge, though a story editor may go with someone who came up with the best take on the idea, rather than whoever submitted the concept first.

INTERNAL DEVELOPMENT: On some series, it works out better for the producer, story editor, or others at the production company to come up with the story ideas first, then hand them out to writers. Most commonly, these will be springboards, and you'll be asked to develop them into a premise first.

LENGTH: For a half-hour show, a premise should consist of not much more than two double-spaced pages or one single-spaced page. The premise doesn't have to be broken into acts, but it's a good idea to do so if you're writing a longer, more detailed premise.

THE "A" STORY AND THE "B" STORY: The main plot is called the "A" story. Most of the time, you're expected to also have a "B" story. The "B" story is a smaller subplot that parallels and intersects with the "A" story. It usually involves characters different from those used in the "A" story (because those characters are busy dealing with the main plotline), and often tends to reinforce the theme of the "A" story. For example: X character is wrongly put in jail. X's friends try to prove his innocence (the "A" story). Meanwhile, X might have an encounter in the jail (the "B" story) that gives him an insight regarding his situation.

Or you might start with all your characters involved in the "A" story and need to spin off a couple of them into a "B" story. For example, a team of heroes needs to attack a stronghold. The main attack is the "A" story, but two of the heroes (the "B" story) are separated during the action and face a different danger that tests their loyalty to the rest of the team.

The "B" story can directly tie into the "A" story or have a more indirect effect. Sometimes the "B" story provides a complication or obstacle for some part of the "A" story. For example, your hero learns that his car is wired to explode and he has one hour to defuse it (the "A" story), but a car thief makes off with the car (the "B" story). The main story is the hero having to find the car in time, while your subplot revolves around the unlucky thief who is unaware he's driving a ticking bomb.

Once in a while, you might even insert a third thread, a "C" story. This can be tricky when you have only twenty-two minutes to tell a story, but it can be done if the plot threads are simple enough.

Here is the premise for "Spykecam":

X-MEN: EVOLUTION
Spykecam (Premise)

by Christy Marx & Randy Littlejohn

Mr. Vandermeer is at his wit's end trying to get Evan to do an actual book report; that is, one based on the *book*, not the movie version of the book (no, there are no musical numbers in the original version of *Les Misérables*). Claiming he wants to put Evan's media mania to good use, Mr. Vandermeer arranges for Evan to participate in an NPR-style "day in the life" visual journal. Evan gets a cool, hi-tech camcorder, and is told to record every aspect of his life for a few days for a TV show on today's American teenagers. A new Spielberg is born!

Evan thinks this is the coolest thing ever, but his constant in-your-face camera is driving his teammates and friends crazy. He's following them around the halls of the school, recording every little deed and misdeed . . . with the exception of the Toad, who desperately wants to be on film and is edited out constantly. The Toad threatens to get even. Mystique doesn't miss any of this action either. In a disguised form, she gives Evan encouragement and reminds him to get plenty of tape of his home life as well, to "balance" things out.

At the Xavier Mansion, Evan rolls tape with abandon: not only does he tape normal stuff, like Institute defense drills and Xavier operating Cerebro, but Kitty and Rogue have a mutant-style tiff over their musical differences, and Evan gets it all. Kurt stages some swashbuckling action and teleports himself and Scott into the Danger Room for the "action sequence," but Scott loses his shades, making the sequence a bit too hairy for their taste. Jean is caught using her powers to do an extra-fast cleanup in the kitchen, and when she realizes Evan is taping her—CRASH!!! She lets her power lapse, and half the kitchenware is in pieces.

The kids, all annoyed, chase Evan outside, planning to make him eat his blasted camera. But this is what Mystique's crew has been waiting for. Leaping onto the grounds, they attack our heroes in a spectacular frenzy that is actually a diversion—in the ruckus, Toad manages to switch Evan's camera with a duplicate before the villains flee.

Prof. X is concerned and has a heart-to-heart with Evan. The boy glumly admits he knows he can't use any of his cool footage . . . but he has to turn in SOMETHING. Maybe some judicious editing . . . but when he hits "playback," there's just footage of the Toad having what he thinks is that last laugh. Mystique's crew has made off with a videotape detailing some of the Institute's most closely guarded secrets! The X-Men must rush to track down Toad and the others and recover the videotape before Mystique gets information that could seriously endanger them all!

33

The Outline

With luck, the premise is approved, though there may be notes and changes as required by the story editor or producer. It would be extremely unusual to rewrite a premise. Instead, you'll take the notes into account when you write the outline.

An outline is usually a beat-by-beat description of the script, broken into the necessary number of acts, with the major sluglines (interiors and exteriors) indicated. I say *usually*, because you will write the outline according to what the story editor wants, and I know at least one story editor who hates the beat-by-beat format. Instead, you may be instructed to write it as straight descriptive prose without EXT. or INT. sluglines.

Either way, the outline should convey enough information for the story editor and production people to know how many locations there are, how many locations are new (requiring new background art), and other production items that may need to be taken into account even before getting to script.

A half-hour script that has a teaser and two or three acts should be broken out as "Teaser," "Act 1," "Act 2," "Act 3," and so on, but you don't need to include fade-ins, or fade-outs, or transitions.

An outline is written single-spaced in most instances (unless a story editor specifies otherwise). The length of an outline will vary. An outline for a half-hour episode normally runs around five to eight pages, depending on how detailed you get. I've done outlines as short as two to three pages (single-spaced), and up to eighteen (when they wanted it double-spaced). If you're working on a series, the story editor should give you some guidelines for the length of the outline. If not, ask the editor what length he or she would like to see, or get some already-completed outlines to look at.

A good outline should cover everything that will be in the script in quick descriptive passages, minus actual dialogue. It's alright to indicate joke lines, or even to include one or two actual lines, of dialogue within the body of the outline (not broken out in dialogue format, as you would do in a script), but generally speaking, you should not put actual dialogue into an outline.

You need to be sure you cover all the action beats, the essence of what the characters are saying to one another, the humor beats (if any), the emotional beats, and whatever else is crucial to conveying what will be in the script.

In the live-action world, the word *treatment* is used instead of outline. A treatment can be anything from a detailed outline to a shorter summary of the story.

You should be allowed a week to write an outline. If the schedule is very tight, you may be asked to turn an outline around in as little as three days.

In the outline for "Spykecam" we already had one large change from the premise—instead of having Mystique as the villain, we were asked to use Sabretooth. The "A" story remains the same—Spyke has to make a video about family. The "B" story is Sabretooth stalking Spyke to get at Logan. And we also had a "C" story, the rivalry between Kitty and Rogue. The "B" story intersects with the "A" story, but doesn't resolve it. The "C" story is resolved by the "A" story. You will find this outline available at *www.christymarx.info*.

The next step will be to get notes on the outline. The story editor might let you go directly to script, or might ask you to rewrite the outline before giving you the go-ahead to write the script. That will depend on the nature of the notes, how comfortable the story editor is with your ability, and what his or her schedule allows. A story editor on a very tight schedule might even present you with his or her rewrite of the outline and have you go to script from that, simply because it can be faster for the editor to do the rewrite than to give you notes.

One rewrite of an outline is perfectly reasonable; a second rewrite would be unusual but okay. Multiple requests for outline rewrites are not reasonable, unless you're very, very new and the story editor is doing you a favor by mentoring you. In that case, do the rewrites.

If you make it past the outline stage, you go to script.

THE SCRIPT FORMAT

There are significant differences between an animation script and a live-action script. I have also written in "hybrid" formats that are somewhere halfway between animation and live action (more on this under Difference No. 1). There is no one single, absolute, unvarying script format for either animation or live action. However, there are some basic rules. The key things you need to know are how to lay out the page (margins, spacing, indents) and how to use the five basic elements from which every script is built:

SLUGLINES / SCENE HEADINGS
ACTION DESCRIPTION
DIALOGUE
PARENTHETICALS
TRANSITIONS

It's rather like someone handing you a set of five tools from which you can build anything from a 5-minute skit to an epic 3-hour movie. What makes you stand out as a writer is how you use those tools to create an exciting, evocative read that conveys the images and emotions you want the reader to experience.

Too often, I see newer writers obsess over the tools of a script. Know the basic rules, but then make them serve your purpose. The script must look professional, but ultimately the quality of the script is what gets you a sale, not how prettily your slugline or action or dialogue is arranged on the page.

If you don't know how the tools work, read the previous chapter on script terms for definitions and examples.

The Basic Layout

As far as margins, spacing, indents, and font, animation and live-action scripts are basically the same.

A standard layout for a script page is:

SPACING: Double-spaced for everything except the dialogue and action description.

FONT: 12-point Courier font. For emphasis on a word, use either CAPS or underlining. Don't use *italics* or **bold.**

MARGINS: 1.5" (one and a half inches) for the left margin (the extra half inch allows room for the binding), 1" (one inch) for the right, top, and bottom margins.

INDENTS:

SLUGLINES, ACTION are on the left margin.

CHARACTER NAME is 2" (two inches) from the left margin, 1" (one inch) from the right margin.

PARENTHETICAL is 1.5" (one and a half inches) from the left margin, 2" (two inches) from the right margin.

DIALOGUE is 1" (one inch) from the left margin, 1.5" (one and a half inches) from the right margin.

TRANSITIONS are aligned to the right margin; or 4" (four inches) from the left margin.

NUMBERING: Page number in the upper right corner, except on the cover page. You can leave it off the first page of the script as well.

ACT BREAKS: Begin each act on a new page.

You won't get into trouble using this basic layout. You may, however, encounter a company or a story editor who has a specific template that he or she wants you to use. In that case, the editor will have to provide you with the template or give you the specific parameters. These vary only slightly from the format given above (maybe half an inch this way or that), but the layout on the page will look the same. Obviously, you use whatever parameters you're told to use.

Otherwise, use the parameters given here. If you're using scriptwriting software, it will set the standard parameters for you.

The Title Page

If this is a spec script, your title page should contain the name of the series, below that the title of the script, below that "written by Your Name." This should be centered and in the upper one-third of the page. At the bottom of the page, aligned to the right, put the name and contact info for your agent (if you have one), or your own contact information. I do not recommend putting a copyright notice or WGA registration info on the title page of a spec script. Many people consider that the mark of an insecure amateur.

If you're working on a show, you'll see an example of what information the company wants, but generally that's going to be the name of the series, title of the episode, the episode production number, your name—centered and placed as described above. The company may want a date, and usually they'll want the copyright and the company's name centered along the bottom. You don't need to put contact info on this type of script, because you're already doing it under a contract.

COVERS: Most of the time when hired to work on a show, you'll be turning in an electronic version of the script. For a spec script, put on covers (front and back) mainly to keep the script intact, and fasten it with two brass brads (that way, if the script needs to be taken apart and photocopied, there are only two brads to deal with rather than three). Avoid ridiculous colors or patterns or outlandish finish for the covers, and don't go any heavier than 20-lb. stock (many readers like to fold over the pages as they read, and you don't want a cover that is an obstacle). Bizarre covers won't do you any good or garner special attention (except maybe to look silly). What matters is what's *between* the covers.

THE DIFFERENCES

That's how live-action and television animation scripts are the same. Now let's get into how they're different.

Difference No. 1: Calling Out the Shots

A live-action script uses "master scenes." This means that a slugline establishes the location, but the rest of the action and dialogue is laid out without specifying the individual shots. In fact, that's strongly discouraged in a live-action script, because deciding on the shots and angles is the turf of the director. It's the live-action director who translates the script into the final visuals.

A television animation script is exactly the opposite. The person who interprets your script and turns it into visual form is the storyboard artist. As an animation writer, you are expected to call out (specify) *every single shot*. You're storyboarding as you write. You decide how to open each scene and what is in every shot in the scene in order to convey your action and dialogue. You decide the pacing. You decide what the visuals will be. A good storyboard artist may tweak what you've done, but it's still up to you to call out every shot.

An animation writer must be able to clearly visualize the script *as animation*. This is where watching a lot of animation becomes valuable. Some things that you can do in a fully animated feature you can't do in a half-hour TV series episode, due to time and budget constraints for TV. You need to be familiar with the look and techniques of the type of animation for which you're writing. Some things that you can do with 3D (such as swooping around in a 360-degree circle) you can't do in 2D. Many of the techniques developed for anime have less to do with creating a style than with finding ways to do animation on a tight budget, such as the "speed lines" background to indicate movement rather than showing a background speeding past. You need to study and be aware of how a story is visually told shot by shot in animation before you can re-create that in a script.

I developed and was story editor on a half-hour kids' series called *Hypernauts*, which was primarily live action, but featured a substantial amount of CG. We wrote the live-action parts in live-action format, and the CG portions in animation format, which led to scripts that were slightly longer than the live-action that people were accustomed to seeing. Because I was familiar with how both formats paced in airtime, I was able to arrive by instinct at a correct page length for that hybrid style of script, which came out to about twenty-four to twenty-six pages for twenty-two minutes of airtime.

Here are two examples of the same scene: as it would be laid out for a live-action script, and then as it would be broken out for an animation script. First, live action:

```
INT. JACK'S HOUSE

Jack stands with folded arms watching as Dick and
Jane take in his shabby surroundings.

                    JACK
          You said you have a proposition.
          Start talking.

Jane notices something unusual and goes over to it.
It's a CRYSTAL SKULL. She picks it up and looks at
it with wonder.

                    JANE
          How did you get this?

                    JACK
          Long story.

                    DICK
          If I didn't know better, I'd say
          it was stolen.

Jack scowls at him. He goes over to Jane and takes
the skull away from her. He plunks it back down
where it was.
```

```
                    JACK
     Well, you don't know better. You
     don't know Jack, as the saying
     goes. You're wasting my time, and
     I don't like people who waste my
     time.

                    JANE
     I think you don't like people,
     period.

                    JACK
     Perceptive, aren't you?
```

Now an example of how this would be done in an animation script format:

39

```
INT. JACK'S HOUSE

Jack's living room has peeling wallpaper; an old,
patched sofa; a rickety table and one chair; a bare
lightbulb hanging from the ceiling instead of a
fixture. Any windows we see are covered with shabby,
but very opaque, curtains. Off to one side (not seen
in this shot) is an old bookshelf holding only a few
ragged books and a CRYSTAL SKULL.

Jack stands with folded arms watching as Dick and
Jane take in his shabby surroundings.

                    JACK
                 (irritated)
          You said you have a proposition.
          Start talking.

ANGLE ON JANE

who reacts with curiosity and heads toward the
bookshelf.
                              (Continued)
```

ANGLE FAVORING THE CRYSTAL SKULL IN F.G.

as Jane picks it up and looks at it with wonder, her
face partially distorted by being seen through the
crystal.

>   JANE
>   (amazed)
>   How did you get this?

ANGLE ON JACK

>   JACK
>   Long story.

ON DICK

who lounges on the old sofa.

>   DICK
>   If I didn't know better, I'd say it
>   was stolen.

ANGLE FAVORING JACK

Jack scowls at Dick. TRACK WITH Jack as he moves
across the room toward Jane.

>   JACK
>   Well, you don't know better. You
>   don't know Jack, as the saying goes.

ANGLE ON JANE

holding the skull. Jack ENTERS FRAME, takes the
skull away from her, and <PLUNKS> it back onto the
shelf.

>   JACK
>   You're wasting my time, and I don't
>   like people who waste my time.

CLOSER ON JANE

>   JANE
>   I think you don't like people, period.

CLOSE ON JACK

who narrows his eyes at her.

>   JACK
>   (sarcastic)
>   Perceptive, aren't you?

In a live-action script, you can get away with less detail about the surroundings, which will be filled in by the director in conjunction with a production designer, art designer, set designer, prop master, and so forth.

In animation, the artist knows what to draw only if you tell him. You aren't trying to keep the storyboard artist in suspense, so if you need something specific (such as a crystal skull) in the setting that he has to create, let him know up front. Sometimes an important prop will be designed in detail by the prop artist, and that design will be given to the storyboard artist. Either way, the artists need to know that the prop requires special attention. Keep your description as concise and to the point as you can. Animation scripts must be written to a specific length, and you can't afford to waste a single line on superfluous description.

If you're using backgrounds that already exist, don't worry about description, unless you need to add something new to it.

Notice that you don't necessarily need to have an action/description line underneath every slugline, particularly when all you're doing is cutting to a character so he can speak a line.

You can leave most of the choice of angles up to the storyboard artist, and specify only certain angles (high, low) or type of shot (wide, close, pan) where needed.

HYBRID ANIMATION FORMAT: A more recent format has been used of late, and may be on its way to being the norm. In this format, the writer is still required to call out every shot, but without using a separate line for the sluglines. Instead, you would begin a new shot with elements of a slugline, but continue directly into the action description without dropping down to a new paragraph. It would look like this:

41

```
INT. JACK'S HOUSE

Jack's living room has peeling wallpaper; an old,
patched sofa; a rickety table and one chair; a bare
lightbulb hanging from the ceiling instead of a
fixture. Any windows we see are covered with shabby,
but very opaque, curtains. Off to one side (not seen
in this shot) is an old bookshelf holding only a few
ragged books and a CRYSTAL SKULL.

Jack stands with folded arms, watching as Dick and
Jane take in his shabby surroundings.

                        JACK
                   (irritated)
         You said you have a proposition.
         Start talking.
                                        (Continued)
```

ANGLE ON JANE who reacts with curiosity and heads toward the bookshelf.

ANGLE FAVORING THE CRYSTAL SKULL IN F.G. - Jane picks it up and looks at it with wonder, her face partially distorted by being seen through the crystal.

> JANE
> (amazed)
> How did you get this?

JACK grows more irritated.

> JACK
> Long story.

ON DICK who lounges on the old sofa.

> DICK
> If I didn't know better, I'd say it was stolen.

JACK scowls at Dick. TRACK WITH Jack as he moves across the room toward Jane.

> JACK
> Well, you don't know better. You don't know Jack, as the saying goes.

ANGLE ON JANE - holding the skull. Jack ENTERS FRAME, takes the skull away from her, and <PLUNKS>. it back onto the shelf.

> JACK
> You're wasting my time, and I don't like people who waste my time.

CLOSER ON JANE who reacts to him.

> JANE
> I think you don't like people, period.

CLOSE ON JACK who narrows his eyes at her.

> JACK
> (sarcastic)
> Perceptive, aren't you?

This format allows the writers to pack more story into a shorter script (around twenty-four to thirty-three pages), but retains the underlying structure of an animation script and makes for a smoother read. As long you understand that it still gets down to using the five basic tools, in one form or another, you should have no problem with this.

Difference No. 2: Dialogue and the Lip-Synch Factor

Another major difference between live action and animation is the nature of the dialogue. In live action, you can do long passages of dialogue because you have a real person delivering the lines. The director decides how to move the camera or break up the delivery of the dialogue into shots, but no matter how it's shot, you have the reality of that live actor on-screen to carry the dialogue using eyes, facial muscles, body language, and a host of subtle factors.

Full animation in an animated feature can come closer to this at a greater cost in artist hours, but it won't equal what a live actor can do. In the limited animation of television, the last thing you want to have sitting on the screen delivering long speeches is a flat animated face with minimal expression: first, because it's not very interesting; secondly, because lip-synching takes time (and time = money).

Some anime takes a shortcut around this by not bothering with a realistic mouth, so no lip-synch is necessary. You'll find that the requirements of short dialogue still apply, perhaps even more so *because* there's no lip-synch and it looks funky when it goes on for too long. The same has been true for CG. As CG-animation techniques improve, lip-synching will become less of a factor, but if you look at the early CG shows for TV, you'll notice how often they tried to design characters wearing full-face helmets or masks in order to trim down the lip-synching work as much as possible.

43

Dialogue in animation is expected to be minimal, pithy, concise, strong, and punchy. Each piece of dialogue should be kept down to one or two fairly short sentences at most. In the examples I gave under Difference No. 1, notice how I took one of Jack's longer speeches in the live-action format, split it into two shorter pieces, and spread it across two shots in the animation sample.

You might be wondering what I mean by "strong and punchy." When I wrote my first animation scripts, I had no mentor, no guidance, and no one to tell me anything about the craft. It was learn-as-you-go. After I'd done one script, I was able to show it to someone who at the time was one of the major animation producers in the business. When I asked for feedback, he told me, "Your dialogue is too soft." I was baffled. I had no idea what he meant by that. When I asked him to clarify, he couldn't. The producer knew what he meant, but he wasn't able to explain it to me. "Soft" was just "soft," that's all. My dialogue was short, and there were no wasted words in the actual lines. My guess all these years later is that he meant I used too much back-and-forth dialogue to get to the point. My characters would use twenty pieces of dialogue to do what should have been boiled down to maybe five pieces of dialogue or less. Having pages of characters trading one-liners is as much of a mistake as having long pieces of dialogue.

When you craft a story and set up a scene for animation, you need to boil down your dialogue to the bare minimum and make that dialogue have the maximum impact, utilizing visuals in place of dialogue as much as you can. Avoid exposition like the plague. If your character absolutely must say several things in a row, break it up across a number of shots and make those shots interesting. Either give your character something to do (what's called "business," as in "give this character some piece of business here"), or have some other action going on.

Difference No. 3: Script Length

One of the other things you should notice from these samples is that calling out the shots for animation makes for a longer script.

Scripts became codified in their present form of font and layout for numerous reasons, but one of the big reasons is to write scripts that are the right length for specific periods of time, especially when it comes to television.

There's an old formula for how much time = one page of script.

> LIVE ACTION: 1 minute = 1 page.
> ANIMATION: 1 minute = 1.5 pages.

Theoretically, then, a twenty-two-minute live-action script would be twenty-two pages. A twenty-two-minute animation script would be thirty-three pages.

This is why the "standard" length for a live-action movie script is 90 pages to a maximum of 120 pages, because most movies are expected to run between 90 and 120 minutes in length.

To fit their airtimes, television programs require scripts written to fairly precise lengths, but even here you run into exceptions. Some live-action shows that are heavy in dialogue exchanges without a lot of action might run to fifty-five or sixty pages for an hour show. This is because dialogue alone eats up a lot more pages than heavy action or a combo of action plus dialogue, but dialogue usually takes up less airtime.

When I first began writing animation scripts, we were doing fifty-five- and sixty-page scripts for a half-hour action show, and most of it ended up on the screen, in contradiction to the formula given above. Over the years, I've watched the length of half-hour animation scripts shrink to forty-five pages, then to thirty-eight pages, and now to around thirty-two to thirty-three pages.

There are a couple of reasons for this. For one, the actual airtime of these shows has shrunk. The granddaddy of half-hour animation, *The Flintstones*, had twenty-seven minutes of airtime. Over the years, more and more commercials and breaks have been added, so that the current half hour of animation is about twenty-one to twenty-two minutes – for now.

The other reason for today's shorter scripts is that less actual animation per minute is being done (being shot on twos or shot on threes), due to shrinking budgets. Stories by necessity have become simpler, and the pacing slower, to accommodate the shorter script length.

Writing to Length

When a story editor says that the length of the script should be no more than, say, thirty-three pages, you must take that seriously. You should turn in a script that is between thirty-two and thirty-three pages. TV writing is precision writing. If the script is too long, it simply means that pages are cut—and you may not have any control over what gets cut. Naturally, your script shouldn't be too short either—at the risk of annoying the story editor, who will then need material added and may have to do it herself if she's in a rush.

The overall length is one issue. The other issue is act breaks.

WORKING OUT ACT BREAKS

If you're writing a script for a show that's already on the air, you'll get the act structure from watching the show. Otherwise, you'll get the info from the show bible or from the story editor. A very common structure is a teaser and three acts, or a teaser and two acts. An alternative is a teaser, two acts, and a tag (rarely seen these days). One-hour animation is extremely rare, but a live-action one-hour show commonly has a teaser and five acts—some do without a teaser; some add a tag. For a ninety-minute animated TV movie, there are usually eight acts.

You might occasionally encounter a show that does individual eleven-minute segments (two per show), rather than one half-hour story. Those are generally written as one act without teasers or other breaks.

The acts must be roughly equal in length. You might observe that in some one- or two-hour live-action dramas, they will let the first act run extremely long in order to make sure they've hooked the audience before cutting to the first set of commercials. With a longer form, such as a ninety-minute animated TV movie, you can also get away with a longer first act.

In half-hour animation, you have the option to make the first act a little longer, but not by any more than one or two pages. Assuming a thirty-three-page script, you should strive for a formula that is as close as possible to eleven/eleven/eleven (eleven pages per act). If you have a teaser, you have to carve out a couple of pages for that, so your formula might be two/eleven/ten/ten, or two/ten/eleven/ten, and so on depending on the demands of the story and the best place to put an act break. You can probably get away with two/twelve/ten/nine or similar variation.

What you absolutely don't want to do is let any one act get out of control. If you turn in a script that breaks out as nine/six/seventeen, you can count on your story editor wondering what on earth you were thinking, and telling you to fix the act breaks. There's room to be somewhat flexible, but no more than a couple of pages in any one direction.

Act breaks provide an extra challenge in working out the pacing and dramatic three-act structure of your story. By dramatic three-act structure, I refer to the triad of exposition-conflict-resolution that is the blueprint of your beginning, middle, and end. Exposition-conflict-resolution applies equally to a three-minute comedy short or to a ninety-minute epic adventure. Keep that dramatic structure in mind when you're crafting the overall story, without tying it to any specific act in the script. It might seem easy to divide up the dramatic triad to a three-act script, but do you really want to spend the entire third act solely on resolution? It's more likely that the resolution will take place halfway through the third act of the script, especially given the compressed nature of animation stories.

So we'll assume you have a grasp of your dramatic three-act structure as it applies overall to your story. Now you have to figure out how to build to a critical act break that takes place at approximately so many pages into the script. Your act breaks must be gripping, exciting, and dramatic. If you don't have your viewers totally hooked, you'll lose them during the commercial break. The purpose of a cliff-hanger act break is to keep the audience in enough suspense to stick around. The act break doesn't have to be a cliff-hanger based on physical peril. It could be a moment of suspense or mystery, or it could be a moment of emotional confrontation.

Which means that each act must have its own internal momentum that brings it to that critical point at the right time. In a ninety-minute animated film, this means finding seven points at which you can break the story with either a physical or emotional cliff-hanger . . . while not making it look contrived.

This is where having a solid outline is so important. Most of your scenes are going to run somewhere around two to three pages. Simple math tells us that trying to fit, say, ten scenes into an eleven-page act isn't going to work, unless you have an insanely frenetic story. This is where you need good instincts to estimate how many pages you will actually need for a scene vs. how many scenes you can realistically fit into a single act. As you work out your major story beats, you can reasonably estimate being able to fit three to four major story beats into an eleven-page act. You might be able to squeeze in five scenes if one is really short. By the time you take into account dialogue and breaking out all the shots, you'll find that three to four beats, or scenes, will easily fill eleven pages. You might have an instance where you're cutting back and forth between two major story beats rather than having separate scenes, and you'll need to estimate how many pages that will eat.

The best way to become good at this is practice. Write lots of sample outlines and sample scripts.

In the past, it was common to allow two weeks to write a half-hour animation script. These days, it isn't unusual to be given only one week to turn in a half-hour script.

You will find the "Spykecam" script available to read at *www.christymarx.info*.

THE 3D SCRIPT VS. THE 2D SCRIPT

I find myself being cautious in what advice I give about writing for CG (3D) vs. traditional cel animation (2D) because the field of animation is in a state of flux as CG continues to develop, transplanting 2D in some areas of the business, but not others.

At the time I write this, the major animation-movie companies have abandoned 2D entirely in favor of 3D. This is a function of CG getting better and better, combined with dramatic successes in 3D features. At first, CG elements were incorporated cautiously into 2D films such as Disney's *Beauty and the Beast* and *Aladdin*. The steamroller began with Pixar's wonderful *Toy Story* and subsequent successes with *Monsters, Inc.* and *Finding Nemo*, along with the great success of DreamWorks SKG's *Shrek* series. At the same time, some expensive 2D films didn't perform well, and turned into large losses for the studios.

What some of these companies forget is that the best visuals in the universe—whether they are 2D or 3D—won't save a weak story or weak script. Disney's *Treasure Planet* had spectacular CG, but a story that didn't quite work.

Consequently, it's hard to say at this point whether CG will remain the flavor of the decade, or whether 2D will make a comeback in features (as this is being written, Disney recently released a 2D feature, *The Princess and the Frog*. If it succeeds, it could pave the way for a return to the traditional method.) There will likely always be smaller studios that continue to produce 2D features or direct-to-video features.

Meanwhile, in TV, there were some superb CG shows made early on (such as *ReBoot* and *Shadow Raiders*), but they were expensive, and it was tricky to churn them out on a tight TV production schedule. TV animation is trending toward more-stylized 2D work, Flash animation, and whatever else will grab eyeballs to the small screen while keeping the budgets low. There is also a style in which 3D is rendered to look like 2D while retaining the ability to move in 3D. MTV's version of *Spider-Man* is an example of this.

I wrote for some of the early CG TV series, all for the same production company. At the time, we wrote the scripts in a live-action format using master scenes, rather than an animation-script format. This was due largely to that particular company's method of parcelling out the art tasks without using storyboards.

In most TV animation, one artist is given one act of a script to storyboard, so you can end up with three artists drawing storyboards for a half-hour show with three acts. Those three artists determine the look and flow of the visuals.

This company instead assigned a CG artist to handle particular characters, and the artist would create the animation for the scenes containing those characters. Essentially, the artist took the place of the storyboard artist on a rather piecemeal basis, but with a director to pull the various pieces together.

However, the last time I met with someone from that company, I was told they had gone to doing storyboards. Note that even scripts that are written in a live-action format have to adhere to other animation "rules," such as keeping dialogue short.

When it comes to something that is evolving, as CG is, each company or studio will likely have its own approach to how it wants the scripts done. Your best bet is to be familiar with both live-action and animation formats, as well as with the rules and requirements of each.

As for writing TV spec scripts, as you will certainly need to do, my advice is to write in an animation-script format regardless of which technology will be used to animate it. This shows that you know how to do it, and is more likely to be the right way to go. Just be sure that the visuals you create in your script will work for the technology you have in mind. If you're writing an animation script that you intend for 3D, your visuals should utilize the strengths of 3D animation. If you're writing a 2D series spec, your visuals must be in line with what can be done in 2D.

What tends to be "expensive" in CG is creating the 3D characters, especially when doing a TV series. This is because of the time it takes to create the wire frame of the body shape, then add texture, color, and all the other details that go into creating a full model. As the technology develops, this may change, but when I was writing for *Beast Wars*, we had a specific set of characters and a very strict rule against creating any new characters. I pitched a story idea that I thought got around the "no new characters" rule by calling for a new character that would be a conglomeration of parts from the other characters, so that existing components could be recombined rather than something new created. The story editor nearly didn't pitch it, but liked the idea enough that he went ahead. It became the episode "Transmutate," and the company liked the story enough that they went to the extra trouble of creating something entirely new for the Transmutate character.

RESTRICTIONS BREED CREATIVITY

I've heard writers enthuse about doing animation because "you can do *anything* in animation!" This was usually said in comparing animation to live action. This was truer in the past than it is now, due to the increased use of CG elements in live action. It also highlights the difference between feature animation and TV animation.

Features have multimillion-dollar budgets and a long development period. They can afford to pull out the stops. They need to because they have a big investment to recoup.

TV animation is about doing the best you can within the limitations of shrinking production budgets and tight production schedules.

Here are some examples of the type of restrictions I've run up against in animation. These restrictions called for adaptation and creative thinking.

THE CROWD SCENE RULE: One big example is crowd scenes. Movies can afford to use sophisticated programs to generate and control huge crowds of 3D animated characters on the screen (look, a zillion CG orcs are storming the Hornburg!). For a TV episode, you need to avoid crowd scenes. When you need to have a crowd scene for some reason, you find ways to cheat around it. You stick to close shots, or pick shots that show as few random people as possible (such as a few feet rushing by at ground level). In short, you get creative. You also want to avoid lots and lots of small objects flying around. Asking a TV animation artist to draw a hundred Ping-Pong balls bouncing around in a scene could be dangerous to your health.

LIMITED BACKGROUNDS: One show had a very tight budget that prohibited more than a few new backgrounds per show. Remember my example of how quickly one location can eat up several backgrounds? The challenge with that show was to use the maximum number of already-existing backgrounds from episodes in production, and to sharply curtail how many new backgrounds were in the script. It's also helpful to have generic backgrounds such as "jungle" or "rock wall."

LIMITED VOICES: Another show would allow me to use only a relatively low number of voices. Let's say it was ten voices. The trick here is that the cast I was required to use took up eight of the voices. The challenge was to come up with stories that stayed tightly focused on those characters with almost no outside characters.

LIMITED DIALOGUE: Besides limiting voices, I've had shows where I could have only so many lines of dialogue per episode. It was a matter of going through the script and counting the lines. If there were too many lines, I had to either find places to trim out dialogue, or else rewrite the speeches to be more condensed.

TOO MANY PROPS OR MODELS: Shows with a very tight budget might also prohibit the writer from asking for too many new characters that have to be designed, or even for new props that have to be designed. Once again, it's a matter of finding a way to work around the restrictions by changing the scene or altering the story. Whatever it takes.

OTHER THINGS YOU MAY BE EXPECTED TO DO

Once you're given a script assignment, you should be told what additional info you will be expected to provide along with the script. The most common ones are as follows:

- LOGLINE AND/OR SYNOPSIS: The logline is one sentence of the type you'd see in *TV Guide* to give the gist of the episode. The synopsis is about three short paragraphs. This type of synopsis should be crafted to give other writers enough detail to gain a quick knowledge of what's in your script, so they can avoid having situations or scenes that are too similar to yours.
- CAST LIST: For established characters, you need to give only the name. Characters should be listed in order of importance. For any new, secondary, or incidental characters, you will need to give the character name, indicate whether it's a speaking part (if a speaking part, you should give an indication of how many lines), and give a description of the character (usually the same description you put into the script).
- SET LIST: This would be a list of your major INTERIOR and EXTERIOR backgrounds. If it's a new background, include full description.
- PROPS LIST: This isn't as commonly asked for these days, but it would be a list of special or unusual props that would have to be designed for your episode, such as a handheld GPS that transforms into a laser gun, a type of vehicle not used before, or something that is more than just a background object (such as the crystal skull I used in my script examples).

SCRIPTWRITING SOFTWARE

More and more companies, especially with TV series, are requiring writers who work on their shows to use scriptwriting software. The two main pieces of software currently on the market are Final Draft and Movie Magic Screenwriter. So far, every company that has required me to use scriptwriting software has used Final Draft, whether it was a live-action show or an animated show. Final Draft is now very prevalent on live-action shows, and has rapidly become prevalent in animation, including theatrical features.

This doesn't mean you should run out and buy a copy of Final Draft. That depends on your budget. If you have plenty of money to spare, go for it. However, it is perfectly legitimate to ask the company to loan you a copy of the software if they're requiring you to use it. The advantages to already having the software are that it sounds more professional to say you have it (and less hassle for the story editor to get it to you), and that you'll have a chance to become familiar with it ahead of time, thus not having to deal with a learning curve while trying to get a script done under deadline.

Scriptwriting software has its good points and bad points. The software automates much of the process and gives you handy shortcuts. Some of those automated shortcuts have been known to drive me mad. I have to live with that, and you can make some adjustments to how you want the software to work. I haven't had much luck importing previously written scripts into the software, or exporting scripts to a plain Word format from the software. Both actions left me having to do a lot of editing fixing the odd quirks that happened in the process. Because you can print a Final Draft formatted script only from Final Draft itself, you will either need to have the program in order to print out a copy later (for example, for samples of your work), or you will need to have an exported version in Word format or in Rich Text Format (RTF).

Final Draft Viewer is free software that will let you read and print Final Draft documents without having the full version of the scriptwriting software.

THE ANIMATED FEATURE FILM

The animation-development process is different for theatrical projects. Writing actual scripts for theatrical animation is a recent development, beginning mainly when Michael Eisner (as head of Disney) mandated that for *The Little Mermaid*, the script be done before any animation work. This created a major shift in how feature animation was developed. However, it's a far more collaborative process than in television.

On features, usually more writers are hired, sometimes one writer or one team of writers after another. Often, writers are hired as "story consultants" to give their input.

The writers go back and forth in a more fluid process with the animators—with script influencing storyboards, and storyboards influencing script. Big meetings are held in which everyone involved goes over storyboards in detail. Unspoken etiquette dictates that the directors get to comment first, after which everyone else in the room can give an opinion.

Storyboards are turned into "story reels," which are carefully evaluated to get a sense of how the story is working, especially in a visual sense. At its most effective, a feature animation film should convey just about everything the viewer needs to know when viewed without sound or dialogue, as though it were a silent movie. After input on the story reels, there is more rewriting. The rewriting is a constant back-and-forth process.

One of the big differences is the time span of the development and production, which typically runs four to five years. In April 2005, Jeffrey Katzenberg, head of DreamWorks Animation SKG, commented that DreamWorks spends three to four years in production, with budgets of around $125 million per picture. That's a huge commitment.

I should mention that direct-to-video features are developed in a fashion more like television animation, and have the same kind of tight, short schedules of a television series.

I consulted with Terry Rossio, who, with his partner Ted Elliott, has written or worked on numerous feature-animation projects—including *Aladdin*, *Small Soldiers*, *The Road to El Dorado*, *Treasure Planet*, *Shrek*, and *Shrek 2*. Terry generously shared his experience in this area.

A feature-animation script runs about eighty to eighty-five pages (and no more than eighty-five), containing around twenty sequences. In this sense, sequences would be similar to beats. This refers to the major story beats, events, or action, or a series of events that are grouped together because they are related. Terry said, "[Jeffrey] Katzenberg (Dreamworks SKG) will speak of a five/ten/five-act breakdown of sequences (meaning five sequences in Act 1, ten in Act 2, and five in Act 3), but that's very loose and informal. We tend to think of animated movies as having a two-act play structure. In the end, just about any structure fits a good story."

The emphasis in features is on simple story, but complex characters. The focus is on the characters and on the underlying theme, not the plot. Having a clear theme is also at the heart of creating an animated feature. That theme should have a simple, strong core, such as "family is important" or "if you love someone, you must be willing to let them go."

Because of the fluid process I described earlier with the writers working more closely in collaboration with the artists, the studios don't want the writers to break their scripts out shot by shot. Instead, they're written in a live-action script format, which keeps the scripts much shorter and leaves the scene and shot layouts to the animators.

Another reason for using the live-action format is that the first people to read the scripts are studio executives, who are more accustomed to reading live-action scripts. These scripts are shorter than the norm because animated features are (mostly) designed for a young audience with a shorter attention span, so they tend to be shorter movies.

I asked Terry about the inclusion of music, because it often plays a significant role in animation features. Terry said, "If music is important to the film, then it gets included in the screenplay, exactly as it is intended to be in the final cut. A musical sequence can be a montage, or we prefer 'series of shots.' But it can also be a single scene designed to move the story forward, or anything in between."

Aside from these major differences between television and feature-animation scripts, a couple of the rules for television should still apply. You will want to keep your dialogue short and pithy. You will want to remember that you're working with animated actors, and not live actors, when it comes to calling for subtle emotion.

BEYOND THE BASICS (ADVICE, TIPS, AND TRICKS)

Now we'll assume that you're actually working on a show. Here's a grab bag of additional advice, tips, and tricks.

Keep Your Story Editor Happy

There are certain things you should never, ever do to your story editor:

- Never turn in a script late, unless there's a very good reason and your story editor has approved an extension.
- Never fail to return phone calls or email as a way of avoiding having to give your story editor bad news or an excuse. Avoidance is a bad, bad idea—as I learned the hard way. Be honest and stay in communication with your story editor or producer.
- Never cheat on the format. If you're using a program such as Final Draft, this is moot, because the program will set standard margins. But if you're using Word or some other program, never deviate from the template or guidelines set by the story editor. Adding one extra line per page can add one entire extra page to the script. Don't try to cheat the margins or use a smaller font or anything else that will provide the story editor with a headache later having to reformat your script. You only hurt yourself in the end, because when the script is properly formatted and comes out too long, it will have to be cut. Make it the right length the first time around. After all, the reason standard formatting came about was to provide a reasonably accurate way to judge how many minutes of airtime will result from a script of a given length.
- Do not argue excessively with your story editor. This is something I encountered with new writers working on their first scripts. They wanted to argue about *every single note* I gave them. I'm not talking about asking for clarification on a note—I'm talking about a stubborn resistance to changing anything. Not only is this irritating on a personal level, but it takes a lot of time that most story editors don't have. This gets down to two things: (1) if you don't have the temperament to get notes from ten different people whose sometimes contradictory notes must be reconciled, then don't even think about getting into scriptwriting; and (2) *learn to pick your battles*. I can't emphasize this second point enough. To put it another way, don't sweat the small stuff. Make the changes. When it comes to something that you truly consider significant to the story, don't argue it—*discuss* it. This is a fine point of semantics, but an important one. What you really want to do is get at the precise reason for the change, to present your reasoning in a nonconfrontational manner, and—if you can't win your point—

look for a compromise. Often, if you listen carefully, you can defuse the change by coming up with an alternate way to do basically the same thing. Then both sides win. But the minute you get the sense that this isn't a battle you can win, make the best of it with good grace and find a way to make it work for you, rather than risk never working for that story editor again.

- Needless to say (I hope), never flatly refuse to change something. That's the kiss of death. If the notes are really that bad, your only remaining course of action is to give up the job and walk away, regardless of the consequences.

Be Kind to the Storyboard Artist

Don't keep secrets from the artists. If there is an important prop that will be used in a room in a later scene, be sure to include that prop in the *first* description of the room, so that it can be taken into account when that background is being designed and created. Likewise, if you need some special feature in a location, such as a hidden trapdoor, give some indication of it in the first place you describe the location. Capitalizing the prop is a good idea. Even though the door may not be revealed until Act 3, the artist will need to design the room to account for it when working on Act 1. The same rule applies to characters. Don't suddenly mention that your character has a scar on his right cheek several scenes after you have already introduced the character. When you first introduce or describe the character, make sure all the significant information is there.

Be consistent in how you refer to a character, prop, or place. Remember that there can be a different storyboard artist working on each act. You don't want to confuse them by saying "trapdoor" in one act and "flip-up hidden door" in another act, or by referring to an "Aztec temple" one time and an "ancient Mexican temple" another time.

Present Tense and "-ing" Words

All scripts are written in the present tense in third person. If you're not accustomed to writing in present tense, check your scripts afterward to make sure you didn't slip into past tense here or there. Although it's not absolutely forbidden to use something other than third person (such as "we see Jack at work"), you'd better be very good at it, or you may turn off a reader who is expecting standard third person. When ending an act or script, there is one fairly common usage of "we." It looks like this:

```
CLOSE ON JACK

pinned down by <GUNFIRE> from both sides! And as
Jack desperately hunches behind a flimsy wall, we…

                                              FADE OUT
```

This is a stylistic choice. Some people like it; some don't.

It's also a good idea to avoid writing passive sentences or words ending in "-ing." For example, avoid "Jack is looking at Jane." It reads better as "Jack looks at Jane." It's shorter and more dynamic. Make sure your characters "walk" instead of "are walking," "run" instead of "are running," "talk" instead of "are talking," and so on. This is a not 100 percent rule, and there may be times you want an "-ing" word, but for the most part, go for shorter and stronger in your language. This holds true for dialogue as well.

Verboten Words

Have you ever wondered why the villains in a Saturday-morning cartoon will cry, "Destroy them!" or "Annihilate them!" In children's animation, certain words are considered forbidden, with very rare exceptions. Words that are commonly forbidden include "death," "die," and "kill."

I've also been told not to use supposedly offensive terms such as "idiot," "moron," and "cretin." Sometimes it's a personal quirk of the producer or story editor, such as one exec who hated the use of the slang word "idjit."

Employ common sense when writing a script for kids. Avoid the forbidden words noted here, as well as swear words or words with explicit sexual meanings.

55

Everybody Gets Out Alive

You may have also noticed in most action-adventure cartoons, that no matter how big the explosion, anybody inside or riding the exploding vehicle/building/object will get out safely. As with the forbidden words, having anyone (good or bad) die on the screen in children's animation is strictly taboo. There have been some rare exceptions, depending on the type of show, but generally you should take it for granted that you need to *show* good guys or bad guys escaping from explosive or destructive situations. This makes it clear that they didn't die.

Imitatable Behavior

The following "rules" do not apply to full-on comedy, such as squash-and-stretch cartoons (for example, the Looney Tunes characters Road Runner and Wile E. Coyote), where the action is obviously not real. The rules apply to action or adventure shows or to anything that isn't pure comedy.

"Imitatable behavior" refers to any TV show's physical action that a child could imitate—action that would do damage or cause injury to that child or to another living thing (especially to other kids). This is something that anyone producing visual works for kids worries about, and it governs much of what is considered acceptable or unacceptable in a script.

A prime example of this is the use of fire. One of the reasons there was no Johnny Storm the Human Torch in the early *Fantastic Four* series is that the producers worried about kids trying to imitate him by setting themselves on fire. In scriptwriting for kids, use of fire in a way that could lead to imitatable behavior is strongly frowned upon.

Other forbidden behaviors include poking anything into eyes, punching, hitting, kicking, choking around the neck, and so forth. It means no guns, no knives, no weapons that kids could manage to obtain (which is why you see a lot of beam or laser or other unreal weapons).

There are exceptions, of course. Shows geared for an older audience might allow a careful use of weapons, but the show would specifically have to allow that. For a series that has martial-arts characters, the producers or the story editor will lay down guidelines about what type of martial-arts moves are acceptable and where on the body the blows can land.

Then we have something such as *Teenage Mutant Ninja Turtles*, in which the heroes carry martial-arts weapons. When I wrote for *TMNT*, the unwritten rule of indirect use of force applied. By indirect use of force, I mean that the Turtles couldn't use their weapons directly against an opponent. Instead, they would have to use the weapon against some inanimate object, which would then in turn have some impact on the enemy. For example, if the Turtles are in a store, the weapon is used to knock down a pile of canned goods. The cans then fall on the villain or trip him up. Or if the villain is standing under a tree branch, you have the Turtles cut off the branch so it falls onto the villain.

I have seen this go so far that on another show, I wasn't allowed to have a character throw a cream pie directly into the face of another character! Instead, the pie had to levitate out of the character's hand and *then* be thrown.

This rule about indirect use of force applies to a lot of shows, but a truly classic example was when I was asked to develop Robert E. Howard's Conan character into an animated series. Conan is a barbarian. He uses a sword. He isn't squeamish about using a sword. But I couldn't let him kill anyone, not even the villains, or use a sword directly against them. This was a challenge, to say the least.

I began by researching the source material. I pulled an element from one of Howard's original stories, then bent it to my own use. I gave Conan not an ordinary sword, but a "magic" sword. In this case, it was made of star-metal that had fallen from the sky. Any weapon made with this star-metal (and all of Conan's regular companions ended up with some type of weapon made of star-metal) had the ability to reveal and vanquish Conan's main enemies. These enemies were the lizard-men, who could assume a human disguise. Merely getting close to Conan's sword made them revert to lizard-man form, and the merest touch of the sword sent the lizard-men POOF! into an alternate lizard-man dimension, where they couldn't get back to Earth. The end result: Conan gets to "use" his sword (sort of) and get rid of his enemies, but nobody dies. Not even lizard-men.

And of course, any *other* use of Conan's sword against a living foe had to follow the indirect-use-of-force rule.

Or you can have the villains be robots, machines, or rock monsters, or something else far enough removed from humanlike that the rule can be ignored.

One other factor is having an increasing influence on what level of action can be used in animation series. Many shows are being financed as foreign coproductions. Studios in France, Canada, Germany, Britain, India, and elsewhere help finance the production in exchange for having the rights to the series in their own country. However, Britain and other European countries have a lower threshold of acceptability in physical action (some people call it "violence," but I draw the line at calling any kind of action "violence"). These sensibilities will affect what is allowed in a show. In general terms, Europeans want their kids' shows to be less "violent" than American shows. When writing your physical action, you need to have a good mind for coming up with clever alternatives.

And if you think all this sounds extreme, writing children's live-action shows is even *more* restrictive.

Subtle Emotion

Don't write lines such as "There is deep sadness in her eyes." Or "Standing stone still, he radiates cold anger." Most animation, and especially the limited animation of television, can't adequately convey subtle emotion. Flat, animated eyes can't communicate the level of emotion that we can read from human eyes. This has to be done with broader facial movement and body language, as well as emotion in dialogue.

SLANG AND FANTASY LANGUAGE

Using contemporary slang will make you sound hip, but will also quickly date the show (or, for that matter, a comic or a videogame). Many clever writers get around this by inventing slang that doesn't really exist, but sounds appropriate for the show. This is even more useful when dealing with a futuristic or science-fiction show where you don't want modern slang to sound out of place or archaic . . . unless that's by deliberate intent.

If you're going to use foreign slang, *do your homework*! It's embarrassing to read slang for, say, a contemporary Australian that hasn't been used for twenty years except as a joke.

Then there's fantasy. It's easy to forget how modern some of our phrases are when writing a pure fantasy show. "Fast as lightning" is fine, but "faster than a bullet" is a problem if your characters use only swords. You never want to hear Conan say, "Wow, cool." Be careful to avoid anachronistic slang.

57

I came up with the Marx Fantasy Dialogue Scale to differentiate the various ways in which fantasy dialogue could be spoken, ranging from colloquial/ modern (No. 1) to High Epic/Poetic (No. 5). Here's an example:

1. He doesn't know what he's doing.
2. He does not know what he is doing.
3. He does not know what he does.
4. He knows not what he does.
5. He knows not what his purpose is, for confusion lies heavy upon him.

You would rarely want to use No. 5, because it's wordy and sounds least natural to modern ears. Using purely colloquial language can sound jarring in some fantasy settings. Creating the right fantasy dialogue depends a great deal on how you use contractions, on your word arrangement and sentence structure, and on the vocabulary you employ.

Dialect

Let's say you have a character who is Russian and speaks with a heavy Russian accent, or a character who is Irish or Romanian or whatever. How do you express that in dialogue?

Mainly, just indicate the character's nationality when you describe the character, and then leave it to the actor. Don't try to write in dialect unless you're very, very good at it—and then only if it doesn't distract from giving the actors readable dialogue. You might want to play around with grammatical structure in a way that's appropriate to that dialect, or toss in verbal quirks, but make sure you get it right.

If you want a piece of dialogue spoken in a foreign language, but you're unable to come up with a translation yourself, I would recommend this:

```
                            JANE
                     (spoken in French)
             What do you know about the crystal
             skull?
```

This throws the responsibility onto the casting or voice director to find an actor who can speak French. Which raises another point: if you create a major, recurring character who needs to speak another language, make sure you include this in the character description *before* the casting takes place.

The Other Translation Problem

As I've mentioned, nearly all television animation these days is done overseas. This means that the scripts have to be translated into Japanese, Korean, French, German, and so on for non-English-speaking animation-production houses.

This can create some quite funny glitches, particularly when it comes to the use of English idioms. A friend of mine likes to tell the story of a *G.I. Joe* script he wrote in which his characters were in a desert location having an argument. He used the idiom "X decides to stick his oar in the water," meaning X character decides to give his opinion.

When the animation came back, his characters went from standing in the desert to sitting in a rowboat with oars in water that suddenly appears out of nowhere!

It has become necessary to avoid using English idioms in animation scripts that will go overseas for production. This can also apply to using references that are too obscurely American and might mean nothing to an overseas animator. An overseas animator might understand something as internationally known as "he had ears like Mickey Mouse," but a phrase such as "he had hair like Don King" will probably leave them mystified.

Getting Around the Lip-Synch Problem

As I mentioned earlier, lip-synching is expensive, and anytime you can come up with a useful way to have dialogue without requiring lip-synch, it helps the schedule and the budget. Here are a few tips:

- Have dialogue begin during your EXT. establishing shot (as V.O. dialogue). Partway through the dialogue, cut to the interior shot with the character completing the speech. Or vice versa, have the character begin a speech about something, then cut to the location or object under discussion and complete the dialogue as V.O. or O.S.
- A variation on this first tip would be to start the character's dialogue during a long pan when the character is O.S. at the beginning of the pan, and then finish the speech when the camera brings the character into view.
- Have the character turned away from camera in a way that hides most of the face (such as an OTS or POV shot).
- If it fits the story, have something else (helmet, scarf, mask) obscure the face. In CG shows, they often create secondary characters with helmets or face masks for exactly this reason.
- Go to an ECU on the eyes so the mouth doesn't show. I wouldn't recommend this for more than one very short speech, because of what I said about the lack of emotive power in animated eyes.
- Self-reflective dialogue (such as the character's inner thoughts) can be done as a narrative V.O. rather than having the character talking out loud to himself. However, whether or not this method of hearing inner thoughts is appropriate in your script depends on whether it's been established in the show already. You wouldn't want to suddenly have a character's inner dialogue be heard when that technique hasn't been used in the series previously—unless the story editor or producer says it's okay.

Capitalizing Character Names

It's a common practice to put the name of a character in CAPS the first time that character appears in the script, but not afterward. This refers only to naming the character in the action description paragraph—not to sluglines or dialogue, where the character name is always in caps.

Be a Good Net Citizen

Animation writing became one of the first sectors of writing to get wired. I attribute much of this to Steve Gerber, who in the 1980s required writers on *G.I. Joe* to do their scripts on a computer, to communicate via his bulletin-board system (BBS), and to send scripts by modem. That was what propelled me abruptly into the world of computers.

Since then, animation and television in general have become very wired. In animation, the majority of pitches, outlines, scripts, and notes are exchanged via email or FTP. Sometimes artwork for a series is posted on hidden Web pages for the writers. In addition to having a good handle on using email and browsers, it's very important to have good antivirus protection in place so that you don't become the pariah who spreads an infection to the story editor or other writers. Or conversely, so you don't get hit by someone else who's being careless.

The "Spykecam" Outline and Script

You will find the outline and the full script of the "Spykecam" episode of *X-Men: Evolution* available to read and study by going to *www.christymarx.info*. If you happen to see the finished episode, you'll notice differences between our script and the finished version after rewrites by the story editor. For example, we used a Shakespearean play in our version, not realizing that another writer had already used a Shakespearean play as a key element in her script. Rather than be repetitive, the story editor changed our script to accommodate using a different play. Noting such changes can be instructive when studying scripts vs. finished episodes.

CHAPTER 3

Basic Animation Writing Structure

Jean Ann Wright

DIFFERENCES IN STORY STRUCTURE

Structure exists to help you write a better story, but differences in the length of your story make a difference in the complexity of your structure. Differences in type (feature, kid's cartoon, Internet short) or genre (action/adventure, comedy, preschool) can also make a difference in complexity and style. A feature script is longer and requires more structure to hold our interest. An Internet short or one-minute TV cartoon requires very little plot. In fact, structure may get in the way of the gags. Generally, action/adventure shows require more plot than gag-driven comedy shows. Primetime animated shows generally use a sitcom structure with more clever dialogue and less action.

BASIC STRUCTURE

All stories must have a beginning, middle, and end. A short series script (for TV or the Internet) must be about the stars of that series and be centered on them. The star or hero of each episode must have a goal or motive, and someone or something must oppose that goal. These are the basic story musts, and the same applies to a film. Of course, there are also independent animated films that are more abstract and make no attempt at telling a tale.

Normally scripts use a three-act structure:

- *Act I* This ends after the problem has been set up. (The girl is on top of a flagpole.)
- *Act II* This ends before the **climax**. (Someone is pelting her with squishy tomatoes and rotten oranges.)
- *Act III* **Resolution**. (She finds a way to get down.) Wrap up with a **tag**.

DOI: 10.1016/B978-0-240-81343-1.00003-0

Occasionally a TV animation script will be written in just two **acts**, but even with only two acts, the basic three-act structure will be spread out over the length of those two acts. The three acts of a typical television script may be about the same length, although the last act will probably be the shortest. Sometimes the first act is shorter. Television act breaks normally come at commercial breaks, so suspense should be built up to help keep the audience in their seats through the commercials. There may be an opening teaser.

A three-act feature script will probably have acts that are apportioned: 25 percent for Act I, 50 percent for Act II, and 25 percent for Act III. The rules are not carved in stone.

CREATING THE STORY

First Method

This is a simple step-by-step method for creating a story for an established series or for your own characters. Here you're writing a story for characters you know.

- Who is your protagonist, star, or hero for this episode? We will use the terms *protagonist*, *star*, and *hero/heroine* interchangeably in this book because the protagonist, or the person who drives the story, is normally the star or the hero/heroine in an animation story. What is the star's character flaw, fault, or weakness? How does this flaw hurt or annoy others?
- Go to the end of your story. What does this character learn about himself and how to treat others by the end of this episode? What was the lesson that the story taught him—the theme of your story? A series star may have to repeat some of these same lessons time after time, since series characters don't undergo much change. For instance, Scooby-Doo remains a coward.
- Back to the beginning. What does your protagonist want? This goal should start low and snowball throughout the story until it's almost an obsession by the end.
- Who (what villain or opponent) can best attack the star's character flaw, oppose his values, and try to stop him from reaching his goal? This villain should ideally want the same thing as the star. (It could be something specific like a treasure chest of gold, or the characters might be fighting over something general like control or a way of life.)
- What's the **catalyst** or inciting incident, the person or thing from the outside that causes the protagonist to come up with his goal and start the story moving? It may be the villain that puts the story into action, especially in a mystery. (The villain appears as a ghost at the old house.)
- Make sure that all story points are related and tied together so that you're telling only one story.

- The star or hero develops a **game plan** to reach his goal. The villain attacks over and over. There is usually a major reversal or **turning point** in the way that the action is going at the end of Act I, spinning the action around in another direction. Now there's no turning back for the hero.
- In Act II new information is coming out. Our hero keeps revising his plan because it's not working. A high point is likely about halfway through the script. Everything looks good for the hero, and it appears that he'll attain his goal. But the hero has a defeat or apparent defeat, giving the villain or antagonist an advantage. This starts the downward slide for the hero.
- There's another turning point toward the end of Act II, spinning the action around again.
- The **major crisis** is the lowest point in the story for the hero. It's the reverse of what the hero wants. Often it's here that he's faced with his critical choice (whether to go after the gold in the chest that's nearing the edge of the falls or to save his best friend). This crisis might be the turning point at the end of Act II (more likely in a feature), but it can't come too soon or the third act will drag. If the major crisis is at the end of Act II, it requires a short third act.
- In Act III the hero comes back and tries harder. This is the biggest battle. It's best when it's a physical battle and a battle of values. The hero wins! This is the climax! Everything must build to this point.
- Resolution. Wrap up quickly.

This method works best for longer material: a feature, or an hour, or at least a half-hour story. It works best when you want more character, more plot, and less belly laughs. The steps are general, a structure to work toward. Your story may be slightly different.

Second Method

This method is the same as the first method, but if you don't yet know your characters, the steps will be in a different order. Here you may want to start with the theme or lesson that your protagonist is going to learn—what the story is really about, the second bullet in the first method. Then go to back to the first bullet: Create a protagonist or hero that can best benefit and learn from that theme and an antagonist that is best suited to fight or oppose that theme and that hero.

Third Method

Some longer stories have all the elements of the previous methods, but they have more than one plot: an **A-plot** and a **B-plot**, and sometimes even a **C-plot**. The B-plot is a subplot that complicates the main plot or places an obstacle in its way. One plot may be an action plot and the other a character-driven plot. The character plot may revolve around the hero, and the action plot may revolve around the villain. Both plots must advance the story. The subplot must add to the story, giving it more dimensions. The subplot should start after the main plot, interweave, and wrap up close to the main plot. It should remain less important. Getting the two plots to come together into only one story with nothing extraneous can be the hard part. Stories with A- and B-plots are too complicated for shorter stories under the half-hour length. Even some half-hour stories do not deal with subplots. If you're working with a story editor on a series, ask if he wants a subplot.

Fourth Method

Primetime animated shows are written like sitcoms. A sitcom is a comedy based around a situation. A protagonist still has a goal, develops a game plan that's opposed, and battles someone or something for the outcome. But sitcoms have less action. They're not as visual and lend themselves less to classic animation techniques. The comedy is centered on the characters, who may be more realistic. Sitcoms stand out for their clever dialogue and multitude of jokes, one or more on each page. One or two writers may write an initial script, but somewhere in the process, a whole group of staff writers sits around a table and works together, punching up the humor and polishing the script. These scripts usually have a subplot.

Fifth Method

A few animation writers work very differently. They feel that plot tends to get in the way of the gags and the laughs. Preferring to keep it simple, they work with a basic idea for the star's goal and opposition (Coyote wants to catch the Roadrunner, but Roadrunner doesn't want to be caught). They add an arena, the necessary characters, and some props. Then they build the gags toward a big climax, placing the best, wildest, and funniest gag there. The story is simple with a beginning, middle, and end. Create one escalating conflict with at least one reversal. Stories over five minutes need multiple obstacles or complications. But funny is what it's all about! This style tends to work best in shorter cartoons: thirty seconds to twelve minutes max. The classic animators worked this way. They worked together often in one room, developing stories by topping each other with gags. They developed ideas and animated the stories themselves. Characters developed gradually through gags, dialogue, and bits over a period of time. They knew and loved their characters, sometimes becoming their characters as they worked. Imagination, surprise, and exaggeration are very important in this style. There is not enough plot here to keep the audience's interest for a longer story or feature film.

And More!

There are many variations and combinations of these styles. Each feature, each series, and each story editor is different. One other suggested structure method leapfrogs a plot-developing or story scene with a gag scene throughout. So you have story scene, gag scene, story, gag, story… until the end!

STORY THEME

The theme is the lesson that the protagonist learns, the central message or values of the story. We just touched briefly on theme when we talked about what the main character learns about himself. Not all animation stories have themes, but many of the best stories do. A theme is something for the audience to think about later. It gives the story some substance. It helps us understand each other and the world around us. It's an observation about life and the people in our world. It helps us to identify with the characters. We recognize our own problems and root for the character to work through those problems, flaws, and needs in order to survive and grow.

Think of a theme as one value coming into conflict with another and winning out. Forgiveness is better than revenge. Living for the present can make life fuller than constantly worrying about the future. Pestering your older brother is more fun than playing by yourself…at least until you get caught. These are the basic everyday values of life, and they have been the subjects of stories from the beginnings of time. Oral tales of old; myths; legends; the Bible; Greek, Roman, and Shakespearean plays; novels; films; and even games have all been centered on these conflicts in values.

Remember your audience. Because male teens are the biggest ticket buyers, many films center on the theme of childishness losing out to adulthood (coming of age or identity). If your audience is primarily children, then you may want to consider what is appropriate. Universal and timeless themes that touch us all are usually the best themes for films.

Character, plot, and theme are all connected. Your hero may have a character flaw that is getting in the way of his happiness. What he goes through during the course of the story changes the way he looks at life and alters the way he'll live in the future. That's his **character arc**. Ideally, he will become a better person, or at least come to know himself and the world a little better. Will reaching his goal make life better for your hero and for others? Will the values of the hero or the values of the villain win out, and why? It's possible to have more than one theme, but if this is the case, the themes must be interrelated.

A theme is felt, not indoctrinated or preached. No one wants a sermon. Instead we want characters that by their actions show what they value in life and fight for what is good in the world. Values are expressed mostly through action, but they might come out briefly during the course of a verbal conflict as well. Conflict and opposing values are at the heart of any story.

EXERCISES

1. Make a diagram of basic animation structure so that you can see it and better understand it. Be sure your diagram shows how it's all interconnected.
2. Copy one of the structure diagrams on the board and discuss it in class.
3. What was your favorite gag-based cartoon of all time? Why? Discuss the structure of one of the classics.
4. Watch *Shrek*. List and discuss the basic structure points (hero and goal, villain, catalyst, game plan, turning points, major crisis, critical choice, battle, climax, and theme).
5. Discuss the subplot of *Shrek*. How does it weave in and out of the main plot and make the story richer?
6. List 10 possible themes for an animated feature.
7. If a short cartoon has less structure, what keeps our interest? Discuss.
8. What keeps our interest in a short film with no story? Discuss in class.
9. How much structure will your project need? Which structure method will you use, or do you plan to use another kind of framework? If you're using a structure that was not discussed, how will it hold your story together and make it interesting for the audience? Explain.
10. Who is your protagonist in your project? What's his problem or goal? What terrible thing will happen if he doesn't get what he wants? Who or what opposes him? Does your protagonist learn something by the end of the story and if so what?

CHAPTER 4
Developing Characters

Jean Ann Wright

HOW TO BEGIN

Put in as much time as it takes to develop characters that are really original and interesting! You'll want each of them to be as different from the others as possible. Those differences allow your characters to conflict and to relate to each other in funny ways. You'll probably want to start by writing a biography or fact sheet for each of your main characters. If you're an artist, you may prefer to start by drawing the characters. Often writers choose to script scenes between characters to see how they'll react. And actors sometimes prefer to improvise scenes out loud to develop their characters. Whatever works best for you is fine. Think of your characters as real actors. Get to know them so you know what they'll do. Lucky for you, your actors won't indulge in gourmet lunches and then demand a trainer to get in shape for the big battle scene or insist on a stunt double to fight the fifty-foot, flying monster with two robotic heads!

TYPES OF PEOPLE

People have been characterized by types and traits for eons. In the Middle Ages there was black bile (melancholic, sentimental, thoughtful), blood (sanguine, amorous, joyful), yellow bile (easily angered, obstinate), and phlegmatic (calm and cool). Another method divides the body into centers: head (soul, link to God), pituitary (integrated mental, emotional, and physical), throat (conscious creativity, intellect), heart (greater love, brotherhood of man, self-sacrifice), solar plexus (aspiration, group power, personal power), sacral (sex, money, fear), and root center (survival). Carl Jung classified types as the introvert or the extrovert, and then further into those who experience life mainly through

DOI: 10.1016/B978-0-240-81343-1.00004-2

sensing, thinking, feeling, or intuition. People have been characterized as being dependent, independent, or interdependent. Whether or not you believe in these kinds of classifications, any of these methods might help you to develop your characters. Of course, there's also astrology.

Consider these other norms. Real people are often in conflict with their character opposite. However, some people seek out others that complement their strongest traits. Usually, people are a combination of two or more types.

CLASSIC COMEDY CHARACTER TYPES

From its beginnings, comedy has often been based on a character type. It's a stereotype in that it's an exaggerated model we recognize and understand. This kind of character is valuable in comedy shorts like cartoons because we already know that character and what to expect. It saves time. We don't have to set up a new character for the audience, but we can go immediately into the story and the gags. We laugh when the character does the funny thing that we have come to expect, and we laugh when he does something off-the-wall that we don't expect. Inflexible types are great for comedy. These character types have a comic defect. You can set up a character type and bounce the world off him, using conflict and contrast. Think of Homer Simpson, Donald Duck, and the Grinch.

Comedy stemming from character allows for sustained humor, and it's remembered long after the gags and the situations. A good gag builds characterization, and characterization builds gags.

Classic Roman comedy types are still used in cartoons:

- *The Blockhead*—We're smarter than he. He's defeated before he even begins.
  - Fred Flintstone (*The Flintstones*)
- *The Naif*—The kid who's always in trouble.
  - Bart Simpson (*The Simpsons*)

Other typical comedy types include the following:

- *The Fish Out of Water*—The misfit. (Try developing a whole series around this type!)
  - Shrek (*Shrek*)
- *The Naïve*—Forever innocent.
  - Winnie the Pooh (*Winnie the Pooh*)
- *The Conniver*—Not innocent, but *really* guilty.
  - Wile E. Coyote (*Road Runner*)
- *The Zany*—Wild and crazy.
  - Aladdin (Disney's *Aladdin*)
- *The Poor Soul*—The underdog. This character works best today when he's a child or an animal. Be careful about adult characters that appear to be victims. If the adult is a victim, then he must constantly be struggling to get out of that situation for us to identify with him. Also, this kind of

character must retain his cool and remain likeable no matter what injustices are done to him. Charlie Chaplin fought for his dignity.
  o Tweety Pie (*Tweety Pie*)
- *The Coward*—Always the chicken.
  o Scooby-Doo (*Scooby-Doo*)

Classic Comedy Types vs. Negative Stereotypes

For a short cartoon, you may choose to use a classic comedy type that we already know, but take care to avoid negative stereotypes. Commercial broadcast television, especially, is a mass-market medium. Networks have censors that ensure that their comedy is politically correct, especially if the comedy is targeted at children. Some networks are more careful than others. In commercial TV advertisers will refuse to buy advertising in programming that offends. In a global marketplace where the audience is very diverse, a certain amount of political correctness is just common sense. You simply cannot afford to lose a segment of your audience…even if the gag is the funniest ever!

When you're writing about someone of the opposite sex, someone older or younger, someone with disabilities, or someone from another culture or lifestyle than the one you know well, consider what you write. Be aware of nuances. Think of people in terms of multi-dimensions. What do these characters do in their spare time? What are their relationships socially at play, at school, or at work?

Whether you're developing characters or just writing a scene, consider who would normally be in that location in real life. Who would be there in New York or Detroit? Who would be there in New Delhi or Beijing? What races, nationalities, social/economic classes, occupations, sexes, and ages would be there? Develop different characters into your series and films in places where you would normally find them and in places where they could be.

Value diversity! Prize differing beliefs and cultural values besides the traditional ones you know. Make minorities active, not passive. Avoid casting minorities as victims, or if they must be the victims, let them overcome this by themselves. Both bad guys and good guys come in many diverse types. You might want to create characters and then add a gender or race afterward. The key is in not isolating minority characters. One child in a wheelchair is a role model, but it's hard to make role models interesting and unique. If you have two or three characters with disabilities in the same script, then each can be unique and interesting, good guys and bad.

Do your research before you develop and write characters and scripts that are different from what you know best. Read the latest scientific studies. Get to know people who are not like you. This is a part of your job! Understand people's thought processes and really care about others. Try to get someone from another culture, lifestyle, age group, or sex to give you feedback about characters and scripts that are different from what you know so that you get it right.

Don't be afraid of a point of view! Let characters stand up for their culture and experiences and provide the rest of us with new insights.

Recent studies on gender differences are compelling: Most, but not all, women are more relational, better at reading emotions, nuances, and social cues. They're apt to be more sensitive to touch, pain, and sound. Their body movements may use more of the small muscle groups. They might score better in verbal skills and short-term memory. Men generally score better in mathematical, mechanical, and spatial skills. Assertiveness is likely to be higher in males. Males tend to do more exploring and may be more creative. Women often overcome problems with support from their friends. Men tend to deal with problems more on their own. Remember, however, that not all males or all females are the same. Today there are plenty of stay-at-home men and plenty of women who are CEOs. Try seeing sexuality in broader terms with warmth and love for all ages. Instead of describing people by their attractiveness, try describing them by intelligence, style, or uniqueness. Try giving your characters traits that are opposite from the norm.

Everyman vs. One-of-a-Kind

As human beings, there are qualities that we all possess. A character who is everyman is someone who represents us all, and we'll always be able to identify with that character. Real people are a combination of the qualities that we all possess and specific, unique traits. Characters should also be a combination of those global qualities and the unique characteristics that make them one-of-a-kind.

Complex and Original Characters

If you want to develop characters for a feature or a series that you hope will become a classic, then you probably want to develop more complex characters than the character types just listed. Classic characters who will be loved and remain on the toy shelves for decades are usually unique characters that we can all relate to and like. You want to give those characters a complete personality and an attitude toward each other. The more personality and individuality your characters have, the better your stories will be.

STARTING A PROFILE

Not every question that follows will be applicable or necessary for each character you develop. The most important information is what will help you delve into the thoughts, feelings, and emotions of your characters. Feelings and emotions are key to good writing! You might even want to write down your own character profile and delve more deeply into the things that make *you* tick. Tapping into your own emotions, often buried deep inside you, may help you hit pay dirt in understanding the complexity of your characters and getting inside their skins. Some people feel that it's better to write a character profile in the first person, as if it were an autobiography, so you really get inside the soul of each character. Your characters should be allowed some room to grow as you write more about them. The more you know about your characters, the better.

CHARACTER PROFILE

- Name (name may give us a clue: Precious, Cowboy, U.R. Steel, or Ted D. Bear)
- Sex
- Age
- Appearance (height; weight; hair color; eye color; physique; size; posture/poise/carriage; outstanding physical characteristics, such as dimples; dress—taste, neatness)
- Movement
  - Does he move like a dancer or someone who's sleepwalking? How does he walk?
  - Does he use expansive gestures when he talks?
- Mannerisms
- Voice (diction, vocabulary, power, pitch, unusual attributes)
  - What does the character say, and how?
  - Give your character a **dialogue tag** (Fred Flintstone's "Yabba dabba doo!").
  - Make your character's voice distinctively his or hers.
- I.Q., abilities, talents, qualities (imagination, judgment).
- Personality/attitudes/temperament. Attitudes are key to comedy and situation drama.
  - Is your character ambitious, loyal, sensitive? Inferior, optimistic? Shy? Sloppy? Eager?
  - Character flaws, bad habits, weaknesses
    - What is your character's biggest secret? What will happen if someone finds out?
    - What is your character's biggest fear? Why? What caused this?
    - What was your character's biggest disappointment?
    - What was his most embarrassing moment?
    - What was the worst thing that ever happened to him?
    - How does this affect your character today?
    - What makes your character angry? Frustrated? Ashamed?
    - Does he have self-esteem?
  - Is your character a loner? Does he belong to lots of groups? Which ones?
    - How does he connect with the other characters during your story?
  - What makes your character laugh?
  - How does he relax?
  - **Motivations**, goals, ambitions. What does your character want?
  - What is your character's **spine**? What's his unchanging driving force throughout life?

71

- o Does your character put his own self-interest first, or that of the group and its survival?
- o What are the shifting allegiances in your character's life?
- o Does he feel pressured by other people or circumstances?
  - ▪ What are your character's hard choices? Crises? Urgent decisions? How does he react differently from the norm?
- o Values. What's important to your character?
- o How does he feel about the past? What in past situations have specifically affected the important choices he is making in this story?
- o What are your character's current circumstances (rich/poor, good luck/bad luck)?
  - ▪ What effect do these things have?
  - ▪ What current threats exist in your character's life?
  - ▪ What opportunities does he have?
  - ▪ How does your character feel about the future?
- Situation
  - o How did your character get involved in this situation?
  - o What about his background or personality made him get involved?
  - o What kinds of changes has your character been going through?
    - ▪ Birth of a child? New brother or sister?
    - ▪ Marriage? New stepmother or stepfather?
    - ▪ Death in the family?
    - ▪ A major move?
    - ▪ A major school or job change?
  - o What external or internal stresses is your character facing?
- Birthplace
- Ethnic background (when needed, research for authenticity) and any cultural baggage?
- Social/economic/political/cultural background and current status (research)
- Education
- Occupation—research well if he has one. Values derived from the work (an accountant vs. an actress)
  - o Pace, stress factors, other characteristics of the job.
- Lifestyle
- Family
  - o Siblings? Parents? Husband or wife? Extended, adopted, or alternative family?
  - o How do these relationships now or in the past affect your character?
  - o How did he grow up? With love? Closeness? Neglect? Abuse?
  - o How did your character's family affect his self-image?
- Hobbies, amusements
  - o What does your character read, watch on TV/in the movies/on the Internet?
  - o What sports, exercise, or hobbies does your character engage in?
  - o What does he do on Saturdays? Sundays? Tuesday evenings?

- What makes him funny?
- Give your character one dominant trait, with a couple of other less important traits.
- Era—if this is historical, research well.
- Setting or place
  - What kind of people would be in this setting?
  - How would your character react to this setting? Would he be happy here?
    - Why or why not?
  - Where was your character before this? Why?
  - Is he likely to leave soon? Why or why not?
  - Does this setting or where he was before give your character a different outlook or attitude? A different rhythm?
  - What sounds, smells, and tastes are in your character's surroundings?

You don't need to answer every single one of these questions, but do take the time to get to know your character. Use the Character Profile to help you explore personality.

TYPES OF CHARACTERS

Different kinds of stories have different kinds of characters. Realistic characters are often found in modern stories and in dramas and are multidimensional. These characters have feelings and attitudes just like real people. We can see what motivates them. They act like people we know.

The classic hero is found in classic tales, often oral histories. The story is meant to teach us some important truth. The classic hero had some realistic traits and some that were more symbolic that made him bigger than life. He's an adventurer, a person of action, a warrior. Often the hero goes on a quest with much demanded of him along the way. He may find a mentor, undergo tests, and win a final battle to attain his goal and save the day for all. His journey makes him stronger and wiser. Classic heroes and heroines are found in myths, westerns, crime and war stories, science fiction, comics, and many children's stories.

Fantasy characters are romantic. Often they live in a magical world with powers that can be used for good or evil. They're more realistic and less exaggerated. They usually have a limited number of traits. They may look different, and these physical characteristics might extend to their personalities. Much of the fun of these characters is the fish-out-of-water conflicts they have. This world could be a nightmare world or a world of our fondest dreams. Stories can be funny or tales of good and evil. It's possible for humans to enter into these fantasy worlds and for fantasy characters to suddenly find themselves in a world that is real.

Nonhuman characters often personify certain human traits. Pooh is always hungry; Scooby is always scared. Usually, only a few traits are given to the character, and the audience can identify with those traits. These qualities may stem from the properties or physical appearance of the animal or object itself. A cat uses its eyes like a soldier with a night vision weapon, or a stick of gum clings.

Symbolic characters are meant to represent a trait or idea. They're one-dimensional and stand for qualities like love or evil, justice or fear. We find these characters in myths, comic book stories, fairy tales, and other fantasy. The Ancient Greeks and Romans used these characters, and they appeared in the morality plays of the Middle Ages and in the Punch and Judy shows later. There are no gray areas in these personalities.

Everyman represents the ordinary man or woman or every kid. This character is less specific and more symbolic. He has more than one trait, but he is generalized and we should always be able to see ourselves in this character.

TAKING YOUR CHARACTER FURTHER

Consider other ways to develop characters. Is your character like anyone you know? Who? Does the character resemble an actor or actress or one of the characters they play? In what way? Stay away from characters that have been overdone. Does thinking about this real or fantasy person give you any ideas to make your character funnier or more realistic? Is this character a combination of people? Juxtaposing traits gives you something we wouldn't expect. You might want to take this real or fantasy character, and then give his personality a new twist.

Observe people and use your observations. Try taking some real traits that you've observed, and add a funny trait to make your character unique.

Quality characters are often more complex. This may explain why they tend to have more lasting appeal. Make a list of inconsistencies in your character: He's this, but he's also that! What's illogical, surprising, and unpredictable about him? What makes him interesting? Different? Fascinating? Compelling? Never too bland? Always larger than life? Use "what ifs" to dig deeper into your characters. Once you've decided on these inconsistencies, they should remain constant. They do not change on whim or in keeping with the current episode's story.

What makes your character funny? A comic character needs to have a flaw that makes him funny. What are his funny attributes? What very human mistakes does he make that would make us laugh? Recognize ourselves? Be typical and recognizable to kids of a specific age category? We tend to like comedians who let us feel superior (like Charlie Chaplin). We know that we're much smarter, more resourceful, and luckier than they. For animation comedy we often want to create loveable and larger-than-life characters to whom slapstick things are almost certain to happen. It's human nature to like to see slapstick things happen to people with power or authority, especially if they're pompous or misusing that authority (the mean boss, the overbearing substitute teacher, the bully who's a hall guard). Most of us humans struggle to be normal, to be perfect children or parents, to be the ideal student or employee, and fail at these things every step of the way. Much of current television is based on these failings.

Do you really understand this character and what makes him tick? How is this character similar or different from you? Let his feelings and emotions show. Do you like him (even if he's the villain)? Accept the shadow side of yourself so you can accept those flaws in your characters. If you truly understand and like your characters, others probably will, too. If you still don't quite "get" your character, do more research. Delve more deeply into yourself. Write or act out scenes that won't be in your script to learn more about him. Make your character real to you.

Then exaggerate! Make your characters larger than life. Think James Bond or Superman! When the average person is the main character, he or she often walks taller than in real life. The character becomes a model of all average people. Make your slob a superslob, the bore a superbore. Exaggerate! Exaggerate! Exaggerate!

More realistic characters are harder to animate convincingly. You can't squash and stretch a real person. The less realistic ones lend themselves more to the medium and to the gags, especially if it's a comedy.

What **behavioral tags** does this character have? These are repeated actions that are specific to that character. Does he go into a one-armed handstand when overjoyed? Does she shake her hips from side to side or tug on her ear?

Set up relationships. One way to create a series is to start with a character type, or one really strong character, and let all the remaining characters bounce off. How does your character feel about each of the other characters, and how do they feel about him? Why are these characters friends or enemies? Contrast characters (a smart guy with a dumb guy). How does this character affect each of the others by the strength of his personality, by his actions? How do they affect him? Does he team up well or conflict with the others? Each of your characters should be as different as possible from each other. You might want to make a list of characters and then itemize the traits of each to make them as different as you can.

There may be two stars. What brings your characters together and keeps them together? What pushes them apart and provides the sparks? Is life better for others around this team or worse? Is life sweet or bitter when they're together? Are there enough believable reasons that this team will stay together, or is the conflict intense enough that they must eventually split up and end your series? Too much attraction and the show is boring; too much conflict and the characters may become unlikable. Roadblocks may come from the situation rather than the characters themselves to avoid this problem.

Avoid using too many characters. Keep economy in mind. Also, it becomes much harder to identify with characters who don't receive a lot of screen time. If there are many, we don't care about any of them.

Can we identify with this character? Bond? Does the audience have real recognition of that character? We need enough information about a character to empathize. What are the real-life, down-to-earth traits that we immediately recognize? What are the character's little eccentricities, small compulsions, and very human characteristics? Or you may want the audience to feel superior to (rather than identify with) a character. Think of Scooby-Doo. You could let your character be the scapegoat, the butt of her own or someone else's jokes. It's okay to let your character appear foolish and find life difficult. The audience sympathizes.

Do we really respond strongly to (or against) this character as a person? We need to feel that this character is family. What makes us root for her or hate her? How can we strengthen this? It's been said that it's hard to sympathize with someone who is too naive or dumb, but one moving relationship with another person may save an otherwise unsympathetic character. If you must have an unsympathetic character who's not a villain, then start by showing what happened to make her that way. Avoid showing your **protagonist** as a complete misfit in the beginning. Your audience must like her and admire her enough to want her to recognize character flaws and try to change. We like characters with positive goals and dislike characters who are evil or selfish and have negative goals. If something is important to your likeable character, then it will probably be important to your audience as well.

Buyers like a cartoon character with an edge, someone you love to hate. Think of bad Bart Simpson. The audience will identify with someone who's not sickening sweet but has tastes, dreams, and weaknesses.

Is your villain *really* bad? Your hero or heroine is only as strong and as good as your villain is evil. A truly great villain can add inches to the stature of a hero. Is your villain a life-and-death threat? A monstrous **antagonist** requires a stronger hero to beat him. But you may want to add those shades of gray, a wisp of human kindness where you least expect it. Give your villain emotions and feelings to make him vulnerable. Motivations keep any villain from becoming cardboard. In a very short story you may require a fairly cardboard villain due to the lack of time to develop anything else. Why does this villain want what he wants? Is he aware of how evil he seems to others? How does he convince himself that this is right or at least justified? A funny villain isn't very frightening. Watch out for bumbling antagonists. They need to be at least as strong as the hero to make it a fair fight. A bumbler might work in a comedy, especially for younger children. If you want a funny villain, try making him the secondary antagonist, with a stronger and more evil villain as the main foe. The antagonist doesn't always have to be a villain and be evil, but the antagonist *usually* is evil in animation.

MORE TO THINK ABOUT

Today's characters should be able to extend across media. Think in terms of film, TV, home video and DVD, the Internet, wireless, books, games, toys, and other merchandise.

Layer details, gestures, speech, imperfections, behaviors, original reactions, and approaches to action. Layering makes your character more interesting and attracts different demographic groups for different reasons.

If this character is for a series or a game, is your character interesting and unique enough to not eventually become boring? Is there some mystery there, a feeling that there's more to find out, more we want to know? Can your character grow? How? Is she strong enough to sustain conflict and be funny week after week? Characters must have enough history to allow the audience to continually be discovering something fresh. Two or more characters who have known each other in the past can keep tapping into this history.

In a series characters probably change a little over the course of each story, but if they change too much, then their relationships have changed, and you no longer have that same series. You have to watch out for that.

For television keep your characters simple, something you can establish (without detail) in a speech or a half page of script. Your characters should have only two or three major attributes. Keep them visually simple as well. A simple character makes a better stuffed toy. The character animates more easily and ends up looking nicer in a TV series because the artists can draw or model him better and quicker. Every detail and extra color adds pencil time or modeling time during the animation process, adding up to increased animation expenses. When designing, think three-dimensionally for toys and for animation because the character must be drawn or modeled and seen from every angle as she moves.

As you're designing these characters, you'll want to show what they look like from all angles (front, back, and side, and possibly from a low angle and a high angle as well). You'll want them drawn in action and flaunting an attitude, showcasing their personality. You'll want them posed so that we can see easily what they're doing if we can only see a silhouette. We want to also see them in relationships with one or more of the other characters, preferably in typical backgrounds of the series or film.

Okay—now you've developed your characters. Is a character missing…someone to set off the other characters, set sparks flying, take the **plot** off in another direction? Try creating a situation in which your characters have to react. The way they react is the way you get to know them and test their relationships.

Any character that is similar to another character shouldn't be there. Remember that characters should be as different from each other as possible to keep interest, provide conflict, and comment on the theme. Their traits and visual appearances should be different; they should contrast in values, attitudes, lifestyles, and experience. A comedy, especially, requires that each character contrast sharply with each other character to provide the humor.

Let your characters evolve as you work with them. Changing one part of the puzzle usually means adjusting others. This is a process; do some research of your own. Try out your characters on your own kids, on your nieces and nephews, on a youth group. You might test them at children's wards in hospitals or as mascots. Make up a story about them to tell your kids at bedtime. Watch reactions, ask questions, and make developmental changes accordingly.

77

Keep your characters consistent. They must remain true to their core traits and to what has made them who they are. Keep their choices consistent with their values.

Put your best character in the right concept for him. The concept and the character should be a tight fit. Stories should stem from the personalities of the main characters.

YOUR CHARACTER IN A STORY

If you're creating characters for a feature or a short as opposed to a series, then you want to develop them to best tell your specific story. Characters have conflicts in dramas and do funny things in comedy because they are so different. So their values in life must be different. Your characters must be created with personalities that best express a conflict in their values. Values indicate a **theme**. The theme centers on the core values that are expressed in a story, the basic message, or lesson that the protagonist learns. You may want your main character to reveal something about the theme to us but probably not in words. Maybe he represents one point of view about your theme and the villain who opposes him represents the opposing view. Maybe the other characters all represent differing points of view. One character could even express the point of view of the audience. But each character should have his own good motivations for feeling the way he does.

Your audience needs to be able to identify right away who the major characters are and be able to tell them apart easily by name, sight, and personality. We should recognize, too, which characters are minor and unimportant. Use height, weight, ethnic type, voice, hairstyle, clothing style and color, attitudes, and movement to help identify characters.

The hero or heroine must be the most interesting character in the story. If he's not, then you might want to consider centering the story on the colorful character instead, making him the protagonist. Supporting characters don't have the burden of driving the story forward, and so they may become more interesting and colorful. Don't let them take over! If your characters get too pushy, stand up to them, and threaten to erase them from your hard drive!

You may want your less important characters to help in defining the role of the hero. Is your hero a leader, a father figure, the class clown? Minor characters can help us to understand the star's role in his peer group and in the story.

All characters need a story function, or they shouldn't be there. What's the essence of this character—the core or nub? What is the one dominant characteristic that most affects the plot? If a character doesn't affect the plot, then remove him. A character should always be motivated by this essential characteristic, and every other trait should ideally come out of this one or support it. What event or circumstance or decision in the past made him this way?

Character information is sprinkled throughout the script, not crammed into the beginning. Use only the essence, and be concise. Use conflicts, contrasts, reactions, gags, or visual symbols to convey information and define character.

Consider your protagonist or hero. What plans does he make, and what does he do to attain this goal? What decisions does she make along the way? How do they affect her? How do they affect others? What terrible thing is at stake if our hero doesn't reach this goal? Animation protagonists invariably do reach their goals at the end.

What are each character's goals? What do they want? Do we care? What are their hidden agendas? What do they *really* want? (If this is animation for kids, what drove you personally as a kid?) What does each character promise? You should only set up traits and circumstances that apply to this story and the goal. But if a character is playing with matches, we need to see the inferno, the payoff. Don't cheat your audience out of the juiciest parts of your story.

Think in terms of scenes. What are your characters' goals in each scene? Which character is driving each scene? What are your characters' feelings in each scene?

Is there a broad range of emotions throughout your story? What are the conflicts your characters go through to reach their goals? The goals of different characters should conflict to set off sparks. We need to see the effects of conflict on the main characters. Characters should confront difficult choices, and they must make those choices themselves. The more difficult the choice, the more interesting the story. Because of difficult choices we get to know the characters better, and we come to admire them more. What's hidden along the way from your characters or from the audience? What things do some characters hide from themselves? As all this information comes to light, the choices become ever more difficult, leading to the most difficult choice of all, the **critical choice**, near the end of the story. These choices make your characters drop their masks. They react instinctively, revealing what's been hidden. What do we learn about a character then? What does that character learn about himself? How does he change because of it? Characters change each other. Does your character always stay in character, acting and reacting in ways that only he would do?

In the end, this is what's important: What event/circumstance/decision in the past is still affecting your hero today, making him who he is and driving the plot of the story you're writing today? Anything that you discovered about your character in developing him that doesn't relate to this is unimportant and doesn't belong in your story.

ANIMATED CHARACTERS LIVE

The technology exists to control animation and lip-sync of characters in real-time. What this means is that kids can call into a show and speak to their favorite character on the air live as an actor/animator controls the animation and lip-syncs in a booth. Interactive games can become a part of a live show with callers using telephone keypad game controllers. Actor/animators could develop their own characters for this kind of production. Or writers could provide a cast of actor/animators with detailed bios, backstories, and guidelines for the characters they portray.

ANIMATED CHARACTERS AS ICONS

Internet providers are just one source of supply for animated character icons with personality. These characters have built-in animated behaviors that respond to real-time input. They can accompany instant messages, responding to the text with motion, sound, color, and humor. File size for these characters must be small, and many of the character expressions are exaggerated to give them more visual impact in the limited space. There appears to be a great future for characters like these in cell phones, sales pitches, and so many other areas. Changing technology will continue to open up new opportunities for animated characters.

MARKET RESEARCH

Studies seem to show that kids like characters that they can identify with, characters that appear to be like them in one or more ways. The youngest children like characters that are safe and nurturing or that they can nurture in return. They like characters that they can emulate: heroes and heroines, teen or adult role models, sports figures, entertainment figures. Children, too, are fascinated by the dark side of life and are entertained by villains. Perhaps it's a way of learning to deal with life on a more adult level. Children generally prefer characters who are older than they are, or at least that's what they want other kids to think. Boys often prefer male characters, although girls apparently have no preference. Boys are more apt to be attracted to power and control, to defending the right, to the gross and silly. Girls still seem to be more romantic in the broadest sense and more nurturing. Animal characters often are nonage and nongender specific, making them less likely to be rejected for those reasons.

We all like characters that satisfy our basic emotional needs and values while still appearing fresh and "in." Children and adults alike seek love, acceptance, belonging, and security. We all strive for independence and control. Parents want to instill the very best of all qualities in their children.

Popularity usually starts with the oldest and drops down in age. When characters become too popular, then the fad subsides. Part of being a fad means being the first. By the time a character is beloved around the world, it has started to lose its appeal.

PROTECTING YOUR RIGHTS TO YOUR CHARACTERS

If you hire an artist to design your characters for you, then that artist needs to sign a simple "Work for Hire" agreement *before he sets pencil to paper*. It's recommended that you obtain the services of an entertainment attorney to draw this agreement up for you. If you don't have an agreement signed *before* pencil is set to paper, then you don't own the character—the artist does.

You must protect the characters you've created, but if your project includes a **bible** or a script, then it's best to file for protection and copyright when the project is completed. You may wish to file for trademark protection then as well. In the meantime, place the following information on each piece of completed artwork, title page of script, and bible: © (copyright symbol) 2009 (year of completion) Jean Ann Wright (your name). Your work is not protected without that information.

EXERCISES

1. Think back to when you were a child. Who were the people that you liked the best? Who frightened you? Why? Can you use any of these people as the basis of a character? Exaggerate!

2. Use kids you know for the following: Listen to kid dialogue. Write it down. Make a list of hobbies and activities, especially noting anything that is interesting and out of the ordinary. Ask the kids about places they especially remember and like. What places made them afraid? What do they hate? What hurts their feelings? What embarrasses them? What makes girls scream? What makes them laugh or cry? What does their sister or brother do that they hate the most? Save the lists.

3. Go to a mall or park and watch people. How are they different? How do they walk? What funny mannerisms do they have? How do they change their behavior when interacting with different people? Do they react to their environment? Now create two opposing characters from those that you've seen. Add new traits. Give them motivations. What's the conflict? How can you make them funnier?

4. Observe half a dozen animals or everyday objects. What stands out about each one? Pick an "essence" that you can develop into character traits: the happy-go-luck dog, the sly cat waiting to pounce, or an elegant tapestry pillow. Develop them into characters first as the animals or objects that they are and then into animated people.

5. Choose a classmate to work with. You'll each think like a character, any character. Ask each other these three questions:
   A. What do you want?
   B. How do you move (your walk, things you do with your hands, etc.)?
   C. What do you enjoy doing?
   It's okay to make up wild and funny answers. Now change partners and ask each other three different questions:
   A. What's your biggest fear?
   B. What do you sound like?
   C. Who or what are you (male, female, person, animal, object…like a banana)?
   Individually, develop a unique, new character using most of these attributes. Discuss your characters in class.

6. Think of the funniest thing that ever happened to you or a friend. If you can't think of anything, make something up. What kind of

81

character would make that situation even funnier? You may improve the details, if you wish. Discuss.

7. Develop three to six characters that you can use in a TV series, a short, an animated feature, or a game. You may work any way that is most comfortable for you, filling out a fact sheet, scripting short scenes, doodling and drawing, or improvising monologues or scenes between characters.

8. Grab a piece of paper and list at the top each of the three to six characters you're developing for your project. Underneath list the opposing attributes and traits of each, making sure that each character is as different from each of the others as possible. Will these characters conflict or rub against each other in a funny way?

9. Write out a detailed biography of each of your characters and give them a name.

10. Design your characters or work with an artist who can.

SECTION 2
Widening Your Perspective

CHAPTER 5

Animation Comedy and Gag Writing

Jean Ann Wright

WHAT MAKES *YOU* LAUGH?

What makes you laugh? Or, more importantly, what makes your audience laugh? "Why does Brutus the Brave refuse to cross the road?" "Because he's no chicken!" Humor varies from culture to culture and from age to age. In comedy we set up a situation, increase the tension, and suddenly we're stopped dead by something unexpected. Emotion gushes out, tension is relieved and exploded into laughter. At least that's the way it's supposed to work. And it *will* work if you set up the gag right. Comedy is a contrast between two individually consistent but forever incongruous frames of reference linked in an unexpected and sudden way. A stereotype is twisted. You lead the audience down the garden path (the setup) and then—zap! Surprise is very important. Generally the bigger the surprise, the bigger the belly laughs. Two classic baby jokes, peek-a-boo and the jack-in-the-box, demonstrate at an early age what makes us laugh. There's the buildup, the expectation, then the pop or shock.

Some forms of comedy, like satire, don't rely on a single effect but a series of minor explosions or a continuous state of mild amusement. A running gag gets funnier with each repetition. Think of *the Road Runner* series, one long running gag.

Experts believe that all comedy contains an impulse of aggression or fear. The fear may be combined with affection, as it is when we tease. It's this fear or aggression that's released when we laugh. Shock works well. Repression can contribute to a bigger laugh. Repression is the reason that gross-out and bathroom humor get belly laughs. The energy of the comedy is important. Whether a situation is tragic or funny depends on the audience's attitude, whether that attitude is dominated by pity or animosity. Who is slipping on the ice? Is it the sweet, little old lady or the school bully? If it's the little old lady, the two frames of reference remain juxtaposed. We're apt to feel sorry for her. But if it's the bully,

DOI: 10.1016/B978-0-240-81343-1.00005-4

the two frames of reference collide, and we laugh. The experts claim that kids naturally laugh at cruelty and boasting. They laugh when a hoax is played or when others are in some way made uncomfortable. A witty remark may go over their heads. Of course, in children's media we need to consider good taste and good role models as well and use common sense in what we want children to see. Humor for kids is politically correct, but that does not mean it's boring!

ANIMATION COMEDY

How is animation comedy different? It's above all visual with plenty of sight gags. The very basis of your idea must be visual. Animation uses motion and misuses the laws of physics. Timing is important. The comedy is exaggerated, often taking reality one step beyond. It may be illogical. There might be a use of fantasy, occasionally with musical numbers and dances. Dialogue may be "smart" with comebacks, put-downs, puns, rhymes, or alliteration. Titles are funny. Names of people, places, and things are funny. Most executives that buy or approve stories prefer material that will make both the kids and the adults that could be watching with them laugh. Of course, this means higher ratings and higher box office receipts. However, a few executives prefer the comedy material to be specific to a single age group. So you must find out what the executives who are going to approve your material want. Never write down to the kids!

COMEDY OUT OF A CHARACTER'S PERSONALITY

The funniest comedy develops out of a character's personality. Take a classic character type and twist it. What makes your unique character naturally funny? Use a character's attitude, mannerisms, and dialogue to increase the comedy. Reactions and comedy takes can often be funnier than the gag that has gone before. You might also play against character type or expectation for your humor: a rough and tough dog that cringes at the sight of a bug. Exaggerate appearance, diction, behavior, and attitude. Act out your scenes as you write. How would that action really happen? How would you feel if you were that character? How can you exaggerate and make it funnier? Spend some time developing comedy and gags from the personalities of your characters. Good characters and the comedy that their relationships can provide is the best recipe for a classic script. Characters with a comic defect and fish-out-of-water characters are types that work well for comedy. Use characters as different from each other as possible so that these conflicting personalities can bounce off of each other in a funny way.

WRITING A FUNNY TELEVISION SCRIPT

Start by putting yourself in the mood to *think* funny! Then begin to analyze. Where does the humor of this series originate? Is it belly laughs, giggles, or smiles? Is there visual humor or funny, smart dialogue? What's funny about the star's personality? Be consistent to the kind and amount of humor of that show.

Combine people, places, and props, juxtaposing one idea with a totally different one (an angry man and an office cooler in the middle of the desert). Place the unexpected in a surprising context. Place the obvious where the viewer would least expect it. Place incongruous words or things in juxtaposition to create surprising relationships. Make sure that your script is sprinkled with spot gags throughout. Come up with a script that's funny and fresh, or at least put a new twist onto a classic idea.

Try creating an episode around a funny situation: perhaps the fish-out-of-water or an unresolved predicament (like a lie or a secret). You can give your star a tough choice between two good things or two that are bad. Often there's a catalyst that rocks the boat. The star may make a plan, but it turns into a textbook case of Murphy's Law, and everything that can go wrong does. Complicate the predicament your star finds herself in by adding additional layers of problems. Escalate the trouble so that she digs herself in deeper and deeper. Maybe there's a race against time with your star in really big trouble if her parents come home early or if she doesn't get something fixed before they find out what she did. Or maybe your star is trapped somewhere embarrassing.

Be sure you have plenty of props available because these are necessary for the gags. Misuse your props. Make up your own wild gadgets.

Set up your gags with the basic information of the joke. You might intentionally mislead your audience in the setup with false clues. A beat or two of complications or incongruity adds tension, but keep the setup short. Exaggerate everything. Build your gags, **milk** them, and top them. Add a **capper**. Comedy is a process of setup and **payoff**, and this is often done in a rhythm of three…dum, dum, de-dum! Setup, setup, payoff! Sometimes you can set up now and pay off later with the **punch line**. You may have multiple punch lines, each one funnier than the one before. Friz Freleng often timed his animation to the beat of a metronome. He'd get a rhythm going and then break it for the surprise. Get a feel for the timing, and work on your gag until it feels right.

Getting the laugh often depends on using the right words in exactly the right order. If something isn't funny enough, try adding C's and K's to the dialogue. These sounds are funnier!

Use timing, tension, and hints, letting your audience bring a little to the whole and bridging the gap. Use simplification and selection. Give the audience A, B, C and F, G. The audience should have to supply D and E. Use implicit, not explicit, punch lines. Instead of saying, "Miss Petunia eats like a pig!" you want to say, "Miss Petunia is invited to lunch. Should I get out our best trough?" Don't tip off the surprise—the punch line—but save it for the end. Save the biggest, wildest, and best gag for the climax. Scenes usually go out on a laugh line, a **stinger**, or a **button**. End your script with a twist!

Get feedback on your gags from story editors or trusted friends. Listen with an open mind, and don't get defensive. Try to put the script away for a couple of days; then look at it with a fresh point of view, consider the suggestions carefully, and do your rewrite. If something bothers you even a little, then it's not right. Fix it! Turn in your very best work.

PUTTING TOGETHER COMEDY SCRIPTS

Established writers have several theories for putting together comedy scripts. Some believe that comedy plots need to be simple to have the room to make the story funny. They like to focus on doing comedy riffs around a basic subject. This works best on short cartoons, where a complicated plot isn't necessary to hold the viewer's interest. Some writers like to use the leapfrog method (a story-developing scene, then a comedy scene, then a story-developing scene…all the way through). Even action scripts in cartoons usually have some comedy scenes. These scenes are used to break up the tension from the intense action. After all, this method was good enough for Shakespeare. In a longer story with more depth, consider the effect of tension and when you want it released. Tension built up in a mystery can be released in a good comedy scene. But if you want the tension built up for the climax, perhaps you don't want a comedy scene immediately prior to that climax. Most writers just use their judgment on what will work best for the length and depth of the story they're writing.

COMEDY DEVICES

Cartoon gags have an old history with roots in vaudeville and magazine cartoons, as well as comic books and silent films. Here are a few comedy devices that you can use in writing gags:

Old Gags

Don't be afraid to take an old gag and update it with a twist.

Impersonation/Disguise

A character in costume or drag. This is great for kids' cartoons. Children like this best when the character is embarrassed by the disguise.

Multiple Personalities or Role Reversal

These devices allow characters to do things that they wouldn't normally do.

- For multiple personalities: A witch places a spell over a rabbit, and the rabbit changes into a flamboyant frog, then an unlikely looking prince, then a meek but gigantic lion.
- In role reversal: A normally responsible girl pretends to be flighty in order to attract the attention of the football captain.

Anthropomorphism

Like impersonation and role reversal, you have two forms of reference, and you oscillate between them. *Scooby-Doo*

Multiple Reference

Two or more frames of reference in one gag or joke. "His mom repaired the microwave with extra parts from an old jet. Now when she opens the oven, the bagel circles the table twice before coming in for a blue-plate landing."

Pretense and Exposure

Pretending to be someone the character is not, hypocrisy unmasked. Pretense usually involves character mannerisms and business, perhaps a change in voice. *The Emperor's New Clothes*

Reactions and Takes

These are usually used in an ending to a gag, rather than as gags themselves. They rely on funny expressions, reactions, or a funny take, even a double take. The character is often left in a funny pose, perhaps with something on top of his head.

Pull Back and Reveal

The basic gag element is at first hidden from the audience. We see a tic-tac-toe game in progress. We pull back to see that the game is being played by two very dignified scientists in the middle of a dry erase board covered with complicated, mathematical formulas.

Hidden Element

The gag element is hidden from one of the characters.

Twist Around

Things are the opposite of what we expect. *Alice in Wonderland/Through the Looking Glass.* The twist might be in the dialogue: "That teacher's so mean that when a pit bull sees her, he runs for his blankie." Or the gag could be visual: At a spa snooty pigs, dressed to kill, are taking a tour. They turn up their noses as they watch people wallow in mud baths.

Misunderstanding

Old is mistaken for young, man for woman, and so on. Sitcoms use this technique often. The teacher says to the principal, "I won't put up with those pests!" In the next scene we see a classroom of kids waiting for their teacher. Instead…in walks the pest control man!

Twisted Clichés

Take a cliché and twist it.

- Twisted—a visual twist is part of the cliché gag. "They're playing our song!" We see performing birds ringing bells as they peck out a once-romantic ballad.
- Turnabout cliché—one important word is changed. Two kids at recess are fighting. One says, "She called me a dirty number."
- Literal cliché—The gag centers on a word in the cliché that has more than one meaning. We use the wrong one. "One pitcher is worth a thousand words."
- Cliché visual—A new gag is made out of a cliché picture. Uncle Sam is pointing his finger. We pull back to see Uncle Sam's son, looking defiant. Uncle Sam says, "You pick up your toys before you watch the fireworks!"

Customs

The juxtaposition of references from two different occupations, ethnic customs, or time periods. *The Flintstones, The Jetsons*

Pop-Culture References

Shared cultural experiences. *Shrek*

Topical Humor

Jokes based on the news of the day or time period. You can use any old joke and bring it up to date. Topical humor is harder to use in animation because of the extensive lead-in time until the television show or film is shown. Also, topical humor may be dated by the time a show is rerun or released on DVD. *The Simpsons, South Park*

The "In" Joke

"In" and upscale. "In Beverly Hills 911 is unlisted."

The Dumb Joke (usually a belly laugh)

Blonde jokes, women driver jokes

Kid's Mistakes

Not always funny to kids. This is hard to use in kids' cartoons unless the joke involves a younger brother, sister, tagalong, or (in the same vein) a pet. *Bill Cosby's Kids Say the Darnedest Things*

The True Story

Usually this is a real belly laugh. Often it's something embarrassing that has actually happened to you.

The Ridiculous Situation

The opposite from The True Story. The gag is exaggerated so far that it couldn't possibly be true, but the sheer ridiculousness of it is funny. The cowboy riding the nuclear bomb.

Understatement

Chaos may be all around, or something very unusual is happening. The main character ignores it or says something very understated. A huge crowd is watching the take off of the first flight to leave our solar system. The spaceship rockets toward the sky, then explodes like a firecracker. Cool Surfer Dude: "Looks like a dud, dude."

The Excuse

We've all made them, and we recognize ourselves. Usually there's a lie involved. The character tends to keep digging himself in deeper and deeper.

Insult and Name-Calling (often a belly laugh)

These are some of the easiest to write. You have to be careful in children's television, but it can be done. *Teenage Mutant Ninja Turtles* used this frequently.

Comebacks and Put-Downs

Modern cartoon staples.

Malapropism

The wrong word. Dr. Seuss's holiday dinner of "roast beast."

Literal Use of Words

Take a slang word and use it literally.

Whimsy

"I feel like burying myself in a box of jelly beans and committing spearmint!"

Definition

"A lie is like a watering can. It usually has holes in it."

Pun, Witticism, Poetry with Rhymes and Alliteration (all a snicker to a chuckle, not a belly laugh)

These should be used along with (and not in place of) sight gags. They don't work internationally because they can't be translated properly. Association based on pure sound. Kids love the sound of words: "The monster mumbled through a mouthful of still-morphing marshmallows." Also, a play on words and ideas where two different reference scales meet. Think cliché, then twist: "Eager beagle."

Caricature, Satire (verbal caricature), Irony

We see ourselves and yet something else. Fun-house mirrors. Irony appears to take seriously what it really does not. This might be over the heads of kids.

Parody

A funny put-on of someone or something. Often these are twists on books, movies, or television shows.

Funny Sounds

Anything with a C or K. Some sounds and letters are funnier than others. Sound effects. Accents. For children's media accents should not be demeaning.

Misplaced Emphasis

This can be a child's lack of understanding or a ditsy adult. But something is not right in the sentence context.

Transition, Digression, or Non Sequitur

A mood or mental picture is broken by a complete transition of thought or inflection in the punch line. The punch line isn't logical and doesn't fit the setup.

False Logic

"How do you get milk from a kernel of corn?" "You use a low stool!"

Say One Thing and Show Another

What is said is the setup. What is shown is the punch line.

Metamorphosis

In animation someone or something can totally change physically into someone or something entirely different.

Shell Game

People, props, or animals shuffle, hide, and pop up where they're least expected.

Funny Chase

Chases right out of the Keystone Cops.

Food Is Fun

Characters can have food fights. Food can be gross or crazy like fried bugs or purple ice cream with green spots.

Rube Goldberg Inventions

Kids love fantastic machines, devices, and contraptions—the more complex and sillier, the better.

Try-Fails

Kids love a character who keeps trying and goofing up. They can relate. Build this series of failures so that each failure is bigger than the one before.

Action Gag

Based on action rather than a funny situation. Action gags are very visual and depend on timing and the funny way in which the action is performed.

The Running Gag

Keeps repeating during the course of the story or series. It's funnier as it goes along. Often has a twist each time it repeats. Bugs Bunny's "What's up, Doc?"

Gag Series

All based on a single situation or prop. This series builds and gets funnier and wilder with each new gag topping the one before. Here you're milking one basic idea for all it's worth: A cat watches a goldfish in a bowl. The fish peeks out, and you see two huge, cat eyes magnified by the bowl. The goldfish dives and flips a piece of seaweed onto the cat's nose. The cat reacts and leaps for the bowl. In the next shot we see the bowl on top of the cat's head. The fish blows a huge bubble. It lands on the cat's tail. The cat turns around and bats at the bowl, flipping the goldfish up into the air. By the end of the gag series, the whole room is in a shambles, with the fish playing a victory song on its own scales.

93

Artist Gags

The artists devise these. They involve funny drawings, the use of funny staging, design, animation, effects, and color. The writer may try to describe them, but it's really up to the artists to make them funny.

Playing with the Medium

These gags surprise the audience by going against expectations in timing, cinematography, design, animation, and filmmaking.

Speeded-Up/Slow Motion Action

Use a change in normal speed for your gag.

Laws of Physics

Animation often rewrites the laws of physics. Wile E. Coyote runs in the air before falling to the bottom of the canyon and flattening, but he always reappears in the next scene unhurt.

Proportion

Play tricks with big and little, fat and skinny—perspective.

Motion Gags

Any gag that uses motion is especially suited to animation. A treadmill becomes an escalator.

Death

This is a hard one, but it can be done! The point is that anything can be made funny.

The Surprise Ending

A scene or an entire show may be fairly standard and cliché. But the ending has a comedy twist and saves it. Often this twist is heightened if what goes just before is especially everyday and normal. This doubles the surprise.

MORE COMEDY TECHNIQUES TO TRY

To build a gag, try taking a situation, building it, exaggerating it, and then making a sudden reverse. Or use Gene Perret's "Uh-oh Technique": Everything is going all right, then something happens and the audience says, "Uh-oh!" Or the character doesn't realize just how grave the crisis is, but the audience does.

Use switching techniques, taking one basic situation and then making a funny variation on the situation. Make lists of words, phrases, events, places, people, facts, things, and symbols that relate or are opposite to the main topic. Conjure up surprising and ridiculous images from your list. Write about what makes you passionate or angry. Attack authority. Look at a problem from all angles and home in on what's illogical. Verbal humor works well when the budget is small and animation is limited. Visual humor works better internationally, as any word play can get lost in translation. And it's okay to be silly! Have fun!

GLOBAL COMEDY

Comedy can be culture-specific. Certainly, a people's history influences their comedy. If you're writing comedy for a specific country, you should be aware of their preferences in humor. Study what films and television shows are successful in that country and which ones fail. Visual humor is almost universal.

COMEDY IN YOUR ORIGINAL PROJECT

If you're developing an original project, rather than writing comedy for someone else, you want your comedy to be particularly fresh. One thing you might want to consider is character point of view. If you give one of your main characters a point of view that's totally unique and off-center, that view of reality will change the entire world around him, and you'll have a funny script. Another way to develop fresh material is to create a new storytelling style that's uniquely suited to this one project. Or you might want to develop a style that's especially suited to you! You can brand yourself with an original style as some stand-up comics do. This will make you stand out from the pack, but it will also limit you. Developing a unique style can take time. It may develop naturally over the course of several projects if you let it. Then try to write what you know well and what you feel strongly about. If you're honest, the details will ring true. We'll laugh at what we recognize in ourselves and the others we know.

REFERENCE

Watch the old silent films. Charlie Chaplin and Laurel and Hardy are especially good for learning animation comedy. Watch the Our Gang comedies and The Three Stooges early sound films. You can learn from clowns as well. All of these are visual.

CHECKLIST

- Is the very premise of your script a funny one?
- Are the majority of your gags visual? Did you use the types of gags that work best in animation, motion gags, gags that defy the laws of physics?

- Does all of the comedy relate directly to the story and characters with nothing extraneous?
- Is much of your humor based on your characters' personalities? Have you used these attitudes and reactions to the best effect?
- Are all your gags in character, true to the established personalities in that script?
- Can your star dig herself in deeper and deeper for funnier and funnier results?
- If you're writing for a current series, is your humor similar to the humor already established for that series, and do you have about the same ratio of gags per page?
- If this is an original script, are all of your characters as different from each other as possible in order to heighten the comedy?
- Have you exaggerated as much as you can for the level of humor of that series?
- Do all of the gags have a setup, increased tension, and a sudden surprise at the end (the payoff)?
- Does the timing feel right, or is there a way to make your gag funnier?
- Have you twisted at least some of the running gags so that they remain funny and don't get monotonous?
- Do your gags build throughout so that the funniest gags are near the climax of your cartoon? This is especially important for short cartoons with little plot.
- Will your gags be appropriate for your audience? If this is a kid's series, are the gags those that you'd want your kids to see and appreciate? If you're writing for a series, who is your audience? Are you writing for kids of a certain age only or for both kids and adults? What do the executives who approve your script expect? Will an international audience understand the gags?
- Are you using a variety of types of humor?
- Have you refrained from spelling out the joke so that the audience can bring something to the party? Is the joke still clear?
- Focus on the dialogue, making it wittier with funnier comebacks. Remember to keep up the conflict to heighten the repartee.
- Have you used the funniest words (some with C's and K's), placing them in the funniest juxtaposition and the funniest order?
- Is your script sprinkled with gags throughout?
- Now forget the rules. Are your gags funny?

EXERCISES

1. Watch a classic cartoon. List as many of the gags as you can. Rewrite five of the gags by updating them, giving them a new twist, or switching the personality of some of the characters.
2. How many different gag techniques can you list that haven't already been listed here?

3. Take a book of jokes that you like and analyze the sentence structure of five of them. Are the sentences long or short? Did the writer use lots of adjectives and adverbs, or is the structure lean? What kinds of verbs are used? What's the imagery like? How is the joke set up? How is the punch line delivered? What about timing?

4. Develop five funny premises, each using funny situations. Be sure that your star digs himself in deeper and deeper.

5. Write five funny premises based on character.

6. Make a list of props around a specific subject (such as mysteries, dogs, magic). Write ten gags using many of these props.

7. Write ten sight gags. Then rewrite these gags, pushing them up a notch by exaggerating even more.

8. Dash off ten gags using at least ten different comedy devices.

9. Take five of your gags and rewrite them several ways. Set them up differently. Change the character reactions. Experiment with the wording and the timing.

10. If you can draw, board a gag sequence. Concentrate on funny staging, funny drawings, and funny movement. Explore several ways of doing the same sequence.

11. Can you think of other ways besides those listed to make your humor fresh and unique? Discuss these in class.

12. If you're developing a project of your own, try increasing the humor and uniqueness of one or more of your characters by making their point of view a little more off-center.

13. Develop a unique and humorous storytelling style for an original project you're working on. Be sure that this style is right for this particular project.

CHAPTER 6
The Animated Feature

Jean Ann Wright

CONCERNS IN GREENLIGHTING AN ANIMATED FEATURE

A major animation feature is very expensive to make, and studios are reluctant to take too many risks when they've got millions of dollars at stake. Many studios purchase the rights to a book or well-known character for their feature rather than buy an original **spec animation script**. Or they retell a classic myth, fairy tale, or story that's in the public domain. Some films, like *The Wild Thornberrys* and *The Powerpuff Girls*, were popular TV series before they expanded to the big screen. These stories with marquee value practically guarantee a built-in audience. Often studios commission a script for their feature based on a subject that they think will sell a lot of tickets at the box office. Features normally require a broad audience to justify costs.

Many features do badly at the box office due to poor quality in the script or in the production itself. This can be caused by a budget that's too low or a lack of experience by the studio. It might be brought about by a story that's watered down, or it could be caused by formula stories that rely too heavily on what has worked in the recent past. Audiences from a media generation who have seen so many stories long for something different. A good story is essential. When animated features do poorly at the box office, this frightens the people who will back films financially, and it becomes even harder to sell a feature story.

After *Toy Story* and *Shrek*, audiences seemed to prefer CGI films, and both Disney and DreamWorks began to shut down their traditional animation departments. Audience preferences are constantly cycling and in a state of change. In this case I think the quality of the traditionally animated stories, and

DOI: 10.1016/B978-0-240-81343-1.00006-6

the power of the press, had more to do with box office results than how the films were made. I look for great traditional animated films again in the future.

THE FEATURE SCRIPT AND PRE-PRODUCTION

The feature animation script is normally written in a format like a live-action script using master scenes that do not detail the camera shots, but it has fewer pages. Feature scripts average roughly one page per minute of screen time. Normal length varies from about 75 to about 110 pages. Most theatrical animated features have a running time of approximately seventy-five to ninety minutes. The direct-to-video features run about ten minutes shorter. The Motion Picture Academy in the United States requires an animated film to be at least seventy minutes to qualify for feature awards.

At many studios in the United States an initial story treatment, rather than a finished script, is given to storyboard people (or storymen), who take it for further development visually. A treatment or outline breaks down the basic story into scenes. The storymen may then develop character, further plot out the **story arcs**, and develop scenes from this treatment. At some point the story might go back and forth between a full script and visual development, with the creative executive supervising the process. Just how much the storyboard artists contribute depends on the studio; some studios let the board people develop and change a great deal, and some don't. A writer may be writing drafts of a script at certain stages after meetings with the storymen. This development can easily take a year or longer. Some sequences may go into production while the rest of the film is still in development. Sometimes an entirely new writer or team of writers is hired to polish a final script, improving dialogue and making the film funnier. Disney's sequels to *Peter Pan*, *Dinosaurs*, and *Fantasia 2000* were each in story development for several years. Often the developed film hardly resembles the original treatment or script. And changes may be made throughout the production of the film.

Management at DreamWorks prefers a finished script before going into production. Jeffrey Katzenberg usually gets involved personally with the writer on rewrites. He closely monitors the storyboarding process and reserves the right to revise until practically the final mix. On *Sinbad* the visual development influenced the story, as the designs of Tartarus changed the concept of that domain. The character of Eris evolved so much that new casting was done, and the character was rerecorded with a new actress.

DreamWorks has also been experimenting with animatics. They include not only what's indicated in the storyboard but also intercuts or different angles so the editor has a choice, resulting in a finished film that looks more like a live-action film in its cinematography.

The Disney method, traditionally, was to go into the early stages of production using only a treatment. The treatment was further broken down into sequences. The sequences were given to teams of writers and storyboard artists, where they were tweaked until they were the best that they could be. Of course, this process sometimes improved each section to the detriment of the whole. But there might be many pitch sessions during the story process as the teams pitched sequences, brainstormed gags, and solved story problems. Pitching your sequence of drawings with enthusiasm became an art in itself. The best story elements survived.

There is no single way to approach the feature story. Each studio, and even each feature, is different, and old ways are always subject to changes as the business of animation changes.

THE DIRECT-TO-VIDEO OR DVD FEATURE

For direct-to-video or DVD features the process is closer to that of TV animation due to the budget restraints. The lower budget may justify targeting an audience that's not as broad as that for the theatrical feature. Who is the audience for your studio or your original project? Aim specifically for them. Original projects with no marquee value are very difficult to sell to the large companies. Before development, consider what might be needed. What is each studio's niche? Where are the gaps in their product? Differentiate your project from what is already out there. High quality will pay off later. As a rule, the script is still initially written in master scene format. There are far fewer changes to the finished script than there are to that of the theatrical feature. At the major studios direct-to-video or DVD features are often sequels. In writing a sequel you must analyze your original cast. Who is the best character? You might want to write the sequel around him. Which characters do you keep in, and which can you afford to drop? What's the best angle for a new story? What's important to retain from the original? DVDs need added value (games, behind-the-scenes clips, artwork, etc., geared for both adults and kids). Small animation studios can produce an original direct-to-video or DVD feature on a much smaller budget than a theatrical feature and still expect to make money, as they are cheaper to make, easier to distribute, and require less money for promotion. As with TV animation, each studio has its own twist on the process.

THE TELEVISION FEATURE

Once in a while television buyers are interested in broadcasting a feature or a feature package. In that case the budgets are probably even lower than those of the direct-to-video features. To get budgets down and interest in the films up, the television feature story will probably have marquee value rather than being an original. Sometimes old classics that are now in the public domain will be used and updated with a new twist. License fees will probably not cover the costs to make the feature, but if the title is saleable on its own, then the film can recover costs later by international sales. Of course, with budgets that are so low, the television feature may be even lower in quality than the direct-to-video feature, but that doesn't mean that the writing can't be top notch.

FEATURE FINANCING AND DISTRIBUTION

There are many methods used to obtain film financing. Features can be financed by internationally preselling certain rights (book rights, video rights, TV rights, game rights, certain merchandise rights) or territories (the distribution rights in certain areas). Some governments will help provide financing. Film funds or grants may be available for independent films. Europeans can obtain financing with the help of Cartoon Movie, an annual forum for European animated films. At least one company financed its feature by issuing new corporate stock.

Interesting the consumer products group or the music division of a large corporation in your concept could help to gain support for your feature pitch at that corporation. Projects need instant appeal from a logline pitch, and budgets must match realistic marketing possibilities.

Product placement is the practice of obtaining marketing assistance or fees for placing certain commercial products in a film. The animated film *8 Crazy Nights* (2003) expected almost $100 million in marketing support from the product placement in their film. However, companies that ante up good money for their product or company logo might also expect to see instant stardom for their product on film, and they could demand story or artwork changes for that ka-ching of the cash register.

Some small studios do their own financing, working on the development and production slowly in between other projects. This method, of course, can take years. Some companies have tried setting up a Web site about their film to help obtain financing. A Web site that allows visitors to see digital **dailies**, see designs, hear newly composed music, and get information about the film might help build an audience as well. Potentially successful soundtracks or toys on a Web site can help attract financing. Often studios participate in co-productions to split the costs and the risks and speed the process along the way.

The completed film may then be taken to markets like Cannes in hopes of garnering awards and good buzz in order to get distribution. Or a film can qualify for an Oscar® nomination in the Feature Animation category if it has had a short prerelease showing.

PRODUCTION SCHEDULE

Most features will take anywhere from eighteen months to four years to produce. CGI features take about the same amount of time as a traditionally animated film. Serge Elissalde's French production *Loulou and the Other Wolves* was completed in only two months of pre-production (including the script), five months of production, and one month of post-production. Dario Picciau's Italian production of *L'Uovo* was completed by a crew of only six people, including the writer and producer, working on their Macintosh computers. A television feature will probably take less time than the average theatrical feature and will probably be produced more like any other television show. Budget, experience, and the number of full-time staff working on the film determine the time it takes. Because the lead time can be much longer than that of a TV show or a game, it's more important to have an idea that will still be popular years down the road.

THE STRUCTURE NEEDED FOR A FEATURE AUDIENCE

Although animated features are usually assumed to be for children, the film must appeal to all ages, including teenage boys (the primary demographic group targeted for films). A story with universal appeal means the kind of story that people of all ages everywhere can understand and appreciate. These stories, and the characters in them, resonate in some way in our own lives. Basic human needs and emotions are found in the myths, legends, religious stories, folktales, and fairy tales humans have loved since the beginning of time. Without some substance—some importance—an animated film may not be worth taking the time, money, and effort to make. Many look for a timeless quality that will keep the feature popular for generations.

An original project with a high concept, something that will hook the executives with its obvious marketability, may be easier to sell as long as the characters and story are compelling. The premise of a film, like that of a television show or a game, should be simple enough that you can communicate it in a logline. In the United States the film should have a "cool" factor. Teens may feel that an animated film is only for kids, so your film needs something extra to get them to the theater. In recent years this something extra has often been CGI animation. However in the United States it's usually women who make the decision to go see an animated film. Mothers don't want to take their young kids to something that will give them nightmares or model behavior that's too negative. The kids themselves want writing that respects them rather than writing that talks down to them. They usually look for something familiar. The major companies have discovered that the big-budget feature needs be an event.

Writing an original feature is much more fun and more challenging than writing for TV animation. Of course, the script must be written better, too. Each major studio has its own style. Your story should have uniqueness and universality.

Fully developed and well-motivated characters that are appealing and have an attitude are especially important in a theatrical feature. Today's kids need to be able to relate to that attitude. Many animated features are buddy comedies. Characters are usually broader than typical live-action film characters, and they're action oriented. They should be dealing with events that lead to a life change. They are less likely to be clichés. They might be less direct than characters for television, talking around problems and hiding their fears. Interesting characters make an interesting story, so animated stories may be told through the point of view of the character actors of the story (the animals, the villains, the humorous characters) rather than the more ordinary hero or heroine. The hero is often accompanied by a funny sidekick.

Animated features have a theme—frequently about coming of age (Miyazaki's *Spirited Away*). There is action, drama, and there are tears. There's humor, often smart, edgy, and sophisticated. Many recent features have included pop-culture-related gags and smart dialogue, including double entendres. There's innocence as well. Often there's a love story. Love stories provide something special to relationships by sending sparks flying.

The structure must be well written and almost as complex as that of a live-action feature; however, there must be some room in the plot for the elaboration that will be done by the storyboard artists. There will be an A-plot and a B-plot, and maybe a C-plot. The B-plot is often the love story. A minor story point may be set up early in the story, only to be paid off much later in the script. This may relate to theme, action, or character as well as humor. The older viewers in the audience will remember and "get" it. Scenes are usually shorter. A short cartoon can hold our interest with a simple plot that's merely a string of events leading to a climax, but a feature needs a tight interwoven structure to keep our interest. A feature script starts slower than a television animation script. The actual plot may take ten minutes or so to really get going. But remember there is always something happening in an animation script— something to animate, whether it's fast action or gags. The audience must be constantly wondering what will happen next. That does not mean that there shouldn't be some quiet scenes in a feature where we get to know and care about the characters and their hopes and dreams, but even quiet scenes need attitude and conflict to make them interesting. There must be an emotional component that speaks to everyone. And the story must be visual! The more visual your story is, the better. Don't worry about having enough dialogue. If you can tell the story better without much, do it! The story must have wonder and heart and appeal for all ages. The best features have a deeper reflection about life that we can take away with us. A feature must be fresh and original. It must be well written!

The feature may open with a sweeping panorama, a stunning visual shot that takes your breath away. Think of the eagle's flight through the western canyons and forests and out into the valleys in *Spirit*. Think of the animals gathering for the presentation of the new lion prince early in *The Lion King*. *Bambi* opened with a pan of the forest where he was born. Or instead, the feature may start with a look at character, challenging us to fall in love with the rascally cast right away. Remember Scrat trying to bury his acorn in *Ice Age*? Or what about Woody coming to the rescue of Little Bo Peep in the playroom in *Toy Story* even before the main title comes on? Or there may be jeopardy right away. In *The Iron Giant* we open with the satellite spinning in space; then within two minutes we witness a horrible storm at sea with a ship in terrible trouble. In *Lilo and Stitch* we open with a teaser before the title, showing the alien scientist on trial for genetic experimentation. His creation, number 626 (Stitch), is exiled from the planet.

However a feature may start, the main characters must be introduced and the story set up within the first fifteen or twenty minutes—the sooner the better. By then we must have a hero or heroine that we can really care for. We should know who the villain is. We need to know what the story problem is, what our hero wants, and what terrible thing is going to happen if the hero doesn't get it. We must know some of the reasons that the characters are acting as they are. The catalyst has started the story rolling, and the hero has come up with a plan. At the end of Act I something happens that spins the plot around in a different direction.

The tight structure continues. In Act II new information is revealed. Midway through we may find a high point where everything seems rosy. Then the hero has a defeat or apparent defeat, starting a downward spiral toward the major crisis. There's another major twist at the end of Act II. This might be the major crisis when all hope is gone. There's the inevitable big conflict, usually a physical conflict as well as a conflict of values. But the hero makes a critical choice. He pulls through to the climax and wins! He has learned something from the whole experience, and so have we (the audience). After the hero wins, the loose ends are tied up—quickly.

SELLING AN ORIGINAL FEATURE

It's usually very difficult to sell an original feature animation script because of the monetary risks that companies must take in putting out so much money for something unknown. Some writers suggest that you write a novel first and then try to sell the book for a feature. It's probably easier to sell a feature story to a smaller company willing to produce a direct-to-video or DVD feature than it is to sell to a major entertainment giant to make into a theatrical feature. But after the success of *Jimmy Neutron: Boy Genius*, there's now proof that it's possible, with the right planning, to produce a hit with a property that has no prior marquee value at all. For a feature pitch you'll need a fifteen- to twenty-page treatment. If you have little or no screenwriting track record, then I'd recommend that you write a good screenplay as well. The screenplay might help you get an agent; the treatment is the normal feature animation, pitching tool. You'll need higher-quality artwork than you needed for a television pitch. You'll want a wish list of actors for your cast, some musical components, and perhaps even some sample orchestrations. If you can get an agent interested in your project, it'll be easier to get pitch meetings at the major companies. If not, use any contacts in the entertainment industry that can help you get those meetings. But be sure that your pitch materials are the very best they can be first.

FEATURE FILMS GLOBALLY

The animated feature is coming into its own globally. More animated films are being released in more countries. And these films aren't always in the model of the U.S. animated film. France's *Kaena: The Prophecy* and Miyazaki's *Spirited*

Away are just two of the more serious international films, unlike most of the U.S. animated films, which are likely to be comedies. Both were targeted at an older audience, teens and adults. *Les Triplettes de Belleville* appealed to adults more than children; many Japanese films have done the same. The more diverse films that do well internationally, the more diversity there will be in feature films everywhere.

EXERCISES

1. Take the idea that you've been developing for television and develop it instead for a feature film. Remember to add a subplot. Write a treatment.

2. Do you think your feature project would make money? Why?

3. Discuss how you might make your feature project better known before you try to get financing.

4. Make a list of animated features that have been released lately. Do research on box office figures for each. Which ones were successful? Why?

5. What do you personally like to see in an animated feature? Talk to several kids. What did they like about the most recent animated films?

6. Who buys the tickets for animated films in your neighborhood? Take an informal survey.

7. How would you develop your short into a feature?

8. Make a list of animation festivals around the world that might accept the entry of an independent animated feature or an animated short. Designate which festivals will accept which (or both).

SECTION 3
Opening the Doors

CHAPTER 7
The Pitch

Jean Ann Wright

DO YOUR HOMEWORK

Before you pitch your project, do your homework. If you're not familiar with animation companies, make a list from the credits of a video or series. Or, better yet, get a directory. You can find a directory online at AWN (Animation World Network at *http://www.awn.com*) or buy a directory from *Animation Magazine.* Know what each company has on the air or out in the marketplace and, if possible, what they're looking for now. Find out a little about the executive that you'll be pitching. What does this decision maker like? If this is a network, study their current children's programming schedule printed in the newspaper or *TV Guide.* If this is a production company, find out what kind of animation they've produced. Consider the style and content. Ask around. If possible, go to selling markets like NATPE (National Association of Television Program Executives at *http://www.natpe.org*). Attend animation seminars and events where programming and development executives speak. Do research on the Internet by searching for the company and their executives. Check out the archives at AWN. Or research at the library (*The Hollywood Reporter, Daily Variety, Animation Magazine, Kidscreen, Animatoon*).

When you call a company to set up a meeting and you don't yet know who is in charge, ask for Animation Development. Stand up as you phone so that you have more energy. Spend a couple of minutes getting to know the assistant who is the gatekeeper. Be prepared with a logline pitch. Sound enthusiastic about your idea. The assistant is probably very busy, so don't get longwinded, but she can give you valuable information, and she can help you get an appointment. Get to know her, and treat her courteously! If you're new at this, you may have to call several times until you convince her that you're a

DOI: 10.1016/B978-0-240-81343-1.00007-8

professional and deserve the time. If you have no agent, then you might want to hire an entertainment attorney to avoid signing a release form for your project. (See the information about agents.) Remember that companies always need good, new material. Call once a month, but don't be a pest! Try to make your appointment with the head of the company or the person in charge of development, if you can. You may be stuck with the lowest executive on the totem pole, but that's okay. The only difference is that the lowest executive must pitch your project all the way up the ladder. The best pitch times are probably midmorning. The executive should be awake, not yet hungry because he hasn't had lunch, not sleepy because he just had lunch, or eager to get out of the office!

REHEARSE

Rehearse your pitch, but don't memorize it. If you have a partner, it helps to pitch together. Get your presentation down solid with the timing just right. If you can practice with a camcorder, do it. Stand if you wish. Hook your audience. Be passionate. Think of yourself as a storyteller. Your entire meeting will likely run twenty minutes or less. Some experts recommend that intriguing pitches be kept under two minutes and that the whole meeting be kept to ten or fifteen minutes maximum.

Start your series pitch with title, genre, and brief concept. Pitch the essence of your concept first. Think of a commercial. Pitch the goal of the hero in the series. Why do we have sympathy for him, what danger is he in, and how does he always win? Pitch your most colorful character caught up in the events and conflicts of your concept and its arena. Pitch the characters and their relationships, not what happens. What makes your characters interesting and unique? Pitch a character's main one or two traits and his conflicting trait. Talk about the villain. He's usually interesting. Find the element that people can relate to, and pitch that.

Sell the executives with your concept and pitch. Never tell them what they or the audience will like. Don't map out a merchandising or business plan. That's their job.

Be prepared to pitch your best and most complete idea first. Have a maximum of three or four shorter, less complete, ideas ready as well. If the buyers aren't interested in your main idea, you don't want to waste this opportunity. These secondary ideas can be as short as a logline. Allow time for questions after the pitch, and be well prepared to answer them. An agent may or may not go to the pitch with you.

If you're pitching a script, pitch title, genre, hero, why we should root for him, and the danger he's in. Bullet points only! Stick to the essence. Be clear. Do not pitch individual scenes in a story. Tease, tantalize, leave the executives wanting more.

COMING IN FOR THE PITCH

Dress as you would for any business meeting—nothing distracting. A neutral color is probably better than hot pink. Look neat and well groomed. Don't eat garlic or onions just before your pitch!

Bring in a few things for a series pitch. First, you need a professional-looking bible complete with artwork for your pitch. The average length is five to ten pages. Bibles that are too long tend to get put aside for later and forgotten. Bring in larger artwork on cards that are easy to see as you pitch. Six to twenty-four cards are about the right number. Bring in a small prop or a gimmick if you can find one that really represents your project well and helps in visualizing it. Don't bring in too much. Costumes are too much, as is a keyboard. This isn't *Phantom of the Opera*. Keep it simple!

Your project is a gift! Be confident. When you arrive, make eye contact with the executive. There may be more than one. Go in with high energy, and keep it throughout the pitch. Shake hands firmly, but otherwise keep your hands to yourself. During the pitch, don't give the executives any reason to say "no."

First you might want to relax the executive by showing an interest in her. This is where that research about the executive comes in handy. You might ask a question that has to do with your project to get her involved. But do *not* start with a joke. Be relaxed, open, and outgoing. Keep this introductory part of the pitch very short. Development executives are extremely busy.

THE PITCH

Tell the buyer the name of the script and the genre. Give him your agent's name, if you have one. Keep eye contact throughout your pitch. If there is more than one executive, some experts advise that you pitch mainly to one person. Hook the executives with your best idea first. Excite them! Keep your pitch entertaining. Put on your best acting and storytelling performance. Use your hands to gesture; use your face. Executives are more likely to buy an idea that is fun for them, too. Pitch in the style of the series or story you're trying to sell. If it's a comedy, pitch the fun of that series or story. Try to connect emotionally.

Maybe the buyer didn't think she needed a project like yours before you arrived, but make sure that she needs it before you leave. Don't give too much information. The more you say about a project, the more reasons someone might find to reject it. Do be prepared to pitch three or four brief episode ideas, if you're asked. Adjust your pitch to the interest level. Change your tone of voice to wake up lagging interest. If you're told that the company already has a similar idea in development, stop immediately and go on to the next idea. Don't pitch more than three or four ideas. Let the executive know that the pitch is over by asking her if she'd like to read the series bible or if she has any questions.

When your pitch is over, let the executive talk. Be prepared to answer questions like these:

- What's the basic concept? (The logline version.)
- Who's the star?
- Who's the main villain?
- Why is your series or story different? What's the twist? What's the hook? Why is your project exciting?
- How does this relate to the child viewer? Why will she like the series or story? How do the characters relate to her? Why does she care about your star?

Can they work with you? They are judging you. You don't want to do or say anything that will give a negative impression. Be honest, be positive, and go with the flow. If you don't know the answer to a question, say so. Tell the development executive that you're not prepared to answer that question right now. You can call back with the answer. If an executive interrupts you with a new idea about your project during the pitch, go with that. Even if they hand you something entirely different, run with it and don't look back. An idea that a development executive just gives away is an idea that she wants to buy. Fight for what's important to you, but be willing to make changes. There will be many changes during development.

Hand the executive a copy of your bible as you leave. Thank her for her time.

AFTER THE PITCH

The next day you may want to send a thank-you letter. Thank the executive for her time. Reinforce any major selling point. Answer any question that you were unable to answer at the meeting. I know one writer who encloses (or leaves behind) a stamped postcard with the title of the project, his name as developer, and a line that mentions that this project was pitched to that company on that date. There is a line for a signature. He feels that this gives him added protection. Others might feel that this is too negative.

Continue to work on new ideas. Give yourself a year to pitch your old project before dropping it. Keep up your contacts for the next pitch. Email or call about once a month or so (never more often) to touch base. Take someone to lunch if you wish. Or send out a regular (or irregular) newsletter letting people know what you're doing professionally. Projects get sold most often through long-term relationships.

OTHER PITCHING AND SELLING OPPORTUNITIES

A number of other opportunities exist to pitch your project or make a script available to companies that might be interested. First, let me say that there are a lot of scams out there. So if you choose to pitch in one of the following ways, do check out these opportunities *very* carefully first.

Screenwriting expos often have contests that allow you to pitch your project to a list of available producers or development executives. There are also organizations that conduct regular pitching sessions. For a fee you can attend a luncheon or other meeting where decision makers are available to meet and to hear the short pitches of the attendees.

Then there are companies on the Internet that promise writers help in getting their scripts read by those who might buy. These companies list scripts for free or for a fee. Some charge a finder's fee if the script is sold in addition to the listing charge. These companies deal mostly with live-action scripts.

It's possible to make the right contacts in these ways, but it is also possible to waste your money or risk losing your idea. I would recommend setting up meetings and making a traditional pitch, if it's at all feasible.

STUDENT PROJECTS

As a student you may have to pitch your project to a teacher or someone who is going to help you with financing. Does your project fit the guidelines set for the class? Can you obtain financing? Do you have plans to repay the loan, if necessary? Are safeguards in place so that the funds are used wisely and you won't run out before the project is finished? Is your project practical to do? Can you do it in the required time? Is the necessary equipment available when you need to use it? Do you have production plans, and are you able to get the necessary help? If you want to use this project as a calling card to the industry, is the subject matter something that industry people will want to watch? Is this the kind of project that the industry sells? Are you able to do a professional job, or would it be better to do something less ambitious that will have a more professional look? Is this the type of film that is likely to win awards in festivals? Would it be popular in contests? Carefully think your project through! You may want to include the answers to some of these questions in your pitch.

EXERCISES

1. Develop a pitch for a project that's already on the air, and practice the pitch at home.
2. Sponsor an evening panel of animation professionals to give pitching tips.
3. Rehearse pitching with a partner. Is this easier than pitching by yourself?
4. Practice pitching in class. Videotape the pitches, if possible, so those in the hot seat can see themselves as others see them. Discuss the pitches in class, giving suggestions for improvement.
5. Invite animation professionals to class to hear your practice pitches and give you tips.
6. Research places to pitch your project.
7. Think of other ways you might find buyers to pitch your project. Discuss in class.
8. Rehearse your pitch for your own original project.

CHAPTER 8
Breaking and Entering

Christy Marx

There is no one way to break into writing, especially in television or film. There is no magic way to go about it, no secrets that will guarantee getting a break, but there are ways to improve the odds. Because it's one of the things everyone asks, I'll relate how I broke in.

I was living in Los Angeles and had managed to sell a couple of stories to Marvel Comics editor Roy Thomas, who had recently moved to L.A. One of the stories I sold was about *The Fantastic Four*. I began attending the monthly meetings of a group of professional comic book writers and artists. I got to know people and made friends in that circle.

One day, one of the writers I'd gotten to know passed me a tip that an animation studio called DePatie-Freleng Productions was looking for writers, especially writers who had worked on *The Fantastic Four*, because they were doing an animated version of the FF.

On the basis of the one comic book story, I was able to get a meeting with one of the founders of the studio, David DePatie. He was a small, dapper man with a huge antique desk and two nice, but absolutely enormous, dogs. As I sat across from him, the dogs pressed up to me, and I spent the meeting bookended between them, doing my best to get a job. Apparently, I passed the test. DePatie asked me if I knew what an animation script looked like. I said no. He tossed a script across to me to use as a template, and off I went to work on "The Diamond of Doom." I studied and studied that script, though I was completely clueless about what the terms meant or how to create a TV script. Somehow I managed, and that led to more work with DePatie-Freleng.

Nowadays, you would certainly be expected to know what an animation script is and to have a very good spec script already written. Back then, animation scripts were so new, it was perfectly understandable not to know. Though it would be hard to re-create this type of break given today's competitive field, my experience does contain one of the most important steps: networking.

BREAKING INTO TELEVISION ANIMATION

If you're a writer who already has credits in another field, such as comics or games, you should have an easier time making a lateral move into animation writing. You likely have contacts that can get you in the door, and you probably won't have much trouble getting a meeting at an animation studio based on your other work. I would still recommend that you have one or two sample animation scripts that will show that you know how to handle the format, but it may not be necessary if your other credits are impressive enough.

If you're brand-new, you should consider the words of Louis Pasteur: "Chance favors only the prepared mind." No matter how much raw talent you may have, it won't do you much good unless you are prepared to take full advantage of whatever piece of luck or opportunity comes your way. This means knowing the animation field, being familiar with what shows are on, and having some strong animation spec scripts as samples of your work for a studio exec or story editor to read when that opportunity comes along.

Spec Scripts

A script is called "spec," or "speculative," because you don't actually expect to sell it. The purpose of a spec script is to show your writing chops and your ability to "get" the show you're writing for. Remember that your primary goal is to be hired to write, whether it's for that show or another one. Actually selling a spec script would be the cherry on the whipped cream.

There are two schools of thought about writing a spec script for a show and submitting the script to that show's story editor or producer. One school of thought favors it because there is always at least the slim chance they could buy your script. A more predominant school of thought is that it's a bad idea because unless your script is absolutely, positively spot-on in every respect, it's more likely to fail. The reasoning is that the story editor or producer is judging the spec script by more-exacting standards because it's their show and they know the characters so well. I would go with the shows you feel the most compelled to write, rather than worrying about this choice.

Choose a show that's been on the air more than one year, is going strong, and is well known. Don't pick a show that is so obscure that no one will know what it is. Write to your interests or strengths, meaning write spec scripts based on the genre of animation that you most want to write for. If you're great at light humor, pick that type of show. If you're great at hard action, pick one of those. If you're crazy about the anime-style shows, pick an anime series. If you're versatile, do one of each. If you write a spec script for a show that goes off the air, set it aside and write something new.

Avoid the three prime mistakes many newcomers make:

Mistake No. 1: Don't write a story that is clearly contradicted by something that happened in the series or contradicts how the characters normally behave. Obviously, you must be *very* familiar with the show's characters, tone, themes, and everything that is unique to that show. If you haven't seen every episode, go to Internet fan sites and research the story lines, or you might even find the episode available on youtube.com or other video-streaming sites.

Mistake No. 2: Don't write a story that causes a significant change or life upheaval for one or more of the major characters, or an event that would turn the series upside down (such as killing off a major character). Only a story editor or producer gets to write those kinds of shows. You want to write a really great, but *typical* stand-alone episode of the series, something that wouldn't feel out of place if it were aired in the middle of the series' other episodes.

Mistake No. 3: Don't introduce a new, unknown character and build the story around that character. Stay focused on the central characters of the series. You *can* take a secondary character that already exists in the series and do something interesting with him or her, but make sure you have plenty of action focused on the central characters as well.

Do your best to get hold of copies of scripts for that show: *(a)* because it's helpful to see what format that series uses; and *(b)* because sometimes the story editor or producer has some special quirk related specifically to that show. For example, in *X-Men: Evolution*, they used a special X-Men graphic they called the "X-Wipe" in place of a generic wipe. Not that it's critical to know that, but it can't hurt either.

Getting hold of animation scripts isn't easy. They're not commonly put out for sale. I would try a few different methods:

- Contact the production company or studio that makes the show, explain that you want to write a spec script, and ask them if they will send you the bible and/or sample scripts. This is iffy, but worth a shot.
- Do a search on the story editor and writers of the show to see if they have Web sites with a way to contact them. Ask to buy scripts from the show for the purpose of writing a spec script. Do NOT at this point ask these people to read your script when it's done. Asking for that kind of favor might prevent them from answering you at all.
- If you live in L.A., go to the Writers Guild Foundation Shavelson-Webb Library (formerly the James R. Webb Memorial Library). This will allow you to at least read scripts, though you won't be able to take them with you or photocopy them. I would recommend calling the WGA library first (323-782-4544) and inquire whether they have animation scripts for that show. The library is working to obtain more animation scripts. Unfortunately, not many animation writers think of donating their scripts to the library. The odds of finding the most current scripts are

slim, but the library has both series and feature scripts that are worth studying.

- Look for shops and Web sites that might have animation scripts for sale or for downloading.

Networking

You've done your research, studied animation, written your terrific spec scripts… now you network. This is the single most important activity you must engage in if you want to get the lucky break that, because you are prepared, you will be able to use to your advantage.

Animation, as with any area of scriptwriting, is a people business, so a great deal of succeeding at networking is having good social skills, strong communication skills, knowing how to interact with people, how to make a good impression, how to be witty and chatty without coming across like a sycophant, all the while subtly conveying that you're a professional who would be fun to work with. Even if you're not a professional yet, you want to put forth a professional attitude consisting of awareness of the business, self-confidence, enthusiasm, and pragmatism. Easy.

It's way beyond the bounds of this book to teach you those skills, but you need to have them.

Networking is about making the business contacts any way you can, but in a way that leaves a positive impression. You must walk that fine line between putting yourself forward and being obnoxious.

WAYS TO NETWORK

Don't restrict yourself to these methods. Be creative. Consider these as starting points, but do it any way you can.

- Use the Internet: You may, stress *may*, be able to strike up a relationship with a story editor or producer via Web forums or email. Most pros are frankly too busy to carry on an extended email exchange. Forums exist here and there where you might be able to bump into some pros. I don't consider this to be a highly effective route, but I wouldn't rule it out. The Net will probably be more useful as a research tool to learn about the animation business and about people in the business.
- Media Conventions: The mother of all conventions is Comic-Con International, which is held every summer in San Diego. Comic-Con began decades ago as a little comic book convention. It is now a massive monster convention that covers comics, animation, anime, TV, film and videogames with almost equal fervor. Hundreds of pros show up. Some are there to promote new projects, some do panels and lectures, some do signings at the big company booths, and some show up just to have fun. The WGA Animation Writers Caucus does a panel every year.

This is *not* a place to shove your résumé or spec script in someone's face. That's the last thing a speaker wants to deal with during a busy convention, though a business card is always acceptable. However, it gives you a chance to at least meet pros and then follow up afterward in the hope they'll remember you. Plus, the panels and lectures can be extremely informative.

- Trade Shows/Conferences: There are writing-craft conferences you can attend such as events sponsored by the **WGA Foundation** (*http://www.wgfoundation. org*). Although these events may not be specifically about animation, there is sometimes overlap with people who write for animation (for example, I have been a speaker at their events). You need to search out other such conferences, lectures, or panels that might touch upon animation writing or feature-animation writers, story editors, or producers. Again, the point is to make some sort of contact and attempt to follow up on it later.
- Join animation-related organizations: Professional groups out there have a variety of members, but may have writers and story editors among them. Any way you can get to know people is worth it. **Women in Animation** requires professional credentials to join (and men are welcome), but they also have a student membership, if you qualify. **ASIFA** (Association International du Film d'Animation, or International Animated Film Association at *http://www.asifa-hollywood.org*) is an international group dedicated to animation.
- Get an entry-level job: This is an old, standard method of breaking in. You get any kind of entry-level job you can at an animation studio or production house, learn the ropes, meet people, make a good impression, and try to leverage your way into a writing job. Getting a writing job may not happen while you're working at that particular place, but could happen later if you maintain contact with the right people.
- Parties: It may sound humorous, but one of the all-time best ways to make contacts is to get invited to parties where the pros hang out. I can't tell you how to do this, other than meeting or knowing someone who can invite you. Animation writers are not, in general, big party animals, so it's going to take some luck to go this route.
- Schools and classes: There aren't a lot of formal courses for teaching animation writing, but if you can find one that's taught by someone who is actually working in the business, find a way to take the course.

119

Writing Contests and other Outlets

In the world of live-action writing and feature writing, there are many contests that can prove an extremely good way to gain entry-level attention if you can win or place highly. Unfortunately, there's nothing comparable in the world of animation writing. Here are some possibilities:

- Scriptapalooza: This television-writing contest is held twice a year, with the current deadlines for submissions being in April and October, with the winners announced about four months later. It has categories for screenplays and various types of teleplays (television scripts). The contest welcomes writers from around the world.

Although Scriptapalooza is not specifically for animation writing, at least two writers won Emmy Awards for writing animated programs after having used the Scriptapalooza TV competition to get their breaks into the industry. For more information, visit *http://www.scriptapalooza.com*.

- Nickelodeon Productions has a Writing Fellowship Program for both live action and animation, though one can never predict how long such programs will last. According to their Web site, "Nickelodeon Productions is continuing its search for new creative talent and is looking for writers to work full-time developing their craft at Nickelodeon. This program stems from Nickelodeon's commitment to encouraging meaningful participation from culturally and ethnically diverse new writers." At this time, however, they are accepting applications only from American writers. For more information, go to: *http://www.nickwriting.com*. Or contact them via:

  Nickelodeon Animation Studios

  ATTN: Nick Writing Fellowship

  231 W. Olive Ave

  Burbank, CA 91502

- You may also want to consider online sites such as InkTip.com (*http://www.inktip.com*), an Internet database of scripts that are made available for reading by registered, legitimate producers, production companies, or studios. You pay a fee to upload your script to the site. You also receive a regular newsletter in which producers or production companies indicate specific types of scripts they're looking for. Every once in a while, a producer will look for an animation script. Because we're talking about feature scripts with this particular type of site, any live-action-style script you've written that fits the requirements could be considered as a feature-animation script.

Learning about the Business

It's also extremely important to learn as much as you can about the business in general. You need to know who produces animation, which channels air animation shows, what type of shows each channel puts on the air, and how the overseas producers of animation and the overseas market are affecting animation in the United States.

I recommend these sources:

- *Animation Magazine* (*http://www.animationmagazine.net*). It covers not only television and film animation, but also increasingly the world of games. It does a good job of covering overseas animation and anime. The magazine comes out once a month, and your subscription will also give you access to their daily Internet newsletter, which will give you news more quickly than the monthly magazine (but the magazine is a lovely thing to hold in your hand and have for reference).

- Animation World Network (*http://www.awn.com*). This is a highly useful Internet site bursting with information about the world of animation, along with forums, festivals, and a place to post your résumé. It also features job listings, though you need to be wary of the people who want you to work for free. You should also subscribe to their informative email newsletter, *Animation Flash* (*http://www.awn.com/user/register* - scroll to bottom of page to find newsletter options).
- *Cynopsis: Kids.* This is a compact but useful email newsletter that arrives every weekday morning. The original *Cynopsis* newsletter is described as "a free daily early morning trade news composite featuring pertinent updates from the entertainment business, with just a dash of editorial." *Cynopsis* deals with television and film data, including ratings and box-office results, with a slant more toward the marketing and sales end of the business. *Cynopsis: Kids* focuses on the entire kids' market, including games. Subscribe to either or both by going to: *http://www.cynopsis.com*.
- The Trades: By "the trades," I mean the two major trade papers that deal with the entertainment business: *Variety* (*http://www.variety.com*) and the *Hollywood Reporter* (*http://www.hollywoodreporter.com*). They cover all aspects of the business, but once or twice a year (mainly around Oscar time), each one also puts out a special issue covering animation. Because the trades are quite expensive, it might be worth trying to pick up only those issues dealing with animation. You can also get an online subscription, rather than a paper subscription, which might be more useful for doing searches related to animation. This is also pricey, however. It's a matter of what you can afford.

BREAKING INTO FEATURE ANIMATION

Terry Rossio (whose long list of credits includes *Pirates of the Caribbean, Shrek, The Road to El Dorado* and *Aladdin*) put it rather succinctly: "There is no strategy that doesn't fail over 99 percent of the time, and no strategy that is far more effective than any other. I would say it makes more sense to write a live-action screenplay, because there actually is a market for live-action screenplays!"

From everything I've gathered, landing a job writing an animation feature is the ultimate crapshoot. The trend is toward big-name feature writers, or someone who happens to be hot in the live-action-feature realm, or someone who already has a feature-development deal with a studio and is tapped for an animated feature under that deal (in other words, the studio is already committed to paying them to write a feature, so they may as well write an animation feature).

The studios are not open to an unknown walking through the door to pitch an idea for an animation feature. The exception to that would be that you've created or own the rights to a property that the studio is dying to have. A highly successful children's book (preferably a series of them), for example. This is still no guarantee that you would be offered the chance to write the script, unless you have a strong script sample or other credits that would convince them.

Selling an Animation-Series Concept

Far too often, I'm asked by someone with no credits or experience how to sell a series. It's hard enough for established pros to sell a series. However, there are some general guidelines and things you need to know if you want to attempt to sell a series or property at some stage in your career.

First, you will need to create a pitch bible.

The Animation Bible

Every series has a bible. In reality, there are actually two different kinds of bibles, and they serve two different purposes. Though their purposes are different, the bibles contain the same basic elements. Those two kinds of bibles are the PITCH BIBLE and the SHOW BIBLE (or series bible, or writers' bible).

> THE PITCH BIBLE: This is a short version of the bible, no more than maybe ten to twelve double-spaced pages, often with large type and lots of white space, and often with sample artwork—in other words, designed to be a very quick and exciting read with the purpose of *selling* the series idea. A pitch bible must be written entirely with one thing in mind—that you are selling how exciting and fresh and fantastic your idea is.

> THE SHOW BIBLE: If you're being hired to develop a bible for a show that is a definite go, the bible will be intended primarily for the writers who will work on the show. When I do that kind of bible, I use single-spacing, I get into detail, and I don't worry so much about length. It still needs to be a good read, of course, but your purpose in this case is to make sure the writers have enough information about the show to go off and write the appropriate scripts.

I've also heard mention of the so-called MINIBIBLE, which usually just means they want to pay you half the price to write a smaller version of a regular bible. Be wary of someone asking for a "minibible." Clarify what they really want, and don't let shortness be an excuse for cheapness.

It's not unusual for the pitch bible to end up being the show bible/writers' bible, with perhaps a few extra pages of info added. Those extra pages are usually from the story editor, dealing with production details (such as "keep the length to between thirty-three and thirty-four pages"), or giving specific guidelines about the show (such as "we don't want time-travel stories" or "it's a fantasy show, so don't use modern slang"), or whatever else the writers need to know that might not have been covered by the pitch bible.

It's also not unusual for a show bible on a new series to be rewritten even while you're in the middle of doing a script. There can be a lot of last-minute and ongoing adjustments to a show that's in development. You need to be flexible and go with the changes.

In the live-action world, a bible or a proposal for a series is called a *format*. This is due to the specific language used in the WGA's Minimum Basic Agreement.

What Goes into an Animation Bible

A more or less standard format has developed that calls for these elements:

- TITLE PAGE
- CONCEPT/HOOK: The opening pages must immediately convey what the show is. It must tell in a quick and exciting way what the concept is, what the hook is, who the significant characters are, what the show is about, where it's set. For a pitch bible, it must draw the reader in and make that reader want to know more. For a show bible, it must also convey necessary information.
- THE SETTING: If there's something special about where the series is set, you might want to do a section about that, especially if you're doing a science-fiction or fantasy series. Or you may be dealing with a special time period (past, future, alternative time line), and need to go into more detail in order to convey that aspect of the series.
- CHARACTER BIOS: For a pitch bible, these would be short, exciting descriptions of each major character (heroes, villains, important pets/creatures). For a show bible, these are hopefully more detailed, and accompanied by a section describing character interactions or relationships—meaning how does Jack, for example, get along (or not) with Jane and Dick; how does Jane relate to Jack and Dick; how does Dick interact with Jane and Jack. This section can be put under each character's bio, or off in a section by itself, depending on what seems to work better for your bible or style. A short paragraph for each interaction should suffice. You would want to touch on character relationships in a pitch bible, but perhaps not at this level of detail.
- SPECIAL ELEMENTS: Depending on the nature of the show, you might want to add sections that deal with weapons or vehicles or other unique elements. In a pitch bible, this is a good place to show what sort of toy-property potential your show has (if that's appropriate). For science-fiction/fantasy shows, it can be helpful in establishing more detail about how this series will handle these special elements. If the show is set in a future world, for example, how has the technology evolved, or have we gone backward and are living a more primitive life, or are the characters using alien technology, and so on. Some of this would be covered earlier under your opening-concept pages or your pages about the setting. These special elements would be specific additions to that, and only if really needed.
- STORY/SPRINGBOARDS: In some bibles, I've seen the entire pilot episode laid out—told in an exciting story form, but with enough detail that you have everything you need for an outline. This can come earlier

123

and can be a part of your concept/hook pages, if that works in setting up the series. But toward the end of the bible, it's a good idea to include anywhere from five to twelve story ideas, done as springboards, to indicate that you have lots of good ideas and the series has plenty of potential.

Bear in mind that these are only guidelines. The basic elements should be present in the bible, but how you present them and how it's all put together can vary tremendously. Each writer who creates a bible will develop a personal style and approach. Some writers like to use larger type and bold emphasis on certain passages or words to make them stand out. Some writers like to get into a lot of story description; others stick with generalities. The main thing in a pitch bible is to have plenty of white space (no pages crammed with tight rows of text) and a fast, engrossing read.

You will find an example of a pitch bible at *www.christymarx.info*.

Using Artwork in a Pitch Bible

This issue gets a lot of debate among writers, and there is no easy answer. Many people will swear that having artwork is a must. Having a hot, popular artist do the artwork might be an asset if you aren't that well known yourself. On the other hand, I've heard a studio executive tell me that he'd rather not see artwork—because if he doesn't like the art, it might turn him off to the whole idea. I've also, however, encountered studio executives who had no interest in the written work and wanted to see only images. It's the luck of the draw, and there's no way to predict it.

It might be that you have a truly special approach to the *look* of the show, and showing what the look will be might be vital to selling your idea.

Or, if you're working from an established property, you may have art that is already associated with that property. This is ideal.

One thing is certain: if it isn't good, professional-grade, quality art, *don't use it*. Far better to have no art at all than to have poor or obviously amateur art. You'd better study enough animation art to know the difference.

Finding an artist is another issue. Can you afford to pay someone? Or would you have to find someone who would be willing to work for free? Free generally implies someone young, such as an art student, who is willing to do the art in order to get exposure.

You could attend comic book conventions, where both professional and aspiring artists abound. You could go to local colleges or art schools that have illustration or graphic-design classes and connect with students there. You could contact schools that specialize in teaching comic book art, such as The Joe Kubert School of Cartoon and Graphic Art, Inc. (*http://www.kubertsworld.com/ kubertschool/KubertSchool.htm*). You could also to your local comic book store and inquire about *really good* local artists.

If you're paying a professional artist, have a signed, written agreement that specifies that you retain all rights to your work. You should also at least offer to use your best efforts to get the artist work on the show if it should sell.

If you have someone working for free, definitely have a signed, written agreement that clearly states that you retain all rights to your work (but not to the artist's work), and that you have free use of the artwork. However, you should work out a payment for the artist if the show should sell, as well as offering to use your best efforts to get the artist work on the show.

You can't make hard and fast guarantees to get an artist work on a show (that would usually not be under your control), so be careful to phrase it as "best efforts" or a similar term.

What Will Sell and Why

The most difficult thing to sell in today's market is an original concept. You have a better shot at selling an established property—whether it's a published children's book, a comic book, a computer game, or a toy. Marv Wolfman and Craig Miller (jointly as Wolfmill Productions) produced an animation show based on a line of popular sculptures, *The Pocket Dragons*.

However, you can do this *only* if you have legally obtained the rights from the creator or owner of the property to make this adaptation. I've encountered far too many people who want to write a script based on some big property, thinking they can somehow magically sell it and then somehow equally magically get the rights. Put this notion entirely out of your head. With a very big IP (intellectual property), something major such as *Batman* or *G.I. Joe*, the studio or company that owns the rights will want to have it developed and written by well-known people with strong credits and status in the field. They won't turn over such an important property to an unknown.

But let's say it's something not as well known that has potential. You have to option the property first. This means a signed contract that clearly spells out what rights are being granted, what you're paying or offering in return, and the time period allowed for you to sell the idea. You would want to have an option for at least two years. These things take more time than you might think.

The trick with optioning an established property is *(a)* beating out people with bigger reps, more power, and more money than you; and *(b)* having the means to buy an option and pay a lawyer to draw up an option agreement. If you're very lucky, you might be able to work out a deal that doesn't involve money up front, but you can't shortcut having a professional written agreement. To do it on the cheap, you could try to find a sample option agreement on the Net, but you'd better know a lot about intellectual-property law, copyright law, and trademark law first. Otherwise, you need to use an attorney who specializes in intellectual-property and/or copyright law. Sometimes they're called entertainment attorneys.

125

Alternatively, you can take your original concept and try to get it made in some other format first, such as putting out a comic book, or putting it on the Internet as a Web comic or Flash animation. To protect yourself, first register your copyright with the U.S. Copyright Office (*http://www.copyright.gov*).

Whatever you decide to pitch, it will need to be so extraordinary, so unique, so special that it can grab the attention of studio or production executives who have hundreds, if not thousands, of ideas pitched at them year in and year out. Believe me, they've heard it all. You will need to be good at delivering a quick, coherent, cohesive, and interesting verbal pitch of your idea. You must be thoroughly prepared for any question they might throw at you, which means having your concept fleshed out enough to cover anything they could want to know about it, possibly beyond what is in the pitch bible. If the exec expresses interest, you can leave them a written version (often referred to as a "leave-behind").

Then, if the gods smile upon you, you may get a development deal and be paid money to continue working toward developing your idea into a full-fledged series. This is often known as "development hell." Bear in mind that studios develop many more projects than they actually make. They might develop dozens of ideas for only a handful of series openings.

Getting in the Door

There is the obstacle of even getting in the door to pitch an idea to someone. Your strongest chance lies in having a list of animation credits to your name, and an agent who can make the call to set the pitch meeting.

If you have strong credits in a related field—such as comics, games, or children's books—or if you have an established property, you might still be able to pitch your concept, but you may not be considered as a candidate to write the show if you don't have animation-writing credits. One alternative is to write the pilot episode or a sample episode as part of your presentation in order to show that have a grasp of writing an animation script. Of course, your sample had better be a very good script, or it could have the opposite effect. It's still likely they'll want to pair you up with an experienced animation producer and story editor whom they trust.

Without an agent or someone with connections to do it for you, you would have to make a cold call to the studio, network, or company to ask for a meeting. Your first step is to watch a lot of animation to determine which studio/network/channel is producing the type of animated show you want to pitch. In today's market, that narrows it down to only a few places such as Disney, Nickelodeon, and the Cartoon Network. Research them on the internet, find out where they're located, and try to get the names of their development executives. The title will be something along the lines of Director of Development, VP of Development, VP Creative Affairs, Senior VP Original Programming, and so on. If you want to pitch comedy, you want to make sure you get to the development executive who handles comedy rather than action-adventure, because these jobs are sometimes divided into genres.

If you make the call yourself and ask for the executive's office, you will end up dealing with an assistant. The assistant's job is to be the gatekeeper—to weed out unwanted calls and make sure any calls that get through are valid business. The best thing you can do is *win the goodwill* of this assistant, who is very important to you in getting anywhere. Be unfailingly polite and professional. Have a clear and concise explanation of who you are and what you want. If the assistant deems you worth consideration, the odds are high that you will first be requested to send a query letter and material for evaluation. Be prepared to do that, and confirm that you have the proper mailing address. If they request you to sign a release form, do so. It's a standard legal method of protecting themselves.

Keep your query letter short and to the point. Remind them that you spoke by phone and that the material was requested, so they don't think it's an unsolicited submission. Don't waste a lot of time in a query letter trying to describe the property or do a big sales job. Give just enough to get a taste of who you are and what you're offering, and let the material speak for itself. If you want your material back, include a stamped, self-addressed envelope. Otherwise, indicate that the material doesn't need to be returned.

Wait three to four weeks for a reply. If you don't hear anything, place a very polite follow-up phone call to inquire. This will take patience, because it could take a long time for the exec (usually surrounded by reading material up to their eyebrows) to get to your material. If you hit the bull's-eye, then you might be invited to come in and have a face-to-face meeting. It's a long shot, but my attitude is: the worst they can do is say no.

GETTING AN AGENT

One of the frequent questions about animation is "Do I need an agent?" Although I wouldn't say it's absolutely necessary for animation in the way it is to write for live action, I strongly recommend getting an agent. An agent gives you legitimacy. It immediately says to a potential employer that you've gotten through a significant gate that separates the amateur from the professional.

Having an agent also allows you to keep clear of the negotiating and money end of things, which is what you want. Let the agent run interference for any problems that come up, so that you remain above the fray.

Back when I started out, I had no animation agent for the simple reason that television and film agents dealt only with live-action and either had no awareness of animation or didn't consider it worth the effort.

Then Candace Monteiro, who formed what is now the Monteiro Rose Dravis Agency, had the brilliant idea to gather up all those loose animation writers for representation. For a long time, this resulted in Candace's repping the majority of animation writers. Gradually, other agents and agencies realized there was something to be had here, but the overall pool of agents who specifically handle animation today is still rather small.

Probably the best way to determine who the current agents are is via the online database set up by the WGA's Department of Organizing. Go to *http://www.wga.org*, click on *if you're an employer*, click on *find a writer*, and enter the names of an animation writer whose credits you've seen on the screen. If that writer is listed in the WGA database, it will show his or her agent and contact information. Do that for enough writers, and you will begin to see the same agent names showing up consistently. This will give you a good place to start.

Also, there is a general list of agents at *wga.org*. Click on *writer's resources*, then click on *agency list*. It's a good idea to double-check an agent here to make sure they're legitimate.

Getting an agent to read your spec script is the next hurdle. Do not send an unsolicited script to an agent. It will most likely be returned unread. Many of these agents have as many clients as they feel comfortable handling, and may not be open to taking on a new person. The task is to find one who will be open to at least reading your spec. Never pay a fee to have an agent read your script. Anyone who asks for a reading fee is not someone you want to deal with.

Your best bet is to get a personal recommendation, either from someone already represented by that agent, or from someone (such as a producer, director, or story editor) who has read your script and liked it enough to recommend you to an agent. This gets back to the value of networking and personal connections. A personal connection of some sort will get you the agent's attention more effectively than coming in cold.

If you don't have that sort of personal connection, your first step is to send a query letter or email. As with any query, keep it short, simple, and to the point. Agents have highly attuned b.s. detectors, so keep it factual. Explain who you are, list any pertinent accomplishments (college degree, work in other media, winning contests, and so on), and ask whether the agent would be kind enough to read one of your spec scripts. Be patient. After a few weeks, follow up with a polite inquiry. If you never get an answer back, strike that one off your list and keep going.

A licensed script agent's commission is 10 percent. Avoid anyone who wants more. If you happen upon someone calling himself a manager, check carefully into his credentials. Whom else does he manage? What has he accomplished for his clients? Managers are not held to the same licensing standards as agents, and they can charge whatever commission they want. Anything over 15 percent, however, is questionable.

If you want to or choose to proceed without an agent, consider using an entertainment attorney when you need a deal negotiated or a contract finalized.

You're going to pay at least $250 to $350 an hour, so be prepared for that. Those hours can pile up quickly. Work out ahead of time *exactly* what you can afford. State that very clearly to the lawyer, and stick to it. In some instances, a lawyer *might* consider handling you for a commission instead, but usually only if that lawyer considers you a good prospect to be a long-term, high-earning client.

Once you Have an Agent

The worst mistake any writer can make is to think, "Great, I've got an agent. Now I can kick back, relax, let the agent get the jobs, and wait for the phone to ring." Certainly, a good agent will be putting your name out and scouting for work, but you must continue to network, promote, get scripts out there, and do everything you can to bring in the work.

Agents are not the magic answer to success. An agent is a calling card, a confidant, an adviser, a negotiator, and a money collector. But *you* must bring in the work, using any and all techniques that you would utilize without an agent.

Be positive and honest in your dealings with your agent. It's a professional partnership that needs to be nurtured from both sides. Remember that you are not your agent's sole client. Your agent won't be calling you every day or every week, maybe not even every month. You should stay in touch regularly with little reminders that you exist. That doesn't mean pestering your agent every day, but once every couple of weeks is a good idea. Having new material or bits of good news will help keep your agent excited about repping you, and gives the agent something to work with when putting your name out.

GETTING PAID

Ideally, you will have an agent who will handle all negotiations, contractual affairs, and payments. If you're new to the business and perhaps have just gotten an agent, I will share the primary rule that my first agent quickly drummed into my head with a sledgehammer: never, never, NEVER talk money. Always let your agent handle the money discussions. The agent's job is to get you the best money possible. Your job is to do the writing. Keep those things separate.

If you don't have an agent, consider using an entertainment lawyer, as mentioned earlier, and let the lawyer talk money. If you insist on doing it yourself, it will be up to you to handle the contract; to find out from the company to whom, when, and how you send an invoice; and to follow up on getting paid.

Don't expect to get rich writing animation. There are exceptions (as in any business), those exceptions being people covered by a WGA agreement or who have the clout to command large money.

The dirty secret of the majority of television-series animation is that animation writers are making about the same fees as they made in the 1980s. There has been virtually no improvement; in fact, and in some cases, it's gotten worse.

Back in the mid-1980s, getting $6,000 for a half-hour script was considered terrific money. But how many people do you know whose income has barely budged in twenty years? Two decades later, some shows pay only $5,000 per half hour. Anything less than that (for a half-hour show) should be considered completely unacceptable.

What a company or studio pays depends on how big or how successful they are and what market they operate in. The smaller, independent studios, foreign coproduction, or the company doing syndicated animation can't afford to pay as well as a major studio, network, or big cable channel.

For half-hour fees, the average low end is between $5,000 and $6,000; the average high end is between $7,000 and $8,000. Writing a pilot can earn you anywhere from $10,000 to $15,000. Some writers with sufficient clout have gotten more, but that was the general range as of the time this book was written.

There will also be no residuals (additional payments for repeat airings of the episode) and no royalties from DVD sales or anything else unless the show is covered by the WGA.

Which means it's time to talk about unions.

UNIONS AND ORGANIZATIONS

There are two labor organizations that deal with animation writers: the Writers Guild of America (WGA), and IATSE Local 839 (The Animation Guild). This is an especially tricky and complicated topic, due to the history of animation development and the quirks of federal labor law governing unions.

As you may recall in my brief opening chapter on animation history, actual scriptwriters entered the process very late when the needs of television required writers in addition to storyboard artists, or "gagmen." Consequently, there were no writers taken into account by the two unions involved until very much after the fact, by which time the animation business was set in its ways and had no interest in seeing animation writers get the benefits of union protection.

Without the protection of a union, animation writers were (and are) subject to a great many abuses. Typical abuses include the following:

- Getting writers to work for unacceptably low amounts of money or to do ridiculous amounts of work for one payment.
- "Cattle calls," in which dozens of writers were called together at once to pitch for a series that had only a limited number of scripts available. Writers would generate pitch after pitch with no guarantee of getting a job, against the dozens of other writers doing the same. This practice has been pretty much stamped out by animation writers taking a stand, but there is nothing to prevent it from happening again.
- Giving writers only a gang credit or no credit at all. A gang credit would be one long list of every writer who worked on a series, ganged together

in the end credits so that it was impossible to know who had written which episode. Although most shows now do a much better job of giving a writer a proper credit up front, there is nothing to guarantee this except the goodwill of the company or studio.

- Writers have no right to sell their scripts (copies of the script itself) as WGA writers can do.
- No residuals or other participation (for reruns, DVD, and so on).
- No health insurance or pension.
- No arbitration over disputes, nor anyone to help a writer with a dispute.

Along with many of my fellow writers, I have been part of a fight going on for more than twenty years to achieve WGA union protection for animation writers. We are finally making inroads in this tough battle, but we still have a long way to go.

The WGAw and the Animation Writers Caucus

The Screen Writers Guild was formed in 1933, reorganized into the Writers Guild of America, west and Writers Guild of America, East in 1954 (members living west of the Mississippi River belong to the WGAw, and members living east of that boundary belong to the WGAE). The early union was focused on the only game in town at the time—live-action movies. Because animation of the time was created by artists, it was excluded from later bargaining negotiations. Coverage for television was included much later.

The document that lays out every detail concerning how scriptwriters are paid and treated is the MBA (Minimum Basic Agreement). The MBA covers what the minimum payment will be to the writer. Minimum payment is known as scale (example: "My agent negotiated a deal that was scale plus 10 percent"). The minimum payments for any project are based on several factors, such as:

- Whether it's a theatrical feature, TV feature, series, or whatever.
- The project's budget (mainly for theatrical features).
- The time length (mainly for TV).
- For TV, the time slot in which the show will air (daytime vs. primetime, and so on).

The MBA also covers how writing credits are determined, what the residuals will be (a residual is a payment that is made each time a TV show is rerun), rules on how writers have to be treated, provisions for arbitration in case a credit is disputed, payments to cover health and pension, and a myriad of other details designed to protect the rights and interests of writers. The MBA is renegotiated every three years.

When a studio or company signs the MBA, they become signatories to that agreement, meaning they are legally bound to abide by these rules in every detail. Although the company must pay no less than the *minimum* amount set out in the MBA, it's up to your agent, lawyer, or you to negotiate a higher price, if you can. There is no upper limit to how much you can be paid.

Most movie and television production entities that produce live action are signatories to the MBA, but until fairly recently there were among the signatories few studios or companies that produced exclusively animation. Because scriptwriters became a serious factor in the animation process only in the 1960s, it wasn't until around the 1980s that we began the first serious efforts to be covered by the WGAw. I won't go into the tedious details (which is a book in itself), but we found ourselves up against two major obstacles. One was the tangled complications of federal labor law that governs how guilds and unions can operate. The other—no surprise—was (and is) stiff resistance by the animation companies and studios.

In the early 1990s, I joined the Steering Committee of the newly established Animation Writers Caucus. The WGAw formed this caucus as a means for organizing and representing animation writers under the guild. For a minimal fee (waived if you already belong to the WGA), anyone who has written the equivalent of a half hour of produced animation can join the AWC. A member of the AWC is considered an associate member of the WGAw, which provides certain benefits that include receiving *Written By* magazine, all guild mailings, the AWC newsletter, access to the credit union, reduced member rate for registering scripts, joining the WGA Film Society, and access to an alternative health plan. The AWC arranges panels, awards, and other events.

Most importantly, the AWC, under the auspices of the WGAw, works to bring animation writers fully into the WGAw by having studios or companies sign the MBA.

I had the pleasure to work on the first animation series covered by a WGA agreement, *Pocket Dragon Adventures*, in 1997. The first show fully covered by the MBA was the primetime animated series *The PJs* in 1998. Since then, more shows have been organized and have become signatories to the MBA, though nearly all of them are primetime series. This is because of what I said earlier about primetime animation shows being written mostly by sitcom and live-action writers who are accustomed to writing as WGA members and expect to have those rights, benefits, and protections.

In 2004, an agreement was put into place between the WGA, IATSE Local 839 (see below), and eight companies: Adelaide Productions, Cartoon Network Studios, DreamWorks SKG, Fox Television Animation, Sony Pictures Animation, Universal Cartoon Studios, Walt Disney Pictures and Walt Disney Television Animation, and Warner Bros. Animation. The eight companies/studios have agreed that they must give notice to writers with their first monetary proposal as to which union (WGA or 839) will cover the writing work. The writer can then request that her work be covered by a WGA agreement, or, at the very least, receive WGA equivalent benefits (meaning payments to health and pension, credit arbitration, residuals, and so forth).

If you are hired by a company or studio that is not one of these eight, you need to request WGA coverage yourself. Don't be afraid to ask!

The important thing to know about all of this is that should you ever find your-self in a position of power or have the necessary clout, you should fight to have your show done as a signatory to the WGA. To get help in doing this, contact the WGAw Organizing Department at 323-782-4511.

Having worked in live action as a WGA writer and in animation without the benefit of the WGA, I cannot emphasize enough how important this struggle is. The WGA is the right home for animation writers. We must make that happen.

IATSE LOCAL 839 (a.k.a. THE ANIMATION GUILD)

The cartoonists union began as the Commercial Artists and Designers Union, which won their first contract after a courageous strike in 1937. This was followed by a Screen Cartoonists Guild in Hollywood and numerous battles to organize the artists and animators at major studios such as Disney and Warner Bros.

In 1951, the animators voted to join the International Alliance of Theatrical Stage Employees (IATSE), and a year later they became Local 839 under IATSE. More recently, Local 839 has renamed itself The Animation Guild (TAG).

Local 839 covers layout artists, ink and paint artists, 2D and 3D animators, storyboard artists, and other related categories. Because there were no actual scriptwriters early on, the people who came up with story were simply called "story men." And by the odd manner in which writing developed in anima-tion, the people writing animation fell under this category of "story men" (later "story persons"). Thus, rather by accident, Local 839 has ended up with scriptwriters (now at least referred to as "animation writers") within the body of union members who are otherwise working in the art end of the business.

If you get a job to write for a show that is covered by Local 839 and you are unable to get WGA representation instead, you will need to pay an initiation fee and dues to Local 839. Depending on what you earn, you may also be eligible for health insurance, and there will be payments made to a pension and welfare plan. There are, however, no individually paid residuals in the manner of the WGA.

LOCATION, LOCATION, LOCATION

In the United States, if you want to break into animation writing in a serious way, you need to be in Los Angeles. That is still where the bulk of animation development is done, where the major studios are, and where most of the work originates. This is also where you need to be to meet the people who hire writers and to do personal networking.

There are some animation companies in San Francisco and New York City, and those would be other possibilities to explore, provided those companies actu-ally hire writers. In many cases, the animation company provides the art while the scripts come from somewhere else—for example, L.A.

133

There is independent animation production being done elsewhere, such as in Florida, but the trick once again is to find places that hire writers. If you're in Canada, you need to go to the major centers of animation production—Vancouver or Toronto.

Finally, there is the overseas factor. More and more animation is being done using coproduction financing from studios in France, Britain, Ireland, Australia, Korea, Japan, China, India, Taiwan, and elsewhere. There's no easy, straightforward way for an American to get work for those companies. It would once again be a matter of networking. If you live overseas, however, you would be advised to find out where the largest producers of animation are in your country, and then move to that location. Your goal would be to meet people at that company who can hire you, and you need to be close enough physically to do that.

CHAPTER 9

Agents, Networking, and Finding Work

Jean Ann Wright

WRITING A SAMPLE SCRIPT

Before you can write for an animated television cartoon, you have to write a sample script to submit to the story editor of that show. This is not a script that will be sold. Try surfing online to find an actual animation script in the genre you're writing so that you can use it as a template. Write your sample script for a show that's similar to the show you want to pitch. Or if you want to write for a specific show, ask the story editor of that show what kind of sample script he wants to see. Do not write a sample for the same show you want to pitch because the story editor will know that show too well; and he'll see only the script's flaws. You may be able to get work with only one sample script, but it's better to have several: a sample for a sitcom like *The Simpsons*, for a half-hour action/adventure, for a seven minute squash and stretch comedy, and for any other animation genre that interests you. What's most important is that your sample script is fresh and exciting. This is not the time to break the rules. The story editor wants to see if you *know* the rules. When your sample script is ready, contact the story editor you want to pitch to and ask if you can submit a sample of your writing. Be sure it's your very best! Add a colorful script cover. You can submit a copy of your sample script to an animation agent as well, but an agent is not a must to find work.

LOOKING FOR WORK

Networking is very important in the animation industry. Because the industry is relatively small and writers must do quality work quickly, many story editors hire only writers they know. Join animation organizations like ASIFA and Women In Animation. Go to animation events where you might meet animation writers and story editors. Go to seminars and workshops and introduce

DOI: 10.1016/B978-0-240-81343-1.00009-1

135

yourself to the writers and story editors there. The important thing is to get your name out there and repeated over and over again. Check out animation-related Web sites. Many animation writers have their own Web site, and you can email them there. Just remember that good writers may be extremely busy with tight deadlines, so be brief and to the point when you ask for advice. A few professional writers have been forced to use pest control!

AGENTS AND MANAGERS

There are animation agents who represent animation writers. But even if you obtain an agent, you will still need to look for work on your own. Most agents are not eager to take writer-developers with no track record. And even if they do, they prefer to spend their valuable time finding work for those who can provide a better monetary return on their time. Many working animation writers have no agents at all. Most story editors will read your sample script without an agent. However it's difficult to get development people to look at an original project without an agent or entertainment attorney. Contact the Animation Writers Caucus of the Writers Guild of America, in west Los Angeles, for a list of agents who handle writers. This is a list of all literary agents, not just those that represent animation writers. An entertainment lawyer will submit scripts for you if you wish to hire them for that purpose, and they'll negotiate any resulting contracts. But be sure you contact only entertainment lawyers so that they know the industry. Without either an agent or an entertainment lawyer, you may be asked to sign a release form, giving up some of your rights. Companies are in mortal fear of being sued!

OTHER SUGGESTIONS

You should be immersed in the animation medium so that you know instinctively what sounds right and what doesn't. Watch cartoons on television, and go to see the latest animated films. Rent animation at your video store. Get to really know the current series on TV. In order to write convincingly, you need to know those characters so well that you know exactly what they would do at any given time. Read entertainment magazines like *Animation Magazine*, *The AWN Spotlight*, AWN's *Animation Flash*, *The Hollywood Reporter*, *Daily Variety*, and *Kidscreen* so that you know what's happening in the animation industry, who's buying what and why, what series are popular with the kids.

When you watch cartoons on TV, make a list of the writers, story editors, and producers for each series. The story editors are the ones who will hire you. Producers can also give you an "in." Every second Tuesday *The Hollywood Reporter* publishes a list of production companies and the series that are in production. This listing includes TV animation series with credits for the series' producers and story editors. If you don't subscribe to *The Hollywood Reporter*, you may be able to find it at the library. Often the listing is out of date, but this gives you a starting point in your job hunt. Call these companies and ask for the story editor you find listed. If that story editor is not available at that company, try to talk to another. Remember that today most writers and story editors in the United States are freelancers and work at home, moving often between companies.

Ask any story editor that you contact if you can send them a sample script and if they're accepting ideas for premises (written for free) for their series. Ask them to send you a bible of the series they're working on, a script from the series, and a few sample premises. Overworked story editors have tight deadlines, so keep it very brief. Keep a card file on each story editor. List their latest series and any other series they've edited. From articles you've read and from talking to them, list what they like and dislike and any useful personal information that will be helpful in conversation when you talk to them again.

If you're pitching your own original projects to development people around town, keep a card file on development executives as well. You'll eventually meet a lot of story editors and development people, and you won't remember it all when you need it later. Then write and keep writing each day.

Take time out from your writing to promote yourself and what you're doing. Be creative. Be funny. Be different in your promotional efforts so you stand out. Keep up these contacts, and don't be afraid to use them; just remember to keep it brief. Make friends with the assistant who answers the call. They can often help you get through the gate. Calling once a month or every couple of months is probably okay; calling every day is definitely counterproductive. Better yet, email or write, send out funny promotional material. Eventually, story editors will start referring you to other story editors who are currently looking for material.

When you get that first assignment, write exactly what that story editor wants and needs. Ask! And always, always turn in your assignment on time.

The process sounds difficult and it is, but new writers break in all the time. You just need to be good…and fast…and most of all persistent!

Consider looking for work internationally as well. Many U.S. writers do much of their writing by email for companies overseas. Contact companies outside of the United States. There's a huge market out there for U.S. animation writers. Send sample scripts, credits, and so on. If you don't live in the United States, be sure to contact local networks and production companies in your search for work.

Whether your employers are around the world or down the street, keep up your contacts. Get your own Web site. List credits, a bio, awards, and make sample scripts available there. Add a photo. Send out a periodic email newsletter. Include helpful information along with the self-promotion, but keep it short. Call your contacts occasionally in order to establish a more personal relationship. Talk pets and family. Send flowers. Take them to lunch. Keep up the networking. Try to meet your international contacts at trade events or on business trips. Think of your writing as an international business. You are the person responsible for business development. For a freelance writer, taking the time to look for work is an important part of your career.

EXERCISES

1. Watch cartoons. Start an index card on each writer, story editor, and development person you find. Normally, development people are not listed in the credits. How will you find out more about them?
2. Write a sample script. Be fresh. Make it the very best you can. Write in a different genre from what you already have.
3. Research animation agents and compile the class results. Make up a directory that can be photocopied and handed out in class.
4. What are networks and production companies buying today? Do some research on the Internet or in the library.
5. Invite an animation writer or a development executive to speak to your class.
6. Join an animation organization like ASIFA (worldwide) or Women in Animation.
7. Check out AWN. Join in some of the discussion forums.
8. Conduct a class discussion about the most popular animation series in your area. Can you see international trends? Where are these programs being produced? Animation seems to cycle in employment opportunities. How is it doing currently? How can you make a living during the down cycles?

PART 2
Writing for Games

INTRODUCTION

The word "games" is a convenient shorthand term for a wider field of interactive entertainment that can take many forms. Currently, we see a huge business for videogames as defined primarily by platform (PC, consoles, mobile devices, etc.) and genres (First Person Shooter, Role-Playing Game, Massively Multi-player On-Line Game, casual, puzzle, adventure, etc.). Yet there are so many other possibilities, such as interactive fiction, true mass-market games on Facebook with millions upon millions of players, interactive series on the Web, and attempts to create genuine interactive drama rather than being bound by the constraints of "game" expectations.

The development of electronic games draws heavily on the millennia-old interest in passing one's time at games of chance (rolling the dice, tossing coins), skill (sports), or strategy (chess, go, backgammon, poker). The earliest electronic offerings reflected simple skill-based games: Pong and arcade shooters. As the field of videogames matured and the technology advanced, savvy players began to demand more satisfaction from the stories that provided the rationale behind increasingly complex games that combined elements of chance, skill, and strategy with the additional aspect of making the player a character within the game. Videogames have become a blend—often an awkward blend at war with itself—of gameplay and storytelling.

At the same time, interactive writing is in its infancy. As with animation writing, it draws from an ancient history of audiovisual storytelling, but with a modern twist—the player is no longer a passive viewer/listener. The player's actions are vital components in how digital storytelling and games work. This extra twist is what differentiates the craft of writing for games from any other form of writing. It requires an entirely new way of looking at and thinking about how "story," in the traditional linear way we understand it, can be integrated into a nonlinear form that demands active participation in how that story will be expressed.

In this half of the book, five authors share a range of expertise, experience, and knowledge about this ever-changing, ever-mutating field of interactive entertainment. In addition, there is a section on the newly developing area of *serious games*, in which the familiar formats of videogames are used not to entertain, but to instruct, teach, or inform the "players" on real-world subjects—everything from Army field training to dealing with world hunger to helping kids fight cancer cells.

We will cover topics such as these:

- Basics of game design
- The nature of interactivity
- Tools and terminology
- Script and proposal formatting
- Linear vs. nonlinear narrative
- Simulation stories
- Design and writing of serious games
- Breaking into videogame writing

If you find that the contributors' chapters spark your interest in learning more, you can delve more deeply into the books listed here. Let's meet the authors.

Terry Borst, *Story and Simulations for Serious Games: Tale from the Trenches* (ISBN-13: 978-0-240-80788-1)

Terry Borst is a Writers Guild of America member with screenwriting credits in feature films, episodic television, and videogames, including the award-winning Wing Commander III and Wing Commander IV. He has also taught screenwriting and multimedia design at UCLA, USC, the College of Santa Fe, the Banff Centre for the Arts, Moorpark College, and various conferences and workshops. Borst and co-writer Nick Iuppa contributed Chapters 19, 20, 21, 22, and 23. You can learn more about Terry Borst by going to www.terryborst.com.

Timothy Garrand, *Writing for Multimedia and the Web* (ISBN-13: 978-0-240-80822-2)

Timothy Garrand is currently a principal user experience architect with TandemSeven. TandemSeven designs, architects, and builds world-class applications and portals.

Garrand brings nearly 20 years of usability and user interface design experience with special expertise in rich Internet application design, content development, and content strategy. Garrand's experience spans multiple industries, with an emphasis on financial services, consumer products, educational media, and publishing. Garrand has worked on more than a hundred Web and multi-media programs for major companies such as Houghton Mifflin, Pearson Education, Reed Elsevier, Rockland Trust, Fleet Bank, Hartford Life, the State of Massachusetts, Citibank, Giant Eagle, JPMorgan Chase, Career Education Corporation, Chubb Insurance, Standard Chartered Bank, and Fidelity Investments.

Before joining TandemSeven, Garrand worked as an independent consultant, senior interactive architect for the agency Immersant, and he served as owner-operator of his own company, InterWrite, which specialized in information architecture, content strategy, and online design educational multimedia.

Garrand is a frequent speaker at conferences and professional gatherings and occasionally teaches a course on interactive writing for the University of Massachusetts.

Timothy Garrand contributed Chapters 13, 16, 17, and 18. You can learn more about Timothy Garrand by going to www.interwrite.com/book/index.html.

Nick Iuppa, *Story and Simulations for Serious Games: Tale from the Trenches* (ISBN-13: 978-0-240-80788-1)

Nick Iuppa is an award-winning designer of instructional media and game-based training. He has held creative positions for world-renowned entertainment companies such as MGM, Walt Disney Productions and Paramount Pictures and served as a training executive at Silicon Valley giants Hewlett Packard and Apple Computer. Nick also spent 10 years as Vice President and head of Instructional Media Development at Bank of America. He has more recently headed The Iuppa Creative Group, a team of experienced instructional designers, writers and serious game producers who first came together as The Paramount Pictures Simulation Group in 1997. After successfully designing and building leadership-training simulations for the DoD and the US Army, the team has gone on to do instructional and game design on two large projects for the US Fire Service. Additionally, IA has designed a course in Becoming American, a framework for teaching civic literacy to immigrants (for Retention Education), and designed learning packages in creativity, music and math skills for Leap Frog. They have also created entertainment and instructional games for Walt Disney Company, Worlds of Wonder, and Electronic Arts. The Iuppa Creative Group is currently involved in developing confidential and proprietary learning systems for a number of clients. Nick holds a BA in Communication Arts from the University of Notre Dame and an MA in Psychology of Communication from Stanford University. He and co-writer Terry Borst contributed Chapters 19, 20, 21, 22, and 23. You can learn more about Nick Iuppa by going to www.nickiuppa.com.

Christy Marx, *Writing for Animation, Comics and Games* (ISBN-13: 978-0-240-80582-5)

Christy Marx's eclectic career includes writing for animation (television and film), live-action (television and film), comic books, graphic novels, manga, videogames, and educational books. She began her work in videogames by designing award-winning adventure games for Sierra On-Line: *Conquests of Camelot: King Arthur and the Search for the Grail* and *Conquests of the Longbow: the Legend of Robin Hood*. She has done writing and narrative design for games in the PC, console, and MMOG categories and most recently spent two and a half years creating an original storyworld for an MMOG in development. Her related activities include panels, lectures, workshops, and seminars for all three fields of writing. In her spare time, she herds cats.

She contributed Chapters 10, 15, and 26 to this book. You can learn more about Christy Marx by going to www.christymarx.com.

Carolyn Handler Miller, *Digital Storytelling: A Creator's Guide to Interactive Entertainment* (ISBN-13: 978-0-240-80959-5)

Carolyn Handler Miller is one of the pioneering writers in the field of nonlinear entertainment. As an award-winning Hollywood screenwriter, she brings a unique perspective to the craft of digital storytelling. She has worked as a writer, writer-content designer, or consultant on more than four dozen new media projects. Her work as a digital storyteller includes not only videogames but projects for the Web, interactive TV, smart toys, and transmedia entertainment, as well as innovative educational, informational, and promotional endeavors. In addition, she teaches courses in interactive narrative for the University of New Mexico.

She contributed Chapters 11, 12, 14, 24, and 25 to this book. You can learn more about Carolyn Handler Miller by going to www.carolynmiller.com.

SECTION 1
The First Things You Need to Know

CHAPTER 10

Writing vs. Design

Christy Marx

I am frequently asked how one goes about becoming a game designer, because people still tend to think that *designer* means the same as *writer of the game*. To add to the confusion, the two are often combined. However, as game production becomes more specialized, so do these two roles. Given the scope and complexity of writing for videogames, it's important to understand the difference between design and writing. If you want to work as a writer, you need to understand how these two roles differ and what a designer does, so that you'll know when you're being asked to be a writer or to go an extra step toward being a designer. To get some of the confusion out of the way, let's deal first with the issue of being a game designer.

THE GAME DESIGNER

The role of game designer has evolved considerably since I began work as a designer. As explained earlier, the first designers were programmers for the simple reason that they were the only ones who knew how to design. As the games business grew and games became more complex, the role of designer became more of an entity unto itself. Back then (at least at Sierra On-Line), it seemed as though anyone who could come up with good ideas for a game and put them down in a reasonably coherent manner could be hired to design. It was more about having the creative vision and enough technical skill to know what could or could not be done within the existing programming and animation capabilities.

Today, the position of designer has become a more technical job. The designer must have the overall vision of the game, must understand the mechanics and fundamentals of game design, must have a very good grasp of what makes a

DOI: 10.1016/B978-0-240-81343-1.00010-8

game fun, is expected to know programming and art tools, *and* (in most cases) is expected to be a writer. Boiling it all down, it is the job of the designer to ensure that the game is entertaining, interactive, and functional. Bad design will kill a game faster than you can blink.

As game development teams grew larger, other designer roles were born. At the very top there may be a creative director who oversees all aspects of creating the game, but at a higher level rather than in terms of the hands-on details. There can be other high-level director jobs for the individual in charge of an entire department, such as the art director, the audio director, the technical director, and the design director. The use of such titles or positions varies from company to company.

The designer at the top of the totem pole with the highest level of responsibility for actually making the game is usually called the lead designer, who might be the same as the design director. There can be one overall lead designer in charge of the project, along with other leads of individual departments, such as the lead system designer, the lead world designer, and so on, who answer to the lead designer. Next on the rung would be a senior designer. Below that level the roles generally default to the type of position, such as systems designer, tool designer, level designer, world designer, and so on.

World building designers and level designers do essentially the same thing—they craft and create the virtual terrain to make sure the player has the best possible game experience while playing through it. A level designer possesses a combination of design, art, architectural, and programming skills.

Additionally, there can be quest designers (creating quests/missions, dialogue, and so on) and content designers (often a rather technical job involving programmatic scripting to make events or scenes happen in the world, as well as other tasks). Although both of these jobs could potentially involve creative writing, they aren't writing jobs per se.

The more recent addition of a position called narrative designer (or sometimes story designer) is for the writer/designer in charge of working out how story will be integrated into the game and delivered to the player. The narrative designer may or may not do the actual writing and might be the one who hires and works with the game writers.

The best way to understand what companies think any kind of game designer is, is to look at the skill requirements in job listings for designers. Many Web sites list designer jobs. The best place to go is Gamasutra (http://www.gamasutra.com), a site that is intensely useful for all things related to game development and features plenty of job listings. High-tech headhunters have Web sites looking to fill the positions for the companies. The game companies often have job listings on their own Web sites.

For those who are interested specifically in being a game designer, looking at these lists of requirements will tell you exactly where you stand and what you need to acquire (experience, skills, education, and so forth) in order to qualify. Today, some colleges teach courses in game design, so there is at least a starting point now that didn't exist years ago.

You'll notice that 99 percent of these job listings will include "a passion for games" as one of the requirements. If you get an interview, you can be sure they'll test you for your knowledge of, and experience with, playing games. If you go after a job with Company A, make sure to play as many games as you can that Company A makes. Feel free to rave about the games to the person interviewing you. If you think the games suck, you'd better find something else to be positive and enthusiastic about (though one wonders why you'd want to work there anyway if you don't like the company's games).

No one will hire you right out of the gate to be a lead or senior designer. The most likely path to become the top person designing a game is to find an entry-level job and work your way up. Some people recommend finding any kind of entry-level job—for example, as a game tester (QA, for "quality assurance"). Other people contest this. The advice is all over the place. From what I've been able to distil, it depends on three big factors: the internal attitude of the company (will the company's managers promote from within, or do they look down on lowly game testers?), how good you are at proving you can do design work, and luck.

DESIGNER OR WRITER

The rest of these chapters will deal with being a writer for games, rather than a game designer. There will be additional information about game design in this chapter, because it can be intertwined with the writing discussion. It's so intertwined that it can be hard at times to sort out where writing ends and design begins, but you need to be able to sort that out because you should be paid differently if you are doing design work in addition to writing, and you should receive a proper credit for it in the game credits.

Possible credits for your work could be writer, story writer, scenario writer, scriptwriter, dialogue writer, story designer, narrative designer, writer/designer, or something else invented on the spot. These titles aren't yet standardized.

This is extremely simplified, but my take is that the line between the two rests on whether or not you are asked to create the *interactive* elements. For example, on one game I was hired to write a story and character bible; however, it was a martial arts fighting game, so none of the backstory or biographies affected the actual game design or the gameplay. This material added background and flavor, but it created nothing interactive.

In contrast, on another game I was hired not only to create the world bible and biographies, but I also had to come up with the backstory, game story, overall quest, the story-related subquests, how the story would be expressed from the beginning of the game through all the quests to the end, plus write cutscenes and dialogue. I didn't design the combat system or the magic-using system or the interface, but the game story and quests are at the heart of the interactivity of the game, so that is design work all the same.

If you're hired as a writer and are asked to create new elements that are definitely generating interactivity in the game, you should discuss with the client whether or not this should be considered as some form of design work.

This doesn't extend to writing dialogue. It's true that dialogue is interactive, but if you didn't create the interactive elements that generated the dialogue, it isn't design work.

VIDEOGAMES AND HOLLYWOOD

There's much traffic between Hollywood and the games business. Movies, TV series, and animation are turned into games, whereas games are turned mostly into movies, but could easily become TV series and animation as well. One announced project was an MMOG and Syfy channel series created in tandem.

Words that mean one thing in Hollywood can mean something extremely different in games. The most important of these is **development.**

In Hollywood, development is mainly a writing process. It's about acquiring a concept (script, book, newspaper article, or whatever), hiring or acquiring a scriptwriter, getting it written and rewritten, while possibly attaching creative elements such as a director or star actor to help ensure it will get made. Once development—meaning the script—is finished, the project is either killed or is greenlit. If it gets a green light, the movie or show can go into preproduction, and finally, with luck, into actual production. A studio or an executive or whoever has the power can take credit for "developing" the project.

In games, development is the process of *making the game*. The development team (the developers, or devs for short) consists of the people creating every aspect of the game design and game assets. That includes the producers, designers, programmers, artists, animators, composer, sound editor, QA, and so on. Game development begins with the initial concept for the game and continues until the game is done and shipped.

Another term that can cause confusion is **scripting.** In Hollywood, everyone knows what a scriptwriter is—the person who writes the TV or movie script. In games, however, a "scripter" or a "scripting" job refers to writing code using software such as Python or Lua, programming languages commonly used in game development. If you're a writer looking for writing jobs in the games business, be careful not to get snagged by jobs looking for scripters or people able to do scripting. It's a programming job, not a writing job.

Another term to avoid is **world building** or **world builder.** It's a term that sounds useful for a writer, but in games it's a technical term for the work of a level designer who creates the geography/architecture for a level or region in the game.

Using a hyphenated term to describe oneself is another area where games depart from standard Hollywood terminology. I have done both game design and game writing, so for years I referred to myself as a writer-designer (or designer-writer). I was so accustomed to the use of hyphenates in Hollywood, it never occurred to me that people in games would have a negative reaction to the usage. In film or TV, if someone is a writer-director, writer-actor, or writer-producer, it's well understood that this person can do either or both of these jobs, not necessarily at the same time. Oddly enough, though, there seems to be more acceptance in the games business of the term designer/writer or writer/designer when a slash is used instead of a hyphen.

In general, the belief is that the combined terms confuse the issue and leave game people unsure whether you want to write or you want to design; or worse, they'll worry about hiring you as a writer, and you'll end up trying to meddle with design when they don't want you to. Most games people think it's essential to have two separate résumés: one purely for the game writing work, and one purely for game design work (if you do both).

Terminology

The terms below are a tiny fraction of the huge vocabulary that surrounds the process of making games. I've subjectively grabbed a batch of the terms that I think are useful for a writer to know, especially if you're not already familiar with games.

The first few definitions pertain more specifically to terms that a writer absolutely needs to know. The rest of the definitions relate more to playing games in general.

Writer-Specific Terms

ASSETS

Any digital file that makes up part of the game—such as art, animation, code, sound, music, voice recording, text dialogue, or whatever. If you write dialogue for a game, each piece of dialogue is an asset.

CINEMATIC

A noninteractive scene that is part of the game story and is rendered in real time by the game engine. It's a scene that the player can only watch, but cannot affect (other than to skip over it). A cinematic can be used to convey a key story point, give the player an extra "pat on the back" for completing some important section of the game, create atmosphere, provide clues to the player about what to do next, and so on. See also *Cutscene*. The two terms, cinematic and cutscene, are used interchangeably, however, and most people no longer make a distinction between them.

COMMENTING OUT (USING ; OR //)

Putting a semicolon (;) or double backslashes (//) in front of a line indicates you are "commenting" or "commenting out" that specific line as a piece of information, rather than writing a line of script or a line of code. When a line is commented out, it tells a programmer (and the program itself) that this is information only, and not something to be acted upon. It's used to make a note of explanation or other information about the piece of code or script that immediately follows it.

CUTSCENE

A noninteractive, prerendered scene written for the game, the same as a cinematic in purpose. A cutscene, however, might use art assets beyond what the game itself can provide. For example, a cutscene could be shot with live actors, or it might use a higher resolution of animation. The two terms, cinematic and cutscene, are used interchangeably, however, and most people no longer make a distinction between them.

DELIVERABLES

A term commonly used to refer to game assets that have to be delivered to meet a milestone (a game development deadline). In the case of a game writer, deliverables would be such things as a story treatment, a quest, dialogue for a particular character, or some other specific chunk of writing.

DESIGN DOCUMENT

This can vary from company to company, but ideally a design document contains the design specifics for every aspect of a game: examples include story outline, explanation of the interface, world-building description, character biographies, lists of important NPCs, and indications of all the interactive elements and what they are and how they work. In short, it is the complete blueprint for the game.

FMV (FULL-MOTION VIDEO)

Prerendered video (animation or live action) done in broadcast-quality resolution (thirty frames per second) and played like a minimovie. Note that as game platforms continue to advance in their ability to render high-quality animation, there may no longer be a need for FMVs. They have been used primarily as opening trailers for the beginning of the game to set up the story, situation, or environment, or for cutscenes.

MILESTONES

Game schedules work to milestones rather than deadlines. A milestone is a date by which a certain chunk of the game design must be done, or the assets created, or code implemented, and so on. For a writer, chunks of game writing will be assigned as milestones.

WALKTHROUGH

A written description of how to follow one or more paths through a game. A walkthrough generally tells the player how to get to locations, how to find the necessary NPCs, what to do there, and other details that help the player find his way through the game.

Game-Development and Game-Playing Terms

AGGRO, AGGRO RADIUS (AGGRO = AGGRESSION)

Aggro refers to how likely it is that a mob (see definition below) or object in the game will attack your avatar (see definition below). If the mob has high aggro, it's more likely to attack you. Your own level as a player can also affect this—for example, a higher-level mob will tend to have more aggro toward you if you're a lower level, while a very-low-level mob may completely ignore you if you're a much higher level than it. Aggro radius is the size of the area around the mob that your avatar must enter in order to trigger the aggressive action. You might be able to run right into or through some mobs without triggering an aggro response, but other mobs might attack you when you're yards away.

AI (ARTIFICIAL INTELLIGENCE)

In computer science, AI is a computer system that is programmed to "think" like a human, to reason, to learn, and to perform cognitive functions that mimic human intelligence. In games, AI is more loosely used to refer to the level of intelligence programmed into the computer-controlled NPCs and other objects to determine how they'll respond to the player or to other objects in the game. The AI given to the human characters in *The Sims*, for example, is much higher than a role-playing game's AI for a minor NPC who needs to have only a specific and limited set of things to say or do.

ATTRIBUTES

Used mostly in role-playing games to refer to the vital statistics that a player can control and improve for their avatar, such as strength, agility, speed, stealth, spirit, and so on.

AVATAR

The avatar is the player's character in the game and is always controlled by the player. There are games in which a player can control more than one character, but the player has only one avatar. The secondary characters are NPCs, even though the player controls them. The avatar may be a specific character that is created for the player (such as Lara Croft in *Tomb Raider*), or a character the player builds from scratch and assigns a unique name, as in RPGs and MMOGs.

Note that although the term "avatar" has been around for a long time, some companies may use other terminology, such as "player character" or "hero character." (See also *Toon*.)

BETA TESTING

Stages of game testing in which people outside the company (meaning potential customers) are invited to test the game shortly before it is officially released. There is first a closed beta which allows a limited pool of players, followed by an open beta that allows a larger pool of players to put the game through its paces. The idea is to find as many bugs (see below) as possible and fix them before the game is released, and to look for weaknesses in the gameplay that can be improved. It can also build a loyal customer base and give the game good word of mouth (you hope).

BOSS

A boss is a mob that is a higher level than the others around it (the "boss" of the lower level mobs), thus posing a greater challenge to the player. A boss is usually the last one the player fights, as the payoff for getting past all the lower mobs. (See also *Elite*.)

BUFF

A spell or other effect cast in the game that benefits the player's avatar, usually for some limited period of time. For example, an avatar might get a boost in strength or an increase in agility or stamina, or might gain an ability, such as turning invisible, and so on.

BUG

An error in the code or other assets that causes a game to work incorrectly.

DEATHMATCH

A player-vs.-player mode of combat that occurs in the multiuser versions of a first-person shooter. In deathmatch mode, a player can respawn (reappear) in the game either immediately after dying or after a very short delay.

DPS (DAMAGE PER SECOND)

A common stat that indicates how much damage your avatar or avatar's weapon/spell can do to mobs or other players, and vice versa.

DUNGEONS

In game usage, this refers to special spaces set aside for dangerous exploration and combat—often, but not always, underground. It typically indicates a large and complex space with lots of room for the player to get into trouble, rather than a single room or simple cave. "Dungeon crawlers" are games built entirely around large, multilevel dungeons where all the action takes place.

ELEGANT

If you hear a programmer refer to something as elegant, he means that it's a beautifully written piece of code that is clear, clean, easy to understand, well commented, and works with minimal problems.

ELITE

A boss mob or NPC that is high level, extra-powerful, and difficult to battle. It can also refer to a dungeon or quest in which such bosses or NPCs are found.

EMOTES

Typed commands that cause the avatar to perform some emoting action, such as waving, dancing, cheering, flirting, bowing, blowing a kiss, slapping, and so on.

EXPLOIT

A bug in the game or a loophole in the game design that allows a player to exploit the flaw in some way that wasn't anticipated, isn't necessarily desirable, and is advantageous to the player, giving him an unfair advantage over other players. For example, a player might discover a bug that allows him to get unlimited numbers of some item and sell them, thus becoming very rich very quickly in a way that wasn't intended and unbalances the game's economy.

153

FEATURE

To put it simply, the features are the actions you're able to do in a game via the interface. Being able to save a game at any point is a feature. Being able to craft or manufacture something in a game is a feature. Being able to customize the appearance of your avatar is a feature. There's an old joke among programmers: "It's not a bug—it's a feature!" This is another way of saying: "It's not really broken—we meant it to work badly like that." The joke is sometimes applied to bad design decisions. Another aspect of feature is "feature creep," which refers to new features being added to a game after the initial game design is done because they seem like a cool idea, but which can seriously mess up the budget and schedule. Adding a feature means adding code, art, and possibly other assets, so a good producer or game designer needs to keep feature creep under control.

FRAG

Killing another player, most commonly used in the deathmatch mode of FPS games.

GRIEFERS

People who play multiuser games for the purpose of interfering with or taking unfair advantage of other players. They cause grief, hence "griefers."

GUI (GRAPHICAL USER INTERFACE)

The Mac operating system was the first to use GUI (pronounced "gooey") when it created graphic elements on the screen (symbols, icons, drop-down dialogue boxes, and so on) that could be clicked on in order to perform a program action, rather than having to type in text instructions to tell the program what you wanted to do. This was a revolution in interface design because it made interacting with programs friendlier and easier (or that's the theory). Now GUI (such as Windows) is the standard.

HIT POINTS (HP)

A mathematical value that represents how much damage the player's character can take before dying.

INSTANCE, INSTANCING

This applies to MMOGs in which there can be hundreds to thousands of players sharing the same game locations or zones, so special locations will be set aside to be instances. This means that many copies of the location can exist on the same server, so that one particular group of players can enter that version of the location and carry out a quest or mission without the intrusion of any other players. Basically, an instance is your own private universe for your group of players. Simultaneously, any number of groups can be playing the same quest or mission within their own versions of that location. For example, a particular dungeon can be set aside to be an instance. As soon as the player or party of players enters the dungeon, they are in a unique version of it that is accessible only to them and not to any other players. Instancing is often used to avoid overcrowding in significant quest areas so that players get a quality experience for that quest. There is much debate among designers over the use of instancing, and what constitutes too much or too little.

INTERFACE

The software and hardware controls used by the player to interact with the game. The hardware part of the interface can be a keyboard, mouse, console controller, joystick, and so forth. The software part of the interface can be icons, symbols, or other input areas on the screen that are used to play the game.

INTUITIVE

Game designers use this word a lot when discussing the design of the game interface. Every designer strives to make the game interface and design as intuitive as possible—meaning extremely easy and natural for the player to understand and use. The idea is that the player intuitively understands what something does or how it works, rather than having to be trained in how to use it or having to read a manual.

LEVELS, LEVELING UP

Level is a dual-purpose term that can refer to a zone (region or location) of the game (for example, a desert, a range of mountains, a swamp, a dungeon, a city,

154

an entire country, a neighborhood, or even the single floor of a huge building structure). It can also refer to the levels achieved by the player when she has racked up a certain number of experience points (or similar stat). The player then "levels up" (usually a numeric level, such as going from level 40 to level 41) and gains enhancements, such as increased strength, spirit, stamina, or other abilities.

LEVEL DESIGNER

Again, there can be variance in this job description, but basically a level designer is responsible for using art and programming tools to create a geographic region or zone for the game, including the design, placement, and functions of flora, fauna, terrain, architecture, NPCs, and mobs.

MOB (MOBILE OR MOBILE OBJECT)

A mob is any NPC or other humanoid, creature, monster, or object that is mobile within the game and is controlled by the computer. More commonly, it refers to mobile objects that can move around and attack or chase the player, rather than an NPC who interacts socially with the player or gives out information, such as a quest giver.

NPC (NONPLAYER CHARACTER)

An NPC is any other game character that is not an avatar. NPCs are usually controlled by the computer, but there can be NPCs, such as a squad of soldiers or a set of quest companions, that are controlled by the player.

NERF

Means to weaken the abilities of a character class or other game object that is considered too powerful. For example, *World of Warcraft* players who feel that the Paladin class is too powerful will ask the devs to "nerf the Pallies." In order to have a weakening or negative affect on them, this would mean having to change the underlying rules that govern what that character class can do.

PATCH

In general computer terms, a patch is a software update that is meant to fix bugs or other problems with an earlier version of the software. In games, the patch would not only fix bugs, but might include changes to the gameplay (nerfs, buffs, new features, and so on) and new graphics, new sound, or new music to go along with new features. One example of a patch to improve gameplay would be adding the ability to have changing weather, such as a rainstorm, in a game region.

POLYGONS

What cells are to the human body, polygons are to 3D digital art. A single 3D character or building can be made up of thousands of polygons, which are tiny individual shapes that fit together to create the whole object. The more polygons, the more detailed and the better the resolution of the art, but also the greater the demands on the processing power of the hardware and software.

POWER-UP

A game item or commodity that can be acquired that gives the player's character an advantage over other players or against mobs. These items often have a limited usage or limited time.

PVE (PLAYER VS. ENVIRONMENT)

An MMOG option where the player is primarily playing against the game environment and the NPCs and mobs in it, rather than against other players (unless the player specifically chooses to do so). It's considered a safer form of gameplay because the player can enjoy the game without constantly having to worry about being jumped by some other player.

PVP (PLAYER VS. PLAYER)

An MMOG option where the player is always playing against other live players in the game environment, as well as with the NPCs and mobs in it.

QA (QUALITY ASSURANCE)

The process of testing a game (by playing and playing and playing it) to find bugs so they can be fixed before the game ships. Most companies have a lead QA person who runs a team of QA testers.

REPLAYABILITY

A game that contains enough entertainment value and variability that the player will play it two or more times to see what the alternative game experience is. *The Sims* has infinite replayability. A strongly linear game with little difference in how it plays out from one time to the next has low replayability quality.

SPAWNING

When a mob or monster or NPC suddenly appears in the game world, it has "spawned"—that is, the game engine has caused the entity to appear in a designated spot to carry out its function.

SIDE-SCROLLERS

Games that use 2D graphics so that the background scenery has to scroll from side to side (or top to bottom) as the player moves his avatar.

SPAWN CAMPING

The practice some players use in order to keep killing over and over again (for loot or experience) by first killing the mob then sitting and waiting at that spot for the mob to respawn, then doing it all over again.

STATS (STATISTICS)

Stats are vital to every sort of game, whether they're an obvious part of the interface (such as RPG character and weapon stats) or a hidden part of the game (underlying code). In RPGs in particular, the player is constantly trying to improve the stats of her characters—stats governing characteristics such as strength, speed, agility, stamina, spirit, and so forth. Stats also apply to what damage or effect an attack, weapon, spell, or other effect will have on the player, other players, NPCs, and mobs.

STRAFE

In combat, moving the avatar from side to side (often while using a weapon) rather than moving forward and then turning. It's a technique for dodging attacks.

TOON

Slang word for an avatar, used mainly by people playing MMOGs.

TRIGGER, FLAG, HOOK

These are all programming terms that indicate a piece of code that checks for specific conditions and activates the correct response depending on those conditions. The response can be an action (fight, run away, give something to the player, and so on) and/or it might be a piece of dialogue. For example, if the player clicks on an NPC that's a dwarf, the NPC code might check to see what character class the avatar is, what level the avatar has achieved, whether or not the avatar is shown as friendly or hostile to the NPCs character class, what the avatar is carrying in inventory, or any other number of variables. Thus, the NPC might respond one way if the avatar is a hostile, low-level warrior ("Get lost, bud"), and a very different way if the avatar is a friendly, high-level dwarf ("Hail, friend—here's some gold to help you out").

Mobs and some NPCs may have a trigger radius around them, meaning a set distance around them which the avatar must enter before an action or response is set into motion.

TWINKING

Done when a higher-level player helps a lower-level player rise more quickly in levels and experience than would be possible in normal play, usually by providing the lower-level player with money or useful game objects (such as money, weapons, gear, or armor). Also used when a player with a high-level avatar gives money or better-than-usual items to a lower-level avatar used by the same player.

WAYPOINTS

In the virtual terrain, these are specific points that are used to determine the movements of NPCs or other moving objects (which are coded to move from

157

one waypoint to another, or within a set of waypoints). Another example might be satellites positioned in space in order to serve as waypoints (spatial and navigational guidance) for the player in a spaceship so she can figure out how to get from one star system to another.

XP (EXPERIENCE POINTS)

The points an avatar gains by accomplishing missions/quests, killing, exploring new locations, and so on. These points are used to determine when the avatar will level up.

FUNDAMENTALS OF GAME DESIGN

Before getting into writing specifics, such as script formats (see Chapter 15), let's take a look at the larger issues that affect writing for games. These issues have to do with the nature of interactivity and the peculiar demands of videogames. Although many of these issues are the responsibility of the designer, a game company will want to have a writer who understands how this type of writing differs from the linear modes of writing. In order to understand that, we'll need to address some fundamental issues of game design.

Linear vs. Nonlinear

The biggest learning curve for someone entering games with a background in writing for linear media (books, movies, TV) is how to think of story and dialogue in a nonlinear way. That is, how do you convey story or allow a character to grow and change, or allow a story to unfold, when you can't entirely control the sequence in which the player will experience the story elements? As a writer, I'm all about putting as much storytelling into a game as I can. As a designer, my mantra is *empower the player*. The trick is to find a way to both empower the player and infuse the game with story and character development.

There's a constant tension between storytelling and interactivity. Storytelling, in the traditional linear sense, depends upon a specific sequence of events. This sequence includes a beginning, a middle, and an end. The writer controls how the reader/viewer will experience this sequence, and the sequence leads to only one conclusion. Thus, the writer determines the structure of the story.

Note that linear storytelling can be nonlinear in the chronological sense, such as using flashbacks, flash-forwards, telling the story backward (from end to beginning), or showing events out of chronological sequence (*Pulp Fiction* being an excellent example).

However, in games, what we mean by nonlinear is that it is the player—not the writer—who has significant control over when and how and in what order she experiences those events. Furthermore, the input of the player can potentially be significant in the direction or resolution of the story.

For example, in both of my adventure games, I offered the player options that were moral choices. In *Conquests of Camelot*, the player's avatar was King Arthur. Along the way, Arthur was put into situations where he could either rescue or decide not to rescue three of his knights, including Lancelot. If the player let his knights die, he could still complete the game, but when he placed his hands on the Holy Grail (the object of his quest), he was found not worthy and was burned to dust, rather than taking the Grail home in triumph.

In *Conquests of the Longbow*, the player's avatar was Robin Hood. On numerous occasions throughout the game, Robin Hood had various options for dealing with NPCs—which could include killing, helping, bribing, convincing by talking, and so forth. The options chosen by the player, along with various other actions during the game story, determined which of four endings the player would get—ranging from the best result (a full pardon from King Richard plus the restoration of his title as earl and the hand of Maid Marian) to the worst result (being hanged as a good-for-nothing robber).

The essence of games is interactivity, which means putting the player in control as much as possible. There is still structure and there are still rules, but they are designed to give the player as much freedom as the structure can allow. Videogames can be nonlinear and interactive and still have a basic three-act structure. More about this later under Game Structure.

It's easy to see how a linear story (Figure 10.1) can progress from one story node to another, with later story nodes able to build on or make reference to earlier story nodes.

In a completely nonlinear story (Figure 10.2), each story node has to stand alone and be self-sufficient without depending on the other story nodes or making reference to them in a specific sequence.

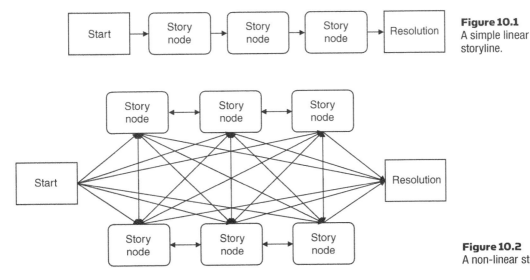

Figure 10.1
A simple linear storyline.

Figure 10.2
A non-linear storyline.

Most games will fall somewhere between these two extremes, as other examples will show.

Basically, what it gets down to is this: the more interactivity (player freedom) the game allows, the less linear story the writer can tell. You can visualize it as a seesaw, with story at one end and interactivity at the other. A game that is weighted heavily with story is light in interactivity. If heavy in interactivity, the game will be light in story. Trying to balance the two issues so the seesaw is horizontal isn't necessarily the right answer. The type of game will determine where on this seesaw scale the game will fall.

Many console games have quite linear stories threading through them, and the interactivity is mainly about the combat system and what/whom the player gets to fight along the way. PC games demand a higher level of true interactivity, with the player able to command a wider range of choices. MMOGs demand a high level of choice. Because they are ongoing, these games provide an additional design challenge in how to keep thousands of players hooked on the game world, the story, and the quests for months and years on end. MMOGs in particular are more about creating a compelling environment—the game world—and the activities in which the player can take part within that environment.

Some games are designed specifically for the hard-core gamers, in which case the design emphasis is definitely on gameplay at the expense of story. Hard-core gamers aren't known for caring about story. Other games look to attract a wider market of players who like a more rewarding story experience or want something more out of a game than twitching their thumbs on a controller.

When writing for games, you'll encounter many variations of this design mind-set, and you'll often feel that story must take a backseat to gameplay. How much story or character development is woven into a game will be up to the attitudes and preferences of the designer or producer—which leaves you, the writer, with the task of balancing your writing input with the requirements of the game design.

GAME STRUCTURE

Game structure is a huge subject. To fully understand it would require reading a book entirely about game design, but if you're hired to write a game story or text for missions/quests or dialogue for the NPCs, you'll need to understand the structure of the game in order to do a good job of it.

Understand that "game structure" is my own wording, and other game designers may have any number of words or terms to cover this. To me, the structure of the game is its underlying architecture, which determines how linear or nonlinear it is, and what parameters are used to create or control the nonlinearity. I would further divide this term into two major components: gameplay structure and story structure.

Story Structure

Although all games have at least a beginning, a middle, and an end, a game that contains story structure should fall under the basic three-act structure of drama—Act 1: *setup (exposition)*, Act 2: *conflict (complications)*, and Act 3: *resolution*. The three-act structure is about the development of emotional response in a story, the building of dramatic tension, and the final release of that tension in the resolution. Games that contain these elements have story structure. Games that lack any of these elements consist entirely of gameplay structure.

An example of a game consisting only of gameplay structure is a casual game such as *Tetris*, which is about manipulating colored blocks as they fall from the top to the bottom of the screen. It has a beginning with the starting positions of the colored blocks, a middle as the player must deal with the new blocks descending, and the end when the player either wins or loses the game. What it doesn't have is story.

Myst was about 95 percent gameplay (the puzzles) and 5 percent story. I'd put most MMOGs at about 90 percent gameplay, 10 percent story (though not story that the player can truly affect). The story-driven action game *Max Payne* is about 50–50. My adventure games probably fall somewhere around 60 percent story to 40 percent gameplay structure (in other words, in these games, the story dictated the gameplay slightly more than the gameplay dictated the story).

Setting aside games that don't depend on story (such as puzzles, cards, chess, sports, sims), every game requires some kind of Act 1 story setup. There must be at least minimal backstory about how the current situation, world, or conflict came to be; information about the avatar or character that the player will be playing (if applicable), or about the general race or class to which the avatar belongs; and what the current situation is that faces the player at the start of the game, which includes some sense of what the player is meant to achieve.

Along the way, there need to be the Act 2 complications that affect either the gameplay or the story, or ideally a combination of both. A more-story-driven game might even have an *inciting incident*. In drama, an *inciting incident* (or catalyst) is usually the turning point between Act 1 and Act 2, and is the event that starts the forces of conflict in motion.

Max Payne had a good example of that. The setup of the first game is that Payne's family has been killed by crazed drug users. At the beginning of the game, Payne is an undercover cop who is out to find and stop those killers, as well as to find the source of the drug. Very quickly, however, he finds himself framed for the murder of his partner, and is on the run from the law while on the hunt for the criminals. This is a classic inciting incident. It ups the ante and reshapes his goals. Now Payne must not only find the killers and stop the drug trade, he must clear his name while on the run. The game storyline throws various other turning points and conflicts in his way as Payne's search leads him from location to location (each location being a "level"), and from NPC to NPC.

Conflict doesn't just mean physical conflict. Top-notch TV writer Stephen J. Cannell has an online advice column (http://www.writerswrite.com/screenwriting) in which he also mentions "social conflict, emotional conflict, spiritual conflict, cultural conflict, internal conflict, relationship conflict, psychological conflict."

Finally, games with story require an Act 3 resolution. The hero wins or fails, achieves the quest or not, finds the killers or dies. Those resolutions may vary (more than one or two endings for a game), but there has to be a resolution. If the player wins, that resolution needs to be a satisfying payoff for the effort she has put into the game. The satisfaction level will depend on how thoroughly the player has gotten involved in the story and the characters, and how the player is rewarded for that involvement.

To be most effective, the three-act structure should be applied to individual scenes or sequences, to entire levels, to entire missions, and finally to the overall game story. In other words, the game should have a large three-act structure, but should also have numerous mini-three-act structures within it.

Resolution is a sticky problem for MMOGs. An MMOG can have the usual amount of setup, but is more about presenting the player with an ongoing world and leveling up within that world than it is with creating a through-line of story complications. There can be references to the background story, but it's extremely difficult for an MMOG player to impact an MMOG world in a significant way along with many thousands of other players doing the same things. All the same, the levels need to add up to something once the player reaches the top level. In *World of Warcraft*, for example, there is a climactic scene for level 60 players and a big quest to pay off reaching that level. It's a resolution of sorts, but not a true resolution because the game doesn't end there. There must be new material, new quests, and higher levels to achieve, or it will feel as though the game has reached a dead end.

Game Parameters

So we begin with the assumption that a game with story will have something akin to a three-act structure. The next big question in how to implement that story structure will be to work out the parameters of the gameplay structure.

"Parameters" is my own terminology. It's not an official game design word, and there can be any number of ways of expressing this part of game structure. The important thing is to understand the underlying concept of game parameters. Those parameters have a major impact on how, when, and where story can be injected into gameplay, or how the story elements will be carried out.

If game structure is the architecture, then parameters are the walls, floors, ceiling, doors, windows, and pertinent fittings. For example, if the room is a bathroom, it may or may not have a window, but it will have enclosing walls, floor, ceiling, and a door as the basic structure parameters. It will also have a sink, toilet, tub, and fixtures for running water as the basic interactivity parameters.

Parameters for a game structure control where a player can go, when she can go there, and what she can do there. A sandbox game has fairly wide-open parameters, allowing the player to go nearly anywhere at any time. A more linear console FPS game might have more-restrictive parameters that determine where the player can go and when and what she can do there. Sometimes two or more parameters work together to control or guide the player. Some parameters will apply mostly to gameplay, some will apply more to story, and many will apply to both.

Here are some examples of typical parameters:

- Zone (location, region, terrain)
- Time or phase
- Player level
- Acquisition of game objects
- Acquisition of a quest
- Predetermined events

Zone

Note that "zone" is only one word that might be used for the concept of a restrained area, and each game company could use a word of its own, such as region or level. The concept is the same. A zone could potentially be a single room, an instanced dungeon, or an entire geographic region. Using a zone to strictly control a player's movements means that the player is restricted to that zone until the right conditions are met to move on to the next zone. In *Conquests of Camelot*, Arthur's castle was one zone. It consisted of various rooms, corridors, garden, and the main gate with portcullis. Arthur had several tasks (subquests) to complete before he could safely leave through the main gate. Once outside Camelot, there were other geographic zones available that could be visited in any order and that required various local subquests to be completed (Figure 10.3).

Once the subquests for all the zones in England were completed, it opened up the ability for Arthur to get on a ship and travel to the Middle East, where the next zone was the town of Gaza, then a desert to be crossed, and finally the zone of Jerusalem. Because we didn't have the ability to make the game terrain endless, we had to build in restricting parameters. There was a safe path through the desert, but players who wandered off in other directions died of thirst.

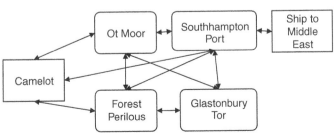

Figure 10.3
The various zones for the England portion of *Conquests of Camelot*.

163

If a zone is inside a building, the parameters will consist of doors that are either locked or can be opened only under the right circumstances, or other ways to get in and out. If the exterior geography or terrain is wide open, the player must eventually be blocked by something—whether it's an ocean, a sheer cliff, impassable mountains, a locked tunnel, monsters that can't be defeated, or severe conditions that block the player from going in that direction.

Zones don't have to be entirely restrictive. Certainly in MMOGs, the player has the freedom to travel extensively through various zones, but those zones will have mobs and other conditions of varying difficulty. In beginner zones, the mobs are low level and easy to defeat by any player, so those zones are fairly safe to wander around in. Other zones increase in difficulty. If a beginning player wanders into a zone populated with higher-level mobs, the player tends to get killed in short order. Players are quick to figure this out, and the zone boundaries become as effective as impassable mountain ranges. This is where two parameters (zone, player's level) work together to guide where the player should go or not go.

Zones are defined by appearance, theme, surface textures, color palettes, sounds, music, and other elements that help set the visual and audio boundaries for that locale. Those elements can potentially relate to story parameters—for example, a dark, forbidding atmosphere, unsettling sounds, and creepy music set the stage for certain types of quests or story elements. A haunted, misty forest will create a different mood for a quest than would a bright, sun-filled valley of flowers. As a writer, you want to mesh what you're writing with the look and feel of the zone in which it will take place, as well as understanding the parameters of the zone.

Time or Phase

In some games, the parameter might be time based or defined as a "phase" or similar term. In *Conquests of the Longbow*, I divided the gameplay and story elements into "days." The player was free to wander around Sherwood Forest and various other locations, so the zones were only a partial restriction. A set number of quests and events were programmed to occur each day in varying zones. They could be done in any order, but the day didn't end until they had been done (Figure 10.4). Then there was a nighttime cutscene that wrapped up the events of the day, depending on how they had gone. The game progressed this way through day after day, night after night, until reaching the resolution.

For another game, we divided a large, sweeping overall story into five phases, which were defined by evolving story elements, plus the player's level in which he advanced from the pilot of a single fighter spacecraft to squadron leader and up the ranks to Admiral of the Fleet. As the player advanced in rank, the story elements for each phase increased in scope and complexity to keep pace with his greater ability to have an effect on the gameplay. This meant that missions written for phase 1 had to work for someone who could operate only a single fighter as part of the space battles, but missions written for phase 4 had to

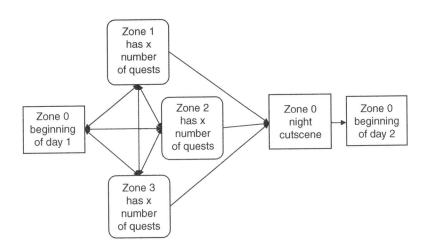

Figure 10.4
Story structure divided into day and night components.

165

work for someone who had advanced to commander of a group of battleships. However, missions also had to be written for every rank below commander, because there was always the chance that the player had failed or had chosen not to advance in rank.

Some games also introduce a timer that requires the player to complete a quest, task, or set of actions within a specific amount of time, such as having to kill some number of mobs within fifteen minutes. Usually such timers will be limited in use, applied to a single quest or small section of the game. Some players like the extra pressure of having the clock ticking down as they try to do something; other players prefer to do things at their own pace. And of course, some sports games use timers to mimic the playing times of the real games, as in football and basketball.

Player Level

As touched upon above, games such as RPGs and MMOGs advance the player by levels that govern his stats and abilities, what sort of weapons he can use, what sort of armor he can wear, and so forth. Some aspects of story and gameplay might be unavailable to a player depending upon his level. That level might be numerical, or it might be expressed in some games as a rank (squad leader, captain, admiral). The player-level parameter often works in conjunction with a zone parameter, as already mentioned.

Player Race, Faction, or Class

There can be any number of terms for this, and it applies to RPGs in which the player selects a particular race, faction, class, or type of avatar—such as Elf, Orc, Human, Dwarf, Gnome, Terran, Martian, or whatever. Within that larger race or class, there are usually subcategories for what type of that race or faction the avatar will be—for example, Warrior, Priest, Merchant, Rogue, Thief, Paladin, Explorer, Trader, and so on. The game engine can track the faction or race to which the avatar belongs.

Both parameters could be used to determine who gets to do a certain quest. There might be quests written that are offered to a Human or Elf, but not offered to an Orc or Troll, and vice versa; or quests that are offered to a Warrior but not a Rogue. If not every player gets to do every quest, it can obviously affect whether the player sees any story elements tied to those quests.

Zones can also be restricted to certain class or faction types. In the *Earth & Beyond* MMOG, there were three factions, and each faction had certain planets that only their members could visit in order to access special trainers for that faction. The effect this had on writing dialogue is that for those faction-only sites, dialogue had to cover only the one faction. In other sites in the game, dialogue had to take into account which of the three factions the player belonged to, and alternate dialogues had to be provided.

Acquisition of Game Objects

A smaller parameter that could affect story or gameplay structure would be requiring the player to acquire or win certain game objects before the next step of the game can unfold. An example would be requiring the player to acquire a cloak of invisibility before being able to sneak into a prison and free a prisoner. Freeing the prisoner could both set up the next stage of gameplay and reveal key story elements.

Acquisition of a Quest

A type of parameter is to require the player to be on a specific quest before other game elements become available. For example, a player takes a quest to enter a fortified area. Taking the quest triggers the appearance of an NPC who provides the means for the player to get in.

An example of a combination of the two types of acquisition parameters working together would be a key that the player can find and acquire only after she has taken a mission to get through a certain door. Once she has that key, she can unlock the door to access a new level of the game.

Predetermined Events

A game could be structured around predetermined events that will always happen as the player progresses through the game. These are usually going to be cinematics or cutscenes that drive the story forward, rather than being gameplay elements. *Max Payne* has a cutscene in which Max is knocked out, has a nightmare about his slain family, and wakes up in a new situation that he has to deal with. The scene provides a transition from one gameplay and story level to another, as well as adding to the emotional story content of the game.

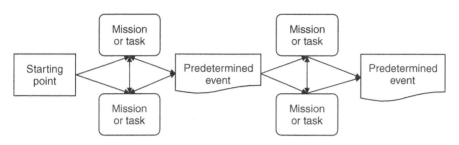

Figure 10.5
Example of a structure organized by predetermined events.

In *Conquests of the Longbow,* I had key scenes or moments that happened on various days in which Robin would have to encounter Maid Marian. The first one was a rescue to bring the two together, whereas other scenes included both story and gameplay elements with the purpose of making the player feel connected to Marian so that in one of the major predetermined events—Marian is sentenced to burn as a witch—the player would feel compelled to save her, which in turn had additional major story and gameplay effects. It was a secondary thread running in parallel to the primary body of the gameplay and game story (which was to raise enough ransom to free King Richard from captivity). A writer would think of it as a subplot, but those predetermined events shaped both story and game elements.

A predetermined-event parameter indicates a more linear or story-driven game structure (Figure 10.5), and can be combined with other parameters.

167

MORE THINGS YOU NEED TO KNOW

Next up are some additional topics that deal with other key aspects of being a game writer. The following topics are covered:

- What if . . .
- Variables and flexibility
- Gradients
- Choice
- The interface
- Immersion
- The player's mind-set

What If . . .

When a writer sits down to create a linear work, there is a constant process of asking "What if . . ." Creating our characters involves asking endless questions. We ask what if we use this or that type of character, what if this character were female instead of male, what if they have this trait or that trait, is old or young, have this set of beliefs, live here or live there, and on and on. What if my character leaves her cell phone uncharged when she's about to get into danger? What if my character says no instead of yes to a proposition? What if I give the character a child to protect? What if there is an ex-wife or ex-husband in the mix?

There are the countless what-ifs as we create the plot and the locations, determine the sequence of events, decide how those events will play out, and pick the one ending that feels right out of all the possible endings.

The nonlinear writer goes through the same process of asking the what-if questions—with the key difference that she doesn't necessarily have to pick only one answer. Instead of, "What if Robin Hood has to get inside Nottingham?" having only one answer, the game writer may have to cover several what-if answers: what if he tries to enter as himself? (he dies); what if he tries to enter disguised as a foolish merchant? (he gets to trick the Sheriff out of money); what if he enters disguised as a beggar? (he can enter safely and explore the town); what if he enters disguised as a monk? (he gets the corrupt Abbot drunk and steals a precious ring from him); what if he enters as a one-eyed yeoman? (he enters the archery contest and wins the golden arrow); what if he never enters at all? (Maid Marian dies for lack of a rescue).

Now, all of those things could happen in a linear story, but in order to empower the player, a game needs to make them all available as options that the player has to (*a*) discover, (*b*) choose to act upon (or not), (*c*) choose *how* to act upon them (Robin wants Merchant's clothes—does he kill, threaten, or bribe the Merchant to get the clothes), and (*d*) carry out the action (which could succeed or fail).

This is also expressed as "*if this, then this . . .*" because each of the what-if decisions requires a subsequent game response. For example, *If* Robin decides to bribe the Merchant, *then* we have dialogue between the two, money leaves Robin's purse, there's an animation of the Merchant removing his clothes, animation of the Merchant leaving, and the Merchant's clothes appear in Robin's inventory as a usable item. *If* Robin decides to threaten the Merchant, *then* we have animation of Robin aiming an arrow at the Merchant, a different set of dialogue between them, animation of the Merchant disrobing and leaving in anger, and the Merchant's clothes appear in Robin's inventory as a usable item. And so forth.

Other what-ifs can deal with story consequences. What if Robin simply kills the Merchant for his clothes? *If* he kills the Merchant, *then* the Merchant doesn't appear during the trial at the end of the game to testify in Robin's behalf, with his absence thus reducing Robin's chances of winning a pardon. What if Robin threatens the Merchant? *If* the Merchant appears at the trial, but has only bad things to say, *then* he has a negative effect on the ending. What if Robin bribes the Merchant instead? Then the Merchant will appear at the trial with good things to say, which will benefit Robin.

Granted, most of these are design decisions you might not be called upon to make as a writer, but being able to think in terms of *what-if* variables and the "*if this, then this*" connections are key components to nonlinear thinking.

Besides which, you *will* be called upon to base what you write upon such what-ifs, which brings us to the subject of variables and flexibility.

Variables and Flexibility

Every one of the options (the various disguises) for getting into Nottingham is a variable. Each method for dealing with the NPCs is a variable. Additional variables might include where they occur in the game sequence (for example, before or after Marian is sentenced to be burned as a witch), or other events that affect using the disguise (for example, whether or not the Sheriff has seen Robin in that disguise before). For example, if Robin uses the merchant disguise to trick the Sheriff out of money, what if Robin tries to enter Nottingham a second time using the same disguise? What if Robin uses the merchant disguise once, but doesn't interact with the Sheriff? Does he get a second chance to enter in that disguise and trick the Sheriff?

You can expect to be asked to write story components or dialogue that takes into account the numerous variables in the game. To be a game writer, you need the mental skills to keep masses of interrelated details in your head. You need to be well organized and detail oriented.

Another important quality for a game writer to have is flexibility. A game writer must also be ready, able, and willing to make sudden, sweeping changes to the story and writing if technical requirements or last-minute changes in game design take place. A change in one part of a game might affect variables in other parts of the game. The game writer must be able to follow the cascade of potential effects, catch any problems, and compensate for them. This requires having the overall structure of the game in your mind, from a large overview down to the small details. You might be the main person who can know whether pulling out a particular thread will unravel a large part of the game tapestry. This is a critical ability for a game writer to have.

169

Most often when significant changes are made to a game story, it's due to time or budget considerations. On one console RPG, I wrote a large, complex story full of secondary quests in several different geographic areas, with allowance for the player to return to those areas more than once with some variability in the story. For reasons of both time and budget (because in games, *time = money,* the same as in TV and film), we had to cut one large chunk out of the story to eliminate returning to one region. Although returning to that region didn't require new art assets, it did require significant programming work, which in turn affected how long it would take the programmers to complete the game. Fortunately, the story was modular enough that it was possible to remove that chunk and still make the overall story work, but I had to run through the entire range of variables that would be affected by the deletion and make sure they were accounted for during the rest of the game. Regarding the change, a number of questions needed to be asked: how did it affect the overall story quest; how did it affect other secondary quests; where there significant objects the player needed to get there; how did it affect the behaviors or use of NPCs; and how did it affect NPC dialogue, which might refer to it or be dependent on it?

Gradients

Good game design incorporates the use of gradients, in which the player is presented with easy tasks in the beginning, then tasks that become increasingly more difficult and complex as the game progresses. The idea is to give the player a lot of wins at the beginning in order to encourage her and keep her playing. This allows the player to become adept at the interface on a gradual basis, rather than trying to master too much all at once. A player who is given a batch of fairly quick and easy tasks at the start will feel empowered and more motivated to master the next level.

If you're writing quests or dialogue for them, you'll want to have an understanding of where they fall in the design gradient, so that you can have that in the back of your mind as you write. This may not have a significant impact on what you write, but it deepens your knowledge, which is always beneficial. It's not that you want to talk down to a player who is at the start of a game, but you do want to make sure the information you need to get across is clearly explained or stated for someone who isn't familiar yet with how the game works.

Choice

Boiling interactivity down to its essentials, it's about *choice*. In linear writing, the writer is making all the choices. In games, the player makes the choices from whatever options the designer and writer make available. The options made available to the player may be restricted by how much of the game budget and schedule can be spent on creating the extra assets to go along with those options. If every choice offered to the player requires a significant amount of new animation and programming, that will affect how many choices can be offered. This is where game design and story choices have to strike a balance between what you'd like to offer and what you can realistically afford to offer.

Choice empowers the player. And the choice must be a real choice, or else the player will feel cheated. As Spock said in the James Blish *Star Trek* novel, "A difference that makes no difference is no difference."

Getting back to Robin Hood's disguises, there is a different consequence for each choice in how to get the Merchant's clothes (killing, threatening, bribing). If there were no difference in the consequences, it would make no real difference which option the player chose. If killing the Merchant yields the same result as bribing him, there's no reason for the player to care about the choices.

Looking at a simplified example, let's set up a situation in which a player has to choose between taking one of two corridors. In this example, we see that whether the player chooses to go left or go right makes no difference, so having two corridors to choose from is a fake choice (Figure 10.6).

However, if there is something significant to be experienced or found in one corridor that affects the rest of the gameplay, those choices become real choices. Ideally, the player will be "pushed" (given some hint or guidance earlier) as to which corridor to take. For example, the player may have been told ahead of time to watch out for the corridor to his left because it's dangerous, they're

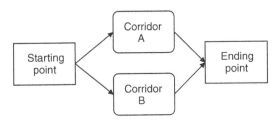

Figure 10.6
Example of a fake choice.

guarding something there, whereas the corridor to his right is safe. But the player is looking for something that is being guarded, so this is a hint that what he's looking for could be in that corridor. The player has been presented with genuine choices (Figure 10.7)—take the safe path and risk passing up something useful, or take the dangerous path and get a valuable object that leads to the next step of gameplay. Notice also that although the player arrives at the same end location either way, you effectively have two different paths of action to track: one with the object and one without the object.

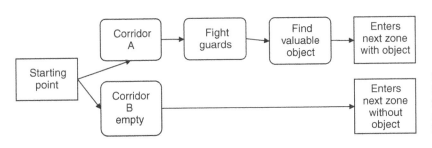

Figure 10.7
In this example, the choices are meaningful because they affect gameplay.

As game producer Ellen Guon Beeman sagely puts it, "Players want to win." Writers should think about that before they create a lot of alternative content that is seen only if the player continues down a losing branch.

Choice has a profound effect on linearity and storytelling. The greater the player's freedom of choice, the more the writer has to account for the variables created by allowing those choices. In the most linear storytelling form of games, such as many console games, the "choices" are nonchoices from a storytelling point of view, and are mainly gameplaying choices, such as battle strategy, type of weapon or spell to use, how to fight types of mobs, and so on. In an adventure- or action-oriented game with a distinct storyline, the choices should affect how the story plays out as well as what the gameplay elements will be. In a sandbox or MMO game, the player has enormous choice in a range of activities and gameplay, but there may be little to no storytelling impacted by those choices.

The Interface

Although a writer will have no control over the design of the game's interface, I consider it vital to understand how important the interface is, for two reasons: (*a*) a bad interface is almost guaranteed to doom a game, and (*b*) the interface dictates precisely how story and dialogue are implemented in the game.

Much of what I wrote about the evolution of games dealt with the changes in game interfaces. There's a significant difference in writing for a game that has a minimal interface *(Myst);* compared to writing for a console game with an interface that can contain many on-screen elements, but are all controlled by a limited set of buttons; compared to writing for a PC-game interface, which can allow a wide range of actions using keyboard and mouse or other devices.

Interface is where the rubber meets the road. Think about the interface for driving a car. What are the essential parts of that interface? You must have a wheel to steer, a pedal to make it move, a pedal to make it stop, something that controls the gears, and a set of tires. That's about it. The essence of controlling that car—speed, direction, avoiding obstacles, and reaching the goal—is dependent on those five basic interface elements. Everything else—such as speedometer, oil gauge, heater, air conditioner, windshield, radio, rearview mirror, side mirrors, adjustable seat, seat belts, and so on—provide nice extra features that make the experience more enjoyable or safe while not being essential to the fundamental interface.

So it is when designing a game. There are interface components that are absolute necessities, and there are the extra features that further enhance the gameplay. One of the designer's main responsibilities is designing a good, clean, intuitive interface and balancing the essential gameplay needs with the additional features (Figures 10.8, 10.9). The needs of the game and the requirements of the

Figure 10.8
This screenshot from *World of Warcraft* shows an interface at the beginning level that conveys important gameplay information at a glance, yet is intuitive and easy to use. Note how only a few options are given to the player at first. © World of Warcraft® provided courtesy of Blizzard Entertainment, Inc.

Figure 10.9
This screenshot from *World of Warcraft* shows an interface at level 80 where the options have grown in complexity and variety, yet remain easy to master because they were presented in a reasonable gradient from simple to complex. © World of Warcraft® provided courtesy of Blizzard Entertainment, Inc.

173

gameplay will dictate the interface, and the interface will be the only means you as a writer have of providing story or character interactions to the player.

In *Conquests of Camelot*, the player had word riddles to solve, and I could do that because my interface included the player's being able to type in words that the game engine could parse. In *Conquests of the Longbow*, I had a specific set of mouse-click icons I had to use, and no text-typing input, which eliminated doing a puzzle such as a riddle. Then we look at the MMOG, which has keyboard input only for chatting with other players or for using emotes, but nothing that affects the gameplay. For most PC and online games, the mouse click is the vital hardware interface—whereas, in console games, it is mashing the buttons on the controller that is the vital hardware interface. Yet both methods can have a wide range of effects depending on how they interact with the game interface on the screen.

The interface elements on the screen fall into two categories:

- Those that are under the control of the player—such as deciding the direction in which to go, moving the camera around, selecting a battle mode, picking a weapon or spell to use, putting on or taking off armor, getting and buying and selling objects, and so on.
- Those that are controlled by the game—such as which NPCs or objects will be clickable, and what that clickable action will be. Examples include a "talk," "buy/sell/trade," or "quest giver" icon for an NPC; a "fight" icon

for a mob that can be targeted; an "open" icon for a treasure chest; a "magnifying glass" icon for an object that can be looked at in more detail; and so forth.

Study the many types of interfaces that exist in a variety of games. Study the use of icons and symbols in conjunction with mouse clicks or button mashing. Study how, when, and where the interface allows the player to make a story choice or interact with an NPC in action or in dialogue. Imagine how you would try to convey story elements using the interfaces you encounter.

Immersion

Good designers and writers strive to create a game world, story, and gameplay that are so well meshed that the player can easily feel immersed in that virtual reality. Achieving immersion for the player means finding a way to disguise the obvious game mechanics and make them organic parts of the game world. This can be tricky when the player needs to learn to "Hold down button 1" to achieve a particular move. Anything that reminds a player that he is only playing a game is something that destroys the player's immersion in that game-world reality. Some players dislike traditional cutscenes because during a cutscene, control of the game is taken away from the player, an obvious reminder that this is a game rather than an alternate reality.

174

Most of the issues of creating immersion are the designer's responsibility, but as a writer, you should always look for the ways you can contribute to creating immersion. Is there some way to convey a particular piece of training to make it sound more "real" and less gamelike? Can training be seamlessly integrated into a series of easy initial quests rather than being a stark tutorial? Is there a way to convey a particular piece of story element without putting it into a cutscene? Can the cutscene be interactive instead of noninteractive?

Immersion is also about word choices, tone of language, avoiding anachronisms, and setting a consistent story mood or theme that meshes with the overall game world.

The Player's Mind-set

To write well for games, it's helpful to play enough games to have a sense of what the mind-set is of a person who plays the type of game you want to work on. If you want to write console games, you need to understand what a console player expects. If you want to write MMOGs, you need to play one or more MMOGs to understand that mind-set. This isn't an absolute necessity for someone who wants to be hired purely as a writer, but it improves your ability to deliver something that fits the gamer mind-set.

For those who have played a lot of games already, this may be a no-brainer, but when I began, I knew nothing about games at all. The first thing I did upon being hired by Sierra On-Line (today known as Sierra Entertainment) was to sit down and play all of the games that Sierra had produced. I wanted to become familiar with how their games worked, but also to tap into the mind-set of a typical Sierra player. I needed to meet—and hopefully exceed—that typical player's expectations. Playing a lot of games also helped me decide which design flaws I wanted to avoid. If something annoyed me as a player, I assumed it would annoy other players.

Being a person of logical mind, I tended to write dialogue and text responses in the order I figured a player would try. My mentors quickly pointed out that I was being too linear. I thought I understood their guidance, and I reworked my scripts trying to take that into account.

But I didn't have the One True Revelation until we had *Conquests of Camelot* about halfway done (the entire England chunk of the game) and took it to a convention to let random people bang away at it. I spent the afternoon watching how players interacted with the game, how they tackled the puzzles, how they approached dealing with the NPCs. By the end of the day, I had the One True Revelation. I finally *got* it.

The One True Revelation is this: players are the Forces of Chaos. They will do *anything* in *any* order, whether it makes sense or not. They use trial and error rather than figure out your clever clues. They throw logic out the window.

Therefore, I share this with you, the potential game writer: expect anything and write accordingly, and always remember—players are the Forces of Chaos.

CHAPTER 11
Interactivity and Its Effects

Carolyn Handler Miller

How does the use of interactivity radically change the way an audience experiences a narrative?

How does the use of interactivity radically change the narrative material itself?

What are the pros and cons of giving the audience some control over the story?

What techniques can be used to help create cohesion in works of digital storytelling?

DOI: 10.1016/B978-0-240-81343-1.00011-X

WHAT IS INTERACTIVITY?

Without interactivity, digital entertainment would simply be a duplicate of traditional entertainment, except that the medium in which it is presented, such as video or audio, would be in a digital form rather than an analog form. To the audience member or listener, however, the difference would be minimal except perhaps in the quality of the picture or sound. Essentially, the experience of "consuming" the entertainment would be exactly the same.

It is interactivity that makes digital media such a completely different animal from traditional storytelling forms, like movies, television, and novels. All stories, no matter how they are told—whether recited by a shaman, projected onto a movie screen, or played out on a game console—have certain universal qualities: They portray characters caught up in a dramatic situation, depicting events from the inception of the drama to its conclusion. Interactivity, however, profoundly changes the core material, and it profoundly changes the experience of those who are the receivers of it.

We've all probably heard and used the word "interactivity" hundreds, even thousands, of times. Because of overuse, the word has lost its fresh edge, somewhat like a kitchen knife that has grown dull because it's been utilized so often. Let's take a moment to consider what interactivity means and what it does.

Interactivity is a two-part word. The first part, *inter*, a prefix, means "between," implying a two-way exchange, a dialogue. The second part, *active*, means doing something, being involved or engaged. Thus the word as a whole indicates an active relationship between two entities. When used in the context of narrative content, it indicates a relationship where both entities—the audience and the material—are responsive to each other. You, the audience member, have the ability to manipulate, explore, or influence the content in one of a variety of ways, and the content can respond. Or the content demands something from you, and you respond.

Essentially, interactivity is one of only two possible ways of relating to narrative content; the other way is to relate to it passively. If you are passively enjoying a form of entertainment, you are doing nothing more than watching, listening, or reading. But with interactive content, you actually become a participant. This is radically different from the way narratives have traditionally been experienced.

INTERACTIVITY AS A CONVERSATION

Interactivity can be thought of as a conversation between the user and the content, a concept articulated to me by Greg Roach during a conversation about the subject. Roach is CEO of HyperBole Studios, the company that made such award-winning games as *The X-Files Game* and *Quantum Gate,* and as a digital media pioneer, he has given a great deal of thought to the subject of interactivity.

Roach compared the act of designing interactivity to the act of writing a sentence in a language like English, which uses the grammatical structure of a subject, object, and verb. As an example, he used a simple interactive scene in which you give your character a gun. The interactive "sentence" would be: He (the subject) can shoot (the verb) another character (the object). Carrying Roach's grammatical analogy a step further, the sentences you construct in interactive media use the active voice and are not weighed down by descriptive phrases. ("He watered his horse" rather than "He was seen leading his dusty old horse down to the rocky creek, where he encouraged it to drink.") These interactive sentences are short and to the point, far more like Hemingway than Faulkner.

Roach is not alone in using grammatical terms to talk about interactivity. Many game designers use the phrase *verb set* in referring to the actions that can be performed in an interactive work. The verb set of a game consists of all the things players can make their characters do. The most common verbs are walk, run, turn, jump, pick up, and shoot.

LEAN BACK VS. LEAN FORWARD

Passive entertainment and interactive entertainment are often differentiated as "lean back" and "lean forward" experiences, respectively. With a passive form of entertainment like a movie or stage play, you are reclining in your seat, letting the drama come to you. But with an interactive work—a videogame or a MMOG, for instance—you are leaning forward toward the screen, controlling the action with your joystick or keyboard.

WHAT HAPPENS TO THE AUDIENCE?

The way one experiences interactive entertainment is so different from the way passive entertainment is experienced that we rarely even use the word "audience" when we are talking about interactive works. More often than not, we talk about such people in the singular rather than in the plural. This is probably because each individual journeys through the interactive environment as a solo traveler, and each route through the material is unique to that person.

Because each user is in control of his or her own path through the material, interactivity can never truly be a mass audience experience. This is the case even when thousands of people are simultaneously participating in an interactive work, as they may be doing with a MMOG or an iTV show. Think how different this is from how an audience partakes of a movie or TV show, watching the same unvarying story unfold simultaneously with hundreds—or even millions—of other viewers. Of course, each member of the audience is running the story through his or her own personal filter and is probably having a somewhat different emotional response to the material. Yet no matter how intensely people might be reacting, there is nothing any member of the audience can do to alter a single beat of the tale.

It is an entirely different case when we are talking about interactive entertainment, and we may call upon one of several terms to describe the person who is in the process of experiencing it. If we're referring to someone playing a videogame, we will use the term "player" or "gamer," while if a person is surfing the Web, we may use the term "visitor," and for simulations and immersive environments, we often call the person a "participant." One term that fits all types of interactive experiences is the word "user," which is the standard term we are employing in this book.

THE USER, THE AUTHOR, AND INTERACTIVITY

The people who participate in interactive entertainments are given two gifts that are never offered to audiences of passive entertainments: choice and control. They get to choose what to see and do within an interactive work, and the decisions they make have an impact on the story. Less than 50 years ago, such freedom to manipulate a work of entertainment would have been unimaginable.

The user's ability to control aspects of the narrative is called *agency*. Essentially, agency gives the user the ability to make choices and to see and enjoy the results of those choices. Agency is one of the unique pleasures of digital storytelling. It is not limited to the kinds of verb sets we discussed earlier (run, jump, shoot, and so on) but also allows the user to navigate through the story space, create an avatar, change points of view, and enjoy many other kinds of interactive experiences that we will discuss later in this chapter.

Agency is something that is built into an interactive work right from the start, as an integral part of the concept, and in fact helps define what kind of work it will be. It is up to the creative team to decide what kind of agency the user will have and how it will be integrated into the work. Experienced interactive designers and producers know that great care must be given to crafting the way the user can interact with the work. Interactivity must be meaningful to be satisfying. In other words, the choices offered must make sense, must have consequences that make sense, and what the user does must have a true impact on the story. Users will quickly become dissatisfied with pointless, empty interactivity.

HOW AGENCY CAN BACKFIRE

Experienced designers know that it can be a risky proposition to give users agency without thinking ahead to the various ways they might use or misuse it. A 2007 interactive advertising campaign for the Chevy Tahoe SUV underscores how agency can be used in unintended ways and can backfire on the producers. This online ad campaign gave users the chance to make their own commercial for the car, offering them a generous selection of videos of the interior and exterior of the vehicle, exotic settings to place it in, and background music, plus the ability to write their own text. To encourage participation, Chevy presented this as a contest, a version of Donald Trump's TV show, *The Apprentice*.

But the campaign went terribly wrong for Chevy. People who detested the Tahoe and hulking SUVs in general gleefully used the tools to make scathingly satirical commercials about the vehicle's role in creating pollution, waste, environmental destruction, and global warming. To its credit, Chevy actually ran some of these commercials on the contest Web site, but it was an embarrassing situation for the company, and the commercials were pulled after a short time.

Many kinds of interactive works, most particularly virtual worlds and MMOGs, have been plagued with run-amuck agency, with a handful of players threatening to spoil the fun the designers had intended to offer. These ill-spirited players have had their avatars bully other players, engage in lewd acts, and even rob, steal, and murder.

As the Chevy Tahoe campaign illustrates, agency is a gift to the user but can cause serious trouble for the creative team. Designers invest a significant amount of time in devising ways to prevent the agency they offer from getting out of hand, while not unduly restricting the sense of freedom they want to give to the users. Agency can also thrust writers of interactive works into an unfamiliar and uncomfortable position, particularly if they come from the worlds of more traditional forms of writing, like screenplays, novels, or television shows. In those fields, the writer has God-like powers over the narrative. The writer gets to choose who the characters are, what they do, and what they say. And the writer controls what happens to them. But in an interactive work, this kind of God-like control over the material must be shared with those individuals who, in an earlier era, would have been powerless and in your thrall—the members of the audience.

Although agency gives users exciting new powers, not all the benefits go to them, and the creators of interactive narratives benefit, too. While it's true that those of use who are writers must give up a certain amount of control, we now have the opportunity to work on a far vaster canvas than in previous media and with story tools never before available. We also have the exhilarating chance to create brand new kinds of narratives. And despite the amount of agency given to the user, we still do retain ultimate authorial control. We, along with our fellow design team members, create the project's narrative world and its possibilities; the kinds of characters who will live there and the kinds of challenges they will face; and the specific actions the users will be able to take there.

IMMERSIVENESS

One of the hallmarks of a successful interactive production is that it envelops the user in a rich, fully involving environment. The user interacts with the virtual world and the characters and objects within it in many ways and on many levels, and the experience might even be *multisensory*, meaning that it may stimulate multiple senses. In other words, an interactive production is immersive. It catches you up and involves you in ways that passive forms of entertainment can rarely do.

The power of immersiveness was brought home to me by an experience I had during the Christmas season one year in Santa Fe, New Mexico. It was my first year of living there, and I'd heard a great deal about the city's traditional holiday procession called *Las Posadas,* so I decided to see it for myself.

Las Posadas originated in medieval Spain as a nativity passion play and was brought to New Mexico about 400 years ago by the Spanish missionaries. They felt *Las Posadas* would be a simple and dramatic way to ignite the religious spirit of the local Pueblo Indians and hopefully turn them into good Catholics.

Las Posadas, which is Spanish for "the inns," recreates the Biblical story of Mary and Joseph's search for a place to spend the night and where Mary can give birth. It is performed with different variations in towns all over the Southwest and Mexico, but the basic elements remain the same. In Santa Fe, the procession takes place around the historic town plaza. Mary and Joseph, accompanied by a group of musicians and carolers, go from building to building asking for admittance, but each time the devil appears and denies them entrance, until at last they find a place that will receive them.

On the evening of Santa Fe's *Las Posadas,* my husband and I waited in the crowd with the other spectators, all of us clutching candles and shivering in the icy night air, waiting for the event to begin. Finally the first members of the procession appeared, holding torches to light the way. Mary and Joseph followed, with a group of carolers around them. The group paused in front of a building not far from us, and all proceeded to sing the traditional song, which pleads for lodging. The devil popped up from a hiding place on the roof and scornfully sang his song of refusal. It was very colorful, very different from anything I'd seen before back in California, and I was glad we had come.

But then I noticed that a number of people were breaking away from the throng of bystanders and joining in the procession. Spontaneously, I pulled my startled husband into the street after them. In a flash, we went from being observers to being participants, and we began to experience *Las Posadas* in an entirely different way. Marching with the procession, we became part of the drama, too, and were fully immersed in it.

For the hour or so that it lasted, I became someone else. No longer was I a twenty-first century Jewish writer. I became a pious Catholic pilgrim transported back to a wintry medieval Spanish village. Some of this I experienced on a personal and physical level: I had to watch my step, taking care not to slip on a patch of ice or trip on a curb or get ahead of the holy family. I was aware of the scent of burning candles all around me and the press of the crowd. Much of the experience was emotional and communal: My husband and I would do our best to sing along with the carolers and holy family when it came time to ask for a room at the inn. Whenever the devil would appear on a rooftop or balcony, we would join in the hearty boos and derisive shouts of the processioners.

The best moment came when Mary and Joseph stopped in front of the heavy gates of the historic Palace of the Governors, the former seat of New Mexico's colonial government. Once again we all sang the imploring song, but this time the gates swung open! A joyous cheer went up from the processioners, our voices among them, and we all surged into the courtyard. Welcoming bonfires and cups of hot cocoa awaited us.

Becoming part of *Las Posadas* instead of merely observing it transformed the experience for me. It was like the difference between watching a movie and suddenly becoming a character in it. To me, it vividly demonstrated the power of immersiveness—one of the most compelling and magical aspects of interactive media.

TYPES OF INTERACTIVITY

Users can interact with digital content in a variety of ways, and different types of interactive media lend themselves to different types of interactivity. For instance, the Internet is particularly good at providing opportunities to communicate with other users; smart toys excel at offering one-on-one play experiences; wireless devices do well at engaging users in short bursts of text or visuals. Each of the interactive media has its limitations, as well. In an immersive environment, a participant's ability to control objects may be limited. Game consoles, unless connected to the Internet, are restricted to just a few players at a time. Interactive TV (iTV), at least for now, does not lend itself to interactions with fictional characters or with participating in a narrative story. When it comes to the types of interactivity offered by the various digital media, no one size fits all.

That said, however, six basic types of interactivity can be found in almost every form of digital storytelling. They are like the basic foodstuffs a good cook always keeps in the pantry that can be used to make a wide variety of dishes. The basic types of interactivity are as follows:

1. Stimulus and response. The stimulus might be something as simple as a highlighted image that the user clicks on and is rewarded by a little animated sequence or hearing a funny sound, or it might involve having to solve a puzzle, after which the user is rewarded by the occurrence of some sought-after event: The door to the safe swings open or a character reveals a secret. Generally speaking, the stimulus comes from the program and the response from the user, although there are exceptions. For instance, smart toys recognize and respond to actions taken by their child owners. The stimulus–response exchange is a universal component of all interactive programming.

2. The ability to navigate and move. Users can move through the program in a free-form manner; in other words, they can simply choose what to do. Navigation may offer a vast 3-D world to explore, as in a videogame or MMOG. Or it may be more limited, restricted to choosing options from a menu offered on a DVD or icons on a Web site. Navigation, like the stimulus–response exchange, is a universal component of every form of interactive programming.

3. Control of virtual objects. This includes such things as shooting guns, opening drawers, and moving items from one place to another. While a fairly common form of interactivity, this one is not universal.

4. Communication. The user can communicate with other characters, including those controlled by the computer and other human players. Communication can be done via text that the user types in or via choosing from a dialogue menu, by voice, or by actions (such as squeezing a smart doll's hand). Generally, communication goes both ways—characters or other players can communicate with the user, too. As with #3, it is a common, but not universal form of interactivity.

5. The sending of information. The type of information that can be sent can range from comments to online forums to videos to YouTube, and it can also include the creation of objects for virtual worlds. This form of interactivity is generally found in devices that have a connection to the Internet or to an iTV service.

6. Receiving or acquiring items. The nature of the material that can be received can range from virtual to concrete, and the methods of acquiring it can range greatly as well. Users can collect information (such as news bulletins or medical facts); purchase physical objects (books or clothing); and receive video on demand. They can also collect virtual objects or assets in a game (a magic sword; the ability to fly). This type of interactivity is common in any medium that involves the Internet, wireless services, or iTV, as well as almost all videogames.

Using these six basic "ingredients," digital creators can cook up a great diversity of playing games. There is an almost infinite variety of games that users can play (trivia experiences for people to participate in). They include:

1. Games, adventure games, shooters, mysteries, ball games, role-playing games, and so on.

2. Participating in a fictional narrative.

3. Exploring a virtual environment.

4. Controlling a simulated vehicle or device: a fighter jet, a submarine, a space ship, or a machine gun.

5. Creating an avatar, including its physical appearance, personality traits, and skills.

6. Manipulating virtual objects: changing the color, shape, or size of an object; changing the notes in a piece of music; changing the physical appearance of a room.

7. Constructing virtual objects such as houses, clothing, tools, towns, machines, and vehicles.

8. Taking part in polls, surveys, voting, tests, and contests.

9. Interacting with smart physical objects: dolls, robotic pets, wireless devices, animatronic characters.

10. Learning about something. Interactive learning experiences include edutainment games for children, training programs for employees, and online courses for students.

11. Taking part in a simulation, either for educational purposes or for entertainment.

12. Setting a virtual clock or calendar to change, compress, or expand time.

13. Socializing with others and participating in a virtual community.

14. Searching for various types of information or for clues in a game.

15. Sending or receiving items, for free or for money, including physical objects, virtual objects, VOD, and information.

This is by no means an exhaustive list, though it does illustrate the great variety of experiences that interactivity can offer and the uses to which it can be put.

HOW INTERACTIVITY IMPACTS CONTENT

These various forms of interacting inevitably affect your content. Users expect to be offered a selection of choices, but by offering them, you give up your ability to tell a strictly determined linear story or to provide information in a fixed order.

To see how this works, let's compare a linear and interactive version of a familiar story, the Garden of Eden episode from the Bible. The Garden of Eden episode is one of the best-known creation stories in the Western world, and thus seems an appropriate choice to illustrate the creative possibilities of changing a linear story into an interactive one.

As it is handed down in Genesis, the story involves three mortal characters: Adam, Eve, and the serpent. Each of them behaves in exactly the same way no matter how often one reads about them in the Old Testament. And the alluring tree that is the centerpiece of the story is always the Tree of the Knowledge of Good and Evil. God has warned Adam and Eve not to eat its fruit, though they are free to enjoy anything else in the garden. The serpent, however, convinces Eve to sample the forbidden fruit, which she does. She gets Adam to try it, too, at which point they lose their innocence and are expelled from the Garden.

Now let's construct an interactive version of the same story. We'll use the same three characters and the same tree but offer the player an array of choices. Let's say the tree now offers five kinds of fruit, each with the potential for a different outcome. If Eve picks the pomegranate, for instance, she might immediately become pregnant; if she eats too many cherries, she might get fat; only if she eats the forbidden fruit would the narrative progress toward the results depicted in the Bible.

As for the serpent, let's allow the user to decide what this character should be: malevolent or kindly, wise or silly. We'll let the user decide how Eve responds to him, too. She might ignore him, or tell him to get lost, or try to turn him into a docile house pet, or she might actually listen to him, as she does in the Bible. We'll give the user a chance to determine the nature of Adam and Eve's exchange, too. Adam might reject Eve's suggestion to try the fruit, or he might come up with several suggestions of his own (open up a fruit stand or make

185

jam out of the tree's cherries). Or they may hotly disagree with each other, resulting in the Bible's first marital spat. Suddenly we have a vast multitude of permutations springing out of a simple story.

Note that all of this complexity comes from merely allowing the player one of several options at various nodes in the story. But what if you gave the players other types of interactive tools? You might allow them the opportunity to explore the entire Garden of Eden and interact with anything in it. They could investigate its rocky grottos, follow paths through the dense foliage, or even snoop around Adam and Eve's private glade. Or what if you turned this into a simulation and let users design their own Garden of Eden? Or how would it be if you turned this into a role-playing game and let the user play as Adam, as Eve, or even as the serpent? Or what if you designed this as a community experience and gave users the chance to vote on whether Eve should be blamed for committing the original sin?

Our simple story is now fragmenting into dozens of pieces. What once progressed in an orderly manner, with a straightforward beginning, middle, and end, and had a clear and simple plot, has now fallen into total anarchy. If adding interactivity to a simple story like the Garden of Eden can create such chaos, what does it do to a more complex work?

USING GAMING TECHNIQUES TO SUPPLY THE MISSING COHESION

Because interactivity can break up the cohesiveness of a narrative, it becomes necessary to look for other ways to tie the various elements together and to supply the momentum that, in traditional storytelling, would be supplied by the plot. Many professionals in digital media believe that the best solution is to use a gaming model as the core of an interactive work and build narrative elements around it. Games provide an attractive solution because they involve competition, contain obstacles and a goal, and achieving the goal is usually a game's driving force. While stories in traditional media use these same elements, they are less obvious, and great attention is placed on other things, such as character development, motivation, the relationship between characters, and so on.

Designer Greg Roach, introduced earlier in this chapter, is one of those professionals who is inclined to turn to games to help knit the various pieces of an interactive work together. "When you discard all aspects of gaming, how do you motivate people to move through the narrative?" he asks rhetorically. "The fundamental mechanisms of games are valuable because they provide the basic tool sets."

Roach sees stories and games as two very different types of artifacts—artifacts being objects created by human beings. Roach says, "A story is an artifact you experience as a dynamic process while a game is a process you enter into that creates an artifact when it ends." Roach feels that interactive works have, as he puts it, "immense granularity." Granularity is a term Roach and others in interactive media use to mean the quality of being composed of many extremely small pieces.

Roach describes films and other types of linear narratives as "monoliths, like a block of salt," and for interactivity to be possible, he says the monoliths must be broken up into fine pieces. "These granules of information can be character, atmosphere, or action. But if a work is too granular, if the user is inputting constantly, there are no opportunities for story." Roach stresses that in order to have an interactive story, "You must find a balance between granularity and solidity. You need to find the 'sweet spot'—the best path through the narrative, the one with the optimum number of variables."

Despite the differences between stories and games, Roach believes a middle ground can be found, a place to facilitate story and character development in an interactive environment.

One of the challenges Roach sees in constructing a nongaming interactive story is the task of providing the player with motivation, an incentive to spend time working through the narrative. But he suggests an answer as well. Roach believes that people like to solve problems, the tougher the better, and he feels that a major distinction between games and stories is the types of problems they present plus the tools you can use to solve them. In a game, he suggested, the problem might be getting past the monster on the bridge. In a story, the problem might be getting your son off drugs and into rehabilitation.

187

GAMES AS ABSTRACT STORIES

Janet H. Murray, a professor at the Georgia Institute of Technology and the author of one of the best-known books on interactive narrative, *Hamlet on the Holodeck*, takes things a step further than Roach. In her book, she asserts that games and drama are actually quite closely aligned and that games are really a form of "abstract storytelling."

To underscore the close connection between stories and games, Murray points out that one of our oldest, most pervasive, and popular types of games—the battle between opposing contestants or forces—is also one of the first and most basic forms of drama. The Greeks called this opposition *agon*, for conflict or contest. Murray reminds us that opposition, or the struggle between opposites, is one of the fundamental concepts that we use to interpret the world around us (big–little; boy–girl; good–evil).

Although Murray does not say so explicitly, every writer of screenplays is keenly aware of the importance of opposition and realizes that unless the hero of the drama is faced with an imposing challenge or opponent, a script will lack energy and interest. For an interactive narrative to work, it too must pit opposing forces against each other. Thus, games and dramas utilize the same key dynamic: opposition. This concept of opposition is so key to drama that it defines how we think of our heroes and villains.

Opposition is not the only way that games and drama are alike, Murray believes. She suggests, in fact, that games "can be experienced as symbolic drama." She holds that games reflect events that we have lived through or have had to deal with, though in a compressed form. When we play a game, she says, we become the protagonist of a symbolic action. Some of the life-based plot lines she feels can be found in games include:

- Being faced with an emergency and surviving it.
- Taking a risk and being rewarded for acting courageously.
- Finding a world that has fallen into ruin and managing to restore it.
- Being confronted with an imposing antagonist or difficult test of skill and achieving a successful outcome.

DRAMA IN AN ABSTRACT GAME

Janet Murray is even able to find a lifelike symbolic drama in an abstract game like *Tetris*. In *Tetris*, players have to maneuver falling puzzle pieces so they fit together and form a straight row. Each completed row floats off the bottom of the game board, leaving room for still more falling puzzle pieces. To Murray, the game resembles our struggles to deal with our over-busy lives, and is like "the constant bombardment of tasks that demand our attention and that we must somehow fit into our overcrowded schedules and clear off our desks in order to make room for the next onslaught."

Games, Murray asserts, give us an opportunity to act out the important conflicts and challenges in our lives and to create order and harmony where there was messiness and conflict.

In many ways, Murray's view of games is much like Joseph Campbell's view of ritual ceremonies—activities that provide us with a way to give meaning to important life experiences and to provide us with emotional release. In its most powerful form, this emotional release is experienced as a catharsis.

STORIES THAT ARE NOT GAMES

In examining the relationship between stories and games, let us not forget what designer Greg Roach asserted: that it is possible to create interactive stories that are not based on game models. We can find examples of game-free narratives in many genres of digital storytelling. One small enclave of such narratives is called, fittingly enough, *interactive fiction* (IF). Works of IF can be found on the Internet, and they are also available on CD-ROMs. Though the creators and fans of IF are a fairly small group, often found within academic circles, they are dedicated to advancing this particular form of storytelling.

True works of IF are entirely text based (although the term is sometimes used for adventure games and other works that are animated or are done on video).

To see/read/play a work of IF, you need to be sitting in front of a computer, inputting your commands with a keyboard. The story advances and reveals itself as the user types in commands ("open the door" or "look under the bed" or "ask about the diamond"). Unlike hypertext, you must do more than click on a link; you must devise phrases that will give you the most meaningful and useful reply.

IF stories can be about almost any topic, and they can be written in just about any fictional genre, although they work best when the plots call for you to be active, to explore, and to make things happen. They need not be plot driven, however. *Galatea*, written by Emily Short, is an intriguing character sketch that is constructed as a dialogue between the user and a *nonplayer character* (NPC)—a character that is controlled by the computer. The story is based on the Greek myth of Pygmalion, a sculptor who carves a beautiful statue, *Galatea*. The statue comes to life after he falls in love with her. It is the same myth that inspired the Broadway musical *My Fair Lady*.

In this interactive version of the myth, you visit the art gallery where *Galatea* is displayed and discover that you are able to talk with her. As you converse with her, you gain insights into her history and troubled emotional state. Her responses to your questions vary, as does her attitude toward you, depending on how you treat her.

IF stories resemble text-based adventure games as well as online MUDs and MOOs (MUD object oriented). Unlike MUDs and MOOs, however, they are played by a single individual rather than with a group. Furthermore, they do not have the win/lose outcomes that are so much a part of adventure games, though they do often include puzzles that must be solved in order to progress. These narratives cannot be as tightly plotted as linear fiction, but they do generally have overarching storylines.

Conceivably, the IF genre could be used as a model for interactive stories that are not merely text based but are told in moving images as well. Throughout this book, we will be examining other works of digital storytelling that contain no overt elements of gaming. These stories demonstrate that even though games are extremely useful vehicles for holding interactive narratives together, works of digital storytelling do not need to depend on game models in order to succeed.

CONCLUSION

Interactivity, as we have seen, profoundly changes the way we experience a work of entertainment. We go from being a passive member of the audience to becoming a participant with an active and meaningful role, wielding a new power called agency.

Interactivity, however, changes the role of the storyteller. Instead of being the sole creator of the story, this role must now be shared with the user. And interactivity makes the telling of a fixed, sequential, linear story impossible.

To knit the story together and make it compelling, storytellers must find new models to use. Many rely on game techniques to achieve narrative cohesion, although some digital storytellers are finding other ways to construct satisfying interactive narratives.

While interactivity creates new challenges for storytellers, it also gives them new powers. Thanks to interactivity, it is possible to tell stories that are deeply immersive and intensely absorbing, that take place on a much vaster canvas, and that can be experienced from more than one point of view. The challenge for storytellers is to find ways to use interactivity effectively so that users can enjoy both agency and a meaningful narrative experience.

IDEA-GENERATING EXERCISES

1. Describe an event or occasion where you went from being a passive observer to an active participant. How did this shift affect the way you experienced the event? Your example could be something as simple as going from being a passenger in a car to actually driving the vehicle, or it could involve a more complex situation, like the *Las Posadas* procession described in this chapter.

2. If you are working on a project for a specific interactive medium or platform, make a list of the types of interactivity the medium or platform lends itself to most strongly and the types of interactivity it does not support well or at all. Is your project making good use of the platform's strengths and avoiding its weaknesses?

3. Take a very simple, familiar story and work out different ways it would be changed by injecting interactivity into it, as with the Garden of Eden example. Your examples might be a story from the Bible, a child's nursery rhyme, or a recent news item.

4. Using a simple story like one chosen for the exercise above, redesign it as two different interactive experiences: one that is very story-like and the other that is very game-like.

CHAPTER 12
Old Tools/New Tools

Carolyn Handler Miller

What can an ancient Greek like Aristotle teach us that we can apply to modern interactive entertainment?

What aspects of traditional storytelling can be successfully used in digital storytelling?

When writers of traditional stories at first move into digital storytelling, what do they find most challenging?

What 10 entirely new tools must creators learn to use when they construct interactive narratives?

AN ASSORTMENT OF STORYTELLING TOOLS

Embarking on a new work of digital storytelling is usually a daunting proposition, even for veterans in the field. Each new project seems to chart new ground. Some call for a unique creative approach; others utilize new technology. And those who work in the newer areas of interactive entertainment—wireless devices, transmedia productions, and innovative types of immersive environments—are faced with having to be a pioneer almost every time out. Furthermore, the complexities posed by interactivity, plus the sheer volume of material contained in most works of digital storytelling, can be overwhelming. No wonder starting work on a new project can feel like plunging into the abyss.

Nevertheless, even though we may feel we are starting from scratch, we actually have a wonderfully serviceable set of tools and techniques at our disposal. Aristotle first articulated a number of these tools over 2000 years ago. Other tools go back still further, to preliterate storytellers. And we can also borrow an array of tools from more recent storytellers—from novelists, playwrights, and screenwriters. Furthermore, we can raid the supply of tools originally developed for pre-electronic games of all types, from athletic competitions to board games.

As is to be expected, of course, the majority of these borrowed tools and techniques need to be reshaped to some degree for digital media. And at some point, we finally empty out our old toolbox and reach the point where we need to pick up and master some entirely new implements. Ultimately, it is a combination of the old and the new, seamlessly integrated together, that enables us to create engaging works of digital storytelling.

LEARNING FROM GAMES

Some of the most effective tools of storytelling, tools that can inject an intense jolt of energy into any type of narrative, were not even developed by storytellers. They originated in games. Games are one of the most ancient forms of human social interaction, and storytellers in both linear and nonlinear media have borrowed heavily from them. Games can be used as a form of glue to hold an interactive work together.

Above all else, games teach us the critical importance of having a clear-cut goal and also show us the importance of putting obstacles in the way of that goal. In games, the ultimate goal is to win the competition, and the players on the other side—the opponents—provide the biggest impediment to achieving that goal. This player vs. player opposition is what provides much of the excitement and drama in an athletic competition, in much the same way it does in storytelling. In addition, participants in sporting competitions must contend with physical obstacles and challenges, such as the hurdles on a track field, the net on the tennis court, or the steep roads in a cycling race.

GOALS IN GAMES AND STORIES

In a good game, as well as in a good story, the best goals are:

- Specific
- Simple to understand
- Highly desirable
- Difficult to achieve

Try to imagine a game or story without a goal. What would the players or characters be trying to do? What would keep the audience interested in watching something that has no clear objective? What would give the experience meaning?

The essential mechanics of stories are remarkably similar to games, especially when it comes to goals and obstacles. In a story, the protagonist wants to achieve a goal, just as an athlete does, even though the type of goal being sought after is of a different order. The objective may be to find the buried treasure, win the love of the adored one, track down the killer, or find a cure for a desperately sick child. A goal provides motivation for the main character, a sharp focus for the action, and a through-line for the plot, just as a goal provides motivation and focus for a game. And in a story, as with a game, obstacles provide the drama, and the most daunting obstacles are human ones—the antagonists that the hero has to contend with.

Of course, some novels and works of short fiction present narratives in which the protagonist has no apparent goal, and so do some art house films. But even though such slice-of-life stories may be interesting character studies or may be admirable for some other artistic reason, the narrative will usually feel flat because nothing is at stake. That is why it is difficult for such works to attract a wide audience.

The conflict between achieving a goal and the obstacles that hinder this victory is what creates conflict, and conflict is the heart of drama. The clearer the goal, and the more monumental the obstacles that stand in the way of achieving it, the greater the drama. The very first storytellers—those who recited the ancient myths and heroic epics of their culture—understood this and made sure to emphasize all the difficulties their heroes had to overcome. Later storytellers, working in succeeding waves of media from classic theatre to television and everything in between, recognized the value of goals and obstacles just as clearly. Not surprisingly, these fundamental story ingredients are just as useful in the creation of digital entertainment.

Games have provided storytellers with other valuable tools as well. From games we learn that the most thrilling competitions are those that demand the most from a player—the most skill, the most courage, the most strategizing. Similarly, a good story demands that the protagonist give his or her all to the struggle. In an interactive work, the same demand is made on the user or the player. The greater the personal investment and the tougher the challenge, the more satisfying the ultimate victory.

In addition, games are governed by specific sets of regulations. These not only add to the challenges but also help to keep the game fair. For example, players are only allowed to use approved types of equipment, or employ certain maneuvers and not others, or score a goal by doing X and not Y. Without such rules, victory would be too easy, and the game would lack interest. Games not only have rules but also follow a set structure or format, though the specifics vary greatly among types of games. For example, a football game begins with a kickoff; a baseball game has nine innings; a basketball game is divided into quarters. No doubt, the first players of ancient sports soon found that without structure or rules, their games would quickly disintegrate into anarchy, and one side would use tactics that seemed completely unexpected and unfair to the other side. Rules and structure provide an equally fair, consistent playing environment to all players.

For the same reason, stories in every medium have a structure and format for how they begin, how they develop, and how they end. Furthermore, although stories don't follow set rules, they are guided by internal conventions. This ensures that behaviors and events within the fictional universe are consistent and logical and make sense within the story. Even a fantasy universe like the one portrayed in the Harry Potter novels, films, and games must remain faithful to its own internal set of rules. For instance, if it is established that characters cannot pass through physical structures unless they recite a secret spell, Harry or one of his classmates should not suddenly be able to blithely walk through a wall without using the spell. That would violate the rules of magic already established in the story. Internal conventions provide a narrative equivalent of a fair playing field.

LEARNING FROM MYTHS

Contemporary storytellers, whether working in linear or interactive media, are also indebted to the great mythmakers of ancient days. These master tellers of tales built their stories upon themes with deep emotional and psychological underpinnings. Many of these old stories feature young heroes and heroines who must triumph over a series of harrowing obstacles before finally reaching their goal, and in the course of their adventures they must undergo a form of death and rebirth.

Joseph Campbell analyzed the core elements of the hero's journey and found that such myths contained characters that were remarkably similar from story to story and that the myths contained extremely similar plot points. He held that the hero's journey tapped into the universal experiences shared by humans everywhere, reflecting their hopes and fears, and thus resonated deeply with the audience.

More recently, Christopher Vogler interpreted Campbell's work for contemporary readers and writers in a book called *The Writer's Journey*. The book profiles the archetypal figures who commonly populate the hero's journey—characters with specific functions and roles to play—and he describes each of the 12 stages of the journey that the hero must pass through before being able to return home, victorious.

The hero's mythic journey has had a deep influence on storytellers throughout the world. Countless works of linear fiction—novels, plays, comic books, and movies—have been built on the model provided by the hero's journey. Among them are the films made by the great filmmaker George Lucas, who has often spoken of his debt to Joseph Campbell and the hero's journey. Even the magnificent film *Spirited Away*, a work of Japanese anime about a little girl trapped in a mysterious resort for ghosts, closely follows the 12 stages of this ancient myth.

This enduring model works equally well for interactive narratives. For example, the immensely involving game *Final Fantasy VII* contains many of the elements of the hero's journey, and a number of MMOGs incorporate it as well. After all, as a player, you set off for a journey into the unknown, meet up with various helpful, dangerous, or trickster characters along the way, find yourself tested in all sorts of ways, and do battle against powerful opponents.

Do writers, producers, and designers of these interactive versions of the hero's journey deliberately use this genre as a model? In some cases, yes, this modeling is conscious and intentional. For example, Katie Fisher, a producer/designer for the game company Quicksilver Software, Inc., is quick to acknowledge that she based the game *Invictus* on the hero's journey and used Christopher Vogler's book as a guide. In other cases, though, the hero's journey is probably an unconscious influence. After all, it is a story that is familiar to us from childhood; even many of our favorite fairy tales are simplified hero's journeys. And many a designer's most beloved movies are also closely based on this model, including such films as *The Wizard of Oz* and *Star Wars*. Obviously, elements in the hero's journey strike a deep chord within audiences both past and present. There is no reason why creators of interactive entertainment should not be able to find inspiration, as Katie Fisher has, in this compelling model.

LEARNING FROM ARISTOTLE

Mythological themes have provided fodder not only for our first narrative tales, but also for our earliest theatrical works. Rituals based on the myths of Dionysus led to the development of classic Greek theatre. Aristotle, one of the greatest thinkers of the ancient world, closely studied Greek theater, particularly the serious dramas, which were then always called tragedies. Based on his observations, he developed an insightful series of principles and recorded them in a slender, densely written volume, *The Poetics*. Though drafted in the fourth century BC, his ideas have held up astoundingly well right up to the present day. The principles discussed in *The Poetics* have been applied not only to stage plays, but also to movies, TV shows, and, most recently, they are finding their way into interactive narratives.

Aristotle articulated such concepts as dramatic structure, unity of action, plot reversals, and the tragic flaw. He also made perceptive comments about character development, dialogue, plot, and techniques of eliciting a strong emotional response from the audience. Furthermore, he warned against using cheap devices that would undermine the drama. One such device he felt was unworthy of serious theater was the deus ex machina, Latin for "God from a machine." This device was called into play when a writer was desperate for a way to get a character out of a predicament and would solve the problem by having a god suddenly descend to the stage from an overhead apparatus and save the day. Aristotle decried such techniques and believed that plot developments should be logical and grow naturally out of the action.

One of Aristotle's greatest contributions to dramatic theory was his realization that the effective dramas were based on a three-act structure. He noted that such dramas imitated a complete action and always had a beginning, a middle, and an end (acts I, II, and III). He explained in *The Poetics* (Chapter VII, Section 3) that

> A beginning is that which does not itself follow anything by causal necessity, but after which something naturally is or comes to be. An end, on the contrary, is that which itself naturally follows some other thing, either by necessity, or as a rule, but has nothing following it. A middle is that which follows something as some other thing follows it. A well-constructed plot, therefore, must neither begin nor end at haphazard, but conform to these principles.

Entire books have been written on the three-act structure, derived from this short passage, applying it to contemporary works of entertainment, particularly to films. One of the most widely used in the motion picture industry is Syd Field's *Screenplay: The Foundations of Screenwriting*. The book breaks down Aristotle's points and expands on them in a way that modern writers can readily understand. The three-act structure is so widely accepted in Hollywood that even nonwriters, professionals like studio development executives and producers, feel completely comfortable talking about such things as "the first act inciting incident," "the second act turning point," and the "third act climax."

The idea of the three-act structure has also found a place in interactive media, most noticeably in games. But it is used in other types of interactive entertainment as well, including virtual reality simulations, location-based entertainment, interactive movies, and webisodes. Of course, inserting interactivity into a narrative project impacts enormously on its structure, so additional models must also be called into play. Often they are used in conjunction with the classic three acts first spelled out by Aristotle.

Aristotle also had valuable things to say about character motivation. He noted that motivation is the fuel that leads to action and that action is one of the most important elements of drama. Just as the players' striving toward a goal is the driving force in a game, a character striving toward an objective is the driving force of a drama. Aristotle believed that there are two types of human motivation. One, he felt, is driven by passion and based on emotion. The other, he said, is based on reason or conscious will. In other words, one comes from the heart, the other from the head.

In interactive media, motivation is also of tremendous importance. It is what pulls the user through a vast universe of competing choices. By understanding motivation, we can create more compelling works of interactive entertainment.

Aristotle also believed that drama could have a profound affect on the audience, eliciting such emotions as pity and fear. The most effective dramas, he felt, could create a feeling of catharsis or emotional purging and relief—the same sort of catharsis Joseph Campbell said occurred when people took part in a reenactment of a powerful myth. Creators of interactive works have not, as a rule, put much effort into trying to produce projects with an emotional punch. Today, however, more attention is being paid to this subject.

LEARNING FROM CONTEMPORARY STORYTELLERS

197

When it comes to interactive entertainment, we can also learn a great deal from the creators of linear narrative, particularly from film and TV. These forms of entertainment already have great similarities to interactive media because they are stories told in moving images and sound, which is also how most interactive narrative is conveyed.

Two of the most important skills that can be ported over from film and television are character development and story construction. These are the fundamental building blocks of any type of narrative. Of course, they cannot be adapted without some adjustments, for interactivity has a profound impact on all aspects of the creative process.

Having made the transition myself from television and film into the interactive field, I am well aware of how closely the techniques of character and story development used in filmed narratives work in digital storytelling. For example, one of my first jobs in interactive media was as a freelance writer doing some work on Broderbund's pioneering *Carmen Sandiego* series, a game that had kids playing the part of a detective and trying to track down the thieving Carmen or one of her henchmen. My assignment called for me to create four new characters for the game and to write dialogue for two of its already-established characters, the Chief of Detectives and Wanda, his assistant. These tasks were almost identical to work I might have done for a TV show, except that I had to write numerous variations of every line of dialogue. Thus, I found myself coming up with about a dozen different ways to say "you bungled the case."

Another early assignment had me working out an interactive adventure story for children based on an idea proposed by actress–producer Shelley Duvall. Called *Shelley Duvall Presents Digby's Adventures* and developed by Sanctuary Woods, the CD-ROM was a story about a little dog who goes exploring, gets lost, and tries to find his way home. It was the kind of tale that could have easily been a kid's TV show, except for one thing: This was a branching, interactive story, so the little dog gets lost in three completely different ways. Each version offers the player numerous opportunities to become involved in the dog's adventures and help him find his way back.

OTHER USEFUL OLD TOOLS

Aside from character development and story construction, what else can be borrowed from traditional storytelling? One excellent tool is tension. Although tension is something we try to avoid in our daily lives, it serves an important function in both linear and interactive narratives. It keeps the audience riveted to the story, experiencing a mixture of apprehension and hope, wondering how things will turn out. Tension is particularly important in interactive narratives because they don't have the benefit of linear plots: the carefully constructed sequence of events that advances the action and builds up the excitement in traditional stories. Creators of interactive stories have to work extra hard to keep users involved with their narratives, and ramping up the tension is a good way to keep them hooked.

One reliable method of inserting tension in a nonlinear story is to put your main character (who is often the player via the avatar he or she is controlling) into great jeopardy: risking death in a snake infested jungle, caught behind enemy lines in a war, or pursued by brain sucking aliens in a sci-fi story. But the jeopardy need not be something that could cause bodily harm; the risk of losing anything of great value to the protagonist can also produce dramatic tension. Thus, the jeopardy can involve the threat of relinquishing everything your hero has worked so hard to achieve in the story, whether it is a vast sum of money, solving a baffling mystery, or becoming a mafia godfather.

Introducing an element of uncertainty can also increase dramatic tension. Which of the characters that you encounter can you trust? Which ones are actually enemies in disguise? Which route through the forest will get you to your destination quickly and safely, and which one might be a long and dangerous detour? Uncertainty is a close cousin to suspense, which is the burning desire to know what will happen next. It is the feeling of suspense that keeps us turning the pages of a novel until long past our bedtime and keeps us glued to a television movie when we know we really should be paying bills or doing something similarly responsible.

To pump up the adrenaline and keep the audience glued to the story, many works of both linear and nonlinear narrative use a device called a *ticking clock.* With a ticking clock, the protagonist is given a specific and limited period of time to accomplish his goal. Otherwise there will be serious, and perhaps even deadly, consequences. A ticking clock is an excellent way to keep the momentum of a story going. The ticking clock can even be found in children's fairy tales. Cinderella, for example, has to rush out of the ballroom before the clock strikes 12 or else she will be caught in public in her humiliating rags. Movies and TV shows are full of ticking clocks, and an entire TV series, *24*, is built around a literal ticking clock counting off the minutes and hours the main character has left to save the day. The awareness of time running out can dramatically increase one's heartbeat, and it is as effective in digital storytelling as it is in films and television.

THE STORYLINE IN LINEAR AND INTERACTIVE NARRATIVES

As we have seen, many techniques first developed for linear narratives also work extremely well in interactive media. Yet when it comes to the role of the *storyline*—the way the narrative unfolds and is told, beat-by-beat—we are faced with a major difference. In traditional linear narratives, the storyline is all-important, and it needs to be strong and clear. It is "the bones" of a story. But narrative works in digital media are nonlinear, which means that events cannot unfold in a tight sequential order the way a carefully plotted linear story does. Digital storytelling also needs to support interactivity, which, as we've seen, can be extremely disruptive to narrative. And, in the case of games, the actual gaming elements of the work become paramount. In order to offer players a pleasurable and dynamic experience, gameplay is often given prominence over a developed storyline.

Works of digital storytelling vary enormously when it comes to how developed a storyline they can or should carry. Some genres, especially *casual games* (short, lightweight entertainments), often contain little or no storyline to speak of. They may not even have characters or a plot; they may be totally abstract, like an electronic version of tic-tac-toe. Simulations might have just enough of a storyline to give users a framework for what they'll be doing. But at the other extreme, we have projects with richly plotted through-lines, dramatic turns and twists, and even subplots, as is true with certain videogames and works of interactive cinema. Given the fact that there is such a vast spectrum of interactive entertainment media, and a great variety of genres within each of the media, it is not possible to formulate a set of rules to govern the "right" amount of story that is appropriate for a given project. The best guide is the project itself. You need to consider its genre, its target audience, its goal, and the nature of the interactivity.

199

WHAT IS "JUST ENOUGH" OF A STORYLINE?

The *JumpStart* line of edutainment games for children seems to have found just the right balance between storyline and other demands of educational titles. The *JumpStart* products are developed by Knowledge Adventure, part of the Universal Vivendi portfolio of game companies, and they are great fun for kids. Their actual purpose, however, is to drill the young users in specific skills they need to master at school, like multiplication or spelling. The drills are incorporated into games that are so entertaining that they feel more like play than like learning. So where do storylines fit in here?

According to Diana Pray, a senior producer on the *JumpStart* titles, the storyline is important to give the game a context; it drives the game toward a particular desired outcome. The *JumpStart* titles feature a cast of highly appealing animated characters, and, in a typical storyline, one or more of the characters has a problem, and the child's help is needed to solve it. "The story encourages kids to reach the end goal," she explained. "We give them enough story so they feel they are in the game. The storyline gives them the incentive to play the games and get the rewards. Incentives are embedded in the story. But kids want to play; they don't want a lot of interruptions. So we don't do very deep stories. We don't want to risk boring the child. We have to be efficient in the storyline."

A HOLLYWOOD WRITER'S VIEW OF INTERACTIVE MEDIA

Writers moving from the linear world of Hollywood screenwriting into the field of interactive media are often as struck, as I was, by the similarities in crafting scripts in these two seemingly antithetical arenas. A number of people interviewed for this book remarked on this. Among them was Anne Collins-Ludwick. Collins-Ludwick comes from the field of mainstream nighttime television and has worked on such successful television series as *Vegas, Fantasy Island,* and the mystery series *Matlock.* In 2002, she made a major career switch and became a scriptwriter and producer for Her Interactive, which makes the *Nancy Drew* mystery–adventure games. It was her first professional exposure to interactive media, and she plunged in headfirst. In just a little over a year, she helped develop four new titles, including *The Haunted Carousel.* (See Figure 12.1.)

"The parallels between what I do here and working on a weekly TV show are phenomenal," she told me. "Lots of the elements are just the same." Chief among them, she noted, was the process of developing the story and characters and the designing of the environments (though they are called "interiors" and "exteriors" in Hollywood scripts). "I found I knew everything I needed to know," she added. "It was just a different application."

For Collins-Ludwick, accustomed to the taut linear scripts of Hollywood, the one major difference was the way interactivity impacted the story. "Giving the player choices was the hardest part for me," she recalled. "We want to give the players as much freedom to explore as possible, but we also want to relate

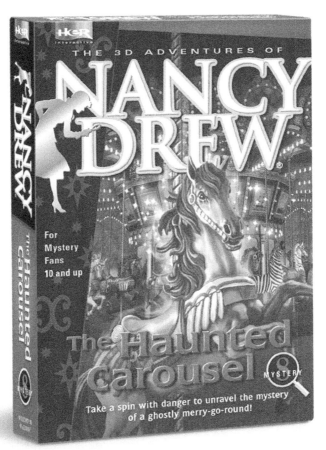

Figure 12.1
Nancy Drew mystery–adventure games like *The Haunted Carousel* utilize many tools drawn from linear screenwriting. Image courtesy of Her Interactive.

a story. We need to move them from A to B to C." The challenge was to find a way to reveal the mystery while also offering the players a significant amount of choice and to balance the need to tell a story against the need to give players the opportunity to explore.

The other big challenge for her, and what she considered to be her steepest learning curve, was mastering an interactive script format. She had to learn how to flag material so that once the player had performed a certain task, something could happen that could not have happened previously. For instance, if a player found a hidden letter, she could now ask a character an important question, or she could enter an area that had previously been off limits.

"It was a lot to keep straight in my head; there was a lot of logic to get used to, and a lot of details. It's a matter of training your brain to think in a certain pattern," she said. But she was taken in hand and helped by a staffer with a great deal of technical savvy, and she also found that the company's thorough documentation process helped her keep track of things. "It's easy now," she reports, "but in the beginning it was very intimidating."

Of course, works of digital storytelling may contain segments that are not inter-active but are, instead, like a linear scene from a movie. Linear scenes are used in different ways in different genres of digital storytelling. In videogames, these linear passages are called *cutscenes*. They are usually found at the beginning of a game, serving as an introduction to the world where the game is set. They also give enough information to make it clear what you as a player need to do in this virtual world, and why. Cutscenes are also sprinkled through most games, often triggered when a player has accomplished a particular task. At such points they function as an opportunity to advance the narrative aspects of the game. They may also give important pieces of the *backstory* (elements of the narra-tive that took place before the game opens and are important to the under-standing of the game's story). These scenes are really no different from scenes you'd find in a movie or a television show except that in today's games they are animated rather than live action. Thus, any of the cinematic or dramatic tech-niques employed in these older media can be used just as successfully in the linear sequences of interactive works, though cutscenes should be kept as short and used as sparingly as possible.

TEN NEW TOOLS

Although many well-seasoned tools of traditional storytelling can, with certain modifications, still be used in digital storytelling, working in this arena also requires utilizing some entirely new tools. And it also calls for something else: an attitude adjustment. In order to create these new kinds of stories, we must release our mental grip on sequential narrative and be open to the possibilities that interactivity offers us.

This is not only true for those who are accustomed to working in traditional screen-based media, like Anne Collins-Ludwick. It also applies to anyone who has grown up watching TV and movies and has developed the expectation that stories should have tightly constructed linear plots. It is usually less of an issue for those people who, from childhood on, have played videogames or surfed the Web. Yet even members of this generation can have trouble functioning in a nonsequential story world.

But no matter which category you fall into—the group who embraces nonlin-earity or the group who is uneasy with it—you still need to learn how to use a new set of tools if you want to work in digital storytelling. Here is a brief run-down of 10 of the most essential tools.

1. Interface and Navigation

The users of an interactive work need a way to connect with the material, per-form actions, and move around. This is where interface design and naviga-tional tools come in. They provide a way for users to make their wishes known and control what they see and do and where they go. The many visual devices used in interface design and navigation include menus, navigation bars, icons, buttons, cursors, rollovers, maps, and directional symbols. Hardware devices include videogame controllers, touch screens, and virtual reality (VR) wands.

2. Systems for Determining Events and Assigning Variables

In order for the events within an interactive project to occur at an appropriate time, and not have the narrative self-destruct into chaos, there needs to be an orderly system of logic that will guide the programming. Most members of the creative team are not expected to do any programming themselves, but they still must understand the basic principles governing *what* happens *when.*

Also, interactive projects typically involve a great number of variables. For example, characters may be constructed from variables including body types, physical attributes, and special skills. To organize such variables, the design team will often construct a *matrix* to help assign and track them. As a member of the design team or as a writer, it is necessary to understand how to work with the variables and the system of logic in your project.

3. Assigning a Role and Point of View to the User

Users have many possible roles they can play in an interactive narrative, and they can also view the virtual world from more than one possible point of view. One thing the creative team decides early on is who the user will "be" in the story and how the user will view the virtual world that is portrayed in the narrative.

203

4. Working with New Types of Characters and Artificial Intelligence

Thanks to interactive media, a strange new cast of character types has sprung into being. Among them are avatars, chatterbots, and nonplayer characters (characters controlled by the computer, usually called NPCs). In some cases, digital characters have artificial intelligence (AI). They seem to understand what the player is doing or saying, and they act appropriately in response. The way characters are developed and given personality and AI calls for considerations never encountered in linear media.

5. New Ways of Connecting Story Elements

In linear entertainment, the various media elements—audio, graphics, moving images, and text—come "glued" together and cannot be pried apart, as do the various scenes that constitute the story. But in interactive media, media assets, scenes, and major pieces of story can be presented or accessed as separate entities and connected in various ways. These various ways of connecting story pieces exist on both micro and macro levels.

Hypertext is one way of connecting assets. It requires an active decision on the part of the user to make the connection. But story elements can also be connected indirectly. Pieces of a story such as a cutscene or the appearance of a new character or the discovery of a clue can be triggered indirectly once the user has performed a specific set of actions or solved a puzzle.

On the macro level, works of digital storytelling can be constructed to exist across a number of media platforms such as mobile devices, broadcast television, and the Internet, with parts of each story available on different media platforms and with the whole story interconnected. This is known as a *trans-media approach*, and it includes a new type of narrative–game hybrid, the *Alternate Reality Game*.

6. Gameplay

As we have discussed, many works of digital storytelling are built around games, and in such works, the creative team must give a serious amount of attention to developing satisfactory *gameplay* for the project. Gameplay is the overall experience of playing a game and what makes it fun and pleasurable; it is what the player can do in the game. It includes the game's challenges, how they can be overcome, the game's rules, and what it takes to win (or lose).

Even works that are not primarily games may require users to solve puzzles, answer trivia questions, or play a series of minigames. Thus, it is important to understand games and have a basic grasp of what constitutes good gameplay.

7. Rewards and Penalties

Rewards are an effective way to keep users motivated, while penalties keep them on their toes and add an agreeable amount of tension. They are usually found in games but may be used in other types of digital storytelling as well. Rewards may be in the form of points, play money, or a valuable object for one's inventory. Players may also be rewarded by rising to a higher level, getting a virtual career promotion, or receiving extra powers for their avatars. Penalties, on the other hand, can be the deduction of anything that can be earned as a reward. The ultimate penalty is a virtual death or losing the game. It is important to know what kinds of rewards and penalties work well for your genre and are appropriate for your audience.

8. New Kinds of Building Blocks

Most forms of linear narrative use the same basic building block or unit of organization: the scene. Scenes move the overall story along, but they are also complete little dramas in themselves. Interactive media, however, uses very different units of organization. Each of these units offers a specific set of possibilities—things the user can do or discover within them. As part of the creative team, you need to have an understanding of the basic building blocks of whatever genre you are working in.

9. The Use of Time and Space

Time and space are far more dynamic factors of interactive narration than they are of linear media. For example, games may present a persistent universe, where time moves on and events occur even when the game or story is turned off. Thus, if users fail to log on to a MMOG they've subscribed to, they may forego the opportunity to take part in an exciting adventure, or if a user has adopted a virtual pet, it may die if not fed regularly.

In a different use of time, the interactive medium may keep track of things like holidays and important anniversaries in your personal life. For instance, a smart doll may wish its child companion a happy birthday or a Merry Christmas on the appropriate dates.

In many fictional interactive worlds, time is cycled on a regular basis, so that during a single session of play, the user might experience dawn, the midday sun, and sunset. The virtual world may also cycle through different seasons of the year, and sometimes the changing of a season will trigger a dramatic event in the story. In some games, you can slow down time or speed it up. And in some works of interactive cinema, you may be able to select which time period of a story you want to visit.

205

In addition, geographical space is experienced on a different scale and in a different way in interactive media than in linear media. Some games contain multiple parallel universes, where events are going on simultaneously in more than one place and you can hop back and forth between these worlds. In other games, the geographical scope of a game can be vast, and it can take hours or even days for the player to travel from one point to another.

As part of a creative team, you need to have a basic knowledge of the various possibilities of space and time in digital storytelling, and you should have some idea of how they might be utilized in the type of project you are working on.

10. Sensors and Special Hardware

Certain forms of interactive entertainment require sensors or other devices in order to simulate reality or control or trigger events. For example, a smart doll might have a built-in sensor that can detect light and darkness, and it can be sleepy when it grows dark and wide awake in the morning. In immersive environments, users need to wear special equipment to see virtual images, and such environments may use a variety of other devices to simulate reality. As a member of the creative team of a project that uses sensors or other special hardware, you will need to know enough about what the devices can do so that you can use them effectively in your project.

THE COLLABORATIVE PROCESS

Working with an unfamiliar and complex set of tools—even a single new tool—can be an anxiety-producing experience. For someone who has never worked in interactive media, the first exposure can be something of a culture shock. Fortunately, professionals in interactive media seldom work in a vacuum. It is not a field populated by hermit-like artists slaving away in lonely garrets. On the contrary, it is a field that almost evangelically promotes the team process. Colleagues are encouraged to share ideas in freewheeling brainstorming sessions. Even staffers low on the totem pole are encouraged to contribute ideas. Since almost every company has its own idiosyncratic methods of operating, newcomers are taken in hand by veterans and shown the ropes.

ONE NEWCOMER'S EXPERIENCE WITH COLLABORATION

Anne Collins-Ludwick, who came from the highly competitive, dog-eat-dog world of primetime television, is one person who has found the working conditions of interactive media to be extremely supportive. She said she was immediately struck by that when she began working on her first *Nancy Drew* title for Her Interactive. "It was one of the most collaborative works of fiction I'd ever been involved with," she reported enthusiastically. "It was collaborative from Day One, when I was first brought into the game."

At virtually all software companies, projects are developed by an entire team rather than by a single individual. The team typically includes specialists from several key areas, such as game design, project management, art direction, and programming. Thus, no one person has the burden of having to be an expert in every facet of the project.

CONCLUSION

Interactive entertainment utilizes an array of tools, some drawn from extremely ancient sources, others from contemporary linear storytellers, and still others that are unique to new media. Although ancient and more contemporary storytelling tools are highly useful, we must move beyond them and master 10 new tools.

Often the greatest challenge for people new to digital storytelling is overcoming the discomfort of working with unfamiliar concepts. Depending on our mindset, the chance to pick up and use the new tools employed in this field can be either exhilarating or intimidating.

For those willing to jump in and try them out, a great deal of help is available. As Collins-Ludwick and others have been pleased to discover, digital entertainment is an enormously collaborative field, and even when the learning curve is steep, newcomers can count on getting the support they need from their teammates.

IDEA-GENERATING EXERCISES

1. Analyze a computer game you are familiar with (such as a videogame or mobile game) and compare it to a specific type of athletic game. In each case, what is the goal, what are the obstacles, and how do you win or lose? In what major ways are they alike or different?

2. Pick a movie, TV show, or novel that you think used tension effectively. What kept you riveted to this story? Do you think this is this something that could be used effectively in digital storytelling?

3. Select an interactive project that you are familiar with, and describe what was built into this material that would make users want to invest their time in it. What would keep them interested and involved?

4. Which of the ten tools unique to interactive storytelling do you feel is the most challenging or intimidating? Why do you feel this is so?

5. Which of the ten new tools do you feel is the most creatively exciting? Can you describe something you'd like to try to do with this tool?

CHAPTER 13
Interactive Media and the Writer

Timothy Garrand

CHAPTER OVERVIEW

This chapter defines important terms and explains the key concepts relating to interactivity, including:

- Interactivity vs. control
- Thinking interactively
- Linking
- High-level design
- Interactive devices

WRITE IT ALL!

Writing for multimedia and the Web may be the most challenging work you will ever do.

- Writing great prose text is not enough!
- Creating engaging video scripts is not enough!
- Writing audio like a radio pro is not enough!
- Making characters come alive with snappy dialogue is not enough!

As a writer for interactive media, you have to do all these things and more.

To be truly effective in this field, you will have to do more than write great text. The most exciting programs today go beyond click-and-read. This includes the latest generation of Web sites, as well as computer games, educational programs and other cutting edge interactive media.

To develop powerful interactive content, you will need to understand how to tame the complex structure of interactive media and write for video, audio,

DOI: 10.1016/B978-0-240-81343-1.00013-3

animation, and online applications. And, most of all, you will have to understand intimately each program's users and the impact of their interactions on your content.

Based on my experiences on nearly one hundred projects and on interviews with dozens of top experts in the interactive media field, I will describe how to master these skills and give examples from detailed case studies of successful programs. The case studies include professional interactive scripts, charts, and other documents that can serve as models for your own interactive writing assignments.

DEFINING INTERACTIVE MULTIMEDIA AND THE INTERACTIVE WRITER

Defining a Few Terms

Why "Multimedia and the Web" in the title of this book? I know the word police will complain that this doesn't make sense, because multimedia is actually a common type of content on the Web. The words "multimedia" and "Web" are not mutually exclusive, I know. I agree, but many users still think of the Web as a place of mainly static pictures and text, while multimedia is the more interactive and media rich world of computer games, edutainment programs, and the like. I wanted to make it clear that this book is addressing the broad spectrum of interactive media content development.

Before we go forward, I should define how we will use the terms "multimedia" and "interactive media" in this book.

DEFINING MULTIMEDIA

As used in this book, "multimedia" and "interactive multimedia" are defined by four basic characteristics:

- Combination of many media into a single piece of work. Combining several media or modes of expression into a single integrated program or piece of work is one aspect of multimedia. Video, text, audio, and still pictures are all examples of different media or modes of expression.
- **Computer mediated.** In multimedia, a computer is used to mediate or make possible the interaction between the users and the material or media being manipulated. "Computer" is used here in the broadest sense, including computers in cell phones, game consoles, and other devices, as well as traditional PCs. No computer involved = no multimedia. A book with pictures is not multimedia.
- **Media-Altering Interactivity.** User interactivity in multimedia is best defined as "the ability of the user to alter media he or she comes in contact with ... Interactivity is an extension of our instinct to communicate, and to shape our environment through communication" (Jordan). Blowing up an alien in a computer game is altering the media.

210

Customizing your broker's Web page so that it presents only the financial information you want is altering the media, as is visually creating your dream car on an automaker's site. Shopping on television does not qualify as interactivity under this definition.

- **Linking.** Linking allows links or connections to be made between different media elements. This can be the menu links connecting different sections of a Web page, or the narrative links in a computer game that are triggered by the actions you choose for the character.

To sum it up, multimedia is a combination of many media into a single work where media-altering interactivity and linking are made possible to the user via the computer. This definition includes all the disc- and cartridge-based (CD, DVD, Xbox, etc.) programs and most of the Web sites in this book.

DEFINING INTERACTIVE MEDIA

"Interactive media" has traditionally been a much broader term than "multimedia." "Interactive media" is used to describe all media with interactivity. It usually refers to computer-delivered interactive media, including both multimedia programs and non-multimedia interactive programs, such as click-and-read Web sites that have limited interactivity and no animations, video, or sound. This is how the term interactive media will be used in this book.

In short, interactive media is computer-delivered media or modes of expression (text, graphics, video, etc.) that allows users to have some control over the manner and/or order of the media presentation.

"MULTIMEDIA" AND "INTERACTIVE MEDIA" IN THIS BOOK

Based on the above definitions, I will generally use the terms "multimedia" or "interactive multimedia" in this book to indicate my major focus is on computer games, E-learning, training programs, Web sites, and other projects that use a combination of computer mediated rich media, complex interactivity, and linking. I will use "interactive media" to refer to all types of computer-delivered media with interactivity, including multimedia, such as computer games, AND simpler interactive media, such as pictures-and-text Web sites.

Types of Interactive Multimedia

The Web is a growing platform for multimedia. Material is presented on sites through multiple media, including pictures, text, video, audio, and animation. The user controls the flow of information and/or performs complex tasks. Examples of Internet rich media applications include interactive animated presentations explaining a product; financial calculators with opportunities to input data and see visual presentation in charts and graphs; product searches with text, audio, and visual elements that allow the user to see how their search terms affect product choices; E-learning courses with exercises, examples, and student-teacher interactions; and online games of all types.

In addition to the World Wide Web, multimedia is presented on local networks, such as corporate intranets; computer hard drives, such as museum kiosks; interactive television, such as MSN TV; dedicated gaming systems, such as PlayStation and Xbox; mobile devices, such as PSPs (Play Station Portables), iPods, and phones; and discs, such as CD-ROMs and DVDs. Interactive multimedia has dozens of uses, with the most common being marketing, sales, product information, entertainment, education, training, and reference material.

> If you are completely new to multimedia and the Web, and feel you need additional basic information on these subjects, you may want to review the Background section of this book, which is available at www.focalpress.com/9780240813431

The Role of the Interactive Writer

The interactive writer may create:

- Proposals
- Outlines
- Sitemaps
- Treatments
- Walkthroughs
- Design documents
- Scripts
- Other written material that describes a multimedia or Web site project

This can include developing the information architecture, on-screen text, overall story structure, dialogue, characters, narration, interface, and more. The key difference between writing for linear media, such as television and movies, and writing for interactive media is interactivity, which allows the user of the program to have control over the flow of the information or story material.

INTERACTIVITY VS. CONTROL

Potential Interactivity

Interactivity means that the user can control the presentation of information or story material on the computer. The potential interactivity of multimedia is awesome. It is possible to interact not merely by screen or page, but by controlling the presentation of individual objects within a screen, such as a single character's actions in a scene, the color of a part of an image, or the presentation of a line of text.

Limits to Interactivity

There are practical limits to the potential of a particular user's interactivity. The viewer's equipment has to be powerful enough to support the level of inter-activity. And even if the viewer has the best system in the world, if the source material is a CD-ROM, a DVD, or some other closed system, the player is work-ing with a finite number of options. He or she can access only what the makers place on the disc. This limitation disappears when multimedia is delivered online, through the World Wide Web or an online service, which allow users to link instantly to thousands, or perhaps, millions of other sources throughout the world. However, for Web surfers who still use a modem, the slow down-load speed can make the online multimedia experience sometimes frustrating.

See the "Playback/Delivery Systems" article in the Background section of this book for a detailed discussion of this issue. The Background section is available at:

www.focalpress.com/9780240813431

Is unlimited interactivity the most effective way to communicate with mul-timedia, if technically possible for the user? It depends to a great degree on what your goals are. If, for example, you are trying to tell a story, such as the interactive narrative *Voyeur*, the degree of interactivity you can allow and still create believable characters, intriguing plot, and suspense will be far less than if you are simply creating a world for viewers to inhabit, such as *SimCity 3000*. Similarly, a Web site with the focused goal of getting you to buy a car will have far less interactive options than an online encyclopedia that wants you to explore its information. *Voyeur* designer David Riordan echoes the feeling of many multimedia developers when he says that: "Infinite choice equals a data-base. Just because you can make a choice doesn't mean it's an interesting one." He says that the creators of multimedia must maintain some control for the experience to be effective.

213

THINKING INTERACTIVELY

Thinking of All the Possibilities

The stumbling block for most new interactive writers is not limiting interactivity and maintaining control over the multimedia experience. Most new writers have the opposite problem of overly restricting interactivity and failing to give users adequate control over the flow of information or story material. This is because limiting options is what most linear writers have been trained to do. In a linear video, film, or book, it is essential to find just the right shot, scene, or sentence to express your meaning.

In writing for interactive media, "the hardest challenge for the writer is the interactivity—having a feel for all the options in a scene or story," says Jane

Jensen, writer-designer of the *Gabriel Knight* series. Tony Sherman, writer-designer of *Dracula Unleashed* and *Club Dead* agrees. Unlike a linear piece in which it is crucial to pare away nonessentials, in interactive media, the writer must "think of all the possibilities."

Viewer Input

It is difficult to predict how the viewer will interact with all the possibilities in a piece. Jane Jensen warns that this can sometimes make multimedia "a frustrating and difficult medium … You have this great scene, but you have to write five times that much around it … to provide options. When your focus is on telling the story, that can feel like busy work and a waste of time."

For example, you have a telephone in one scene that your player must dial to call his or her uncle and find out who the murderer is. This is near the end of the game and getting the telephone number itself has been one of the game's goals. The writer needs to anticipate all the things players might try to do with that telephone. What if players get the telephone number from having played the game earlier, and they then jump ahead to the telephone scene? What should happen when they dial? Should they get a busy signal? What if they dial the number after they have gotten it legally in the game, but they don't have all the information they need, such as knowing that the one who answers is their uncle? Should the writer give them different information in the message? What if they dial the operator? What if they try dialing random numbers?

This can be equally complex in an informational multimedia piece where you must anticipate the related information that the viewers will want to access and all the different ways they may want to relate to the key information. *Compton's Interactive Encyclopedia*, for example, allows users to explore a particular piece of information through text, pictures, audio, videos, maps, definitions, a time line, and a topic tree. The design of the program allows all of these different approaches to be linked together if the viewer desires. This means that students studying Richard Nixon can mouse-click their way from an article about Nixon to his picture, to an audio of his "I Am Not a Crook" speech, to a video about Watergate and Nixon's resignation, and finally to a time line showing other events that happened during his presidency.

Knowing the User

A key way to anticipate users' input is to know as much about them as possible. This is also important in linear media, but it is even more crucial in interactive multimedia, because the interactive relationship is more intimate than the more passive linear one. Knowing the audience is absolutely essential. Knowing what the user considers appealing and/or what information they need will affect every element of a production, from types of links to interactive design.

On most multimedia and Web projects, considerable effort is put into researching the user. Some sources for user information include customer support lines, customer surveys and interviews, bulletin boards, salespeople, user groups, trade shows, and bulletin boards. This information is usually put together in a document called a User Scenario or a Use Case. A Use Case first describes the user and his information and entertainment needs. Then the user's most common paths through the program to get information or complete a task are charted. This helps the designers understand how they need to present the content to meet the user's needs. Before a major project is released to the general public, it is tested with small groups of users in usability studies. The feedback from these studies allows the developers to refine their information design.

LINKING

Links are the connections from one section of an interactive media program to another section of the same program or, if online, to a totally different program. When the information for a program or site is stored in a database, then the linked material can be even smaller or more granular. It is possible to link users' actions to single program elements, sentences, or even words. The simplest link is a text menu choice that the user clicks to bring up new information. When writers develop links, they must make a number of decisions:

- What information, program elements, pages, chapters, or scenes will connect with other sections of the program?
- How many choices will the user have?
- Which choices will be presented first?
- What will be the result of those choices?
- Will the links be direct, indirect, or delayed?

Immediate or Direct Links: An Action

In an immediate or direct link, the viewer makes a choice, and that choice produces a direct and immediate response that the viewer expects. For example, on an investment company's Web site, when the user clicks on the "Rolling Over Your 401(k)" link in the menu, they expect to and will get a page of information about 401(k)s.

Indirect Links: A Reaction

Indirect links, also called "if-then" links, are more complex. Users do not directly choose an item, as in the example above. Instead, they take a certain action that elicits a reaction they did not specifically select. The following example is taken from the walkthrough for the computer game *The Pandora Directive*. The walkthrough describes the program's story and the main interactive options for the user. At this point in the story, you, the user, are trying

215

to escape with the woman Regan, but you have been cornered by the villains Fitzpatrick and Cross.

Excerpt from the Pandora Directive Walkthrough

You get the choice of shooting Fitzpatrick, shooting Cross, or dropping the gun. If you try to shoot Fitzpatrick, you get trapped alongside Regan and Cross; then everybody dies, safely away from Earth. If you try to shoot Cross, he kills you before you ever get into the ship. If you drop the gun, you get to the spaceship.

An example of an indirect link in an informational piece is a student who fails a test in a certain subject area and is automatically routed to easier review material, instead of being advanced to the next level. The student did not make this direct choice. It is a consequence of his or her actions. Figure 13.1 shows how a student who could not answer an arithmetic question in a math tutorial is sent back to an arithmetic review module as opposed to being advanced to the more difficult material. A number of educational multimedia programs work this way.

Indirect links can also cause multiple things to happen when the user clicks one choice. This is most common in a program or Web site where the information is dynamic because it is stored in a database. What this means is that the information is not static in large sections, like the pages and chapters of this book or a traditional HTML Web page. If this book was a database-generated Web site, every paragraph or sentence in it would be a separate piece of information. Depending on what actions the user took on the Web site, these separate pieces of information could be sorted, organized, and displayed in the order requested by the user. For example, on the T. Rowe Price investment company Web site, users can fill out a form and establish the list of mutual funds and stocks that they are most interested in. After they have done this once, when they log on to the site in the future, they are activating a program that searches out the most current data on their topics in the database, organizes this data, and presents it to them.

In the T. Rowe Price example, the multiple actions (sorting, organizing, etc.) are finally displayed in one location, but a single indirect link can also create multiple actions throughout a site or program. For example, on a well-designed Web site for an auto dealer, when a salesperson sells a car and enters the final sales form into the system, the car is automatically removed from the display

Figure 13.1
A reaction to user input.

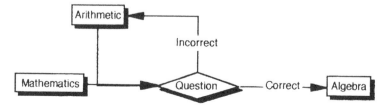

on the public Web site and from the dealer's inventory list. The site might also automatically generate an email message to the customers thanking them for their business.

Intelligent Links or Delayed Links: A Delayed Reaction

Intelligent links remember what choices the user made earlier in the program or on previous plays of the program and alter future responses accordingly. These links can be considered delayed "if-then" links. In a story, intelligent links create a realistic response to the character's action; in a training piece, they provide the most effective presentation of the material based on a student's earlier performance.

In *The Pandora Directive*, for example, you as the player are a detective who is trying to get in touch with Emily, a nightclub singer. You meet Emily's boss, Leach, well before you meet her. If you are rude to him, he mistrusts you. Later in the script when you try to rescue Emily, he will block your entrance to her room, and she will be strangled. If, however, you are nice when you first meet him, he lets you in, and you save her.

Certain Web sites record every click you make and gradually define your preferences. This allows these sites to personalize their presentation to you so that they only show you information and products of interest to you. One example is Amazon.com's recommendation of new book titles to repeat users based on past purchases. The most sophisticated sites might also personalize the way the information is presented. For example, a user who always jumps right to the online videos would be presented with pages containing more multimedia.

217

HIGH-LEVEL DESIGN AND INFORMATION ARCHITECTURE

The complexity that interactivity and linking add to a multimedia project demands strong high-level design and/or information architecture for the program to be coherent and effective. High-level design determines the broad conceptual approach to the project, including the structure, interface, map, organizing metaphors, and even input devices. Information architecture or interactive architecture is the term usually applied to Web sites for the overall grouping of the information, design of the navigation, and process flows of online applications.

Structure as an Interactive Device

The overall structure of a piece is one of the main ways interaction can be motivated in a narrative. In the computer game *Half-Life 2*, scientist Gordon Freeman is on an alien-infested Earth and he must rescue the world from the evil he unleashed in the first *Half Life*. The player's main interactions, which are motivated by this story, are exploring the barren futuristic world and (of course) blowing away bad guys. In another game, *Grand Theft Auto: San Andreas*, you play the role of Carl "CJ" Johnson who is returning home to find out why his mother has been killed. It's not long before you/Carl are rebuilding your street gang in order to get to the bottom of the problems and set things straight. In the narrative informational piece *A la rencontre de Philippe*, the player is motivated to learn about Paris through the role of helping Parisian friends find an apartment. In another narrative information piece, *The Oregon Trail*, your task is to outfit a wagon, join a wagon train, and make the journey safely across the country. This basic premise inspires a whole series of user interactions with the program from buying supplies, choosing a team of animals for the wagon, and shooting deer for food on the trail.

The overall structure and navigation of a non-narrative informational multimedia piece is called the information or interactive architecture. Poorly structured information will cause the user either to fail to interact with the program at all, or to get confused and give up part way through. For example, good information architects know what information to put on the top level of the interactive program, such as a Web site's home page, to engage the user's interest. After hooking the user, this top-level information has to lead the user logically to the information that the user wants.

Interface Design

Another way to help users find their way through the complex structure of an interactive media production is through good interface design. The interface is simply the "face" or basic on-screen visualization of the information or story material in a program. The interface governs how we will interact with multimedia. An interface can be as simple as a list of words in a clickable menu that organizes the information into content categories. The interface can also be more graphical, such as the time clock and icons from the Harlem Renaissance site in Figure 13.2.

The interface can also be much more complex, such as the interface for the computer game *Nancy Drew: Secret of the Old Clock* computer game, which allows the user to interact with the story material in a variety of ways using items in the bottom tool bar and items in the main screen (Figure 13.3). From the bottom bar players can bring up the tools and clues they have found, consult their notebook, track their money, and get help. There are many more options in the main interface, including walking, driving the car, talking to people, solving puzzles, and using the telephone.

The amount of input the writer is allowed to give regarding the interface design depends on the designer and the project, but the writer must consider the overall interface design and information architecture when they are writing. Interface design is crucial in deciding how multimedia content will be organized. It affects the structure of the script for the writer and dictates how the viewer will interact with that content.

Figure 13.2
Timeline and icons from the Harlem Renaissance Web site. Copyright Encyclopaedia Britannica, Inc.

Figure 13.3
Interface for *Nancy Drew: Secret of the Old Clock* computer game. Copyright Her Interactive, Inc.

The interface also affects the navigation of the piece—how the viewer can travel through the information or story and the order in which the information will be presented. The navigation is often demonstrated through flowcharts and diagrams, such as this flowchart from the *Nancy Drew* game (Figure 13.4)

The U.S. White House Web site (*http://www.whitehouse.gov/*) uses a simple hierarchical menu for navigation in which users can first choose from a number of global links in the top navigation bar. By clicking the link "First Lady," the user

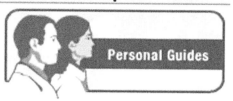

Figure 13.4
A portion of the writer's flowchart for *Nancy Drew: Secret of the Old Clock* computer game. Copyright Her Interactive, Inc.

is taken down a level to the First Lady's page, on that page you have a number of options including "Press Releases and Speeches." Clicking that link will lead to a list of actual speeches, which you can click to read the speech "The First Lady's Remarks After the Christmas Day Lunch." So this is an example of a hierarchical menu where you had to drill down four levels to get to the First Lady's speech you were interested in: White House Home Page → First Lady Main Page → Press Releases and Speeches Menu → "The First Lady's Remarks After the Christmas Day Lunch."

Map or Sitemap

An element of good interactive design is a sitemap or map that represents the overall structure of a piece in a concrete manner. A sitemap illustrates how the player should interact with the interface and navigate through the program. It can be as simple as a text menu that lists all the key pages of a Web site, broken down by categories. Sometimes the map is a flowchart of the entire production, as in the Oakes Interactive training piece for Fidelity Investments retirement counselors. In this program, a student can bring up the flowchart of the whole program and access any area of it by clicking on one of the labeled boxes. The sitemap can even be a literal map, as in *Grand Theft Auto: San*

Andreas, in which the player can consult a map of the cities that make up the island of San Andreas to get oriented and decide where to go next. (The actual interface of the game is a 3D animation of the town's buildings and citizens, with whom the viewer can interact.)

Metaphors

For software developers, the metaphor is a concrete image or other element that represents an abstract concept, making it clear and comfortable to the user. Perhaps one of the best-known software metaphors is the desktop. Windows PCs and Macs present the abstract concepts of computer files, directories, and software as file folders and documents that users can arrange and work with on the desktop.

Metaphors are also used to design individual screens and navigational aids. According to designer Aaron Marcus, "consistency and clarity are two of the most important concerns in developing metaphors" (Marcus, 1995). Familiarity to the viewer is a third item that could be added. Consistency means that users should not use buttons as the main navigational tool on one screen and then suddenly have to switch to a different approach, such as clicking on pictures, in the next screen. Both of these are valid metaphors for linked information, but they are confusing when mixed. Consistent place-ment of the same types of information in the same place on the screen is also important.

Creating familiar metaphors ties into knowing your audience. A valid metaphor for the structure of an elementary school education CD-ROM or Web site might be a street in a town. This is something students are familiar with. It makes sense for them to click on a library to get information or a movie theater to see a film. On a micro level, a common metaphor is a book that opens. Click a dog-ear to turn a page. Click the table of contents to go to a chapter. Sometimes a metaphor can add to the mood of a piece. The Harlem Renaissance Web site uses a tourist metaphor to help make the user feel that they are visitors to another era. The metaphor is strengthened with items such as street maps, email postcards, and evocative full-page visuals. A common metaphor on many Web sites, including the latest version of the Prudential Verani site, is a stack of file folders with tabs that can be clicked on to access the content of another "file folder" of information (Figure 13.5). All of these examples are concrete objects or concepts that help make accessing information more usable.

Familiar metaphors help orient viewers, but this certainly doesn't mean that metaphors have to be clichéd or boring. Certainly a designer who can push the envelope without losing the audience should by all means go for it. There is lots of room to be creative. It is important to make even the minor elements of a production work well. For example, one of the frustrating things in multimedia is the "wait-state" image. Many programs are content to give the standard clock or hourglass, but there is no rule that the wait-state image cannot be fun.

Figure 13.5
Home page for
Prudential Verani
Realty, showing file
folder tab navigation
metaphor. Copyright
Prudential Verani
Realty.

A.D.A.M. The Inside Story, an anatomy program, shows a skeleton with a cup of coffee. Some children's programs have scurrying animals.

Input Devices

Writers might also consider how the users will input their responses to the program. Standard choices include the keyboard, mouse, game controller, guns, writing text on screen, and touch screen, but sometimes the input device can be integrated into the material. Instead of a mouse, the *Guitar Hero* game has a guitar you can play that helps you become a rock star, complete with visual action at six different locations, from basement parties to sold out stadiums. *Redbeard's Pirate Quest* uses a model pirate ship loaded with electromagnetic sensors. Speech recognition is also finally coming of age, and this could have a major impact on interactive narratives. Even more exciting are the potential applications for multimodal interaction. "Multimodal systems process combined natural input modes—such as speech, pen, touch, hand gestures, eye gaze, and head and body movements—in a coordinated manner with multimedia output" (Oviatt, 1999). For interacting with complex multimedia programs, such as virtual worlds populated with intelligent animated characters, a multimodal system will be far superior to the conventional Windows-Icons-Menus-Pointer (WIMP) interface.

INTERACTIVE DEVICES

In addition to the high-level design elements, the designer and writer must develop specific interactive devices that will make users aware of the interactive possibilities they have created. These devices include icons, on-screen menus, help screens, props, other characters, cues imbedded in the story or information, and more.

Icons

In computer usage, an icon is a symbol that represents a command or an ongoing action. For example, the floppy disc image in the toolbar of many software programs indicates the Save function. An hour glass icon indicates that the computer is doing a process and the user must wait. Various types of icons are used for interactive devices. In *Voyeur* they are used to inspire viewers to look into the rooms of the mansion that are visible from the voyeur's apartment. If the voyeur moves the camera over a room in which there is action to view, an eye icon appears. If there's something to hear, an ear appears. If there is evidence to examine, such as a letter, a magnifying glass appears. Clicking on the icons causes the material to be presented. The *Nancy Drew* games do something similar with the magnifying glass glowing when an item is clickable.

In Britannica.com's Harlem Renaissance Web site, icons are used to efficiently indicate the main sections of the site in the Web site's navigation bar (Figure 13.2). The megaphone is for leadership, the page is for literature, the palette is for art, and so on. The meaning of the icons is clarified through the use of rollovers that show text labels when the mouse passes over one of the icons. In the *Oregon Trail*, icons on the bottom of the screen let the player/traveler check the status of supplies and health for the group. The supplies icon shows a bag of flour and some containers; the health icon has a medicine bag and medicine.

Be careful not to overuse icons or rely on obscure icons. Many icons benefit from a text label, and sometimes it's better to skip the icons altogether and rely on text alone.

Menus and Other Text

The text menu and the navigation bar are traditional and still effective ways to access material in informational multimedia. In addition to static text, menus can also be presented as popup or drop-down menus that take less screen space (Figure 13.6). They only appear when the user clicks on them. Text links can also be highlighted directly on a page within the body text, as in Figure 13.2, where the names of important figures of the era are links to additional information.

Although text menus can work well in an informational piece, they can disrupt the flow of a narrative. However, some designers are willing to accept that disruption to achieve a high degree of interactivity. In *Under a Killing Moon*, written by Aaron Conners, menus allow the player a wide variety of action options, including look, get, move, open, and talk. The player can even choose the tone of the lead character's dialogue by picking menu choices such as "Rugged Banter," "Indignant," and "Reeking of Confidence." *Grand Theft Auto: San Andreas* will also use text to indicate actions for the user. Text will appear on the screen at key moments with tips, such as "Ride the bike." or "Keep up with your buddy."

Sometimes words on the screen are optional. In *Under a Killing Moon*, players can pull down an optional hints window. This helps orient them in the game

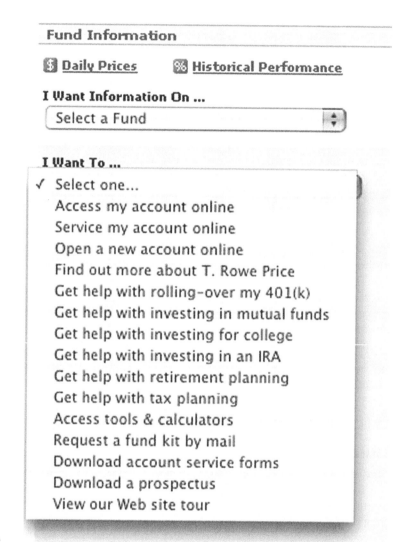

Figure 13.6
Drop-down menu
from the T. Rowe
Price Web site.
Copyright T. Rowe
Price Associates, Inc.

and tells them their interactive options. Sometimes written material is integrated into the story itself. Shannon Gilligan's *Who Killed Sam Rupert?* includes an investigator's notebook that keeps track of what the detective/player has done so far in the game. The *Nancy Drew* games use a similar device. Many online transactions, such as an online account opening for a bank, also have optional help text or product information that the user can decide to access or not.

Props

Props are a popular interactive device. In *Under a Killing Moon*, the character can click on objects in the room to get information. Depending on the object, a player might hear a voice-over wisecrack about a painting, or even see a full-motion video flashback that shows the detective's relationship with the object. In the educational CD-ROM *Sky High*, users can click on various props in a scene, such as toy helicopters and birds, to bring up additional information related to that aspect of flight.

Props that a character can actually use as they might be used in real life are particularly effective. In the educational game *Zoo Vet*, the player can use a wide variety of medical instruments to help sick zoo animals. The game *Half Life 2* has a wide variety of props that the user can manipulate, which encourages interaction. For example, in one scene, the character has to pile a group of boxes a certain way to climb out of a window.

Characters

Characters are another way to guide interactions. Sometimes this is the primary function of the character. In the *Nancy Drew* games, telephone calls from her friends and father nudge her in one direction or another and give additional clues. In the same games, talking with most of the main characters inspire additional actions. The investigators in *Who Killed Sam Rupert* and *Gabriel Knight* both have assistants who remind them of appointments, give them telephone messages, or suggest people to talk to. Other characters, who are not primarily information givers, might say things that suggest a location to visit or a person to interview. This is often used in *Half Life 2*.

A character can also be used as a guide to lead the viewer through the material. This can be successful in both narrative and non-narrative pieces. For example, children's educational programs frequently have characters that suggest what actions to take and what information to explore. The veterinary assistants in *Zoo Vet* perform this function by telling the player/veterinarian when their diagnosis and treatment is off track. Many training e-learning programs will have an expert guide you can call upon for advice when you are trying to complete a task. This guide is usually represented as video, graphics, text, and/or audio of a specific person who can be called upon for help and advice as if they were a live consultant. In the narrative videogame *Astronomica*, the daughter of the doctor who disappeared approaches you, the user, directly by banging on your bedroom window and asking you to help find her father. She leads you to her father's lab, where she works on the main computer, and sends you into the exploratorium to solve the problems there. She also appears now and again on a small communications monitor in the exploratorium to give you tips and encouragement.

Challenge of the Interactive Device

The challenge of the interactive device is to design something that will motivate interaction without radically disrupting the flow of information or story material. A well-designed interactive device will not pull us out of the dream state of storytelling or disrupt our train of thought as we pursue information. In short, interactive devices must be well integrated into the material.

225

CONCLUSION

This chapter has provided a broad overview of some of the key interactive issues the writer must consider when developing a multimedia informational or narrative program. Although the elements discussed above, such as interface design, are not always under the control of the writer, the writer must understand these concepts if he or she is to write effectively for interactive media.

REFERENCES

Davenport, G. (1994). Bridging Across Content and Tools. *Computer Graphics, 28,* 31–32.

Halliday, M. (1993). *Digital Cinema: An Environment for Multi-threaded Stories.* Master's thesis, Massachusetts Institute of Technology.

The *Harlem Renaissance.* (1999). Web site http://www.britannica.com/harlem.

Jensen, J. Telephone interview with the author, July 1994.

Jordan, K. *Defining Multimedia.* NOEMA Web site. http://www.noemalab.org/sections/ideas/ideas_articles/jordan_multimedia.html.

Marcus, A. (1995). Making Multimedia Usable: User Interface Design. *New Media, 5,* 98–100.

Oviatt, S. (1999). Ten Myths of Multimodal Interaction. *Communications of the ACM, 42,* 74–81.

Verani, P. (1999). Web site http://www.pruverani.com.

Riordan, D. Telephone interview with the author, June 1994.

Sherman, T. Telephone interview with the author, July 1994.

Rowe Price, T. (1999). Web site http://www.troweprice.com.

CHAPTER 14

Creating a Work of Digital Storytelling: The Development Process

Carolyn Handler Miller

What is the very first step that needs to be taken in developing a new project, and why is it so important?

What are the five most common mistakes people make when developing an interactive project?

Why is so much time and attention spent on creating certain types of documents during the development process, and are these documents even necessary?

What are the ten most important questions that must be addressed before production begins?

THE DEVELOPMENT PERIOD AND WHY IT IS CRITICAL

Before a work of interactive entertainment is ever built—before the interactivity is programmed, or the visuals are produced, or the sound is recorded—a tremendous amount of planning must first take place. This phase of the work is known as the development process or the preproduction period. It is a time of tremendous creative ferment. In its own way, it is not unlike the period described in ancient creation myths when all was nothingness and then, after a series of miraculous events, the earth was formed and its myriad beings were given life.

The creation of a work of interactive entertainment is a totally human endeavor, of course, but it, too, begins with nothingness, and to successfully bring such a complex endeavor to fruition can almost seem miraculous. To achieve the end goal, a tiny sliver of an idea must be nurtured and shaped, amplified and refined. And, instead of miracles, it requires a tremendous amount of hard work. Bringing a project up to the point where it is ready for production requires a team of individuals with diverse skills who perform an array of different tasks.

Surprising though it may be, the work that goes on during preproduction is much the same for every type of interactive project, whether the end product is a videogame, content for the Web, a VR simulation, or a wireless game. The specific documents that are called for may vary, and the specific technical issues may be different, but the core process varies little, no matter what the interactive medium may be.

THE ADVANTAGES OF GOOD DOCUMENTATION

A well-utilized preproduction period can save not only time and money during production, but it can also help avert the risk of a product that fails. Furthermore, the documents generated during development can go a long way toward keeping the entire team on track while the project is actually being built. Good documentation can mean that everyone is working with the same vision of the end product in mind. It helps avoid confusion, prevents mistakes, and reduces the likelihood of work having to be redone. And if a new member is added to the team midway through, the documentation can quickly bring that individual up to speed.

The tasks that take place during the development period include the conceptualizing of the project; addressing marketing issues; producing design documents, art work, and other materials; building a prototype; and doing testing. Not every task done during this period deals specifically with creative issues, although invariably everything does impact the content, including the drawing up of budgets and schedules and the preparing of marketing plans.

The development process typically lasts an average of six months. However, it can be as brief as a few days or take as long as a year or more, depending on the complexity of the project, the experience of the creative team, and whether or not it involves a new type of technology or content. At the end of the development process, the company should be ready to swing into full-scale production.

FIVE ALL-TOO-COMMON ERRORS

Unfortunately, certain serious mistakes tend to be made during the development process. Some of these errors are caused by inexperience. Others may be fueled by the team's admirable intention of making something remarkable, yet being unable to rein in their ideas and set reasonable limits. And quite often, problems arise because the creative team is eager to plunge into preproduction and is too impatient to invest sufficient time in planning. Based on my own experience and on interviews with experts, here are five of the most common and serious errors that occur during the creative process:

1. **Throwing too much into the project:** In cases like this, the creative team may have become intoxicated with a promising new technology or with exciting new ways to expand the content. But this sort of enthusiasm can lead to many problems. It can cause the project to go over budget or require it to carry too expensive a price tag for the market. The project may take far longer to produce than the time originally slotted for it, causing it to miss an important market date. Or the finished product may be too complex for the end-user to enjoy.

2. **Not considering your audience:** This error can be fatal to a project. If you do not have a good understanding of your audience, how can you be sure you are making something it will want or will have the ability to use? Misjudging your audience can lead to:
   - Creating subject matter they are not interested in or find distasteful.
   - Developing content for a platform, device, or technical ability they do not possess.
   - Developing an educational or training program that omits key points they need to know or that goes over their heads.
   - Developing content for children that is not age appropriate.

3. **Making the product too hard or complicated:** This error can stem in part from Error #2, not considering your audience. You need to understand what the end-users are capable of doing and not make unrealistic demands on their abilities. Sometimes this error is caused by poor design, and it is allowed to slip by because of inadequate testing. Whatever the cause, an overly difficult product will lead to unhappy end-users. As game designer Katie Fisher of Quicksilver Software said: "When a game becomes work, it's not fun for the player." Her comment is true not just of games but for any work of interactive entertainment, be it a smart toy, an immersive movie, or an iTV show. If it is too hard to figure out, people are not going to want to invest their time in it.

4. **Making the product too simple:** This is the other side of the coin for Error #3. We are not talking here, however, about the product being

229

too simple to use—simplicity in functionality is a good thing. We are referring to overly simple content. The content of an interactive work needs to be challenging in some way; otherwise, users will lose interest. It should also contain enough material to explore, and things to do, to keep the users absorbed for a significant amount of time. If it is too thin, they will feel they have not gotten their money's worth. To gauge the appropriate amount of playing time for your product, it is advisable to become familiar with similar products on the market. Focus group testing is also helpful in this matter.

5. **Not making the product truly interactive:** In such cases, users are not given sufficient agency to keep them involved. When this happens, the flaw can usually be traced back all the way to the initial concept. In all likelihood, the premise that the product was built upon was weak in terms of its interactive potential, even if it might have been an interesting one for a noninteractive type of entertainment. In a successful interactive product, the interactivity must be organic from the outset and not just an afterthought.

THE FIRST STEP: CREATING THE CORE CONCEPT

The development phase begins with deciding what, in essence, the new project will be—the core concept. The initial idea may come about in one of several ways, and how it is initiated varies from medium to medium, company to company, project to project. Sometimes the concept is proposed by the CEO or president of the company; sometimes a staff member comes up with the idea; and sometimes it emerges during a staff brainstorming session. In a long-established software company, the concept may be a sequel to an already existing title. In a start-up company, it may be the dream project of a single individual or a small group of colleagues.

WHERE DO IDEAS FOR NEW PROJECTS COME FROM?

Ideas for new projects can come about in many ways. Sometimes they are inspired by a myth or true event from history or from an incident in someone's personal life. Sometimes the starting place begins with someone dreaming up an intriguing fantasy setting or exciting world to explore. Many times ideas take shape just by letting the imagination run free or by a group brainstorming session. In other cases, an idea is sparked by a new technology when someone envisions how it could be used as a medium for an interactive narrative. (For more on creating an original project, see Chapter 25, Creating Your Own Showcase.)

In many instances, of course, a company is given an assignment by an outside client and needs to find a creative way to fulfill it: to come up with an entertaining way to teach high school physics, for example, or to use digital storytelling techniques to promote a movie or sell a line of automobiles.

In many companies, the raw idea is set before the entire creative team and subjected to some rigorous brainstorming. During brainstorming, even the wildest ideas are encouraged in order to explore the full potential of the project.

Once a consensus of the core idea is reached, a description of it needs to be articulated in a way that adequately reflects what the group has worked out. Ideally, one person on the team will boil the concept down to a clear and vivid *premise*. The premise, which is usually just one sentence long, describes the concept in a way that indicates where its energy will come from, what the challenges might be, and what will hook the users. The premise is often written in the second person, "you," to put the listener or reader right into the action.

For example, a description of the premise of a new game might sound something like this: "In *Runway*, you are thrust into the glamorous but cutthroat world of the fashion industry, where you play the head of a small fashion house competing against powerful rivals and try to come up with the winning line for the new season." Or a description for a smart toy might be described this way: "Perry the Talking Parrot can be trained to speak and repeat phrases, but you can never predict what Perry might say because he has a mind of his own!"

In the film business, they call this one sentence description a "log line." The term got its name from the concise descriptions of movies given in television logs and other entertainment guides. However, the idea of boiling down a premise to a few words is equally useful for interactive entertainment. By nailing it down this way, the team will have a clear grasp of what it is setting out to do. They will also be able to communicate this vision to everyone who will be working on it or whose support will be needed to bring the project to fruition. And ultimately, this log line will be a valuable marketing tool.

OTHER EARLY DECISIONS

Early on during the development period, the creative team needs to make certain fundamental decisions about the project, assuming they are not already incorporated into the basic concept. First of all, what specific medium and platform is the project being made for, and what genre does it belong to? Once these basic "What is it?" questions have been addressed, it is time to consider important marketing issues. Who will the target audience be? What competing products are already available? And, if this a retail product, what will the intended price tag be? All these matters can have a significant impact on the design.

To help answer these questions, many companies either use a marketing person on staff or hire an outside consultant. This marketing expert might determine, for example, that the idea you have in mind sounds too expensive for your target audience, and if you don't want to overprice your product, you will need to rethink the design and leave out some of the cutting-edge features you were hoping to build in. Or your marketing expert might tell you your product would have a better chance with a different demographic than you had in mind. This information would require a different kind of adjustment. For instance, if you found out it would have a higher appeal with teens rather than with preteens, you may need to make the product more sophisticated and edgier than you'd intended at first.

Somewhere early on during the development period, the project manager will also be working out a preproduction and production schedule that will include specific milestones—dates when specific elements must be completed and delivered. A budget for the project will also be drawn up. Now, armed with a clearer idea of your project and its parameters, the team can brainstorm to refine the concept and begin to develop its specific features. Unlike the very first brainstorming sessions, where the sky was the limit, these later brainstorming sessions are tempered by reality.

FIVE POUNDS OF STUFF

Designer Greg Roach, introduced in Chapter 11, points out that you only have limited resources for any project you undertake, and you have to decide how best to use them. "It's like being given five pounds of stuff," he said. "You can't do everything you want." Thus, you have to make trade-offs—if you really want Feature X, then you may have to scratch Feature Y or Feature Z. In other worlds you can't build a ten-pound project with only five pounds of stuff.

HOW PROJECTS EVOLVE DURING DEVELOPMENT

As a project moves through the development process, it evolves from a raw idea to a polished state where it is capable of being produced.

During this preproduction phase, many projects require the input of *subject matter experts*, known as *SMEs*. Projects designed for educational, informational, or training purposes will inevitably require help from experts on the content and often on the target learners. But even when the sole goal of the project is to entertain, it might be necessary to seek expert help or to assign someone to do research. For instance, if you are actually doing a game about the fashion industry, you will want to find out everything you can about the world of high fashion, from how a new line of clothes is designed to how a fashion show is staged. Based on this knowledge, you can build specific challenges and puzzles into the game and make the project far richer and more realistic than it would be if you had attempted to rely on your imagination alone.

As the project develops, the team will be setting the ideas down in various types of documents. They will also be producing flowcharts, character sketches, and other visuals to further refine the interactivity, characterization, and look of the project. The various documents and artwork will be described in more detail a little later in this chapter, in the section entitled "Documents and Artwork."

At various points during the development process, ideas and visuals may be tested on *focus groups*—representative members of the target audience. If a client company is involved in this project, it will also need to be briefed on ideas and shown visuals. Based on the feedback that is received, further refinements may be made. The final step in preproduction is often the building of a prototype, a working model of a small part of the overall project. This is especially typical in cases where the project incorporates novel features or new technology or is the first of an intended line of similar products.

The prototype will demonstrate how the project actually operates, how the user interacts with the content, and what the look and feel of it will be like. For many interactive projects, the prototype is the make or break point. If it lives up to expectations and funding for the product and other considerations are in place, the project will receive the green light to proceed to development. But if the prototype reveals serious flaws in the concept or in its functionality, it may mean going back to the drawing board, or it could even be the end of the line for that particular concept.

A TEN-STEP DEVELOPMENT CHECKLIST

As we've already seen, the process of creating an interactive project involves the asking and answering of some fundamental questions. Based on my own experience and on the interviews done for this book, I have put together a list of ten critical questions that must be addressed early in the development process, each with its own set of subquestions. These questions and subquestions apply to virtually any type of work of interactive entertainment. The answers will help you shape your concept, define your characters and structure, and work out the project's interactivity. The ten questions are listed below:

1. Premise and purpose:
   - What is the premise of the project; the core idea in a nutshell? What about it will make it engaging? Try to capture its essential qualities in a single sentence.
   - What is its fundamental purpose? To entertain? To teach or inform? To make people laugh? To market a product?
2. Audience and market:
   - Who is the intended user?
   - What type of entertainment do people in this group enjoy? How technically sophisticated are they?
   - Why should your project appeal to them?
   - What other projects like yours already exist, and how well are they doing?
3. Medium, platform, and genre:
   - What interactive medium or media is this work being made for (such as the Internet, mobile phones, interactive TV, or several media together); what are the special strengths and limitations of this medium, and how will the project take advantage of these strengths and minimize these limitations?

233

- What type of platform (hardware) will it use? (For example, a PC, a game console, a mobile phone, etc.)
- What genre (category of programming, such as simulation, webisode, or action game) does it fall into, and in what ways does your work contain the key characteristics of this genre?

4. Narrative/gaming elements:
   - Does your work contain narrative elements (such as a plot or characters)? If so, has the storyline been fully worked out? What are the major events or challenges that the user will need to deal with during the narrative?
   - Does this work utilize gaming elements? If so, is the gameplay thoroughly worked out? What constitutes winning or losing?

5. User's role and POV:
   - What character or role will the user play in this interactive environment?
   - What is the nature of the user's agency? How will the user effect the outcome?
   - Through what POV will the user view this world: first person, third person, or a mix of both?

6. Characters:
   - Who are the nonplayer characters in this project?
   - What role or function do they serve (allies, adversaries, helper figures)?
   - If your project contains a number of characters, have you developed a character bible to describe them?

7. Structure and interface:
   - What is the starting place in terms of the user's experience and what are the possible end points?
   - How will the project be structured? What are the major units of organization (such as modules or levels), and how many of them will there be? What structural model are you using?
   - How will the user control the material and navigate through it? How will the user be able to tell how well he or she is doing? Will your project be making use of navigation bars, menus, icons, inventories, maps, or other interface devices?

8. Fictional world and settings:
   - What is the central fictional world where your project is set?
   - How is it divided geographically? What are its major settings, what do they look like, and how are they different from each other?
   - What challenges, dangers, or special pleasures are inherent to these worlds?

9. User engagement:
   - What about your project will keep the user engaged and want to spend time with it?
   - What important goal is the user trying to accomplish by the end of this work?
   - What will make the user want to spend time accomplishing this goal?

- What is the nature of the oppositional forces that the user will encounter?
- What will add tension to the experience? Will there be a ticking clock?
- Are you building in a system of rewards and penalties?
- What kind of meaningful interactivity are you offering the user, and will this interactivity have a significant impact on the material?

10. Overall look and sound:
- What kinds of visuals will you be using (animation, video, graphics, text on the screen, a mix)?
- Is the overall look realistic or a fantasy environment?
- How do you plan to use audio in your work? Will characters speak? Do you have plans for ambient sound (rain, wind, traffic noises, background office sounds)? Will there be sound effects? Music?

Once you have answered these ten questions as completely as possible, you should have a pretty good grasp of the major elements of the project or know what needs to be developed more fully.

DOCUMENTS AND ARTWORK

While each company may have its own unique method of doing documentation and preproduction artwork, certain types of written materials and visuals are universal throughout the interactive entertainment universe, even though their names may vary from company to company. The most frequently used forms of documentation and visual presentations are as follows:

1. The Concept Document

The concept document is a brief description of the project and is usually the first piece of written material to be generated. It includes such essential information as the premise, the intended medium and platform, and the genre. It also notes the intended audience for the project and the nature of the interactivity, and it gives a succinct overview of the characters and the main features of the story and game. Concept documents may be used as in-house tools to give everyone on the team a quick picture of what the project will be, and they can also be used as sales tools to secure support or funding for a project. If intended to be used in the second capacity, the concept document should be written in a vivid, engaging style that will convince readers of the project's viability. Concept documents tend to be quite short, generally under ten pages in length.

2. The Bible

A bible is an expanded version of a concept document, and it is strictly an in-house working document. Bibles are most frequently used for complex, story-rich projects; they may not be written at all for certain types of interactive projects, such as puzzle games. A bible fully describes significant elements of the work. It includes all the settings or worlds and what happens in them and all the major characters, and it may also give the backstories of these characters (their personal histories up to the point where the story or game begins). Some bibles, called character bibles, only describe the characters. Bibles vary quite a bit in length, depending on the breadth of the project and their intended purpose within the company. In some companies, the bible is a collection of all the preproduction documents written for the project.

3. The Design Document

The design document serves as a written blueprint of the entire interactive work. It vastly expands the information given in either a concept document or bible, and it contains specific technical information about the interactivity and functionality. It is the primary working document of any new media project. At some companies, the design document evolves from the concept document or bible; at other companies, it is written from scratch.

The design document is a living construct begun during preproduction but never truly completed until the project itself is finished. As new features are added to the project, they are added to the design document, or if a feature is changed, the design document is revised accordingly. Because a design document is such an enormous and ever-changing work, and because so many different people contribute to it, it is vital that one person takes charge of overseeing it. This person coordinates and integrates the updates and makes sure that only one official version exists and that no outdated versions are still floating around.

Design documents are organized in various ways. Some are organized by structure, with a section for each module, world, environment, or level. Others are organized by topic. For instance, the design document for the strategy game *Age of Empires* contained a section just on buildings and how they worked.

To get an idea of the type of information that can be included in a design document, let's take a look at a few pages of one prepared for *JumpStart Advanced First Grade* (Figure 14.1). The document is organized module by module; this module is for Hopsalot's Bridge, a sorting game. It is hosted by a character named Hopsalot, who is a rabbit.

At the top of the first page is a picture of Hopsalot's Bridge, from the POV of the player. Beneath it is a list of the curriculum points the game will teach, followed by brief summaries of the introduction speeches, one for first-time visitors and one for repeat visitors. This is followed by a detailed description of the gameplay, levels, and functionality. The full documentation of this module would also note what objects on the screen are clickable and what happens when the player clicks on them—what the pop-ups will be and what the audio will be, as well as a description of all the buttons on the screen and on the tool bar and what each of them does. It would also indicate every line of dialogue that Hopsalot would speak and would include special notes for the programmer and graphic artist.

Because design documents incorporate such a vast amount of detail, they sometimes reach 1000 pages or more in length. Some companies also produce

Hopsalot's Bridge Module
(Hb)

Access

Click Hopsalot's House, on the Main Menu Screen to get here.

Page Description

The curriculum for this module is the Sorting of:
- – Parts of speech
- – Words
- – Geometry: shapes
- – Science: Health/Nutrition, Animals, Weather

On Your First Visit:

Hopsalot gives long intro. Hopsalot's turbo carrot juice is one of the most prized power-ups for the scooters. Or at least he thinks it is, so he has gone to extremes to protect his supply.

Return Visit:

Gives short intro.

Gameplay

Hopsalot has made an island to hide his high-octane carrot juice on and he has to build a bridge to get to it. He has columns in the water that divide the bridge into 3 sections. He has also created little remote controlled balloon blimps to drop into place and create the bridge.

Each balloon has a word or picture on it (depending on the content selected for the session). For example: each word would be a Noun, Verb or Adjective. You must sort the balloons so that each column of the bridge has the same type of word. Use the left and right arrow keys to steer the balloons and use the down arrow key to make them drop faster.

Continued

Figure 14.1
A few pages from the design document of *JumpStart Advanced first Grade*. Document courtesy of Knowledge Adventure, Inc., and used under license.

If you send a balloon into the wrong column it will bounce back up into the air so that you can try again. Hopsalot will also hold a pin that will pop the balloons that you don't need (distractor blimps in L2 and L3).

When the bridge is complete, Hops will run over to grab a carrot power-up and bring it back. Now for the fun part! He can't leave the bridge up or Jimmy Bumples might sneak across, so you'll need to repeat the activity, but this time matching object will pop the balloon underneath.

Reward:

After you've destroyed the bridge, Hops will reward you with the power-up.

Content Leveling

Note: the levels are related to each topic.

1. Parts of speech
Level 1: Verbs, Adjectives, and nouns
Level 2: Verbs, Adjectives, and nouns
Level 3: Verbs, Adjectives, and nouns
Add words that do not fit into the category such as an adverb or preposition.

2. Syllables
Level 1: 1 to 3 syllables; pronounced
Level 2: 2 to 4 syllables; pronounced
Level 3: 2 to 4 syllables; regular pronunciation

3. Health-Nutrition (food groups)
Level 1: 3 categories: Grains, Meats, Dairy
Level 2: 4 categories: Grains, Meats, Dairy, Fruits
Level 3: 5 categories: Grains, Meats, Dairy, Fruits, Vegetables

4. Animals
Level 1: Habitat: water, land, air
Level 2: Attributes: scales, fur, feathers
Level 3: Zoological type: mammals, reptiles, insects; amphibians as distracters

5. Science – Weather
Level 1: 3 categories: sunny, rainy, snowy; outdoors activities
Level 2: 3 categories: sunny, rainy, snowy; outdoors activities + clothes
Level 3: seasons: winter, spring, summer; fall as distracter

6. Geometry – Shapes and Forms
Level 1: 2D shapes: squares, triangles, circles, rectangles
Level 2: 3D shapes: cubes, cones, cylinders, spheres
Level 3: everyday objects by their 3D shape: cubes, cones, cylinders, spheres

Gameplay Leveling
Level 1: Slow falling pieces.
Level 2: Medium speed falling pieces.
Level 3: Fast falling pieces.

Functionality
I. On entering the Module:
A. Play Background: BkgG1HbBackground
B. Play Background Music: G1HbAmbient.wav

Continued

II. Introduction Functionality
  A. Long Introduction (played the first time a player visits this module)
    Follow standards for interruptability
    a) Play Hopsalot waving at Player
      • Hopsalot's Body: AniG1HbHopsalot, FX Wave
    b) Play Hopsalot giving his Long Intro
      (Note: during Intro, Hopsalot will be Pointing at item as he speaks about them; items will highlight, and Hopsalot will have corresponding "Point" FX going on)

i) Long Intro:
      • Hopsalot's Body: AniG1HbHopsalot, FX Point01
      • Hopsalot's Talk: AniG1HbHopsalotTalk, FX LongIntro01
      • Hopsalot's VO: DgG1HbHopsalotTalkLongIntro01.wav
    c) Go to Gameplay
  B. Short Intro (played on any return visits)
    Follow standards for interruptability
    a) Play Hopsalot giving one of the 3 Short Intros: (Random without repetition)
      • Hopsalot's Body: AniG1HbHopsalot, FX Point{01-03}
      • Hopsalot's Talk: AniG1HbHopsalotTalk, FX ShortIntro{01-03}
      • Hopsalot's VO: DgG1HbHopsalotTalkShortIntro{01-03}.wav
    b) Go to Gameplay

III. Gameplay Interaction
  A. Display
    1. Hopsalot
      a) Hopsalot's Body: AniG1HbHopsalot, FX Still
      b) Hopsalot's Talk: AniG1HbHopsalotTalk, FX Still
    2. Device to throw Balloons
      a) Device: AniG1HbDevice, FX Still
    3. Falling Balloons
      (note: will appear on screen one after the other, according to order set for current level; those will be the same sprite, replicated at {x} instances; use datadict for coordinates)
      a) Play first Balloon ready on the Device: AniG1HbBalloon, FX Still
    4. Carrot Case
      (note: at the right side of screen = case containing the power-up)
      a) Case standing there: AniG1HbCarrotCase, FX Still
    5. Labels
      (Note: located at the bottom of each section of the bridge, they will display the name of each category; they will appear one by one when Hopsalot gives instruction: see below)
      a) Labels sprites are not visible when entering the module

a "lite" version for a quicker read. Companies often keep the design document on the organization's Intranet so it can be readily available to everyone on the team, and some companies only produce electronic versions of the document, finding paper versions to be inadequate.

Not only does the design document help keep things on track during development and production, but it is also the point of origin for many other important documents. For example, the programming department will use the design document for creating its own technical design document, and the test team will use it to prepare a list of all the systems to be tested. The design document also helps the marketing group put together promotional materials and prepare for the product launch. If a manual or clue book or novelization is to be written for the project, the design document will come into play for those endeavors as well.

4. The Dialogue Script

In some companies, as we've seen, the dialogue script is incorporated into the design document, but quite often these scripts are stand-alone documents. The dialogue script sets down all the lines that the characters will speak during the interactive program. These scripts often describe the visuals and the actions that accompany the dialogue, as well. Dialogue may either be spoken by characters on the screen (animated figures or actual actors shot in video) or spoken voice-over by characters who are not visible. Their voices may be heard via a telephone, a radio, or some other device, or the dialogue may be delivered by an off screen character who is offering help and support. In cases when only voice-over actors will be used, and no live characters appear on screen, a separate voice-over dialogue script will be prepared that contains nothing but lines of dialogue.

Formats for interactive scripts vary widely, and no single industry standard exists at this time. Companies will use a format that works best for the types of projects they develop, and many customize their own formats.

One fairly common script style resembles the format for feature film screenplays, except that it incorporates instructions for the interactive elements. This format works particularly well in story-rich projects and games in which the level of interactivity is not too complex. In such scripts, the dialogue is centered in the middle of the page, with the descriptive material extending out further to the left and right margins. When using such a format, it is important to clearly indicate all the dialogue choices being offered to the user, and the responses the other character gives to each one of them. For an example, see Figure 14.2, *Dick and Jane*, a sample script I wrote for instructional purposes. The script incorporates an if/then branching structure.

Some companies prefer to use a multicolumn format. This formatting style roughly resembles the traditional audio/video two-column format used in the making of documentaries and other types of linear programs, where one column is used for visuals (the video) and the other is for voice and sound (the audio). Interactive scripts, however, may use several more columns. At Training Systems Design, the company uses anywhere from three to five columns. The number of columns varies from script to script and even from module to module. The number of columns used depends on the needs of the programming and graphics groups. Their scripts also contain artwork indicating what will appear on the learner's screen. The company calls this type of formatting "scripts and screens."

One example of a five-column scripts and screens format is the company's script for the *Save Your Co-Worker* game, part of the *Code Alert* training program

DICK AND JANE
(Sample script using if/then technique)

JANE, the player character, leaves her house to go for a walk. She is a pretty young woman in her early 20s.

She can 1.) go straight; 2.) turn to the left or 3.) turn to the right.

1. <u>Straight path:</u>
If she goes straight, **then** she must cross a busy street and dodge heavy traffic.

> [The script would continue to follow her actions from this point on]

2. <u>Left path:</u>
If she turns to the left, **then** she will pass a pretty flower garden.

> **If** she stops to pick a flower in the flower garden, **then** a bee will sting her.

> [The script would continue to follow her actions from this point on]

3. <u>Right path:</u>
If she turns to the right, **then** she will come to the house of her handsome neighbor, DICK. Dick is trimming a hedge. Jane can either ignore him or wave at him.

> **If** Jane ignores him and walks on, **then** Dick will continue to trim the hedge.

> [The script would continue to follow her actions from this point on]

> **If** Jane waves at Dick, **then** he will speak to her.

> DICK
> (awkwardly, very shy)
> Oh, hi, Jane. Nice to see you.
> (beat)
> … Uh, any chance you'd be interested in going on a long walk with me on the beach tonight? It's a full moon, and…

User can pick one of three responses for Jane to give:

<u>Response A:</u>
> JANE
> (clearly not interested)
> Oh, sorry, I can't. There's this great sale at the mall tonight… half off designer pumps. Fabulous! Thanks, though.

If A is selected, **then** go to A1.

<u>Response B:</u>
> JANE
> (with genuine enthusiasm)
> Gee, Dick, I'd love to!

If B is selected, **then** go to B1.

<u>Response C:</u>
> JANE
> No way! For heaven's sake, Dick, has anyone ever told you you sound like a total cliché?

Continued

Figure 14.2
Dick and Jane, a sample dialogue script, uses a modified screenplay format and an if/then structure. This script was written for instructional purposes, and thus each *if* and *then* has been emphasized. Script by Carolyn Handler Miller.

241

If C, **then** go to C1.

A1:

> DICK
> (sagging with humiliation)
> Uh, OK. Guess I can take the hint.

B1:

> DICK
> Great! How 'bout I swing by your
> place about 7:30?

C1:

> DICK
> Well, Jane, has anyone ever told you
> you sound like a total [bleep]?!

(Figure 14.3). The script for the game was written by Dr. Robert Steinmetz. The artwork depicts the setting for this portion of the game, an office cubicle, and also shows the bar that keeps track of the learner's score, as well as an icon the learner can click on to receive help (upper left). Column one, labeled Spot, indicates the hot spots on the screen—objects the learner can click on

Figure 14.3
The script for the *Save Your Co-Worker* game written by Dr. Robert Steinmetz for the *Code Alert* training program. It utilizes a five-column scripts and screens format. Document courtesy of Training Systems Design.

(Continued)

Spot	Programming instructions	Value (if selected)	Audio label	Sound effect/voice over
1: Printer	If selected, add value to score bar, play good beep and play audio VO 5.1.2-1A	1	5.1.2-1 A	(Good Beep) it all depends on frequency of use. But, based on where she has her mouse, we can assume this person is right handed, therefore it might be better to swap the phone position and the printer. However, sometimes it is good to move things around to avoid repetitive motion syndrome.
2: Phone	If selected, add value to score bar, play good beep and play audio VO 5.1.2-1A	1		
3: Monitor	If selected, add value to score bar, play good beep and play audio VO 5.1.2-1B	3	5.1.2-1B	(Good Beep) Right! She really should orient herself so that her eyes are level with the monitor and her neck is in a neutral position
4: Head position	If selected, add value to score bar, play good beep and play audio VO 5.1.2-1B	3		
5: Keyboard	If selected, add value to score bar, play bad beep and play audio VO 5.1.2-1C	1	5.1.2-1C	(no beep) The problem isn't really with keyboard…though you could consider it part of a larger overall work habit problem.
6: Mouse	If selected, add value to score bar, play bad beep and play audio VO **5.1.0-3**	0		
7: Lifting position	If selected, add value to score bar, play bad beep and play audio VO 5.1.2-1D	0	5.1.2-1D	(Bad Beep) Nope, he is lifting with his legs, and he is tucking the load in toward his torso.

243

to get some sort of response from the program. Column two, Programming Instructions, gives notes to the programmers, explaining what needs to happen when the user clicks on a specific hot spot. Column 3, Value, shows how the learner's choice will affect his or her score. Column 4, Audio Label, gives the code for the audio that will be heard in Column 5. Column 5, Sound Effect/Voice-Over, describes the audio effects that will be heard and the voice-over dialogue that the narrator will speak.

The multicolumn style of formatting is extremely precise and works particularly well for educational, informational, and training programs. However, it is cumbersome to use for projects that involve a number of dialogue exchanges.

Yet another scripting option is to use a spreadsheet. Spreadsheets are most popular when characters have numerous lines to say and when there are multiple variations of the same speech, such as five different ways for a character to say "Yes! You're right!"

Some companies create their own in-house software programs for script formatting, but off-the-shelf programs are available as well. Two of the better-known commercial products, both of which format linear types of scripts as well, are Final Draft and Movie Magic Screenwriter.

5. Flowcharts

Flowcharts are a visual expression of the narrative line of the program, and they illustrate decision points, branches, and other interactive possibilities. Flowcharting often begins early in the development process as a way to sketch out how portions of the program will work. As the project evolves, flowcharts serve as a valuable communications device for various members of the team, everyone from writers to programmers. They are also useful for explaining the project to people not directly on the team, such as marketing specialists or clients. As a visual method of illustrating how the program works, they can be much easier to grasp than a densely detailed design document.

Flowcharts vary a great deal in style and appearance. The least adorned ones, such as the one designed by Terry Borst to illustrate the interactivity for a short script called *Pop Quiz*, are composed of lines and geometric shapes like a simple diagram (Figure 14.4). More detailed, higher-level flowcharts may also be made for programming, with each element coded to reflect specific functions or types of content.

More elaborate flowcharts may include detailed visuals of the screens and short explanations of functionality, such as the flowcharts produced for *Code Alert* (Figure 14.5). Flowcharts like these are particularly useful for explaining the program to the client or to potential investors.

According to Dr. Steinmetz, the president of Training Systems Design, the company uses two levels of flowcharts. A macro-level flowchart, like the one pictured

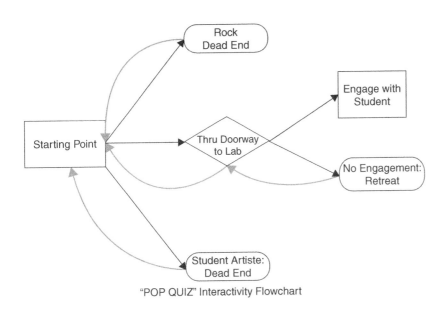

"POP QUIZ" Interactivity Flowchart

Figure 14.4
The flowchart for *Pop Quiz*, a script written by Terry Borst, illustrates the narrative flow of the script and the various branching points. Image courtesy of Terry Borst.

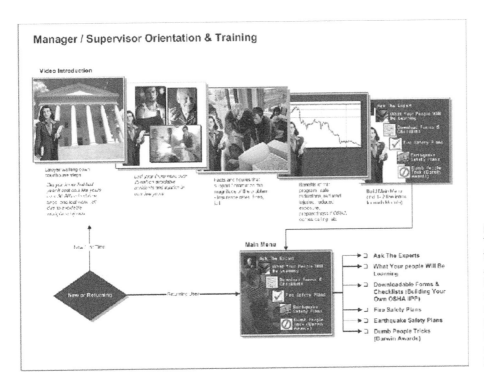

Figure 14.5
The macro-level flowchart for *Code Alert* uses screen images and short explanations to describe how the program works. Document courtesy of Training Systems Design.

here, gives an overview of the training program and is the type of flowchart that would most likely be used in a company proposal. Such flowcharts are made once the major instructional objectives have been identified. A more detailed flowchart, made later in the development period, would indicate all the branching. It would be produced once the specific teaching points had been identified, and it would be cross referenced to the document that laid out the teaching points.

As with scriptwriting, many off-the-shelf software programs are available to make flowcharts. Two that are popular with people in the software industry are Inspiration and Microsoft Visio.

6. Concept Art

Concept art, also called concept drawings or concept sketches, is a visual rendering of some aspect of the program. Such artwork is often used to depict characters and locations. Such images may be used as trial balloons and shown to team members or focus groups to test possible character designs or settings. They will then be refined until a consensus is reached and the team agrees on a final version.

When members of the art department are working on a character design, they might make a series of poses for each character. For example, at Her Interactive, for the *Nancy Drew* games, each character is given a set of eight different poses that reflect the character's personality and emotional state. The clothing the character is wearing can serve as a useful way to reveal character, too. For instance, a depressed young woman may be wrapped in layers of dark clothing, while a cocky politician may stick his thumbs in his suspenders.

7. Storyboards

Storyboards are graphical illustrations of the flow of action and other elements of the content, and they are displayed sequentially. They are somewhat similar to illustrated flowcharts. In the feature film world, movie directors storyboard every scene before filming begins. Storyboarding is often used in interactive media in much the same way. At some companies, it is used primarily for linear sequences, though other companies use them to work out interactive elements as well.

Storyboards resemble comic book art in that each frame advances the story. Each frame will indicate the location of the objects within the scene, the placement of the character or characters, the position of the camera, and the direction of the movement within the scene. Because storyboards are so visual, they are simple to comprehend. They are a useful preproduction tool for many kinds of interactive projects, including VR simulations, immersive environments, and interactive movies—in short, for any interactive endeavor that contains rich visual sequences.

8. Prototype

As noted earlier in this chapter, a prototype is a working model of a small portion of the program. It is the ultimate way of testing a concept. Many people within the interactive community consider it to be a more useful method of trying out the concept's viability than flowcharting or storyboarding because it gives a more accurate indication of the look, feel, and functionality of the program. It's a chance to find out how the navigation works and to actually interact with the material. Prototyping is not necessarily done only at the end of the preproduction process. Small prototypes might also be built along the way to test out specific features. Also, it should be noted that prototyping is not necessarily done for every interactive project. For example, if the company has already made many similar products, and if this is just another product in an already-established line, prototyping may not be called for.

Specialized Documents and Artwork

As mentioned earlier in this chapter, other types of documents are customarily generated during the development process as well, although they do not specifically focus on the creative aspects of the project. They include a technical document containing the technical specifications, a budget, a schedule, a marketing plan, and a test plan. In addition to the fairly ubiquitous types of documents, visuals, and models already described, many companies work with customized tools that are particularly helpful for the type of project they are creating.

For example, at Her Interactive, they use several kinds of special documents when they make the *Nancy Drew* mystery–adventure games. One is the "critical path document," which lists the events that must occur, the discoveries that the player must make, and the obstacles that must be overcome in order to successfully reach the end point in the game. This critical path document is extremely succinct, about a page and a half of bullet points. Another document they produce is the "environmental synergy document," which is organized around specific environments (locations) in the game. For instance, for an interior of a room, it would note how the furniture is arranged, how the room is decorated, what "plot critical" objects it contains, what other less essential clues can be found here, and information about any characters who will be found in this room. It also notes what puzzles need to be solved within this environment. In addition to these two documents, the company also creates a highly detailed puzzle document, which lists all the game's puzzles and specifies how they work. All these documents are cross referenced and collected together as a project bible so that if a team member needs more information on any aspect of the game, it will be easy to find.

When a project contains a great many variables in terms of characters or types of actions, some companies create matrixes to keep track of them. A *matrix* looks much like a table, with horizontal rows and vertical columns. For instance, when I worked on the *Carmen Sandiego* series and was writing dialogue clues to help identify various suspects, I was given a matrix to use. It organized the variable characteristics of the suspects by categories, such as hair color, eye color, favorite hobbies, favorite sport, and favorite foods, and then it listed all the possibilities for each category. I was to write four lines of dialogue clues for each variable.

Within the world of smart toys, inventors and designers create something they call a skeleton logic chart or logic flow document. This tool illustrates how the toy and the child will interact with each other, and it shows the direction of the narrative line. And for projects that are designed to train or teach, a document is often prepared that lists the main teaching points or training goals.

CONCLUSION

As we have seen here, during a well-utilized preproduction period, a concept for an interactive work moves from an extremely rudimentary premise to a well-thought-out project that is detailed enough in every regard to be moved into production. This outcome is only obtainable, however, when teams go through the steps described here or through similar ones that might be more appropriate to their particular project.

Unfortunately, teams are sometimes tempted to jump into production before they've worked out important details, thinking they can do the detail work as they move along. But moving into production prematurely can be a costly mistake.

The development process, when undertaken with care, generates a number of highly useful documents, but it also involves an even more important task: conceptualizing. The creative team needs to work out exactly what the project is, whom it is for, and how people will interact with it. Above all, what about the project will make people eager to spend their time engaged with it? Finding satisfactory answers to questions like these can go a long way toward helping you create a viable project with genuine appeal.

IDEA-GENERATING EXERCISES

1. Pick a work of digital storytelling that you have just begun to work on or that you are interested in doing. The work can be in any medium or for any type of platform. Take this project through the Ten-Step Development Process to determine if any aspect of the project needs more thought or needs to be strengthened before moving more deeply into development.
2. Using the same project from #1 as your model, determine what types of specialized tasks would need to be done during the preproduction process.
3. Again, using the same project as above for your model, determine what kinds of documents you would need to generate in order to effectively take this project through the preproduction stage. What would each type of document contain?
4. Using the same project as your model, consider your marketing specialist. What information do you think this person could give you and the rest of the team that would be helpful? And what documents do you think your team could give to the marketing specialist that would be useful in terms of launching the product?

SECTION 2
Interactive Narrative

CHAPTER 15
The Script Format

Christy Marx

The first thing to know about writing for games is that there are absolutely no standardized formats for game scripts. There is no such thing as "a game script." None, nada, zip. This is especially true when dealing with dialogue writing, where every company may have its own unique method or some proprietary software that is used to create and incorporate dialogue. If you're an in-house writer (full-time employee), there will nearly always be specialized game-engine tools you'll use to create your material.

For the contract writer, there are a few rough guidelines I can give, but don't consider them to be hard-and-fast rules. The producer or whoever hires you may have a clear idea of what she wants you to do. If not, it may be up to you to decide what format to use.

First, you need to know what you might be expected to do. There are certain types of jobs you can typically be hired to do as a game writer. They are:

- FMV or game intro
- Design document
- Game bible
  - Game-world creation
  - Character biographies
  - Game backstory
  - Game story
- Quests or missions
- Cutscenes/cinematics
- Dialogue
- In-game text
- Naming NPCs and game objects
- Technical material or game manual
- Web site and promotional materials

DOI: 10.1016/B978-0-240-81343-1.00015-7

FMV/GAME INTRO

A full-motion video is of broadcast quality and is usually of higher quality than the animation that can be generated by the game engine. With technology constantly advancing, FMV may become obsolete, but what won't change is the desire for a really hot, enticing game intro, something that gets the players' juices flowing and gives a taste of the game world. Essentially, it's the trailer for the game, and runs maybe one to two minutes. It's like writing a trailer for a movie or TV show, except that you'll have to distill the intro from whatever game materials the company provides.

You may be called upon to write an actual introductory scene of some kind—or more likely, it will be a montage of images to capture the mood and feel of the game, as well as to show off the significant game elements (race types, locations, special effects, enemies/monsters, and so on). If it's scenes, you'll be writing dialogue for live actors to record. If it's a montage, there may be some narration to be recorded, or it might have no voice and be done with music only.

This will be non-interactive and will be storyboarded, then created by animators; consequently, you can feel safe using a standard scriptwriting format. My recommendation would be to use an animation script format, because you will almost always be dealing with animation rather than live action.

If you aren't familiar with the animation-script format, go to the first section of this book to read up on animation writing. All the basic rules of animation writing apply here, including the need to keep recorded dialogue (if any) minimal, strong, and pithy.

DESIGN DOCUMENT

It is highly unlikely that you, as a writer, would be asked to write a design document, because this is a designer-level piece of work. However, you need to be aware of what this is in case it comes up in conversation. As defined in Chapter 10, a design document is the complete blueprint of the game. It should be written by the lead or senior designer(s), though many people may contribute to portions of it. The design document needs to contain basically everything that everybody working on the game needs to know about the game—ranging from story elements (descriptions of world, characters, mobs, and so on) to gameplay and technical specs (such as interface, combat systems, lists of items and mobs, stats for items, mobs, and NPCs). Each type of game will naturally require its own sort of design document.

What you would most likely contribute to a design document as a writer are the portions dealing with the game bible, as discussed below.

GAME BIBLE

There isn't a standard format for game bibles either. What you'll be hired to write can vary according to the type and nature of the game, and whatever it is the company wants. Generally speaking, the format of an animation bible works every bit as well for games, so I recommend going to the Animation section of this book and reading up on animation bibles.

How much you do on the bible may depend on what stage the game is in when you're hired. You could be hired at the very beginning of the game development to create the game bible from scratch (with input from the lead designer or game team). You might be hired when the game is already well into development and they want you only to polish up a bible that is in rough form, or perhaps to flesh out only certain portions of it, such as expanding the character bios or adding more depth to the history of the locations.

You could also be asked to describe weapons, vehicles, or other related elements, to come up with a chronology of quests, or any number of other tasks. Consequently, you want to be sure that the company is very specific about what elements you would be covering if hired to write a game bible. You will want to know how much material already exists and how much you will be expected to create on your own.

A game bible will be whatever the person who hires you wants it to be, but these are what I consider to be the main ingredients of a good game bible:

- Game-world creation
- Game backstory
- Game story
- Character biographies (both avatar and NPCs)
- Mobs/monsters/bosses

253

Game-World Creation

Game-world creation is writing the description and explanation of the entire setting of the game, which covers descriptions of geography/terrain, key locations, history of regions or places, descriptions of the various races or NPC types, histories of races, and other related information to create a coherent whole for the world of the game.

To be a good game-world creator, you should have at least some knowledge of a wide range of subjects—such as geography, sociology, politics, economic structures, mythology, personal combat, weaponry, war, military strategy and tactics, religions, foreign cultures, linguistics, physics, art, architecture, technology, weather, biology, plants and animals, trade systems, various professions and skills from primitive to technological, the development of civilization, government power structures, and all forms of human interaction. There's your reading assignment for the afternoon.

Depending on when you're brought into the project, you may be asked to create a world from scratch, or you may be given existing assets that have to be stitched together, or you may be working from a pre-existing property (such as a comic book or movie) that will dictate what you can do.

A good example was the work I did on a PS2 RPG called *The Legend of Alon D'ar*. I was brought in to create the game bible, including the game story. What existed were the art designs for the world and its zones, for the main characters and races, and some mobs. The world was a chunk of land torn from a planet and floating in space, which presented an interesting challenge right there, because by the usual law of physics, nothing could live there. Because it was a fantasy-themed game, there had to be a mystical or magic-based explanation for how this world could exist. It was great fun to work out a history to explain its existence, histories and descriptions for the zones and characters and races, and come up with names for everything and everyone, inspired by the wonderful artwork alone. Plus, it all had to work together and, most importantly, have an inner consistency that allowed it to make sense within the rules that were established.

Imagine how the cataclysmic event that created this Floating World must have affected each of the races, the impact it would have not only on their histories and mythologies, but on their native psyches. Imagine the unique pattern of "day" and "night" such a world would have. What about weather patterns? Imagine how the people inhabiting this terrain deal with having a clearly defined edge to their world beyond which there is only an infinite Void. Why are some of the races human, whereas others are reptilian or amphibious? How does that affect their natures, how they live, what social structures they have, what they believe in, what goals or desires they have? World creation begins with such questions and expands from there.

The same cataclysmic event that created the Floating World provided the hook for the deep backstory of the world, which in turn provided the jumping-off point for the game story and overall big quest that drove the player through the game.

You'll find the game bible and story for *The Legend of Alon D'ar* at *www.christymarx.info*.

The largest amount of game-world creation is done for fantasy and science-fiction games, understandably. In the game bible for *Tao Feng*, I gave the game an alternate-history twist, so that rather than building an entirely new world, it was a matter of detailing how a turning point in real-life history had created a recognizable, but altered, version of the real world in which the Chinese immigrate to what would have been California in the 1840s, establishing the independent nation of New China, spanning most of the western states.

GAME BACKSTORY

The backstory is often woven into the game-world creation. The backstory is everything that is pertinent to the game story up to the point the game begins. With *The Matrix Online*, the first three movies, comics, and animated stories made up the full backstory leading up to the point where the MMOG began. Some characters—such as Neo, Superman, Spider-Man, James Bond, King

Arthur, or Robin Hood—are well enough known that there wouldn't be much need for a detailed backstory. The backstory can be full and deep, or short and concise, depending upon the need of the game. *Shadow of the Colossus*, an award-winning game, had only the sketchiest, most minimal kind of backstory that set up the goal of the game, without feeling the need to explain how or why the hero's situation or the monstrous colossi he must fight came to exist.

How much of the backstory is conveyed in the game is another issue. It may be relegated to the game manual, it may be given in the trailer to the game, or it may be woven into the game itself (for example: The player goes into a library, and there is a book containing details of the backstory that can be read if the player so chooses).

Game Story

This would be the story that drives the game by providing the overall quest/ mission/goal that resolves the game, plus subquests and secondary tasks that provide the twists and turns. It should cover the locations and the NPCs that are critical to the story. It should specify and describe significant puzzles, obstacles, and other vital gameplay elements, along with what, when, and where quest objects are required, obtained, and used. It may need to specify what, when, and where cutscenes or cinematics will occur to convey pieces of the story.

255

The game story is intertwined with the interactive elements of the game because the story is not simply about what the goal is or achieving the goal, but *how* the player can achieve the goal. Some of these stories can be quite linear (often the case with console games), or may need to be highly nonlinear, allowing the player a multitude of possible paths for completing the game, with story components that can be accessed in a nonsequential order. The more linear the story, the more likely the company would be to use an outside writer. The more nonlinear, the more likely that the story will be written by a designer.

It's not unusual to be hired when a game is quite far along and the company has suddenly realized it needs a story or other background material. Game writer Katherine Lawrence called this "reverse engineering," because the writer has to come into an existing game world and work backward to come up with a story that fits into it.

Character Biographies

The two categories of character biographies are the player's main character (the avatar) and the NPCs. An avatar can be a specific character or can be left deliberately vague. How much detail is needed for the avatar's biography will depend on a couple of factors: *(a)* how much detail the company wants, and *(b)* whether the avatar has dialogue in the game. An avatar who will have meaningful (not generic) dialogue in the game needs to be fleshed out well enough to establish that avatar's "voice," meaning how the personality and character traits will come out in dialogue. Will the avatar speak in a formal or casual manner (contemporary approach or based on some historical time period)? Will he use slang? If so, what kind of slang? Is he sly, droll, sarcastic, ribald, poetic, philosophical, timid, loving, hard edged? Young or old? Shaped by what sort of life experiences?

An example of avatars with bios attached would be Lara Croft *(Tomb Raider)*, Max Payne, or hard-edged spy Sam Fisher *(Splinter Cell)*. In *Shadow of the Colossus*, the player's avatar wasn't even given a specific name (he is referred to only as "Wander"), and all the details surrounding the avatar's background and relationship with other characters are left undefined and open to the player's interpretation. For most RPGs and MMOGs, it's up to the player to create the avatar from a set of character options, so the player is creating her own avatar's biography, if any.

Consequently, the bulk of the work lies in creating bios for NPCs. These might be nothing more than a few lines of description, depending on how significant the NPC is. For example, a minor NPC might have a bio that is nothing more than "Mortar Pestwhistle is a Leprechaun engineer with a sly sense of humor and an overbearing pride in his creations." In *The Legend of Alon D'Ar*, the player had three NPC companions that he could control as a group along with his own avatar, so those three characters were given detailed bios—including their own subquests, needs, and goals—which were featured in cutscenes along with the avatar.

In the game bible for *Tao Feng*, besides writing the character bios, I included a paragraph on how each character would interact with, or behave toward, each of the other major characters. Because there were twelve major characters, that meant an additional eleven paragraphs for each character to cover these relationships. This is typical for an animation bible, but somewhat unusual for games.

Mobs/Monsters/Bosses

Most mobs or monsters are usually described by their general race characteristics in the game bible, but if a mob is important enough (a boss or a major villain), it might rate its own special description and possibly a biography.

QUESTS OR MISSIONS

This is another area that dovetails with design, because a quest or mission is a primary interactive element. If a game is big enough, especially something such as an MMOG, there can be a lot of work involved in coming up with and writing quests/missions. A quest needs to have an appropriate reward or payoff—such as XP, money, a quest item, vital information, or unlocking the next piece of gameplay.

256

Here's a list of common types of quests:

- Collecting/gathering: Asks the player to bring back an object or x number of objects—such as "Bring me a bottle of cologne" or "Bring me 5 enemy satellites" or "Bring me 15 black tulips." This could be a quest that simply involves finding and getting the object, or it might involve having to kill mobs or NPCs in order to get the object(s) as drops—such as "Bring me 10 pirate eye patches" or "Bring me 5 chimera snouts."
- Deliver: Asks the player to deliver an object or message to an NPC (sometimes referred to as "FedEx" or courier quests)—such as "Take this letter to X" or "Deliver this crate of weapons to Z."
- Talk to: Asks the player to find a certain NPC and talk to him/her/it. Usually that NPC will have a quest for the player. It can also be used to "push" the player to discover a new location or zone.
- Escort/protect: Asks the player to escort an NPC from point A to point B. This will usually involve being ambushed or encountering danger of some kind while protecting the NPC.
- Fighting mobs: In most cases, tells the player to kill x number of a mob—such as "Kill 10 raging chimeras" or "Kill 20 Putrid Bandits." It can be combined with a collecting quest—such as "Kill 20 Putrid Pirates and bring me their eye patches as proof."
- Fighting elite mob: Asks the player to kill a specific boss mob or NPC, which is more powerful and dangerous than the usual kind—such as "Slay Big Badd, the pack leader of the raging chimeras" or "Destroy the planet-eating Doomship."
- Scouting: Asks the player to scout a dangerous location—as in "Scout the inside of this mine and report what sort of monsters inhabit it" or "Travel to the Sagittarius Sector and determine whether there are enemy ships in the sector."
- Rescuing/setting free: Asks the player to rescue an NPC from a dire situation. This can be similar to an escort quest if it involves helping the NPC get out of the location. Or it might involve bringing something to the NPC instead (such as a potion to cure a mortal wound). A variation on this is completing a task or bringing a quest object that will free an NPC from some form of imprisonment.
- Finding person or object: Asks the player to locate an NPC or game item, which may or may not involve doing anything with them or bringing them back—such as "My husband left for Nasty Valley days ago and hasn't returned. Please find out what happened to him." The player could end up talking to the husband to resolve the quest, or might find the husband's bones and have to return with this info (or a token found on the body) to the original quest giver.
- Capture person or object: Asks the player to capture an NPC, mob, or object, rather than kill or destroy it—as in "Take this rune and use it to enchant a raging chimera, then lead it back here to me" or "Capture the supply depot."

257

- Unraveling clues: Gives the player clues to unravel some sort of mystery. This is often used with a linked quest (see below).
- Chained, linked: Many quests are chained together so that the first quest leads to a second related quest, which leads to a third related quest, and so on. Any of the above quest types (or others not listed here) can be combined in a chain of quests. Usually the tasks become more difficult as the chain progresses.

CUTSCENES AND CINEMATICS

These are more commonly used in the linear types of games and can serve more than one purpose. Most cutscenes/cinematics are used to reveal key pieces of the story and to advance the story for the player. They can have an emotional payoff, or they can be bald chunks of data. They can also be used to validate the player for accomplishing something special (a pat-on-the-back "way to go!" moment).

You will want to have a discussion up front with the producer or designer about what the game engine can or can't do in creating the cutscenes/cinematics. A lot of times, there will be "easy" and "hard" ways to do the scene in the engine. For example, changing the camera angle in the middle of the scene could be either easy or incredibly hard, depending on the engine design. Another example: on one PS2 game, I was initially told that the characters wouldn't be able to move their lips, let alone do lip-synching. With that in mind, I carefully wrote the scenes using animation-writing techniques to min-imize the amount of time the camera lingered on a character's face, such as using over-the-shoulder shots for the speaking character rather than looking at the speaking character from the front.

Most frequently, cutscenes/cinematics are noninteractive. Control of the game is taken away from the player, who is then expected to stand and watch the scene unfold. A wise designer will allow the player to click past the cutscene/cinematic if he doesn't feel like following the story thread.

In *Half-Life 2*, a clever approach was taken in which the cutscenes/cinematics would play out inside an enclosed environment so that the player couldn't conveniently leave right away, but the player was allowed to continue interact-ing with the environment. This gave the player the option to do something else in the location, and either ignore the scene or pay attention to it if she wished. There are occasionally mini-cinematics in *World of Warcraft* where a short scene plays out between a couple of NPCs, with the player free to watch or move on to another part of the game (in this case, however, the cinematics don't affect an overall game story).

The important thing to remember about cutscenes/cinematics is that they should be *short*—preferably one to two pages in a standard live-action-script format, slightly more if written in an animation-script format. Again, apply the general rules of animation writing. Keep the dialogue minimal, strong, and pithy.

If you're writing the story that includes indications for the cutscenes/cinematics, there are two things to bear in mind as you create the story:

- There is probably a budget and time limit to how many cutscenes the developers can put into the game, so determine ahead of time what the limit is. Craft the story so that you could lose two to three or more cutscenes should there be a cut in the schedule or budget.
- Be careful not to craft a story that requires big chunks of exposition or too much explanation of events in the cutscenes. Try to limit each cutscene to revealing *one* key piece of story, maybe two, but not three or four. Cutscenes need to be tiny nuggets of story, not big chunks of exposition.

You'll find a few examples of cinematics from *The Legend of Alon D'ar* at *www.christymarx.info*.

DIALOGUE

Setting aside cutscenes/cinematics, 99 percent of dialogue you might be hired to write will be for NPCs. Common types of dialogue include the following:

- Giving quests/missions.
- Giving information, training, directions (to a location).
- Giving hints: "Did you go to Sagittarius Sector yet?"
- Generic greetings: "Hi, how ya doing?"
- Generic threats: "Die, mangy cur!"
- Generic default replies: "I don't know what to do with that."
- Generic vendors (selling and buying game items): "Buy from me. I'll give you such a deal."
- Adding flavor: for example, a storyteller who relates tales that may not be significant to the story, but adds general flavor to the background material.

259

You'll want to know up front whether the dialogue will be done as text or as voice. Some games will combine the two and play audio while also showing the dialogue as text. Both ways present you with limitations in terms of length, so once again apply the rules of animation writing—keep it short and pithy. If it's text, you could potentially have a more specific limitation, such as a certain number of characters (letters) and spaces per speech so that it doesn't occupy too large a balloon or dialogue box when on the screen.

Because voice is expensive, time-consuming, and creates large sound files, it tends to be used sparingly. You should read audio dialogue out loud to yourself to make sure it's easy to say and sounds right when spoken. Better yet, record yourself speaking the lines and play them back to yourself. A line that looks fine in text can sometimes be a clunker when spoken out loud. Saying the lines out loud will call your attention to speeches or sentences that are too long.

If the developer has devised specific methods of integrating dialogue into the game, you may be required to learn a special piece of software. This method can be different for each company, so you need to be good at adapting to new software. And because of this, there is nothing like a standard format. However, it is a common practice to put game dialogue into a TV/film-script format when it's being given to actors for recording.

Writing game dialogue can involve two of the game-design elements described in Chapter 10: Variables and choice.

Variables

The variables that affect dialogue depend upon the programming "flags" that need to be checked before the correct piece of dialogue is fed to the player. These flags are conditions the game code looks for. This gets back to the "*If this, then this . . .*" formula. "*If* this condition exists, *then* this dialogue is given." There can be an infinite number of such conditions, but here are some of the most common ones:

- What level is the player?
- Is the player on a certain quest?
- Is the player incomplete on the quest?
- Has the player completed the quest?
- Does the player have a certain game item or quest object?
- If buying something, does the player have enough money?
- Has the player spoken to the NPC before?
- Has the player spoken to some other NPC yet?
- Does the player belong to a certain race or class?
- Does the player have a race or class bias in relation to the NPC (for example, friendly, neutral, hostile)?
- Has the player been to a certain location yet?
- Has the player done a specific action yet?

There might be only one variable/condition tied to a piece of dialogue, or there could be two or several in combination—or there could be none, of course. Some games don't have these complexities of dialogue. But for those that do, it will be vital to you as the writer to have a full and detailed understanding of what variables/conditions will affect the dialogue, so that you can tailor the dialogue accordingly.

You'll need to be good at juggling these variables in your head and making sure one piece of dialogue doesn't contradict another, especially if they can be accessed in a nonsequential manner.

For example, an NPC could have dialogue that pertains to a particular quest that can be given only once the player is level 10, and only if the player is of the warrior class, but any player is free to talk to the NPC at any time. The variables and attendant dialogue might look something like this:

```
;This NPC is just there to give the player hints
about the Sagittarius quest if the player is a
warrior, or to push the player to another zone
if not a warrior.

//if player is a NOT a WARRIOR:

                    NPC
    I hear there's a guy in the Betelgeuse
    sector that's looking for somebody like
    you.

//if player is a WARRIOR and is LESSER THAN level 10,
and has NOT spoken to the NPC before:

                    NPC
    You've got the look of someone who's
    hunting for trouble. Get some more
    experience under your belt, and I might
    help you with that.

//if player is a WARRIOR and is LESSER THAN level 10
and has spoken to the NPC once or more before:

                    NPC
    You're too green to bother with. Get
    yourself more experience before you
    bother me again.

//if player is a WARRIOR and IS level 10 or more and
does NOT have the Sagittarius quest:

                    NPC
    You look like someone in need of a job.
    Talk to Larry the Leech over there, if
    you're up to risking your neck.

//if player is a WARRIOR and IS level 10 or more and
does NOT have the Sagittarius quest and has spoken
to the NPC once or more before:

                    NPC
    Do I look like I have nothing better to
    do than give advice?
                                   (Continued)
```

261

```
//if player has the Sagittarius quest and has NOT
spoken to the NPC before:

                        NPC
     So you're the Leech's new sucker . . .
     ah, I mean recruit. Good luck to ya.

//if player has the Sagittarius quest and has spoken
to the NPC once before:

                        NPC
     Why are you hanging around here? Aren't
     you supposed to be in the Sagittarius
     sector?

//if player has the Sagittarius quest and has spoken
to the NPC twice or more before:

                        NPC
     What do you want, a medal? Get a move
     on.

//if player has COMPLETED the Sagittarius quest and
spoke to the NPC BEFORE taking the quest:

                        NPC
     So you worked for the Leech and got out
     in one piece. I'm impressed. I'll spread
     the word that you can be trusted.

//if player has COMPLETED the Sagittarius quest and
has NOT spoken to the NPC before, use any one of the
following dialogues chosen at random:

                        NPC
     Nice day, if we don't get sucked into a
     black hole.

                        NPC
     Something you want?

                        NPC
     What do you want, an autograph? Move
     along.
```

Hopefully, what you have noticed about that example is that the more variables the game design allows in the NPC dialogue, the more specific the dialogue can become (making the game feel "smarter"), but it also increases the amount of both coding and dialogue writing that has to be done. In that short example, there are a dozen or more conditions that a programmer has to code (including flags that must be *created* by talking to that NPC), which is one reason for a push to keep game dialogue limited. In game design, there is a constant tension between wanting to make a game feel smart and more aware of exactly what the player is doing vs. the need to keep the writing and programming from getting out of control.

One more thing about the example on the previous pages—it's one-sided and nonbranching. Only the NPC has lines, assumedly initiated by the player clicking on the NPC, and there is no input of player dialogue. It's minimally interactive because the player can't affect it and can't do anything other than read or hear it. Once you go the extra step of adding player dialogue, you move into the area of player choice and branching dialogue.

CHOICE

The biggest mistake a non–game writer tends to make is assuming that game dialogue always consists of simple branching-dialogue trees. Many games avoid using branching dialogue, or have adapted it to be more variable. However, because you could encounter some form of it, it's a good idea to understand the basics as well as the pitfalls. The trick with branching forms of dialogue (Figure 15.1) is to keep the dialogue from branching out of control. At some point, each branch has to come to an end or become a dead end, or the branches could become infinite. Notice from this simple example how quickly branches can proliferate.

263

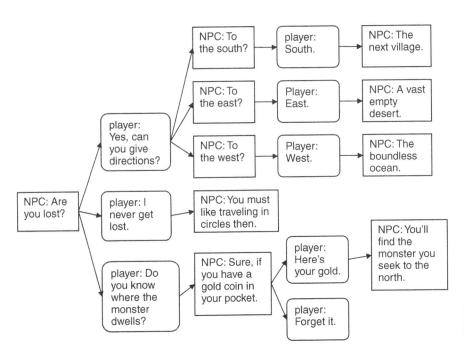

Figure 15.1
Example of branching dialogue.

In the above example, one branch dead-ends pretty quickly. One branch will lead to useful data about a particular direction, but only if the player pays for it. But the remaining branches allow the player to deduce the right direction without paying (assuming the player has the same dialogue options to choose from each time he talks to the NPC).

The other pitfall to avoid is creating branches that don't serve a real purpose and create only an illusion of choice. You would never, for example, want to do this (Figure 15.2).

That's a waste of the player's time—and frustrating to boot. Every branch and each dialogue option should have a purpose, or it shouldn't be there. At the same time, each branch has to end somewhere, with the player feeling that taking the branch was worth it—either in getting useful info, receiving something (reward), opening up an option to do something (such as buy, sell, or trade), getting backstory flavor, or, at the very least, being given something amusing (a joke or insult).

Bear in mind that branching dialogue will be further complicated by the same types of variables and conditions as nonbranching dialogue. On one MMOG, we wrote branching dialogues for numerous variables (checking for player level, phase of the game, what step in a quest the player had reached, whether a reward was due, and so forth), with some of the branches linking to other files of branching dialogue with more variables and conditions. In more complex cases, we had up to six interconnected files of complex dialogue trees that linked via special branches from a main file.

Another variable that could come up in some games is the race or class bias that could be attached to both the NPC and the player. Being friendly, neutral, or hostile toward a particular race or class could require different dialogues to account for the bias.

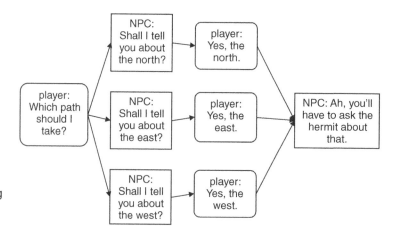

Figure 15.2
Example of branching dialogue with false branches.

In summary, writing dialogue can range from fairly simple to intensely complex, but one thing remains the same—you must be able to write clever, compelling, useful, and entertaining dialogue limited to a few sentences at a time.

SLANG AND FANTASY LANGUAGE

You will find this section in the Animation chapters, but it bears repeating here.

Using contemporary slang will make you sound hip, but will also quickly date the game. Many clever writers get around this by inventing slang that doesn't really exist, but sounds appropriate for the genre. This is even more useful when dealing with a futuristic or science-fiction game where you don't want modern slang to sound out of place or archaic . . . unless that's by deliberate intent.

If you're going to use foreign slang, *do your homework!* It's embarrassing to hear or read slang—say, for a contemporary Australian—that hasn't been used for twenty years except as a joke.

Then there's fantasy. When writing a pure fantasy game, it's easy to forget how modern some of our phrases are. "Fast as lightning" is fine, but "faster than a bullet" is a problem if your characters use only swords. Unless you're writing a total parody, you don't want to hear a medieval knight say, "Wow, cool." Be careful to avoid anachronistic slang.

I came up with the Marx Fantasy Dialogue Scale to differentiate the various ways in which fantasy dialogue could be spoken, ranging from colloquial/modern (No. 1) to High Epic/Poetic (No. 5). Here's an example:

1. He doesn't know what he's doing.
2. He does not know what he is doing.
3. He does not know what he does.
4. He knows not what he does.
5. He knows not what his purpose is, for confusion lies heavy upon him.

You would rarely want to use No. 5, because it's wordy and sounds least natural to modern ears. Using purely colloquial language can sound jarring in some fantasy settings. Creating the right fantasy dialogue depends a great deal on how you use contractions, the word arrangement and sentence structure, and the vocabulary you employ.

IN-GAME TEXT

This is written material the player might come across in the game. One example mentioned previously is finding books that can be opened and read. Other examples would be letters, journals, diaries, dispatches, notes, briefings, decrypted code, and other such items that can be found or are given to the player as part of a quest. It might be text that appears on a monitor, PDA, or other communication device that the player uses in the game.

TECHNICAL MATERIAL OR GAME MANUAL

In addition to the game itself, there is writing that needs to be done to explain to the player how the game works and other technical-writing needs. When I was making adventure games for Sierra On-Line, I wrote the game book that came with the game. The book gave backstory and other general information about the game and interface. I also wrote the "hint book," a separate book that the players could consult for hints when they felt stuck or unable to progress.

You could be asked to write other game-related material that falls outside the game—such as compiling a list of quest objects and where they're found, a chronology of quests, a walkthrough, and so on.

WEB SITE AND PROMOTIONAL MATERIALS

Most games have a Web site to help promote the game and create a sense of community for it. You could be hired to write material—of either a technical nature or purely promotional—for the Web site, or you could be hired to write marketing material for other media.

For example, for *The Matrix Online*, I was hired to take the brief descriptions of the many skills and abilities the player could learn in the game and "*Matrix*-ize" them, meaning rewrite them in a way that would fit with how data are downloaded into someone's brain in the *Matrix* movies. Those descriptions were intended as additional material for the game's Web site. On another game, I was asked to recraft the game bible into a shorter version that could be used by the marketing people in PR releases.

BEYOND THE BASICS (ADVICE, TIPS, AND TRICKS)

Some writers who have expressed an interest in writing for games have worried about what level of technical skill they need to have, in terms of knowing programming or special software. Because each company can have its own approach, there isn't any particular software to learn ahead of time, but—and this is a big but—you should be technically inclined, and able to quickly learn, new pieces of software. Obviously, you'll need to know one of the major word-processing programs, such as Microsoft Word. Microsoft Excel is another program that is heavily used in the business (including sometimes writing dialog) and it's wise to have some familiarity with Excel.

You don't need to know programming or be able to write code. However, you could potentially be asked to incorporate bits of code, so it doesn't hurt to pick up whatever basics you can along the way. If you can write some basic HTML or use Flash, you have taken a good step toward proving that you can handle a basic scripting language. If a company wants you to incorporate bits of code, they'll provide you with the necessary training or instructions. They won't expect you to come in the door knowing it.

Version Control

You need to have good organizational skills and the means to track the many versions and variations of the work you do. It will be vital to have good communication with the producer, product manager, or lead/senior designer (whoever the point person is) on how to name your narrative or dialogue game files. If you're writing only a game bible, this may not be as crucial. But if you're writing numerous files, such as dialogue for lots of NPCs or a large batch of missions, it is absolutely crucial.

Either they, or you, need to establish precisely what identifiers will quickly and easily tell anyone working on the game what that file is about, what it attaches to, what NPC or zone it belongs to, and so forth. Additionally, there must be an identifier (such as a date) that will immediately indicate which is the most current, latest, and/or approved version of the file.

Without careful version control, you end up in the hell of version confusion, with no one quite sure which is the latest or approved version, or what goes where in the game. Some companies have "data wranglers," whose job it is to oversee such assets and make sure there's a workable system of asset identification and version control.

Once you plunge into a game-writing project, make sure to find out whom to deal with and what system they want to use for version control.

267

Recording Dialogue

If you write game dialogue that will be recorded by actors, the chance is slim, though not impossible, that you'll be asked to attend the recording sessions. If you do get the chance to attend, you should go for it. As the writer, your input to the voice director and actors could be invaluable, because you will know better than anyone else what the context is and what the emotional tone of the dialogue should be. Plus, it's a good way for you to learn what works or doesn't work in spoken dialogue.

Because that *is* rare, you should be aware that the overwhelming majority of the time, actors will record their lines alone, not in the presence of other actors. A game that has a superbig budget and uses big-name movie actors might go the extra step (and considerable expense) of getting their big names together at the same time in a recording studio so they deliver their lines to one another in a more natural way. That would be the exception.

Instead, what you have are actors with sheets of paper that usually show only their lines. If they're really lucky, the actors might be given a full script so they can see what other characters are saying, but you can't count on that. A voice director will feed other lines to the actors (if it's back-and-forth dialogue), so that the actors at least have something to respond to. And hopefully, above the line of dialogue, there will be a line or two of additional information that gives some idea of the situation or circumstance in which the line is delivered.

However, if you look at the sample presented earlier in this chapter, the descriptions of the game variables may not provide the actors with much help. A good actor will draw the meaning out of the lines, but some lines may not by themselves clue the actor in to how the dialogue should be delivered.

For that reason, I recommend the free use of parentheticals when writing audio game dialogue. If you've read the Animation chapters, or are familiar with scriptwriting, you know what this means. For those who don't, parentheticals are one or two words in parentheses beneath the character's name, indicating the emotional tone or attitude for the line.

Consider this line:

```
                    NPC
        You don't want to go there.
```

Imagine how many different ways a line like that could be delivered, if the actor had no indication of what to do with it. If you include a parenthetical, you greatly increase the odds that the line will be recorded in the emotional tone you intended.

Here are some possibilities:

```
                    NPC
             (friendly concern)
        You don't want to go there.

                    NPC
             (condescending)
        You don't want to go there.

                    NPC
                (afraid)
        You don't want to go there.

                    NPC
              (impatient)
        You don't want to go there.

                    NPC
             (angry, stern)
        You don't want to go there.

                    NPC
            (cool, indifferent)
        You don't want to go there.
```

This is not to say that you should overdo the use of parenthenticals. Limit them to the pieces of dialogue that could be interpreted in more than one way.

One more item that is tremendously useful for a recording session is to include along with the recording script a paragraph or two of background information about each character. That way, if the actors haven't been provided with other information beforehand, they will at least have something that fills them in on the nature of the characters they're portraying.

GAME BIBLE, GAME STORY, AND CINEMATIC SAMPLES

You will find the game bible, game story, and examples of cinematics for the PS2 action RPG titled *The Legend of Alon D'ar* available to read and study at *www.christymarx.info*. The developer was Stormfront Studios, and the publisher was Ubisoft.

269

CHAPTER 16

Script and Proposal Formatting

Timothy Garrand

CHAPTER OVERVIEW

Multimedia and the Web's use of many media and interactivity make script formatting difficult. Nevertheless, it is essential for writers to present their ideas effectively on paper so that clients and production team members can visualize their ideas. At this point in the industry, there is no one set format for all situations. The format chosen depends on the demands of the individual production. After discussing scriptwriting software, this chapter defines the following formats:

271

- Web site outlines
- Treatments
- Proposals and design documents
- Single-column scripts
- Multicolumn scripts

SCRIPTING SOFTWARE

There are number of software programs dedicated to script formatting and developing large writing projects, including:

- CopyWrite (Mac) is a project management tool for writers. It allows a writer to browse, organize, and manage the documents and information for a project.
- StoryView helps organize large writing projects. It is a visual outliner for writers that lets a writer brainstorm, create, structure, and organize ideas.
- WordMenu is an all-in-one dictionary, thesaurus, almanac, and more.
- Final Draft Screenplay and Movie Magic are two popular screenplay formatting and script development software programs.

DOI: 10.1016/B978-0-240-81343-1.00016-9

Some writers swear by these programs and think that it makes the writing process much easier. The Web sites for these programs are at the end of this chapter. Most of them have free demos so you can try them out and see if they work for you.

My own feeling, and that of many of the writers interviewed for this book, is that if you are competent with a major word processing program, such as MSWord, you don't really need a dedicated scriptwriting program. The key is in becoming skilled with tables and learning how to create macros. Macros allow you to automate certain formatting functions and make writing a script much easier. If you don't know how to use macros, go to the help section of your software, search for macros, and follow the instructions.

Using your current word processor will not only save you money and the time it would take to learn a new program, it will also insure compatibility. Scripts and other documents are often shared with other members of the multimedia team. If you write in a major word processor, chances are that other members of the team will be able to open your files and edit your documents. If you use specialized script formatting software, accessibility may not be the case, unless the software can export to a standard format, such as MSWord or RTF. This export feature should be a major consideration before buying one of these specialized scriptwriting tools.

PRELIMINARY DOCUMENTS: OUTLINES, PROPOSALS, AND DESIGN DOCUMENTS

A project's script or detailed design document includes every word of text, narration and dialogue; descriptions of all the images, videos, and animations; and explanations of the linking and functional elements. Fortunately, projects almost never start with a script. Usually some sort of preliminary written document is presented to the client and other members of the production team before the final script is written. This is useful for clients who may have difficulty understanding an interactive script. It also ensures that the basic goals of the project are being achieved before the fine details are worked out in the script. Sometimes the preliminary form itself, such as a Web site outline, is adequate to get the production green-lighted with the client.

Outlines

Before writing a full text script of all the content on a Web site or another information heavy program, such as an online course, it is useful to write a content outline and a flowchart to explain the content and navigation to the client and production team.

The flowchart illustrates the overall navigation, structure, and size of the site; the outline provides more details about the actual content and functionality of the individual pages. The outline sample that follows is most effectively used with an accompanying flowchart. The client consults the chart for overall structure, and then reads the outline for the details. The structure of each page on the outline below is fairly simple. The outline should be adjusted to match the specific project. The elements include:

- Title: The page title, which should be the same as what is on the flowchart.
- Image: Describes possible images for the page, including animations or videos.
- Text: Describes on-screen text.
- Links: Includes all the links on this page from text within the page and from the navigation bar or menu.
- Navigation: The specific buttons that will have to be created for the navigation bar or menu.
- Functionality: This describes what the user can do on this page besides click and read. For example, if it is a real estate site, as in the example below, can the user search for properties or calculate a mortgage payment?

A useful feature of Inspiration software, which I use to create my outlines, is that it will convert the outline to HTML for publishing to a client's review site on the Web. Part of this conversion creates a clickable menu at the top of the outline for every page in the site, so the client can quickly jump to the page they want.

PARTIAL OUTLINE OF THE *PRUDENTIAL VERANI* WEB SITE

Home Page

TITLE: PRUDENTIAL VERANI REALTY: The Real Estate and Relocation Resource for Southern NH

IMAGE: Images that demonstrate that Verani is a professional, friendly place. Possible images: Prudential logo, friendly Verani staff, Verani office, people enjoying a beautiful home. Might have other images on page to lead user to some of our key features, such as a calculator image for the tools and an email icon for our custom email notification service. Images will be small or designed in such a way that the page will load quickly.

TEXT: Explain that we are part of Prudential, one of the largest corporations in the world, but also a family-owned company with strong roots in Southern New Hampshire. We have the resources to sell your property effectively and/or make your home search efficient and successful. Also should introduce some of the key features of the site, such as our searches, custom email notification tools, extensive information resources, and so on. Near the bottom of the page should be a short disclaimer stating that we have made every effort to make the information on this site accurate but are not liable for any errors or omissions; please see our Terms of Use Policy.

LINKS: Homes & Land, New Construction, Commercial & Industrial, Relocation Services, Verani Mortgage and Title, Real Estate Information & Resources, News & Special Events, Search/Site Map, About Us/Contact.

Might also have a link from a calculator image to the tools and calculator section.

In text on the bottom of the page and on every page will be links to Terms of Use, Privacy Statements and a webmaster email link.

NAVIGATION BAR: Homes & Land, New Construction, Commercial & Industrial, Relocation Services, Verani Mortgage and Title, Real Estate Information & Resources, News & Special Events, Search/Site Map, About Us/Contact.

I. HOMES & LAND

TITLE: Homes & Land

IMAGE: Small image of attractive house. This could be the same picture all the time or a regularly changing featured house.

TEXT: Briefly explain the range of properties we offer and the area we cover. Direct the user to the search page and other services that will help with moving and home buying, such as Relocation Services, the How to Buy a Property Section, Home Preference Check List/ Questionnaire, & New Construction.

LINKS: Home, Search, Contact, Relocation Services, the How to Buy a Property Section, Home Preference Check List/Questionnaire, & New Construction.

NAVIGATION BAR: Home, Search, Contact

IA. CONTACT AN AGENT

TITLE: Contact Us

IMAGE: Photo of friendly agent.

TEXT: Phone numbers, addresses, and emails for all offices. Plus a form that the user can fill out and submit so that we can contact them.

LINKS: Home Page, Search, Contact, Homes & Land.

NAVIGATION BAR: Home Page, Search, Contact, Homes & Land.

FUNCTIONALITY: Users can fill out form with their address and email, click the type of information they want, write a short note and submit it to us. Message will go to different people at Prudential Verani depending on what type of information the user requests.

Copyright Prudential Verani Realty.

Treatments

Although a treatment could be used for a preliminary description of a Web site, it is more commonly used for CD-ROM or DVD multimedia programs. The treatment, a form borrowed from linear film or TV writing, describes the structure and key elements of a project in a form similar to an essay or a short story. Guidelines for treatment writing include:

- Use the third person (e.g., "He shambles," not "I shamble" or "you shamble").
- Use the present tense ("he shambles," not "he shambled").
- Write visually. Be descriptive, but don't call shots.
- Capitalize:
  - Character names when they first appear.
  - Major sound effects.
  - Technical directions, such as ROLLOVER, LINK, etc. (but don't use unless necessary).
- Usually summarize on-screen text, dialogue, and narration, although a few bits of dialogue or narration are allowed if they help present the material.
- Usually double-space treatments, although sometimes they are single-spaced, with chapter or section headings in all capitals.

MULTIMEDIA INFORMATIONAL TREATMENT SAMPLE

The following sample is from the conclusion of the treatment for *The Nauticus Shipbuilding Company*, a multimedia program about shipbuilding presented on a museum kiosk.

Conclusion: After the last component has been selected, a 3D animation sequence depicts the launching of the vessel. If the design is suitable for the mission, the visitor will see a depiction of their design successfully carrying out the mission. If the design is fundamentally flawed, the vessel will be shown sinking.

```
Some evaluation will be provided as to the ability of
the visitor's design to carry out the selected mission.
Finally, the visitor will be given the opportunity to
print out his design and evaluation.
```

NARRATIVE TREATMENT SAMPLE

A narrative interactive treatment is sometimes called a walkthrough. The following is a section of the walkthrough for *The Pandora Directive*.

```
In the introductory conversation with Gordon
Fitzpatrick, you learn that he is looking for a
Dr. Thomas Malloy, who recently stayed at the Ritz
Hotel. Fitzpatrick and Malloy used to work together
(where, unspecified). Fitzpatrick then says he saw a
photograph of Malloy in the Bay City Mirror and found
out that the photograph had been taken at a local
university (San Francisco Tech). Fitzpatrick gives Tex
a copy of the photo.
```

Proposals and Design Documents

A treatment is usually only one component of the first detailed description of an interactive project. This preliminary description is sometimes called a high-level design document proposal, a design proposal or just a proposal.

FORMAT FOR AN INFORMATIONAL DESIGN DOCUMENT PROPOSAL

A proposal can be in many forms. One fairly standard approach includes the following elements.

- Design objective. This is a short description of what the program hopes to accomplish. It is sometimes no more than a paragraph, but it is important because it is the first chance to grab the reader.
- Creative treatment. This is a detailed description of the entire program. It will run for many pages, depending on the size of the project.
- Navigation. This is a description of the interface and how the user will navigate through the program. It often includes a navigation flowchart. The navigation is also described in the treatment.
- Production and marketing. Design documents often have sections dealing with the project schedule or, if it is a mass-market piece, ideas for marketing the program to the public. Biographies of the writer, designer, and other key personnel are sometimes included here.

FORMAT FOR A NARRATIVE PROPOSAL

A proposal for a multimedia program that includes a story would follow much of the same format as above. It may, however, call the treatment a "story summary." There may also be sections describing the characters.

STORYBOARDS, SCRIPTS, AND FINAL DOCUMENTS

Unlike the preliminary documents discussed above that summarize the key features of a program, the script details every element of a piece. The examples that follow are only a few of the interactive script formats in use, but they present enough options that you should be able to find something that can be adapted for your production.

Be aware that many productions don't use traditional scripts at all and instead use combinations of flowcharts, dialogue lists, walkthroughs, and other types of written material.

Linear Screenplay Format

Many approaches to formatting scripts for interactive multimedia use linear screenplay or teleplay format as their basis and then add variations, so it is useful to understand the specifics of the linear screenplay format.

Script format is important because the running time of a video is judged by the number of pages. One page, if it is typed in proper format, is roughly one minute of screen time. There are variations on the example below, such as greater use of double-spacing in television writing, but the example is a standard screenplay format that can readily be adapted to different situations. Note that margins and line spacing are distorted in the example below to allow space for the directions.

The format below includes some technical and camera directions. Be aware that if you are writing a script to hand off to a director or multimedia designer, they may not want such directions included. In that case, you can still use the same format below, but leave out the technical and shot material, such as "Camera Dollies Back."

DIRECTIONS

Top margin = 1". Number pages in upper right-hand corner. No number on page 1.	THE MULTIMEDIA WRITER
Slug lines are typed in CAPS at the beginning of each scene, telling whether scene is INT. or EXT. (interior or exterior), location of scene, and day or night.	FADE IN: INT. ARNOLD'S BEDROOM DAY
Scene Description: Left margin 1.75", right margin 1" (7.5" if measured from left).	The room is a wreck. The floor is covered with papers and trash, the bed is unmade and cigarette butts litter the desk and windowsills.

Break long descriptions into several short paragraphs. The first time a character's name appears in the scene description, type it in CAPS.

Single-space within scene description or dialogue. Add a blank line space between dialogue passages, scene description paragraphs, and slug lines.

Dialogue: left margin = 3.0", right margin = 2" (or 6.5" if measured from left).

Name of person speaking dialogue is in CAPS and centered over the dialogue. No space between speaker's name and dialogue.

Dialogue direction is typed in small letters, centered under speaker and placed in parentheses.

ARNOLD throws the door open and stumbles into the room. **CAMERA DOLLIES BACK** with him. Arnold is in his early twenties, thin and unkempt. His once handsome features are contorted in agony. He clutches what appears to be multimedia manuscript in his hand.

He stumbles to the floor and falls to his knees, pulling the script to his bosom. He falls back with a scream and hits the floor in agony, dropping the script.

The title of the manuscript is revealed to be The Great American Computer Game.

>   **ARNOLD (OS)***
>   (whispering)
>   Why me?

>   **DISSOLVE TO:**

EXT. ARNOLD'S APARTMENT DAY LONG SHOT

The door of the apartment swings open and Arnold stumbles out clutching his script.

>   **ARNOLD**
>   I keep asking myself:
>   What is the secret?

The booming, powerful, authoritative voice from the unseen NARRATOR of our film is heard.

>   **NARRATOR (VO)****
>   (booming)
>   Arnold never did learn the secret.
>   He should have read Tim Garrand's
>   *Writing for Multimedia and the Web.*

Camera movements, such as tilt, pan, track, dolly, and zoom typed in CAPS in the scene description. On right side of page are placed: Fade out and Dissolve to. On left is Fade in.

Bottom margin = 1/2–1". It depends on how dialogue breaks. Don't break dialogue over 2 pages.

THE CAMERA QUICKLY ZOOMS IN TO Arnold. He tosses away his script in the trash and runs off.

His script sits on the top of the trashcan, its pages fluttering sadly in the breeze.

FADE OUT.

---

*(OS) next to the speaker means off-screen. The character is part of the action, but we do not see him or her in this particular shot. A character yelling from the bathroom while the camera focuses on the bedroom is an example of an off-screen voice. Or, as in the example above, the camera could simply be focused on an object in the same room as the character, leaving the character nearby but off-screen.

**(VO) next to the speaker means voice-over. This indicates that the speaker is not a part of the film or video's action. A modern newscaster narrating a World War I documentary is an example of VO.

Single-Column, Simple If-Then Interactive Format

Use: Narrative or informational programs with limited interactivity, usually at the scene level. Because it is a single-column script, it would not be well suited to a program with extensive voice-over narration. That usually requires a multi-column script, which is explained later in this chapter under "Double-Column Format" and "Triple-Column Format."

Description: This script is similar to the linear screenplay described above, except that at various points in the script the user is given two or three choices of different scenes. This type of script can be used when the inter-activity is fairly simple. The following example is part of an interactive museum piece located at the National Scouting Museum in Irving, Texas. In this story, the characters have to choose whether to search the school, the farm or the neighborhood for a missing child. The situation is first outlined in a linear fashion, and then the options follow: first the school scene option, then the farm scene option. The neighborhood option is not included in this sample.

The complete script is included in the "Boy Scout Patrol" section of the book, available at www.focalpress.com/9780240813431

BOY SCOUT PATROL THEATER

by Maria O'Meara

SCENE 2

TROOP HQ

2-1. WS GROUP

                    ALEX

  Okay. We all know why we're here. Bob has
  divided the map up into areas. We're going to
  use the buddy system to cover each one.

                    BOB

  Here's a map of the area we're searching.

2-2. MAP GRAPHIC

                    BOB (voice-over)

  This is where she was last seen—the school.
  Here's where she lives. Between the two is the
  old Wilson Farm.

WHICH PART DO YOU WANT TO SEARCH?

A. THE SCHOOL

B. THE FARM

C. THE GIRL's NEIGHBORHOOD

IF A. THE SCHOOL

SCENE 2A

2A-1. CU ALEX

                    ALEX

  Chas and Don, you guys go see if she's not
  still hanging around the school.

M-1.

TRANSITION MONTAGE TO SCHOOL

1. POV HALLWAY

2. POV SCIENCE ROOM

3. POV POOL

4. POV STAIRS

```
SCENE 3

3-1. 2 SHOT BOYS enter a classroom.
```

[Scenes have been deleted. The boys search the school and fail to find the girl. They return to scout headquarters and must choose again.]

```
WHICH PART DO YOU WANT TO SEARCH?

A. THE SCHOOL

B. THE FARM

C. THE GIRL's NEIGHBORHOOD


[IF B. THE FARM]

2B-1. 2 SHOT ALEX AND BOB

                         ALEX
   Greg and Hal—search the farm.

M-2.

TRANSITION MONTAGE TO FARM AREA

1. POV WOODS

They happen upon their science teacher who is
looking for mushrooms in a field. He looks
very scientific and has a sample bag, notebook,
magnifying glass, etc. He is humming a little
song.
```

Single-Column, Complex If-Then Interactive Format

Use: The previous example had fairly simple if-then conditions. For example, if the scout decided to search the farm, then we cut to the farm scene. For many projects the interactivity is far more complex. In such projects, the questions users ask of characters in the program, or what action users did previously, will affect what new actions, characters or dialogue will appear on screen. This type of complex if-then interactivity requires a more complex format.

Description: The following sample is from the computer game, *Nancy Drew: The Secret of the Old Clock*. This is a highly interactive program where the player gradually accumulates clues and information to solve a mystery. The player gathers the information in a nonlinear sequence. So the game engine needs to keep track of what the player has already discovered in order to reveal the next pertinent bit of information.

For example, if the player has already asked a certain character about another character's middle name, he or she should get a different response than if he or she had not asked that question previously. In the first line of the sample below, there is an elaborate series of conditions that indicates what the player already knows: "If EV_Saw_Questions = True and EV_EC_Said_Lois = False and EV_JW_ Said_Mid_Name = False." This indicates the player does not know the middle name is "Lois" and that the player has not asked this specific character JW about this before. When these conditions are met, the player will be able to click on (ask) the question that follows the conditions tagged with <>, and the character will respond with the line that's in square brackets ([ ]). However, if the conditions are different and JW_Said_Mid_Name = True (see the line below "Go to 1048"), that means the player has asked JW about this before and instead

---

Scene 1047 Information Check

If EV_Saw_Questions = True and EV_EC_Said_Lois = False and EV_JW_Said_Mid_Name = False

<What was Emily's mom's middle name, do you remember?><NJP47>

['Course I do. It was - {frustrated} Oh, piffle! It's right on the tip of my tongue. It was - it was -] [JWP47]

Go to 1048

Flag Set: EV_JW_Said_Mid_Name = True

Info Check: No

Bye: No

===========

Scene 1048

[{with an exasperated sigh} It'll pop into this feeble brain of mine one of these days. Why don't you just go ask Emily.] [JWP48]

Flag Set: None

Info Check: Yes

Bye: Yes

===========

Copyright Her Interactive Inc.

of Scene 1047, Scene 1048 will be used in which the player is sent to another character, Emily. This script format is used in conjunction with a flowchart.

Single-Column, Screen-Based Informational Script with Element Labels

Use: This script is best suited to an informational program that has considerable interactivity and a variety of media, such as narration, text, and video. Screen elements are clearly defined in the script by labels.

Description: This script was used in the training program *Vital Signs*, which teaches medical technicians how to perform various tasks. Each script page is one screen of material. The script page has three parts divided by horizontal lines. The top part describes the lesson and topic. The middle part describes the actions. The bottom part describes the feedback (reaction to the actions) and linking.

VITAL SIGNS

Unit: u1

Lesson: Blood Pressure

Topic:

Title:

Screen: u1.4.13p

Type:

Graphic File:

(GRAPHIC/VIDEO: Colette looking apprehensive)

Text:

Meet Colette, age 7.

You're going to take her blood pressure. You've explained the procedure to her. What do you use next?

(CAPTIONS)

  Cuff   Ball Pump   Valve on cuff   Doll

(AUDIO: NARRATOR VO): Now it's your turn. Meet Colette, age 7. You're going to take her blood pressure. You've explained the procedure. What

(Continued)

do you use next—the cuff, the ball pump, the
valve on the cuff or the doll? SELECT your choice
now.

Feedback: (VO and text)

Cuff, Ball Pump, Valve = (SFX: Little Girl's Voice)
(VO audio ONLY): No. I don't want that. It's going
to hurt!

NARRATOR (VO): Apparently, Colette didn't buy your
explanation. Try again.

Doll = **NARRATOR (VO):** You're good. That's right. From
the look on her face, you can tell Colette didn't
buy your explanation, so you demonstrate on a doll.
(SELECT "GO AHEAD" to continue.)

Branching: u1.4.14p

Special Instructions:

Copyright Harvard Pilgrim Health Plan.

Single-Column, Screen-Based Informational Script Written in a Database

Use: This type of script could be used for a narrative or information piece with substantial interactivity. It would only be needed for a complex program with many team members or where the final pages were dynamically generated from script segments in a database.

Description: My company InterWrite developed a geology Web site and CD-ROM for the textbook publisher Houghton Mifflin. The project was quite large, had numerous assets (video, graphics, audio, animations), several content experts, and a number of editors. Developing a coherent script that would clearly describe all these elements and allow all the content people and editors to add their comments to the script was a challenge.

The solution was to develop the script as a FileMaker Pro database (see following for a sample page). Each of the elements below, such as screen text or visual layout, was separate fields or units of information in the database. This allowed us to have one master script with all the elements, but by using the databases sort and export functions, we were able to create multiple custom scripts and documents from that master script. These documents included: a list of scenes and a flowchart for the project manager; a table of assets needed for the media researcher; a script (free of internal comments) for an outside vendor; a detailed list of instructions for the animator; and so on. This database script could also be used as the basis of an asset database so that video, graphics, and other elements could be easily found for future projects.

GEOLOGY EXPLORER	
Page Number. Title Date	VIII-2b Relative Ages
Screen Text	Now see if you can determine the year in which the car in the center was released. Write your answer in the space provided and then hit "Continue." If you have absolutely no idea, just hit "Continue."
Visual Layout	Layout 2 Text top, Graphic bottom. The graphic consists of the three cars in a row. A text input box labeled "Car Release Date" is above the 1955 Ford.
Screen Action	Input date; hit "Continue."
Feedback	
Links	Correct Answer + Continue. → VIII-2b1 Incorrect Answer + Continue. → VIII-2b2.
A: Graphic 1	D1) Model-T Ford
A: Graphic 2	D2) 1955 Ford
A: Graphic 3	D3) 1999 Lexus
A: Animation	
A: Audio	
A: Video	
A: Shockwave	Three pictures are arranged in a horizontal row with a text input box above D2) 1955 Ford.
Assets Notes	(Continued)

Notes Internal	No need to actually register whether the student is right. We can just give the correct answer.
Notes to Author	
Notes to Vendor	

Double-Column Format

Use: Informational projects with substantial interactivity and voice-over narration.

Description: This format is similar to what is used for documentary video. It has two columns, with images on the left and audio and text on the right. An unusual aspect of this particular script is that it is illustrated, which works very well to present the feel of the completed project. Most double-column scripts do not include images.

This program is displayed in an interactive kiosk at the National Maritime Center in Norfolk, Virginia. This production teaches shipbuilding principles by having the player build a ship. In the following section, users can choose to get information on various hull types and then must pick one of these hulls for the ship they are building. Because there is only a small amount of material on each hull, all the choices are listed sequentially.

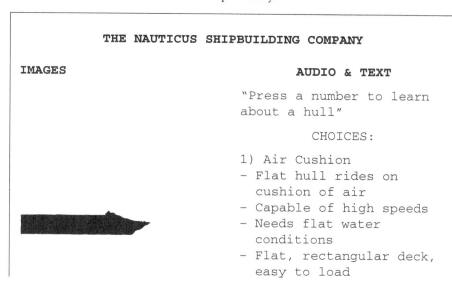

THE NAUTICUS SHIPBUILDING COMPANY

IMAGES   AUDIO & TEXT

                                  "Press a number to learn
                                  about a hull"

                                          CHOICES:

                                  1) Air Cushion
                                  - Flat hull rides on
                                    cushion of air
                                  - Capable of high speeds
                                  - Needs flat water
                                    conditions
                                  - Flat, rectangular deck,
                                    easy to load

2) Planing Hull
- V-shaped hull capable of high speeds
- Performs best in flat water conditions
- High stress levels on hull

3) Displacement Hull
- Deep, rounded hull, very stable in all conditions
- Very large cargo capacity

- Stable platform for large propulsion systems
- Needs very large propulsion system

4) SWATH (Small Waterplane Area Twin Hull)
- 2 submerged hulls, very stable

- Flat deck provides good work area

After selecting a hull to use, cut to Design Assembly screen, animation of hull rollout.

Loudspeaker VO: "Planing hull being moved into position."

Cut to POV animation moving to propulsion subassembly area.

Background sound of motors whirring and machinery clanging. "Next, you'll need to choose a propulsion system."

287

Three Column Format with Narration and Text Transcript

Use: Informational scripts with substantial interactivity and a variety of media, including both audio narration and on-screen text transcripts of that narration.

Description: Often learning programs will have both audio narration and a text transcript of the on-screen narration. This helps learners who may prefer to read vs. listen, do not have audio, or who have a disability. The writer cannot just repeat the narration and the text transcript because there will be subtle differences in the narration, which must be listened to (and read aloud by the narrator) and the text transcript, which is read silently by the user. Note that the narration column is shaded to clearly identify it for the narrator who must read the text. This format also has a fourth column (not pictured here), which was used for production purposes, such as timing the narration. The animations and graphics are simply described by a file name, which is described in detail on a separate animation page of the script.

Images, Text, Programming	Narration (Text Transcript)	Narration (Audio Transcript)
1) (Title) Creating Time Plots		
2) (Main Screen Text) When data are collected over a period of time, they can be represented by a **time plot.**	When data are collected over a period of time, they can be represented by a **time plot.**	When data are collected over a period of time, they can be represented by a **time plot.**
3) (Definition Box) A time plot is a graph showing data measurements in chronological order.	A time plot is a graph that shows data measurements in chronological order. It is important to note that the interval of time between measurements should be the same. So, if you take a measurement once a week, it should be on the same day every week. Or, if you take a measurement every day, the same time period, such as one-half hour, should be used.	A time plot is a graph that shows data measurements in chronological order. It is important to note that the interval of time between measurements should be the same. So, if you take a measurement once a week, it should be on the same day every week. Or, if you take a measurement every day, the same time period, such as one-half hour, should be used.

4a) (Procedure Box) Making a Time Plot [il0262m02c01 anim01F1_ IW.ai]	To make a time plot, use the following procedure.	To make a time plot, use the following procedure.

Copyright Houghton Mifflin Company.

Six Column Format with Live Host, Interactive Media, and Audience Interactivity

Use: Immersive exhibits in museums or complex presentations at major conferences and events that use a combination of live host and interactive media before live audiences.

Description: Script has six columns for the Host's dialogue, user interaction in this case through a PDA attached to each seat, video on big screen, audio and narration, lighting effects on the audience, and cues for the host who controls the program. See Table 16.1 for an example.

CONCLUSION

As you have seen in the variety of script and other document formats in this chapter, there is no one way to format for multimedia and Web documents. The primary requirement is to make sure that whatever format you choose, it is clear to your client and everyone on your production team. And as with most things, keep it as simple as you can. Your format should be self-explanatory.

REFERENCES

Copywrite. http://www.bartastechnologies.com/products/copywrite/.
Final Draft. http://www.finaldraft.com/.
Movie Magic. http://www.screenplay.com/products/mms/index.htm.
StoryView. http://www.screenplay.com/products/sv/.
WordMenu. http://www.wordmenu.com/.

Table 16.1

HOST	VOTE; PDA	VIDEO & LIGHTING	AUDIO, NARRATION, & SFX	EFX	CUES
In our first game, we'll be visiting the year 1813 and exploring the beginnings of the textile industry here in New England. Look down at your screen to see how much you have to start with.		Graphic or animation Bank account icon from PDA.		1813 Gobo effect on queue with movie	Host – next at the word screen activates PDA info
HOST As you see, you each have $10,000 in your accounts. Remember, that's $10,000 in 1813 dollars. But in that time, just as today, you could *earn* money … so let's earn a little more money right now in our Lightning Round.	PDA GRAPHIC on system shows each person how much they have.	MAIN SCREEN Graphic Bank account shows amount of money each person has.			

HOST You'll have a chance to answer 3 questions. For each one you answer correctly, you'll earn $1,000! You'll have 10 seconds after the question to enter your answer. Anyone have any questions? … Let's start the lightning round.	GRAPHIC Lightning Roz und graphic or animation flashes on main screen. Possible lighting effects flash throughout room.
	SFX Lightning round theme song plays.
	Host spot and blue wash fade out. Gobo Lightning effects timed to main screen.
	Host – Next on the words Lightning Round. Movie starts 30 frames after lights fade out.
VISITORS have a pre-set amount of time to answer the questions	GRAPHIC & MAIN SCREEN TEXT BUILD, with graphics What was the relationship between Britain and the United States in 1813? a. They were at war. b. They were allies. c. The United States was a British colony. d. Europeans had not yet come to North America.
	CHRIS (VO) First question. What was the relationship between Britain and the United States in 1813? a. They were at war. b. They were allies. c. The United States was a British colony. d. Europeans had not yet come to North America.

CHAPTER 17

Interactive Multimedia Narrative and Linear Narrative

Timothy Garrand

Portions of this chapter originally appeared in the *Journal of Film and Video*.

CHAPTER OVERVIEW

A narrative is what we commonly refer to as a story. An interactive, multimedia narrative allows the user to explore several variations of a story or stories. Interactive narratives are produced for game consoles, PCs, mobile devices, the Web and interactive TV. Interactive narratives share many elements with linear film and video narrative. Because of this, it is useful to understand the basic elements of linear narrative before exploring the intricacies of interactive narrative.

NARRATIVE AND INTERACTIVE NARRATIVE DEFINED

A narrative is what we commonly refer to as a story. A "story" is one of those terms that we intuitively understand but are hard pressed to define. Critics have written many books defining narrative, but for our purposes we will define a narrative as a series of events that are linked together in a number of ways, including cause and effect, time, and place. Something that happens in the first event causes the action in the second event, and so on, usually moving forward in time.

Narrative interactive multimedia involves telling a story using all the multimedia elements we've discussed in previous chapters, including the use of media and interactivity. In narrative multimedia, the player explores or discovers a story in the same way the user explored information in the programs discussed

293

in the previous part of the book. Often the player is one of the characters in the story and sees action from that character's point of view. But even if he or she is not a character, the player still has some control over what the characters will do and how the story will turn out. Interactive narratives can be used for pure entertainment or to present information in an experiential way.

INTERACTIVE NARRATIVES VS. SIMULATIONS AND WORLDS

A narrative or story is an ancient form of communication, but multimedia can also utilize newer forms that are sometimes confused with narrative. These new forms are simulations and worlds structures. Game and Web designer David Riordan points out that an interactive narrative, a simulation, and a worlds structure are three distinct forms.

In a virtual world program, the player explores an environment. Examples include the classic *Myst* and the more recent online multiplayer games, such as *World of Warcraft*. The designers of a virtual world create a physical space, such as a mysterious island or an entire war-ravaged mythical world, where the player has the freedom to move about and interact with various elements, opening doors, examining objects, talking to other characters, and even completing noble quests against mighty enemies and monsters. Worlds programs are not narratives, even though some of the characters and locations may have background information presented about them.

In a simulation, such as *The Nauticus Shipbuilding Company* or *Amped 3*, a player explores all the different possibilities in an activity, such as building a ship or going snowboarding. Simulations are not narratives. Even if they have a script attached to them, if the elements in the program come up in a random pattern, they do not comprise a narrative.

In an interactive narrative, a player explores a story. Interactive narratives have beginnings, middles, and ends, even though each user may experience these elements differently. There is nothing unplanned in an interactive narrative. Someone who plays the program long enough will eventually see all the material the writer created. An interactive narrative essentially allows each player to discover the story in a different way. The *Nancy Drew* mystery games are excellent examples of interactive narratives.

Simulations, worlds, and narratives can, of course, be combined and that is the most common way they are currently presented. *Dust: A Tale of the Wired West* integrates a narrative into the virtual world of a desert town in the old West. *Just Cause* takes the same worlds approach by making the player a secret agent whose goal is to overthrow the government of the island of San Esperito. The island is a fully developed world that the player can explore and interact with. *Amped 3* takes a different approach and combines simulations and narrative by adding story segment to the snowboarding simulation. Although the original

Sims game was closer to a pure simulation of building a house and creating a family, *Sims 2* creates a more elaborate world for the characters to inhabit and becomes a combination of a simulation and a worlds structure. Many shooter games such as *Shadow of the Colossus* will also add a little story to help set up the action. In the beginning of this game, you are told that the only way you can save your true love is to hunt down and destroy sixteen colossal beasts. Once the setup is in place, the vast majority of the rest of the game is shooting the monsters. All these combinations are valid entertainment, but in this book our focus will be on games where the narrative is the primary, or at least major, component.

COMPUTER GAMES AND VIDEOGAMES: DEFINING TERMS

One of the indications that the interactive media industry is still in its infancy is that even some of the most common terms are not clearly defined. For example, some writers use the phrase "computer game" to mean any game played with a computer involved. This would include all consoles (PlayStation, Xbox, etc.), PC computers, mobile devices, interactive TV, and arcade games. Clearly the Web site "Computer Games Online" uses the phrase this way, because their content deals with all types of games. Other writers, however, think "computer game" just refers to games played on PC computers and not consoles.

The phrase "videogame" has similar conflicting definitions. Some writers think of a videogame as any kind of game using a video display. This would include all consoles (PlayStation, Xbox, etc.), PC computers, mobile devices, interactive TV, and arcade games. Electronic Arts, one of the biggest publishers of electronic games, is using the phrase this way when they title their site, "EA—Action, Fantasy, Sports, and Strategy Videogames." However, other writers think of "videogame" as just applying to console games that are played on the TV and do not include games played on personal computers or a mobile devices.

There is even a third phrase, "electronic games," that also applies to all types of video and computer games. But this term is being used less than the other two terms so will not be used in this book.

In this book, I will use "computer games" and "videogames" synonymously to mean all types of electronic, computer powered games, including those played on consoles (PlayStation, Xbox, etc.), PC computers, mobile devices (phones, PSP, Game Boy, etc.), interactive TV, and arcades games. I think this makes good sense because many games can be played both on a console and on a PC. Having two different names for the same game makes no sense. If I wish to distinguish that a game is played on a personal computer, I will call it a "PC game." If I want to point out a console game specifically, I will use "video game console" or just "console." For games on mobile devices, such as phones,

PDAs, PSP, etc., I will use "mobile game." Just keep in mind that this is the usage in this book, but the final definitions of all these terms are still in flux and may be slightly different elsewhere. So be sure you know how the terms are being defined in a specific context.

INTERACTIVE MULTIMEDIA NARRATIVES

Interactive Multimedia Narratives Genres

Although, there have been some interesting interactive narrative experiments both online and with interactive TV (*CSI* Interactive, *Homicide: Second Shift*, etc.), currently the most sophisticated commercial interactive multimedia narratives are found in video games. But a distinction needs to be made between games that simply have story elements and those that have fully fleshed out narratives. Marc Laidlaw, the writer of the action-adventure games *Half-Life* and *Half-Life 2*, explains it this way:

> If we distinguish stories from storytelling, I'd say that lots of games have stories, but not many games do a good job of storytelling. A story can be very simple, summed up in a screen or even a single line of text. You read it, forget it, and wade into the game. But storytelling is the deliberate crafting of a narrative, with attention to rhythm and pacing, revelation and detail.

The major types of games that include story elements are action games, role-playing games, and adventure games, with adventure games being the only genre primarily devoted to storytelling. The main focus of action games, such as the *Doom*, *Quake*, and *Halo* franchises, is speed and action that usually takes the form of shooting other characters or blowing things up. These games are also sometimes called shooters or FPS (first person shooters). Role playing games (RPG), such as the *Baldur's Gate* franchise, involve a character taking on a role and exploring a world, usually as part of a mini quest with limited story interaction and development of other characters. A subgenre of this game is the Massively Multiplayer Online Role Playing Game (MMORPG), such as *World of Warcraft*, that can involve hundreds of thousands of people at one time via the Web.

As Aaron Conners, the writer of the games *Amped 3* and *The Pandora Directive* explains, in an adventure game, telling the story is the primary focus. There are strong characters and sophisticated story development. Characters overcome obstacles to achieve a final quest. Puzzles are also an important element. *Nancy Drew: Secret of the Old Clock*, *The Pandora Directive*, and *Dust: A Tale of the Wired West* are all adventure games, with *Nancy Drew* being in the mystery subgenre. The appeal of the mystery and adventure story is clearly that they are strongly goal-oriented. The player has something to aim for, obstacles are easy to establish, and jeopardy is built into the genre.

The Current State of Interactive Narrative and Computer Games

After a golden age of story-based adventure games in the mid-1990s, adventure games fell on hard times. Some interactive narrative adventures were poorly done and perhaps deserved to fail. But a number of adventure games with sophisticated stories, such as *Grim Fandango*, were released to rave reviews and critical acclaim and still did very little business. Because of this, many game publishers turned their backs on interactive narrative to focus on action games. Fortunately for lovers of interactive narrative, one of these action games, *Half-Life*, became a smash hit by including more story elements than a typical action game. Although the *Half-Life* story is fairly linear and the game is more action game than interactive narrative, it did show that there was still a hunger for stories in the audience. *Half-Life*'s success made popular the hybrid genre action-adventure—a game that has extensive action elements and a story. Most action-adventure games of this period did not have the sophisticated stories of the classic adventure games of the mid-90s, but they at least pointed the direction for the creation of commercially successful interactive narratives.

The major elements of this new direction for interactive narrative were the combining of different game genres and including more mature content and story elements. But other factors in the industry have also helped strengthen the resurgence of interactive narrative. A key factor is the introduction of the latest generation of game consoles that are capable of presenting content in a more cinematic and realistic fashion. This new capability has helped improve the success of Hollywood and game tie-ins and increased the convergence of narrative film/TV and the game industry. Another factor in more successful interactive narratives, particularly those tied to specific movie properties has been the involvement in games of major film narrative talents, such as Peter Jackson and Steven Spielberg.

All of these factors have produced a new wave of computer games with extensive stories. Although many of the stories appearing in the current crop of games are fairly linear and allow limited interactivity for the user, there is at least a definite interest in including story in games and a growing willingness to experiment with narrative. A few examples from various game genres follow. *The Chronicles of Narnia*, *Pirates of the Caribbean*, and *The Godfather* are all tie-ins to successful movie stories. The controversial *Grand Theft Auto* franchise combines an elaborate urban world the user can explore with mature themes, violent action, and a narrative. (This author is not endorsing the violent content of the *GTA* games.) *Half-Life 2* and later games in that series followed the direction set by *Half-Life* but with a more complex world and story. *Phoenix Wright: Ace Attorney* successfully brought the point and click adventure game to mobile devices with great writing and humor. *Amped 3* integrated story into a snowboarding sports sim. The *Nancy Drew* mysteries are based on the successful books of the same name and are aimed at a female audience. *Indigo*

Prophecy (also known as *Fahrenheit*) has true multipath scenarios where the story changes depending on user choices.

Matthew Costello, the author of *The 7th Guest*, one of the most successful story-based games ever, agrees that there has been a renewed interest in adding story to games. According to Costello, game companies have realized that story, characters, and dialogue are important components. They are hiring more writers with a grasp of narrative, and they are starting early with the story script, instead of just adding story elements to a game after the fact. His own writing talents have been much in demand with contributions to *Just Cause, Pirates of the Caribbean, Shellshock, Doom 3*, and *The Italian Job*.

With the game industry in general looking healthy because of long-term growth in console and mobile games, the outlook for the production of more games with story elements and complete interactive narratives looks strong. There is even some hope that weaker areas of the industry will strengthen. PC gaming has been the one game area in decline, but Microsoft's latest operating system is being billed by the company as the most game-friendly operating system ever. Microsoft has also vowed to put its muscle behind the creation of more PC game titles. And there is even hope that the perennial dark horse, interactive TV, will reach its potential. Digital cable, video on demand, and interactive television (iTV) services are now available at some of the largest cable providers. Now we just need iTV programming to match the technological advances.

Larger game budgets; more powerful consoles capable of a realistic, cinematic presentation; Hollywood convergence and story talent; blended game genres; a willingness to experiment with narrative in games; and broadband speeds on mobile devices and the Web, allowing presentation of video and animation all point to a promising future for the interactive narrative.

CLASSICAL LINEAR NARRATIVE ELEMENTS DEFINED

Although there are many different types of narrative, such as realist and modernist, successful interactive narratives have largely focused on classical narrative, the same type of narrative that dominates linear film and video. Because of this, interactive narrative shares many of the elements of narrative film and video. As these are forms that most readers are already familiar with, I will first review the basics of classical linear narrative in film and TV before diving into the intricacies of interactive narrative.

Character

Classical linear narrative film and video are character driven. It is the character who grabs our attention and whose situation we are drawn into. Most successful film and video today clearly define their characters early in the piece. Who are the characters? Where are they from? What do they want or need, and why do they want it? What the character wants usually provides the action story of the film or video; why they want it provides the motivation for the actions and the underlying emotional story.

As an example, the modern classic film trilogy *The Lord of the Rings* establishes the lead character Frodo as a sincere, loyal, innocent, and cheerful nephew of his more adventurous Uncle Bilbo. We learn all this information about Frodo through the simple clothes he wears, his interaction with friends, his own actions and statements, and the setting. The first time we see him, he is reading a book under a tree in a peaceful orchard. When he first hears of the power of the One Ring, he immediately wants to give it away to Gandalf. A little later he tells his adventurous uncle, "I'm not like you." But when it seems that no one else is suited to be ring bearer, Frodo does reluctantly take on the role. What Frodo wants in the film (his action need) is to destroy the One Ring, forged by the Dark Lord. Frodo wants to do this to save the Shire, but he also would like to prove to himself that he has the internal courage to accomplish the task. If we are going to care about the story, it is important that we identify with this character and his needs. Identification can be achieved in a number of ways, including casting an appealing actor, creating sympathy for an underdog, and having the character do positive things. The best way to achieve identification, however, is to develop the character so that the audience clearly understands the character's needs. *The Lord of the Rings* does all of these things to get us onboard with Frodo.

299

Structure

Once the character's needs are established, the writer can begin to structure the script. The key elements of classical narrative structure are exposition, conflict, climax, and resolution. Figure 17-1 lays out the basic structure of the vast majority of film and TV shows produced today.

Exposition or Setup

The beginning of the story must set up the lead character, the setting, and what the character wants—the goal to be achieved or the problem to be solved. Current films and videos tend to limit pure expositional sequences at the

Figure 17.1
Classical linear structure.

beginning and jump right into the story, integrating the story with the exposition. Some pieces open with an action scene and then slow down the pace in the next scene for exposition. However it is done, near the beginning of a script, the audience must learn who the character is, where he or she is, and what he or she wants.

Conflict

Once the writer knows the lead character and his or her goal, then he or she can start the character on the way to achieving that goal. Of course, if the character achieves the goal in the first scene, it will be a very short story. To avoid this happening, the writer introduces conflicts or obstacles. There are three basic types of conflict:

- Person vs. person.
- Person vs. the environment.
- Person vs. self.

In *The Lord of the Rings* example, there are many "persons" who oppose Frodo, particularly Gollum, the orcs, Ring Wraiths, Lord Sauron, and all their minions. The environmental obstacles include mysterious forests, snowy mountains, labyrinthine mines, and much more. The last type of conflict, person vs. self, is a way of adding considerable depth to a piece. In the case of Frodo, he has serious self-doubts about his ability to carry the task to completion. These doubts are exacerbated by the evil power of the ring itself.

A number of writing critics, particularly Syd Field in *Screenplay*, point to a key plot point or event in the exposition that shoves the character out of the exposition and into the conflict. In Frodo's case, it occurs at the secret council in the elf land of Rivendell when he takes on the task of carrying the ring to Mordor to destroy it. Once the conflicts begin, then each conflict or obstacle should be more challenging than the last obstacle so that the story rises in intensity.

Climax

Finally, the story nears the peak of intensity, and a final event jacks it up to the climax, which is where the character either achieves the goal or not. In Frodo's case, the final event is at the fires of Mordor when Frodo finally reaches his destination. However, because of the power of the Ring, Frodo has been corrupted and is unable to throw the ring into the fire. It is only by chance that another character, Gollum, tries to seize the ring for himself and ends up accidentally plummeting into the fire with the ring. With a little help from Gollum, Frodo has accomplished his physical goal of destroying the ring, but ultimately failed to accomplish his emotional goal of proving he has the strength to withstand the seductive power of the ring. This conflicted climax is one of the elements that adds power to this story. Typically in a Hollywood film, the hero accomplishes both his physical and emotional goal.

Resolution

The resolution wraps up the story after the climax. The resolution of *The Lord of the Rings* involves the return to the Shire and ultimately Frodo's departure with the Elves to a land of peace.

In most stories, the character changes or travels a character arc, a character may start cowardly and by the end prove he is brave, or start the story unsure and by the end be full of confidence. Because Frodo never achieves his emotional goals and because he is so wounded by the evil power of the Ring, he also follows an arc. He travels from a point of carefree, innocence at the beginning to a point of being somber and restrained. Some critics see the journey of Frodo is one from innocence to experience or from childhood to adulthood.

Scenes and Sequences

A narrative is comprised of individual scenes and sequences. A scene is an action that takes place in one location. A sequence is a series of scenes built around one concept or event. In a tightly structured script, each scene has a mini-goal or plot point that sets up and leads us into the next scene, eventually building the sequence. Some scenes and most sequences have a beginning, middle, and end, much like the overall story.

Jeopardy

The characters' success or failure in achieving their goals has to have serious consequences for them. It is easy for the writer to set up jeopardy if it is a life-and-death situation, such as being butchered by orcs in *The Lord of the Rings*. It is harder to create this sense of importance with more mundane events. This is accomplished by properly developing the character. In a well written script, if something is important to the character, it will be important to the audience even if it is not a life and death situation.

Point of View

Point of view defines from whose perspective the story is told. The most common point of view (or POV) is third person or omniscient (all knowing). In this case the audience is a fly on the wall and can flit from one location to another, seeing events from many characters' points of view or from the point of view of the writer of the script. This is the point of view of *The Lord of the Rings*.

The other major type of point of view is first person or subjective point of view. In this case, the entire story is told from one character's perspective. The audience sees everything through his or her eyes. The audience can experience only what the character experiences. Used exclusively, this type of point of view has numerous practical problems. The primary one is that we never get to see the lead character's expressions except in the mirror. Because of this, stories that are told in subjective point-of-view narrative are sometimes told in third-person point of view in terms of the camera. This allows us to see the lead character. Voice-over narration is often used with subjective point of view.

Pace

Pace is the audience's experience of how quickly the events of the narrative seem to move. Many short sequences, scenes, and bits of dialogue tend to make the pace move quickly; longer elements slow it down. Numerous fast-moving events in a scene also quicken pace. Writers tend to accelerate pace near a climax and slow it down for expositional and romantic scenes. A built-in time limit accelerates pace and increases jeopardy by requiring the protagonist to accomplish his or her task in a certain time frame. In *The Lord of the Rings*, Frodo had to destroy the Ring before Lord Sauron and his armies amassed the power to destroy all the good folks of Middle Earth.

CONCLUSION

The above has only scratched the surface of a complex topic, but it should be an adequate foundation for the multimedia narrative discussion that follows. A key issue we will be looking at is how the writing of multimedia narrative differs from writing linear narrative.

REFERENCES

Conners, A. Telephone interviews with the author, December 1995, October 1999, January 2006.

Costello, M. Phone interview with the author, July 1999, February 2006.

Field, S. (1982). *Screenplay*. New York: Dell Publishing.

Riordan, D. Telephone interviews with the author, June 1994, October 1995, December 1995, January 2006.

CHAPTER 18

The Elements of Interactive Multimedia Narrative

Timothy Garrand

Portions of this chapter originally appeared in the *Journal of Film and Video*.

CHAPTER OVERVIEW

Major elements of interactive narrative that must be understood by the writer include:

- The Role of the Player
- Character Development
- Structure
- Exposition
- Plot Points
- Scenes
- Pace and Time
- Dialogue and Other Sound

LINEAR VERSUS INTERACTIVE NARRATIVE

Writer Matthew Costello, who has written successful films, novels, and computer games, points out a key difference between linear and interactive narrative. A film starts from characters. A novel can start with an idea and have characters gather around it. A game starts from the genre and expectations. The story world comes first. A designer comes up with a game story world for a project. Then the writer has to ask, what is the world going to have in it? What are the possible interactions, the environments? What type of story does this suggest?

DOI: 10.1016/B978-0-240-81343-1.00018-2

According to Costello, the story worlds of games are gravitating towards genres. Genres are categories of stories, such as horror, mystery, fantasy, science fiction, and crime genres. Using a genre story world makes it easier to develop a narrative because the user already understands the basic conventions of character and plot lines. The writer does not have to establish everything from scratch as in a nongenre story.

Of course, the key difference between linear narrative and interactive narrative is interactivity. Amy Bruckman of the MIT Media Lab writes, "In making a story nonlinear, the story teller relinquishes the power to control the flow of information to the viewer ... A balance must be struck between giving the viewer freedom and maintaining narrative coherence" (Bruckman, 1990). Finding this balance—giving the player some control over the narrative, while allowing the writer to perform the necessary functions of the classical storyteller, including establishing characters and an engaging story structure—is a key challenge for the writer of interactive narrative.

CHARACTER AND THE ROLE OF THE PLAYER

Characterization in an interactive narrative is vastly more complex than in a linear narrative because of the role of the player. Lena Maria Pousette, the writer of *Voyeur*, identified the key questions the writer must begin with: "What is the [game's] objective? Who is the player? And what does the player get to do?" (Willis, 1993). In an interactive piece, the player expects to be one of the characters in the story, or at least to have significant control over the characters.

Player Control

The degree of the player's control over the characters is one of the first decisions in writing a program. If you are writing for an existing story engine, these choices may be already determined. So be sure to learn the capabilities of the program you are working with. The basic types of control the player is allowed are choice of scenes, the character's actions, or all the character's behavior.

SCENES

In this approach, the player can decide which path of the story the characters will choose, but once launched on that path, the characters function independently until the next branching point. *Boy Scout Patrol Theater*, an interactive narrative at the National Boy Scout museum, is a good example. The Boy Scouts in the story must decide whether to search the farm, the neighborhood, or the school. Once the player makes the choice to search the school, the characters function on their own without player interaction until the next interactive point. The characters are usually seen in third person.

See the *Boy Scout Patrol Theater* section of the book, available at www.focalpress.com/9780240813431

Many games that allow significant interactivity in most of the game will have sections where players can only choose complete scenes. These are often in the form of cutscenes—linear movie-like scenes in the middle of a game.

Actions

In some programs, the player will see the main character on the screen and can control the actions of the character, but not the dialogue. *Grand Theft Auto—San Andreas* works this way. We can see CJ, the lead character, on screen, and we can direct him to steal cars or create other mayhem. This is a third person POV as described in the previous chapter. We do not directly control what the character says or what other characters say to them. The primary place CJ talks is in the cinematic cutscenes where we have no control. Often in games with this type of control, the playable action tends to be seen in long or medium shots so that the player can direct the action.

All Behavior

This is the highest degree of interactivity. In this mode, the player chooses what the character does and what they say. In the *Nancy Drew* mystery games, the player takes on the role of Nancy Drew in the first person POV. We do not see the character of Nancy Drew, but instead see everything through the character's eyes. This approach allows the player to essentially become the character. In the screenshot from *Nancy Drew: Curse of Blackmoor Manor*, shown in Figure 18.1, the player/Nancy Drew is talking to the rather scary aunt who is in charge of the manor. The aunt's dialogue is spoken and also appears in text in the darker color at the top of the window. In this screenshot, the player is clicking the question, "Is anyone else staying here?" which the aunt will reply to in audio and onscreen text.

Many games with interactive dialogue only show the player's choices in text and not the dialogue of the other characters as in the example above. In other games, such as *The Pandora Directive*, the player does not click the actual line of dialogue but instead clicks an attitude, which indicates the type of dialogue the on screen character will speak. This way the actual dialogue becomes a surprise. Interactive dialogue works great for certain types of games, such as mysteries, but some designers feel that it overly slows the pace of some games, such as action games. In *Half-Life 2*, for example, the lead character never speaks at all.

PLAYER CONTROL COMBINATIONS

Few programs function purely in just one of the approaches above. Many programs, such as *Amped 3*, combine different amounts of player control. During most of the snowboarding game play, you have complete control over the player's actions, but you can choose to take a break from snowboarding and view

Figure 18.1
Interactive dialogue Player controlling all behavior. Copyright Her Interactive, Inc.

one of the story challenges. The story scenes are basically linear and there is no interactivity until the scene has finished. Other games, such as *The Chronicles of Narnia: The Lion, the Witch and the Wardrobe*, allow you to change player perspective. In this case, you can choose which of the four main characters to play.

VARIABLE CONTROL

In some programs, players can decide on how much control they want. In *Voyeur*, the player watches the events in the mansion across the street, sees the news on television, and receives telephone calls. If the player just sits and watches, the corrupt politician is the protagonist of the story. If the player decides to try to stop the corrupt politician, the player can have a major effect on the plot.

Impact of Player Options

The degree of player control, player point of view, and the type of character played in a first-person point of view story all have significant impact on the story.

PLAYER AS PROTAGONIST

To maximize player interactivity and immersion in the story, one of the best options is to allow the player to become the protagonist of the story by controlling all the character's behavior and seeing the action in first-person point of view. There are, however, drawbacks to this approach. One is that it is difficult to portray certain types of action in first-person point of view. For example, how do you show someone kissing the protagonist? The player also never gets to see the protagonist's expressions and actions, which are the main ways that character is revealed. Because of this, first-person point-of-view interactive stories often rely on dialogue. Gender issues are also raised with first-person point-of-view interactive. Is the character male or female? If the character is assigned one gender, as in the *Nancy Drew* mysteries or *Dust*, are there character identification problems for the player? If no gender is assigned, how do the other characters address the player/protagonist?

If the player is the protagonist, it is also difficult for the writer to develop him or her as a complex character. If the writer does develop the protagonist in detail, as in the case of Tex Murphy in *The Pandora Directive*, you/the player are left with "a fictitious version of yourself who isn't like you at all and who does things you have never done in a world you have never visited" (Platt, 1995). The writer will also have to hope that the goal of the protagonist is something the player can identify with.

The alternative approach for the protagonist, as practiced in *Dust*, is to have a very general character, in this case, the Stranger. The player knows nothing about him, and so can perhaps more comfortably become him. But will the player be able to understand and empathize with the action and emotional needs of this sketchily drawn character?

PLAYER DETERMINING THE CHARACTER

A way around the quandary of either defining a character that the player cannot fit into or leaving the character vague is to give the player a role in determining the character. In *Amped 3*, at the beginning of the program, the player can choose the character's outfits, gender, voices (male or female) and attitude (cheeky or chill). *Grand Theft Auto—San Andreas* takes player definition of character one step further by having the lead character CJ change depending on what type of activities he does. Lots of exercise, he is buff. Lots of food and riding around in cars, he gets fat. He can also shop for clothes at any number of stores. The nonplaying characters (NPC) in the game will also respond to CJ differently based on his appearance. Even though the basic storyline does not alter from one game play to the next, having a different CJ character can change the experience of the storyline.

PLAYER AS MINOR CHARACTER

A more unusual role for the player is that instead of being a major character, the player can be a minor character, as in *Voyeur*. The player may not seem so central to the action, but the advantage is that the portrayal of the minor character is not as crucial. If the minor character is only sketchily drawn, it will not have as much of an impact on the story as a poorly developed main character. It is also much easier to show the main action of the story in third person. For certain types of training and education programs, this type of third-person portrayal is essential. *A la rencontre de Philippe* is an interactive language program in which the player takes on the role of helping Parisian friends find an apartment. This allows the player to watch the native speakers interact in French, which was one of the goals of the program and which would have been more difficult if the player was a first-person protagonist.

Character Setup and Relationships

The player is only one of the characters in a program. Many others must be set up, but the demands of the interactive narrative do not make it easy to bring them to life. Space is always at a premium, scenes tend to be short, and character setup tends not to be interactive and thus is kept to a minimum.

An interactive writer needs to be able to introduce the characters quickly and simply. And once the characters are established, the writer also has to keep track of the different relationships of all the characters in all the possible versions of the story.

See the Voyeur section available at www.focalpress.com/9780240813431 for examples of character charts and matrices.

ARCHITECTURE: STRUCTURE AND NAVIGATION

Just as in a linear piece, in an interactive narrative, once the character and his or her goal are established, then the basic structure of the story needs to be developed. In interactive writing, however, this is far more complex than the simple linear structure illustrated in Figure 17.1 in the previous chapter, because in an interactive narrative, the writer must also consider navigation between all the elements of the structure.

Will Wright, the designer of the popular *Sims* series of games, explains the difference between linear and interactive narrative well:

> When I watch Indiana Jones escaping from the Temple of Doom (in the movie of the same name), it's not what happens to him that I find interesting; it's what might have happened had he slipped in front of the boulder. Dozens of potential failure states are compressed into a few seconds of action and transmitted to my brain with amazing efficiency.
>
> Game players are given the ability to explore a space of possibilities—the phase space—and this is the real strength of the medium. It's sort of like the difference between a roller coaster and a car. The coaster is on a fixed track. It's a very exciting track, but it's always the same. I can add branches to the track, but it can still be viewed as a finite amount of track. If I put someone in a car, however, they can go almost anywhere. Since I can't simulate the whole world in my games, I have to put up barriers and limit where they can go in the car. (Bunn and Herz)

These barriers, and the road he describes, are essentially the structure of interactive narrative. How the user can move between roads is the navigation. The most common interactive narrative structures are described below.

Linear Structure

Defined: Strictly speaking, this is not an interactive structure but it is often used in interactive projects. Linear structure has no branching choices for the user.

Use: Linear structure is frequently used in narrative multimedia to set up the story. All of the narratives profiled in this book open with linear sequences before user interaction is possible. Linear video is also played during an interactive piece for additional background and to tie interactive segments together. The *New England Economic Adventure* uses linear video to present information that the audience will later use interactively in exercises and games.

Linear Structure with Scene Branching

Defined: This structure allows the user to choose alternative scenes, but after these alternative scenes are played out, the user is always routed back to the same main story line.

Use: This is a common structure in training and educational narratives. In *Boy Scout Patrol Theater* the basic structure is a linear story about trying to find a lost girl. At various decision points, however, the players get to make a choice, such as choosing to search the farm, the school, or the neighborhood. If they choose the farm, then they detour momentarily from the main story and search the farm, but eventually return to the main story (Figure 18.2). A similar structure is used in role-playing, narrative corporate training programs where the user takes on a role and tries to accomplish a task. They can choose alternate scenes for helping to accomplish the task, but are always routed back to the main task scenario.

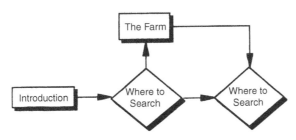

Figure 18.2
Linear structure with scene branching in Patrol Theater.

A variation on this approach is the structure that Chris Crawford aptly calls "Kill 'Em If They Stray" (Crawford, 2005). In this approach, there is only one critical story path through the game. The user can explore different scenes off the critical path, but they usually cannot get very far on any alternate path before they are killed. *Half-Life 2* can be put in this category. It is basically a linear story that sometimes appears to present alternate scenes. But if the players venture down one of those alternate scenes and stay too long, they can expect to be destroyed.

Valve CEO Gabe Newell describes the *Half-Life 2* approach, in the foreword to *Half-Life 2: Raising the Bar*: "A single-player game is really a movie that you create in cooperation with the player, where the lead actor [i.e., the player] doesn't have a copy of the script." (Hodgson, 2004).

Hierarchical Branching

Defined: This architecture involves taking the story in a completely different direction based on the viewer's choice at a preset decision point. This is a common informational architecture but presents problems in interactive narrative.

Used in a Complete Story: Using hierarchical branching to take the complete story into different directions has limited options. For example, as illustrated in Figure 18.3, the character comes to a point where she can choose one of three options: marry Alan, marry Bob, or marry Carl. After that choice is played out, then the character can choose to be faithful, have an affair, or get divorced.

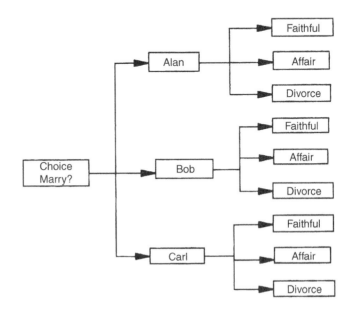

Figure 18.3
Hierarchical branching explosion.

The problem here is obvious: The number of choices increases exponentially. Adding one more set of choices to this chart would mean an additional 27 scenes, the next level would be 81 additional scenes, and the one after that 243 scenes! This is called combinatorial explosion. This is clearly too much material for a writer to present or a viewer to access.

Used with Endings: Although it is rare for an entire story to be completed with hierarchical branching, it is commonly used for the ending of programs. This device gives the viewer a feeling of greater control over the narrative, and branching explosion is obviously limited because the story ends. The end of *The 11th Hour*, where the viewer must choose to save one of three women, is a good example. Each woman equals a different ending to the story. The wrong choice is oblivion; the right choice is bliss.

Used with Dialogue: This type of branching is also used in interactive dialogue.

Parallel Path Stories

Defined: With parallel structure, several versions of the same story play parallel to each other. Depending on choices that the player makes in the story, he or she can move from one path to another. This is a way to give the player an option of multiple paths in a story without the branching explosion of hierarchical branching.

Use: *The Pandora Directive* (Figure 18.4) uses parallel path stories. After a linear introduction, the player enters an interactive scene. Depending on the choices that he or she makes, the player can move up to the A path, which is a Hollywood-type version of the story where the hero wins true love; the C path, a bleak, film noir experience of the story where everything goes wrong; or the B path, which is a middle ground. Each new interactive scene gives the player options to move back and forth between paths depending on the choices they

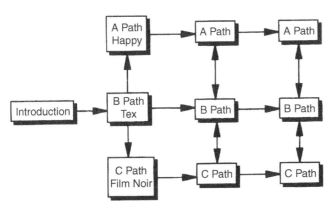

Figure 18.4
Parallel path stories in The Pandora Directive lead to one of several possible endings.

make. Depending on the choices they have made, they have one of several possible endings. Although this can be an effective structure, it is not widely used in complete games mainly because of the difficulty of tracking and creating multiple story paths and the changing relationships of the characters.

It is, however, a little more common to see parallel path structure as part of an otherwise linear game, such as *Metal Gear Solid*.

> This sequence, in which the player is tortured repeatedly but has an opportunity to escape between the torture sessions, has three paths through it: the player can escape in a couple of different ways from the cell between torture scenes, they may admit defeat to the torturer, or if all else fails, they are eventually rescued from the cell by a deus ex machina. This parallel path segment also governs a split in the game's ending: if the player does not give up in the torture scenes, they will end up rescuing the romantic interest—but if they do, she is killed and the player ends up escaping with a buddy character instead. (IGDA)

Linked Worlds—String of Pearls Architecture

Defined: This approach moves away from simple branching. A string of pearls architecture is a linked series of worlds structures connected by plot points or tasks that the player must accomplish to move forward in the narrative. As defined at the beginning of Chapter 17, the worlds approach lets the user explore a location. By itself, a worlds structure cannot form a coherent narrative, but combined with other forms it can.

Use: *Dust: A Tale of the Wired West* uses the string of pearls approach. When the player/Stranger first comes to town in the middle of the night, he is free to roam the town of Diamondback for as long as he wants. There are poker games to be played, hookers to talk to, and mysterious buildings to explore. This is a clear worlds structure—interesting, but by itself there is no story.

To move to the next day and advance the narrative, the player/Stranger must find a place to sleep. He can either stay at the hotel or get one of the town's citizens to take him in. There are a number of ways to accomplish this goal. To stay at the hotel, he needs money. He can get cash at the saloon if he is lucky at blackjack, poker, or the slot machine. If he is nosy, he might also find the four bucks that somebody lost in the hotel couch. But when he does get the money, the hotel owner says there are no vacancies. To get a room, it helps to meet Raddison, another character who lives there and who will introduce the Stranger (the player) to the owner. An alternative to the hotel is to get a citizen to take the player/Stranger home. To accomplish this, the player needs to sweet-talk the abrasive Mrs. Macintosh.

The player can perform all of these actions in any order desired, but eventually he or she has to find the right combination of actions to get a place to sleep and thus exit from the first night of the story and begin the next day or pearl

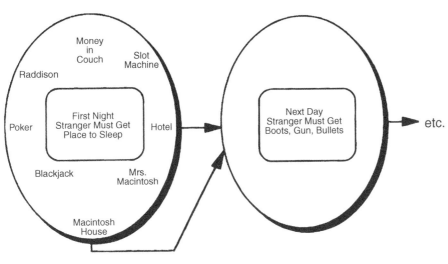

Figure 18.5
String of pearls architecture in Dust: A Tale of the Wired West.

on the string. In the second pearl, the next day's action, the player must get boots, guns, and bullets before moving on to the third pearl (Figure 18.5). All of the player's accomplishments move the story forward to the final shootout and to solving the mystery in one of six possible endings.

In addition to being used in the classic *Dust*, this worlds structure linked by a narrative thread has become a popular architecture in many other games. *Grand Theft Auto—San Andreas* uses this structure. A series of missions form the critical path of the game. These missions must eventually be taken on to move to all the locations (worlds) of the game, but you can decide when you want to take on the mission. You are free to explore GTA's huge virtual world as long as you want. *Just Cause* is set up in a somewhat similar fashion. In this case, a secret agent has the overall goal of overthrowing the government of an island nation. The agent can explore the island, but as in the case of GTA must complete a series of missions to move the story forward. Both of these examples though primarily worlds structures also have simulation elements with the ability to drive cars, boats etc. *Amped 3* is a game that is mostly a snowboard simulation but also provides the opportunity to explore the locations of top boarding resorts. Similar to *GTA* and *Just Cause*, *Amped 3* has a series of story challenges that link together the simulation sections and form the core narrative of the story.

In some ways, the ideal story for a string of pearls structure is a mystery story. This is the structure used in the *Nancy Drew* mysteries. Nancy Drew and any detective's goal in a mystery story is to discover what happened—the narrative of the crime. Initially the detective is in the top or outer world of the crime, but as she gets clues and solves puzzles, she gradually gains access to the inner worlds of the narrative, finally concluding with the mystery's solution.

Variable State Environment and Types of Links

Defined: The most sophisticated interactive narratives, many of which have been discussed previously in this chapter, have moved beyond direct links and simple branching to something that Dave Riordan, the designer of *Voyeur*, calls a variable state environment. With the help of software and sophisticated design that responds in a sensitive way to the player's actions, there are multiple outcomes to scenes, depending on where the player has been and to whom he or she has talked. In short, the environment responds to the player, much as it does in real life.

A variable state environment can take into account hundreds of actions as opposed to just the A or B choices in branching. And as each interaction is played differently, it will yield different responses. Different combinations of different interactions will also yield different responses.

Use: In *Indigo Prophecy (Fahrenheit)*, how and what Lucas cleans up after the murder and how he escapes, affect what clues can be used against him and the testimony of witnesses. *Deus Ex*'s narrative is also affected by player decisions in subtle ways. If you ignore the rules and kill all the terrorists in a blood bath, your fellow trigger-happy officers will applaud your actions and help you with the case, but your "by the book" officers will be appalled. Either choice affects how the story plays out. In *The Pandora Directive*, if you as the player are tactless with your girlfriend, you will get into a fight. This causes you to get drunk, and because you are drunk, you are unable to save a nightclub singer's life. These types of convoluted reactions to the player's actions are far more like real life than the direct reaction to a player's choices in many video games.

Future or Experimental Structures

The primary focus of this book is to document techniques and processes used to create commercial interactive media. It should, however, be mentioned that game theorist, research labs, and academics are working on innovative, experimental game engines and structures that they hope will be far more responsive to user needs than anything now in existence. Some of the purists in this group of researchers do not consider any of the structures described in this chapter as successful interactive narratives architectures. For a detailed discussion of the theoretical basis of interactive storytelling and some of the experimental solutions being developed, Chris Crawford's book, *On Interactive Storytelling*, is worth a read.

EXPOSITION OR SETUP

Exposition is another issue that presents special challenges for the interactive writer. Exposition involves introducing characters, setting, and story situation to the player. Exposition is particularly important in games because the player will need that information to make choices and take actions later in the game. Some designers feel that the key is to make the exposition entertaining and brief. Get the story setup and get on with the game. *Nancy Drew: The Secret of the Old Clock* presents the exposition efficiently and entertainingly. The game opens with Nancy driving her roadster to the Lilac Inn, the location of the mystery. As she is driving, we hear in voice-over what sounds like a 1930s radio show (the era of the game). The radio show/voice-over gives us the key background in audio illustrated with cuts to game scenes illustrating the narrator's description. When Nancy's car pulls into the driveway of the inn, the radio show/exposition is complete.

> You can view this introductory video for the *Nancy Drew* game by going to www.focalpress.com/9780240813431

Amped 3 also chooses a brief introductory scene to introduce the characters and setting. In this case, the characters are riding up the chairlift at a ski resort and the lead character/player is wearing a head to toe pink bunny suit. He is fulfilling a dare, which is to ski the mountain in the bunny suit. Through the banter about the dare and the suit, we get to know the characters and the basic situation.

Other designers, such as David Riordan, try to avoid introductory scenes. "If you spend time introducing the characters, the viewer is not being asked to do anything. In interactive that is death. Instead you need to discover the backstory more as you go." In his game *Voyeur*, he accomplishes this partially through the use of sets and props to give exposition. They can be subtle props, such as a gun in a suitcase, or more overt props, such as a letter the player is allowed to read, or even active props, such as a television set that gives background information on the characters. The use of props in interactive multimedia differs from their use in linear video because in multimedia, the player gets to choose which props to examine, has far more props to choose from, and can do things that would be impossible in linear, such as move closer to a letter to read it or choose to turn on a television set or PDA.

Another key way for a player to learn exposition is through what other characters say to the player as scenes unfold. Early in *Half-Life 2*, the player is pulled into an interrogation room by a cop who turns out to be a friend. He quickly gives the player key background before he rushes him on his way. A variation on this approach is for the game's writer to introduce a stranger character to the location/story. The stranger shares the expositional needs of the player. They both need to be told the situation and introduced to the characters.

Designing a game around an established story genre also helps with exposition. *Just Cause* is a secret agent thriller. Because we know this genre from endless secret agent movies, such as the James Bond series, we understand a lot of the conventions of the genre. Because of this, these elements do not have to be explained again in the game. For example, we know that the secret agent character will have access to extraordinary gadgets, will be sexy, and must operate primarily on his own or with the help of a beautiful lady.

315

Guaranteeing that Essential Exposition Is Seen

Because this is interactive media, depending on the game, the player may have a choice to not view certain scenes, including exposition. One solution is to make the exciting linear exposition scenes, such as those discussed above, mandatory. As soon as the game starts, the exposition plays. Most games will allow the introduction to be skipped on later plays of the game. A somewhat dated approach is to include the backstory in a separate document or book that goes along with the game. A better solution is to design the game to lure the player into choosing the essential exposition, often with engaging interactive devices, such as televisions that can be viewed, mini-games of missions that reveal background, and interesting characters who we want to talk to.

Demonstrating How the Program Works

A type of exposition unique to games is that players need an explanation of how the game works. What can the player do? How do they move? Can they pick things up? How does the interactive dialogue work? The best programs integrate this information into the exposition and do not make the users read vast amounts of instructions before they can play.

One way to do this is to set up a simple situation at the beginning of the program that shows how the game works. For example, in *Dust*, the player is confronted with a nasty dog as soon as he or she enters the town. To get by this dog, the player must pick up objects, talk to characters, access help, and move about. A less integrated approach is to have a tutorial that plays a scene for the user and shows what to do.

PLOT POINTS

Plot points or beats are story information that moves the plot forward. For example, in *Grand Theft Auto—San Andreas*, a key plot point we learn in the first cutscene is that a rival gang has pretty much taken over in CJ's absence. In an interactive story, making essential plot points is as difficult as presenting exposition. Because the user can choose which scenes to view, there is no guarantee that the user will choose a specific scene with a certain key plot point.

One solution is to place essential plot points in a required sequence. With this option, the player cannot learn later plot points and progress in the game until they have seen earlier ones. In the example from *GTA* in the previous paragraph, the player must choose the first cutscene/mission before they can progress in the story to additional major missions and complete the game's story. The first cutscene is not actually forced on the player. They have the option of not choosing it, but if they do not choose it, they are limited to the initial location and basic crime activities of stealing cars and having fights.

Another solution to the problem of guaranteeing key plot points are seen is "to put two or three beats (plot points) in a scene" (Pousette, 1995). This way if the user selects a scene, multiple plot points will be established. Another approach is to have the same information appear in a number of different scenes. The difficulty here is that the information can't be presented in exactly the same way or players will get bored if they select several of these scenes. The solution is to feed the essential information into multiple scenes but to do it differently each time.

In a narrative that includes multiple story variations, such as *Voyeur*, establishing plot points is even more complex than setting up exposition. Often much of the exposition will be the same for all possible stories. For example, in *Voyeur*, the backstory on the corrupt politician and his desire to be president does not change from story to story. Plot points are, however, usually different in each story variation. This means that essential plot points have to be established for each story. It also means that scenes that are common to all variations cannot include plot points that contradict the plot in a specific story variation. Some writers use charts of plot points or beats to keep all of these elements clear.

See the Voyeur section available at www.focalpress.com/9780240813431 for examples of character charts.

SCENES

As the examples above suggest, strong scene writing is important to the interactive writer. Writer Maria O'Meara believes that "crafting a scene well is the most valuable technique of the interactive writer. Every experience in an interactive ought to be a tiny story or scene. Even if it's short, it still needs to have a beginning, middle, and end." Pam Beason of Microsoft agrees: "Every scene must contain a complete thought. An idea cannot be split over two scenes." Writer-designer Jane Jensen says other characteristics of the interactive scene are that "scenes are smaller and there are vastly greater amounts of them. You have to think nonlinearly. As you approach a given location, think what will occur there."

The interactive writer, in other words, must write vertically as well as horizontally. He or she cannot be concerned only with what scene follows another. The writer also has to be aware of what other scenes in other possible stories might be connected to this one. Some interactive writers script ten or fifteen related scenes at the same time in order to keep tabs on all the connections. And rewriting can be ghastly. Change one element in one of fifteen connected scenes, and all the other scenes need to be rewritten.

Stephan Fitch sums it up: "Interactive writing is more like 3D writing. The writer has to see the layers and move through the layers of the script, keeping track of parallel actions in a scene" (Willis, 1993).

PACE AND TIME

Interactive multimedia has no set running time. It depends on how the player plays the game. The challenge here for the writer is to create a consistent sense of time in the piece when a player might spend twenty minutes in a scene or might skip it altogether. Because time is also an important factor in pace, how does the writer deal with the way this variability of time affects pacing?

Player Creates the Pace

Jane Jensen says that there is no way to have the kind of pacing in interactive narrative that there is in a linear movie, in which a writer can carefully create and sequence a number of scenes to create a faster or slower pace. In interactive narrative, the player creates the pace. For example, a player goes into a haunted house and has to find a way out. The writer's job is to make sure that the scenes are dramatic in themselves and that the player is surprised when things happen. The player may think a certain room is safe from the last time he or she played, but this time it might contain a monster.

How the player interacts with this environment creates the pace of the sequence, but that interaction is affected by the kinds of elements the writer-designer gives the player to interact with. Another way to heighten the feeling of pace is to create a sense of urgency. Both *Half-Life 2* and *Grand Theft Auto— San Andreas* feel fast paced because if you dawdle too long in any one location, you have a good chance of being killed. You have to keep moving.

Multimedia Pace = Miniseries Pace

The combined running times of multiple plays of an interactive movie is much longer than the running time of a two-hour feature film. An interactive movie can be thought of more like a miniseries or a serial. For example, the writer can deal with much of the exposition the first time the game is played, which allows the pace to be increased in later plays.

Manipulating Time to Affect Pace

Other writers and designers have actively manipulated time to affect the pace of the story. In Tony Sherman's *Dracula Unleashed* (DVD version), the player has four days to solve the crime. A clock in the game keeps track of the time. In the real time of playing the game, going to a library and talking to someone may only take thirty seconds, but in game time the player may be deducted an hour. And while he or she is at one location, other scenes happen whether the player sees them or not, just as they would in real life. If the player is knocked out, he or she will miss several scenes and be docked eighty minutes on the clock. Sherman feels that although this time manipulation can add a sense of urgency to the game, the players do set pace. The story material stays the same; it is how it is played that affects the overall pacing.

Nancy Drew: The Secret of the Old Clock uses a similar device but it is worked more into the characters. The owner of the inn is a young girl who is getting progressively more upset by all the weird events. Nancy has to solve the crime before the girl gives up and sells the inn—the goal of the crooks.

An even more interesting use of time is in Riordan's *Thunder in Paradise*. In this program, the time spent in one scene affects what happens in later scenes. For example, in one scene the heroes have to battle the villains surrounding an island to save the heroine who is held there. If the heroes take a long time to defeat these villains, the other villains on the island itself have more time to prepare for them, and the heroes' difficulties are increased when they finally land. This use of time is an important step in making games reflect how time is experienced in real life. It can also give the designer more control over pacing. For example, if the player spends a long time on one scene, the next scene could automatically be altered to increase the pace of the sequence.

Of course, games don't have to be about real life. *F.E.A.R.*, a first person shooter, allows the player to put the game into a slow time mode to change the pace of the action. In this mode all the action is slowed down.

DIALOGUE AND OTHER SOUND

One of the difficulties of characterization in interactive media is the limited dialogue that is allowed because many scenes are very short, and it usually takes longer to develop a strong dialogue scene. Writer Shannon Gilligan compares dialogue writing in interactive media to "writing a symphony of snippets." She claims that it is how the writer relates these snippets together through the design that makes a successful sequence.

The potential use of other sounds, particularly nonsynchronous sounds, is also important. *Under a Killing Moon* uses the tradition of the ironic voice-over in the detective story and includes over five hours of voice-over that gives the player information about characters, objects, and situations. *F.E.A.R.* presents a lot of its plot points and backstory through voice-mails. Ambient sounds are also essential for setting mood. The echoing industrial sounds of *Half-Life 2* are nearly as important to creating the eerie, futuristic feel of the game as the visuals.

CONCLUSION

This chapter provides an overview of some of the common elements and structures of interactive narrative, particularly the computer game. In an interview, writer Matthew Costello said that every project is unique. Sometimes storytelling is fairly linear and structured. Other times there is great randomness and more freedom in how the player participates in the story. There is no one right way to create interactive narrative.

REFERENCES

Beason, P. Telephone interview with the author, July 1994.

Bruckman, A. (1990). *The Combinatorics of Storytelling: Mystery Train Interactive*. MIT Media Lab.

Costello, M. Telephone interviews with the author, (August 2005).

Crawford, C. (2005). *On Interactive Storytelling*. Berkeley, CA: New Riders.

Gilligan, S. Telephone interview with the author, July 1994.

Hodgson, D. (2004). *Half-Life 2: Raising the Bar*. Roseville, CA: Prima Games. IGDA (International Game Developers Association). Web site http://www.igda.org/writing/InteractiveStorytelling.htm.

Jensen, J. Telephone interview with the author, July 1994.

Mystery.net Web site. http://www.mysterynet.com.

O'Meara, M. Interviews with the author, December 1995, July 2005.

O'Meara, M. Letter to the author, June 1994.

Platt, C. (1995). Interactive Entertainment: Who Writes It? Who Reads It? Who Needs It? *WIRED Magazine*, 3, 145–195.

Pousette, L. Telephone interview with the author, (December 1995).

Riordan, D. Telephone interview with the author, August 2005, October 1995.

Sherman, T. Telephone interviews with the author, July 1994, September 1995,)

Willis, H. (1993). Let the Games Begin. *Hollywood Reporter*, S–1–S-32.

SECTION 3
Widening Your Perspective—Serious Games

CHAPTER 19

Designing Simulation Stories from Tacit Knowledge

Nick Iuppa & Terry Borst

The idea of creating a learning simulation to teach the tacit knowledge of military leadership was employed in all three projects that Paramount Pictures did for the U.S. Military. But it was most explicitly employed in the final of the three projects, *Leaders*, which was developed for the United States Army in conjunction with the Institute for Creative Technologies of the University of Southern California. Looking at the methodology used in this project can give a good illustration of ways to develop simulations for leadership and other skills that rely heavily on tacit knowledge.

323

STORYDRIVE SIMULATIONS

StoryDrive simulations are those that follow the classic structure of a Hollywood story complete with hero, arc, goal, and obstacle. The participant takes on the role of the hero and sets off on a quest to fulfill that goal. As Robert McKee (author of *Story*) explains, every step toward the goal should be born out of conflict. To impose even greater demands on that model, especially for pedagogical purposes, we can now add the concept that the simulation should be *outcome driven*. Outcome driven simulations require that the steps that the hero takes be based on pedagogical objectives that move him or her not only toward the goal, but also toward better and better skills honed through the challenges of the simulation. It is the task of the author of the simulation then not only to construct the best possible, most dramatic story, but also to construct one that provides the challenges and opportunities needed to acquire and develop skills that reflect the pedagogical goals. How do you do that?

DOI: 10.1016/B978-0-240-81343-1.00019-4

Identifying Tacit Knowledge

Stories are one way to identify correct performance. An easier way may be to find people who are really good at something and just follow them around with a notebook writing down everything they do. Debriefings after each session can then help zero in on the specifics of the tasks and may lead to a correct prescription of correct performance. But tacit knowledge in skills such as leadership and management are hard to identify when you see them and harder to define once you've found them. That is how stories can help. Asking an experienced leader to define leadership might get you a lot of nonconclusive ramblings, but asking that same person to tell a valuable story about leadership can draw out much better, more specific data.

Roger Schank, the noted AI researcher, suggests that people understand the world because they form mental models of it. These internal world pictures are continually revised as they discover new things. The major revisions in people's mental models are so important that they tend to remember the details of what happened when they were surprised enough by something that it made them change their world view. The day the universe changed for them actually becomes a story that they tell their friends, and Schank and others have described the telling of these stories as a mechanism for collective learning. The day we were surprised to find out a very important secret of management we immediately told our fellow managers and we all learned. We keep telling that story and more people learn.

So a good way to learn about important skills like leadership is to go to a number of people who understand it and ask them to tell stories. Within the stories will be the essence of the surprise that changed their worldview. Within the stories will also be an implicit explanation of the old view that was changed when the revelation occurred. As a result of all this you should be able to learn two things:

1. The naive, expected view of the way something should be.
2. The informed, experienced, and true way.

The process of building outcome driven simulations begins when you collect numerous stories about a subject which largely consist of tacit knowledge, and which involve the moment someone learns something about it, which was true even though up until that moment he or she was convinced that it was false. Here is a formula, which helps clarify that point.

Initially you would expect X.
But, with experience, you learn that the truth is Y.
Or to put it more simply:
Expectation = X
Truth = Y

So you have arranged a series of interviews with experienced leaders, you have pressed them for stories of situations where they were surprised by something that taught them a valuable lesson about leadership. Then you and the rest of your team have transcribed the interviews, analyzed them, and determined what was the expectation and what was the truth behind each story. The next step is to turn those stories into decision points based on the underlying lesson of the story. If you believed the lesson then you would do what the lesson said to be true, otherwise you would do the expected thing. Or, put another way,

> If you were in a situation
>
> And you believed the lesson of the story
>
> You would do Y (what the lesson says is the truth)
>
> Otherwise you would do X (what a novice would expect to do)

Here is an example from the *Leaders* scenario.

Situation: You are Captain Young and you have taken over the command of a food distribution operation in Afghanistan. Your subordinate officers have come up with a mission plan that they are very proud of. Later you are talking with an experienced officer outside of your command and he suggests that a different plan might be slightly better.

> *Novice choice:* Accept the plan of the more experienced person and tell the subordinates that this is what they should do.
>
> *Expert choice:* Stick with the plan developed by your subordinates.

Interestingly here, the key word in all of this is "slightly." Since the proposed plan will only be slightly better, it makes more sense to give your troops the motivational lift they will get from carrying out a plan that they designed and selected themselves.

Sorting Out the Story

Once you have completed your interviews and boiled down the scenarios into decision points, organize them according to topic areas. Then validate the decision points by having them reviewed by highly experienced personnel in the positions that you are trying to teach. If there are stories that just don't ring true or cannot be condoned no matter how true they may be, throw them out. In the case of the *Leaders* project we were fortunate to have two highly regarded members of the military training community reviewing our work and commenting on its accuracy and believability. We were also able to cross check the work against the literature on the subject. Sternberg's *Practical Intelligence in Everyday Life* had already documented an extensive study of the military and we were able to verify our data with the Integrated Framework for Tacit Knowledge in the Military that was part of the work. We were gratified to see that the

63 anecdotes that we had collected covered all the categories of tacit leadership knowledge spelled out in the framework.

Once your content has been sorted into groups and verified, you need to organize it into four to six chapters of equal size putting most of the situations relating to specific topics into the same chapter. In the *Leaders* project, the 63 decision formulations that were made by the creative team were sorted equally into five chapters that represented the five components of the mission: establishing a relationship with subordinates, mission preparation, dealing with threats, coordinating with superior officers, and successfully executing the mission.

Building the Narrative

What we have created with the decision formula we have described is a binary system of choices where every decision requires that you make one or the other. These then lead to another choice between two points, which then lead to another choice. These choices can be assembled into a graph or flowchart that takes you from one choice to the next. Given the 63 original decision points and five chapters, we built a simulation that consisted of 12 to 15 choices per chapter. To round out the number of choices needed we sometimes repeated decision points, rewriting them so that the situations and the details of the situation were different. Figure 19.1 shows the structure of the graph for chapter 2 of the simulation.

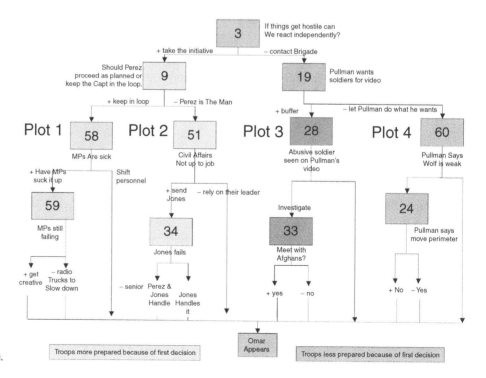

Figure 19.1
Graph of chapter 2 of the Leaders simulation.

In the graph the first choice should be the most important instructional point in the chapter. This should happen for a number of reasons. First, the participants going through the simulation will all encounter this important point. If they go through the simulation again, they will always get this point again, so it is imperative that it be worth it. Second, this point leads to a major division in the action of the chapter, so right and wrong consequences of this choice can be most dramatic. Third, the challenge of this point will hit the participants when they are fresh in the chapter, most clear headed, with the least baggage from previous decisions. It is the most highly focused moment in the chapter, the best chance for undivided attention and dedicated response. Fourth and finally, this is the point by which the participants will judge the entire chapter. The quality of the insight gained at this point can motivate the participants to carry on through the rest of the exercise.

Once the initial point has been made, the decision points that follow should be arranged in clusters based on their content and the personalities involved in the decision. Events should be chosen that match the kind of decision required by the point, and they should be grouped together so that the same characters and location can be featured. As we talk about developing characters we will point out how complex personalities can add great value to story-based simulations. The trick is to recognize opportunities to use the same character to deal with a specific point. Then find decision points that would fit in logically with the situation presented in the simulation. One way to handle this is in brainstorming sessions with a number of participants: a writer, an interactive designer, a subject matter expert who can mix and match decisions with situations and personalities. It is generally not necessary to retell the story on which the decision point is based, but rather to look at the new scenario and try to figure out what kinds of events within the scenario could put the hero into a situation where this particular kind of decision would be necessary. Then review the other decisions and see if there is one that can build on the previous decision with the same characters and location, but with new events and revelations. It ends up being like assembling a jigsaw puzzle, but one where you are creating the pieces as you go along. Once a good event is developed it may not be a perfect follow-on to the previous decision point. If that is the case, set it aside and hold it for a more appropriate moment later in the simulation.

As noted previously, *Leaders* was based on a film about a food distribution operation in Afghanistan. That was the framing device for all the decisions that would follow. In *Leaders*, an initial meeting with Executive Officer (XO) Lieutenant Perez at the start of chapter 2 tests the Battle Captain's ability to handle the first challenge to authority. Perez wants to run the operation. If the participant gives in to Perez, why not let Perez come back and challenge the Battle Captain even further? We found two important decision points about challenges to leadership authority among our 63, staged them at the same place and time, and put them into the hands of Lieutenant Perez. In the process, we made the simulation more interesting, the characters stronger, and the skills more highly exercised.

327

Dead Ends and Shared Outcomes

Two well-established techniques used in branching storylines are Dead Ends (if there is no outcome to a decision, simply say, "Sorry you're wrong. Go back and try again"), and Shared Outcomes (decisions can lead to many outcomes, not just the two pre-planned outcomes specified in the flowchart). Dead Ends provide immediate feedback for the participants, but they destroy the sense of story flow and immersion. For that reason we did not use them in *Leaders*. Shared Outcomes give the participant more choices, but they disrupt the clustering of content that we have just described. The net effect is less dramatic tension and a decreased ability to add levels of meaning that result from highly structured exchanges extended over several decision points. For this reason Shared Outcomes were also not used.

Once the design team creates the basic structure of each chapter, the writer takes over and writes the script for the entire chapter, composing character conversations that present decisions and offer feedback. It is also important to write bridging material: additional scenes featuring other characters that set up each decision point and its problem and later comment on its success or failure.

A sample of the final script follows. It builds on the example that we cited earlier involving the decision regarding implementation of a plan put together by Captain Young's subordinates.

```
Begin decision point 24
EXTREME LONG SHOT of distribution area showing
terrain, converging roads, and position of troops
setting up food distribution and security areas.

COMMAND POST
CLOSE UP: COMMAND SERGEANT MAJOR PULLMAN Pullman
looks down toward the roads.

                    PULLMAN
   Look, I don't want to go stepping on any
   toes, but I was looking over your terrain.
   I'm sure this site got chosen because of the
   road access. But it's sure got some problems.

He points toward the perimeter.
```

                    PULLMAN
I would encourage you to bump your security
perimeter eastward, and put more distance
between the wire and the road. Even after
you've checked a vehicle through, damn
thing could surprise you. That extra
distance between the road and the perimeter
could make the difference.

He points toward a rocky overhang.

                    PULLMAN
I'd also advise you start setting up the
space under that overhang, in case it
rains.

                    JONES
Captain, myself along with the XO and Second
Platoon, we put a lot of thought into this
configuration. Not saying the Command
Sergeant Major has an inferior plan. But
company personnel collaborated very closely
in strategy and tactics.

                    PULLMAN
Captain, your First Sergeant heads a great
team—but if you make these changes, it'll
pay off. Just give it some thought.

Pullman leaves the Command Post. Jones turns to the
Captain.

                    JONES
Would the Captain like changes made to the
security perimeter?

Figure 19.2
Final Leaders simulation scene showing Jones and Pullman addressing Captain Young while Perez looks on.

SUMMARY

In this chapter we have shown how tacit knowledge can be acquired by collecting anecdotes about hard-to-define skills like leadership. We also talked about how these anecdotes can be turned into teaching points, validated, and organized into chapters. We offered insight into the creative process that takes teaching points and turns them into story events and script elements. Finally, we showed examples of decision points set in a story context by providing examples from the *Leaders* simulation (Figure 19.2).

In the next chapter we will consider how to begin giving the participants a greater sense of free will within the context of the simulation story.

CHAPTER 20

Simulation Stories and Free Play

Nick Iuppa & Terry Borst

In the previous chapter we showed how the *Leaders* team constructed a branching simulation storyline from anecdotal information that was gathered through interviews with experienced soldiers. The information was condensed and reorganized into teaching points and turned into a complete learning experience.

Because of the rigors of the branching structure, the participants in such simulations could feel that they are locked into the flow of events in the story, and for that reason have no sense of their own freedom of decision making or their ability to affect the outcome of the simulation. Without this sense of freedom, the simulation becomes less believable, less interesting, less compelling, and generally less effective. Simulations that limit freedom of choice too extensively often negate any sense that the participants are actually controlling the world, and consequently they are distracted from applying the skills that they have learned.

There are a variety of ways to give participants a sense of free will within simulated stories. Two techniques apply directly to branching storylines such as the ones we used in the *Leaders* simulation. We review those techniques in this chapter.

The more advanced and difficult approaches are really experience management systems that move away from branching storylines and aim to give the participants a greater sense of free will.

But let's go back to our *Leaders* simulation and the need to give the participants a sense of free will within the branching story structure. How can we do that?

SIMULATED CONVERSATIONS

In the *Leaders* simulation, participants progress through the story until they have to make a decision. The elements of the decision are presented to them in the form of questions that are asked by one of the nonplayer characters (NPC).

As noted in the example from the previous chapter, First Sergeant Jones asks the participant (Captain) if he should move the location of the food distribution site as suggested by Command Sergeant Major Pullman.

The participant can type in a response to this question using any words he or she chooses, and the natural language interface of the *Leaders* system will interpret the statement and choose a prerecorded response from the many that are available. These responses are audio with attached animation of the characters.

To give the participants a greater sense of free will, they are also allowed to ask questions of the nonplayer character. So, in the case of the question about moving the location, the design team defined as many questions and responses as they could think of. They also wrote and prerecorded the answers to those questions. If a participant asks, for example, how moving the location would affect the morale of the troops who came up with the original plan, First Sergeant Jones has a prerecorded answer.

> JONES
> The platoon leaders and I spent a lot of time
> putting this plan together, Captain, and I'm
> sure that they would be very disappointed to
> learn that you were changing the plan.

To make the interaction as smooth as possible, we tested the prerecorded responses by creating a Web site with still pictures and a narrative story setup, but with the same dialog and choices as in the actual simulation. The site was posted on various military Internet sites and soldiers were asked to participate in the exercise in order to validate the questions and answers. We also tried to discover any new questions that we had not thought of. The answers to these new questions were recorded, added to the system, and contributed to a more robust version of the final simulation. For example, one additional question that was discovered and added to the simulation asked, "What do you think about the probability of rain in this location?" To which we wrote and recorded this additional response:

> JONES
> Captain, it's not supposed to rain here for
> months and certainly not today. I know the
> Command Sergeant Major has served here longer
> than I have, and he may be familiar with
> unusual weather patterns, but I can tell you
> that no weather forecast I have seen predicts
> rain for the rest of this month.

In addition to adding appropriate questions that the participants might ask, we also recognized that soldiers might try and *game the system,* or try and have fun with the conversations by typing in questions that were out of context or inappropriate. We adapted various devices to counter these actions. The simplest one was to assume that the system just did not understand what the participant was saying. So we recorded a series of responses that presented the possibility that they Captain's remark was unintelligible. These remarks also worked in those cases where the participants' comments were off the point. For example:

```
                       JONES
    I'm not sure I understand what you are
    saying Captain, could you restate it?
```

Other responses dealt directly with statements that seemed to be off the topic. These remarks would be highly original or unusual and therefore unlikely to be anticipated. Our responses dealt directly with the fact that the participant was getting off the track. So, there might be words or phrases in the participant's question that made sense, but if the question was not related to the issue at hand it was judged to be a non sequitur. Here's a typical response to a non sequitur question that includes an attempt to get the participant back on track.

```
                       JONES
    I'm not sure I know the answer to that
    question, Captain. I'm trying to find out if
    you want me to move the distribution site.
    What is your decision?
```

The response that the Sergeant gives if the participant asks to be reminded of the original question could also be used as a response to a non sequitur question. In our example the response to being asked "What was the question?" was:

```
                       JONES
    Captain, the Command Sergeant Major has
    advised that we move the perimeter of the
    site to the north. Do you want me to order
    our troops to move the site or can we
    continue with the existing plan?
```

INTELLIGENT TUTORING

Intelligent Tutoring is a unique feature of the *Leaders* simulation that allows instructional statements to appear on the screen to help move the simulation along or get the participant back on track. This response is not from an NPC in the scene (First Sergeant Jones) but from a tutor built into the system itself. We decided not to give this feature a personality or a face but merely to let it appear as text on the screen. This seemed to be the least obtrusive way to introduce tutorial information into the experience. We tested various uses of the tutor and decided to bring in the intelligent tutor after the participant made two non sequitur responses in a row. We also made the statement more direct and included a third person reference to the entire event. In our example, the intelligent tutor statement read as follows:

```
Captain, the First Sergeant is trying to determine
if you want him to order his soldiers to move
the perimeter as Command Sergeant Major Pullman
suggests. Please tell him whether or not you want to
stay with the original plan.
```

Note that the final sentence is a complete restatement of the choices.

The intelligent tutoring system within *Leaders* served two purposes. The first was clarification, as illustrated here. A more sophisticated use of the intelligent tutor was designed to come into play if the participant went through the simulation for a second time and made the same mistake again. In this case the system would remember the participant and his or her response and would explain the teaching point behind the decision node. The participant would still have the free will to choose the wrong answer, but would be much better informed about the point and the intention of the lesson.

In the case of this example, a participant who has gone through the simulation for a second time and encountered this decision point, then asked a series of questions and eventually gave the wrong answer for the second time, would get this statement from the intelligent tutor:

```
Captain, soldiers who have developed a plan
themselves will often show greater enthusiasm for
carrying out that plan. So unless there is an
important reason for changing it, it is better to
stick with a plan developed by the soldiers who have
to carry it out. The First Sergeant is asking if you
want to change his soldiers' plan under the advice
of the Command Sergeant Major Pullman or to let his
men carry out the plan that they created themselves?
```

The *Leaders* team created the full conversation question and answer system for the simulation, and in the process gave the simulation participants a greater sense of free play. We also designed an even more sophisticated solution to the problem of free play, which, though not implemented, was detailed in a report to the ICT and the Army. It is described here.

SPIDER WEBS

One classic way to add a sense of freedom to the story is to create story structures that look more like spider webs than branching trees. In these structures the outcomes of one set of decision elements (decision nodes) can lead to many different nodes. This greater flexibility in the development of the story allows a finer degree of differentiation between possible directives by the participants. If there are five paths out of a decision point instead of only two, the participant has a greater sense of control of the environment because the nuances of their choices matter more. Moreover, the dangers of the ever-branching tree are limited because the same number of decision nodes exist within the exercise, it is just that they interconnect because there are just more paths in and out of each node.

In a branching story structure where there are four levels of decisions and two choices coming out of each decision node, beginning with one decision then going to two possible outcomes, then four, eight, and sixteen nodes, any one path will allow the participant to experience no more than four nodes. That means that, of the 31 nodes that are created for the exercise, 27 nodes are not used. Allowing the participants access to those nodes through the device of spider webbing provides a greater use of the nodes. The result is that the participant can replay the simulation many times and have many different experiences at each playing, even if they do repeat some of their early choices. If AI is employed to keep track of the participants' paths through the story, the system can also direct the player onto those paths that they had not previously traversed and as a result expand the participant's options.

The trick to creating this kind of simulation story is all in the telling. As we will see, it is important that nodes lead one to the next in such a way that the tension in the story—and the logic of the story—builds. The problem with Shared Outcomes (that they disrupt the clusters of content) can be overcome by creative writing and the AI capabilities of the computer. Not every node can lead to another. But it is possible to identify certain characteristics about certain decision nodes so that an AI system can know whether or not one node can be the outcome of another node. Of the 31 nodes in chapter 2 of the *Leaders* simulation only four of them had conditions that made it necessary that another node precede them. That means that 27 of the nodes could follow any of the other nodes and the consequences would seem logical.

To create a spider web-based branching storyline in which most nodes can lead to most other nodes, an analysis of each node must be made, certain characteristics

335

must be identified and coded, and then an AI system must be created which recognizes these characteristics and blocks the use of the nodes in those situations in which their use would be inappropriate. In addition, the story structure itself must be coded (as metadata), along with information about the previous path that particular participants have taken. If these elements can be taken into consideration, it is possible to have a much more flexible version of the simulation chapter which could be replayed over and over again with the participants taking a completely different path each time.

Here is an example. Soldier X has been through the *Leaders* simulation once. He has had made all the possible decisions (four per chapter). The system can tell by his identification number who he is, which decisions he had made, and in what order. The first question the system then asks itself (the next time the participant goes through the system) is: Which other possible start nodes can the participant get this time? Since there are a limited number of nodes that have the qualities needed to start the simulation, that decision is made rather quickly. From that point on the possible path is chosen by the system during the real-time play of the exercise. So the participant goes into a node, makes his decision, and then the system chooses a new target decision point (node) based on several factors. Figure 20.1 shows a sample form that indicates information and ratings that the authors of the *Leaders* simulation gave to the decision node that we have been using as an example in this chapter. That node is called Hand in the Plan.

We can see a number of elements are identified so that they can be considered in choosing the next node:

- Is there a required preceding node or a required follow-up node to this node?
- Which characters are present in the scene?
- What is the background of the scene?

Decision Frame ID:	2–24	
Point Title:	HAND IN THE PLAN	
Set up Scene:	Command Sgt. Major approaches the captain re plan	
Set up Display Text:	JONES: Would the capt. like changes made to the security perimeter	
Characters Present:	Jones, Pullman	
Location Background:	Command Post overlooking site	
Required Preceding Node:	Node 9	**Outcome Scenes**
Required Following Node:	None	POS = 67 - JONES: The good news is he will probably forget all about it.
Number of Answers:	7	
Dramatic Tension Rating:	5	NEG = 69 - JONES: Bravo company prides itself on its flexibility sir.
Pedagogical Importance	5	

Figure 20.1
Molecule
Identification Form.

- What is the amount of dramatic tension in the scene?
- What is the degree of pedagogical importance of the decision?

In addition, this form is used to record other pertinent information about the node:

- Its name and number.
- The text of the question itself.
- Summary positive and negative responses.
- Specific wording of the outcome scenes.
- The number of question and response pairs available to the participant.

In the case of our example we can see that, while this is an important decision, it requires certain prerequisite information not available in the node itself, so that another node must precede it. So while Hand in the Plan could follow a good many nodes, it cannot be the first node in the chapter.

Note the ratings for dramatic tension and pedagogical importance. This is part of the metadata for the node, and is done to make sure that the simulation follows the rules of storytelling and pedagogy. Ideally the nodes get more dramatic as the story progresses. On the other hand, pedagogically it is important to put the nodes with the highest degree of instructional importance early in the chapter so that there is a higher probability that they be encountered.

In the case of the decision in our example, the concept is not especially difficult nor does it carry especially dramatic consequences. Combine that with the fact that it requires a prerequisite node and it looks like Hand in the Plan is an ideal node for the middle of the simulation exercise, not the first nor the final node of chapter 2.

HANDCRAFTED SPIDER WEBS

Though it would be possible to create an AI system that assembled the simulation as it were in progress, sort of like an engineer standing on the front of a locomotive and laying out sections of track as the train roars ahead, it is clear that there are only so many combinations of nodes that follow all the rules for drama and challenge and the presence of characters and available prerequisites, etc. This means that with these limitations it would be possible to construct something like 25 different handcrafted, hard-coded branching storylines that would provide a great deal of participant reusability and represent almost all the possible paths that a player could take through the simulation. The high-powered functionality of having an AI engine that would build the story structure as the simulation progressed might not be achieved in the creation of such an exercise, but the learning experience would be just as good.

All the foregoing, however, assumes a simulation structure like *Leaders*, where the participant stands still at the command center and his or her subordinates ask all the direct questions that need to be asked. If the participant is able to move around the terrain, encounter different characters, and initiate conversations, we have a whole different kind of simulation, one that was not addressed in the limited scope of the *Leaders* project, but certainly one worth exploring. Participant-driven movement over a large terrain populated with numbers of soldiers, all of whom can respond to questions, adds new variables to the simulation and would certainly be better served by something like the auto-assemble spider webs we have just described. In fact, there are even more sophisticated kinds of simulation strategies designed to give participants a greater sense of free will, which address many of these problems.

SUMMARY

Giving participants a sense of free will is one of the core needs of effective story-driven simulations. Even a simulation based on branching story lines such as *Leaders* is capable of employing a number of techniques that improve the participants' sense of free will. One such technique involves giving the participants the ability to ask questions, creating a wide range of answers to these questions, and developing strategies for handling non sequitur statements. Intelligent tutoring operates against the player's sense of free will but can still be used effectively if it is employed as a tool that operates outside the confines of simulation. Spider webs allow branching storylines to give the participants greater range throughout the simulation and, if well crafted, can add greatly to the sense of freedom, but to do this they must follow a rigorous set of rules that assure that they are used effectively. Handcrafted storylines may be just as effective as those driven by artificial intelligence, but become more difficult to manage in simulations where the participants can move around the terrain and have discussions with anyone they meet.

CHAPTER 21

Experience Management

Nick Iuppa & Terry Borst

In the previous chapter we talked about the need to give simulation participants a sense that they have the ability to control the progress and outcome of events so that they don't feel they are merely being swept along in a stream of experiences that will occur, regardless of what they do. It is also important that the interactions that they do perform are not irrelevant. Shunting action over to some side activity doesn't do the job either. The film *Titanic* may be a good example of this principle. In a simulation based on the incidents surrounding the sinking of the *Titanic*, the actual sinking of the ship is not really the story. It's the background. Whether or not any individual character escapes alive is *their* story. Creating a simulation story that allows the participants to prevent the collision and the subsequent sinking of the ship is probably to miss the point here. James Cameron understood this when he wrote and directed the highest-grossing film in motion picture history to date.

He put his heroes on board the sinking ship and left them to their own devices to find a way to survive. Players in a simulated *Titanic* adventure would probably enjoy this aspect of the story the most—saving themselves and someone they love. What they and all simulation participants want the most is interactivity that is relevant and meaningful.

Dr. Andrew Gordon, the lead researcher on the ALTSIM project, may have stated it best when he wrote, "The central problem of creating interactive drama is structuring a media experience in which a good story is presented while participants are still able to have a high degree of meaningful interactivity." There are many key words in that statement: "meaningful" being the most important, followed by "high degree" of interactivity and, of course, "good story." What appears to be a struggle between the free will and free play of the participants and the events of the story itself ends up being, behind the scenes, a struggle

339

between the participants' desires to do what they want and the simulation system's ability to manage, control, and enable the telling of the story.

We have already described the *Leaders* project, which uses a fixed branching storyline to direct players toward the simulation's dramatic goals.

In this chapter, we will look at an alternate approach, the one we took in ALTSIM, which in its own way was even simpler than that of a branching storyline. The ALTSIM approach uses a piece of technology called the Experience Manager, which allows participants to play a very active role in a highly developed story-driven simulation.

In order to do this in the ALTSIM simulation, the Experience Manager needed to understand the story. The device Dr. Gordon came up with to make this possible was a set of formal descriptions of the actions that the player would take as the story moves along. These descriptions were based on the players' perceptions of the events that were happening and the actions they would take based on those perceptions. That set of representations (the metadata of the story), which we called the Story Representation System, in a sense served as the Experience Manager's coded script. When the expectations in that coded script were wrong—that is, when the participants did things other than those written in the Story Representation System—the Experience Manager called up a Story Adaptation Strategy that would adjust the participant experience. If possible, the Experience Manager would do nothing—or, if doing nothing would not allow the story to continue toward its dramatic goals, the Experience Manager would adjust the story, take the participant on a brief but temporary side track, or block the participant's action completely.

The important elements needed to make the Experience Manager work were an effective and accurate coded script using the Story Representation System and, just as importantly, a set of story adaptation strategies that would not seem too farfetched or intrusive, and yet would re-set the story so that it was still allowed to progress toward its dramatic goals.

EXPERIENCE MANAGEMENT

In ALTSIM, the story is told though media elements (individual video and audio clips, text messages, and graphics) that arrive at the computers of the participants in the simulated tactical operations center (TOC). The delivery of the media elements is timed to correspond to the passage of time in the story. Each media element carries with it an expected action by the player. In some cases, the actions are expected immediately or within a very limited time frame; in other cases, they are not, and sometimes it is a combination of elements that require a specific action. In rare cases, there are branches that have been anticipated in the story. These are triggered by specific actions but these branches are extremely limited: so that in fact the story has one, two, or three arcs that split and occasionally come back together as the story progresses.

When the players in the TOC encounter a media element, they take an action. As long as the encoded script of the Experience Manager anticipates the players' actions, the story progresses on track and more media elements are delivered. If the players do exactly what the encoded script describes, they have a rewarding learning experience and the Experience Manager has had to do no more, figuratively, than to sit back and watch.

As an example, consider creating an interactive drama out of the classic western movie *High Noon*. Assume that the story is told through clips from the film but that additional scenes can be added using a style that matches the film while not needing to employ the original actors or new dialog on their part. The reason that we are imagining this is because the copyright issues surrounding a star-studded feature film like *High Noon* would make it prohibitive to turn into an interactive drama. But the story is so clean and direct that the subject is irresistible. Also, *High Noon*, set in the most mythical old west, is perhaps the best example imaginable of a simple story that is all about decision making.

Say that somehow we got the rights to this great film. Now, imagine that in our simulation the player is asked to become Will Kane, the hero of the story, and that each segment presented ends with a question about what to do.

Figure 21.1 shows the arc of *High Noon* recast in the first person so that the player is the hero, Will Kane.

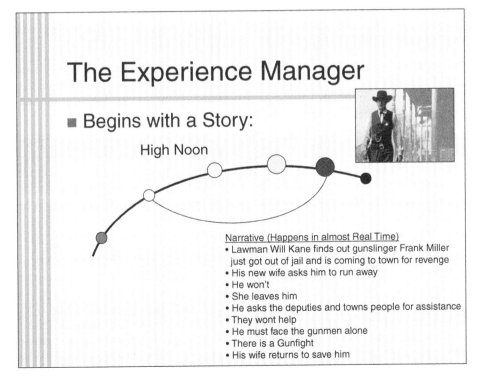

Figure 21.1
The story arc of *High Noon*.

In a sense the entire story of *High Noon* is about the decision to stay or run, but it is presented over and over again in different contexts. In our simulated version of *High Noon* the player decides what to do (if anything) and uses the computer keyboard to compose a response back to the system, e.g., "I decide to let my wife go by herself and I will stay to face the gunslingers." In cases where the player response matches exactly what Will did in the original movie, the story moves forward and the next scene is presented (e.g., "I head into the saloon to ask some of the townspeople for help").

If we were to create another branch to the story (the most probable branch to the events that might occur) and we create all the media to support that path, then we would still have a similar situation. As long as the participant made decisions that conformed to the path of the story the author laid down, there is no need for any kind of intervention. The story just plays out as planned. We can even allow the sheriff to convince some or all of the townspeople to join in the confrontation.

In this case, however, to preserve the dramatic goals of the story, the sheriff needs to have a crisis moment when he knows he must face the villains alone. So the author of this new branch of the story develops a scenario in which some townspeople agree to support the sheriff but at the last minute back out again. That way the dramatic climax of the story, when the sheriff realizes that he must face the bad guys alone, is preserved. The confrontation is represented by the largest circle on the flowchart and is the most dramatic moment in the story—the moment of truth. The smaller black circle that follows is the outcome, the actual gunfight, which, though memorable and exciting, is not really what the story is all about. Once the sheriff finally decides to stay, the dramatic goals of the story have been met.

In a story-driven simulation (which has been expanded to provide one or two additional branches to accommodate the most likely alternate paths of the story, and which maintains the dramatic goals), if the player does not deviate from the established story paths, no dramatic interventions are necessary.

Notice in Figure 21.2, there are two alternate paths for the story. The path from the third circle to the largest circle represents the path when the townspeople decide to join Will and then change their minds. The path from the second circle represents the consequences of the discussion Will has with his wife. The author of this path decided to take advantage of the pedagogical opportunity presented there, so that, if Will handled the conversation badly, then his wife may not come back and save him in the end (which is what she does in the film).

Within this framework, one or two added branches or not, the central problem is how to deal with player behavior that is not anticipated in the Experience Manger's coded script. After all, as soon as Will finds out about the bad guys, the user could respond in a way that is outside the storyline. He or she could have Will leave town the moment he gets the message. If that were the case, the next required scene would not be present in the existing movie. However, a single new scene could be added that could accommodate this action in such a way that the

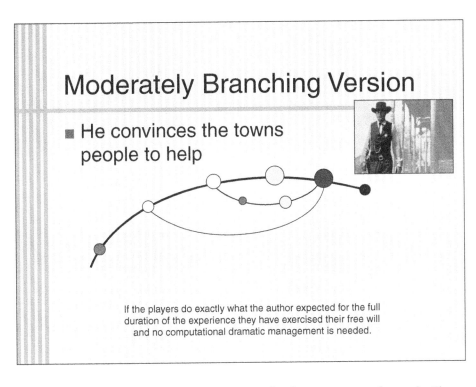

Moderately Branching Version

■ He convinces the towns people to help

If the players do exactly what the author expected for the full duration of the experience they have exercised their free will and no computational dramatic management is needed.

Figure 21.2
Alternate story paths for *High Noon*.

343

rest of the film would still work. For example, the new scene shown in Figure 21.3 would probably work as follows: "As Will walks back home to tell his wife about the message and his plans to leave town, he runs into a young boy who proudly says how much he admires Will and his fearless protection of the town."

In this simple case, the expected action is that the boy will shame Will into staying and facing the bad guys. Note that this specific response works at a single story point as shown in Figure 21.3. But following this approach, and writing and producing the media elements that would allow a separate specific adaptation response for every point in the story, would be all but impossible.

Now, let's look at that response again and rework it slightly as follows: "As Will walks from his office, **ready to leave town,** he runs into a young boy who proudly says how much he admires Will and his fearless protection of the town." That slight redefining of the adaptation strategy would work at any place in the story where Will decides to leave town, no matter when it is (Figure 21.4). The fact is that the revised scene is a **general** piece of adaptation media and it is for such media that ALTSIM's Experience Manager was designed.

Let's assume again that we have created an interactive version of *High Noon* by chopping up the original film into a series of sequences. For example, Will gets the letter; Will talks to his wife who says she will leave him if he doesn't run away; Will talks to the townspeople; Will talks to his deputies, etc. At the end of every sequence the participant who plays the part of Will Kane has to make a

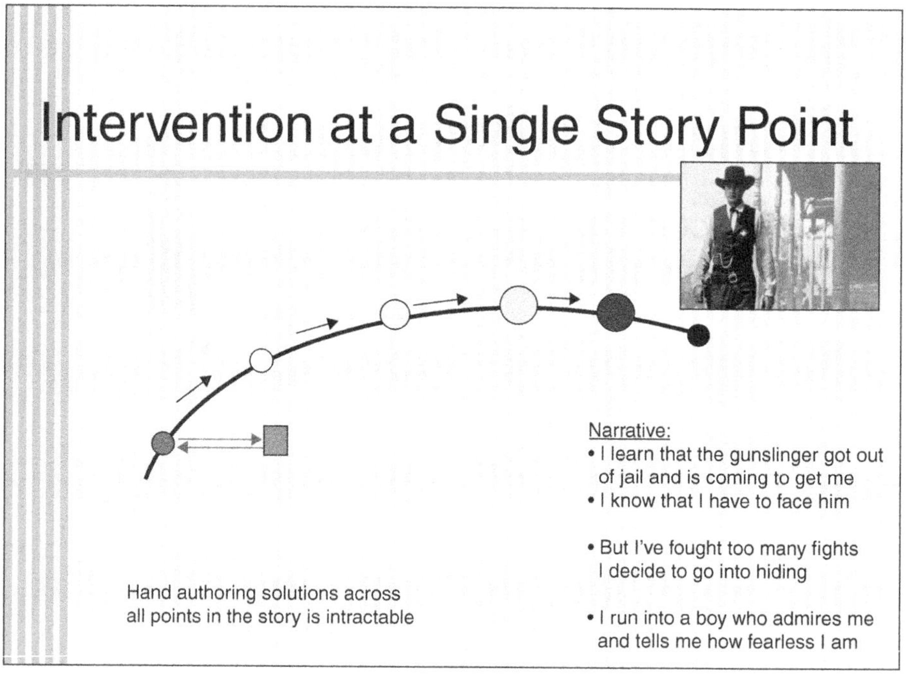

Figure 21.3
A way to handle unexpected player behavior.

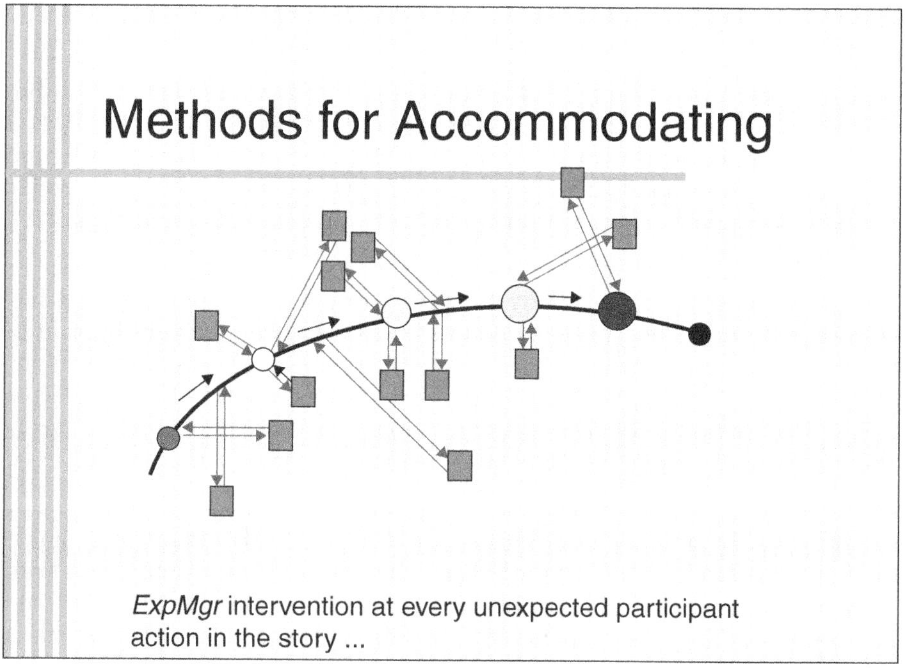

Figure 21.4
Story adaptation strategies applied in reaction to unexpected player behavior.

decision. Most decisions are variations on whether or not to stand and face the bad guys in the light of increasingly negative evidence. For example, Will could decide to join his wife and run away; make up his mind to hop on his horse and ride out of town; or he could get on the next train; or go into hiding.

We could create a decision matrix for Will by plotting the decision points at the end of the movie sequences against Will's possible actions. If we add the option of doing nothing at all, then we really have covered all the possibilities. The Experience Manager's job is to fill in the blanks in such a matrix, that is, to complete the formula that says, "At this moment, with this action, the way to keep the story on track is to employ this adaptation strategy."

Figure 21.5 shows some examples of adaptation strategies that could be used in an interactive simulation based on *High Noon*. They include sending mis-information such as "he's not really out of jail," text messages in the form of telegrams urging Will to stay the course, and weather that makes the roads impassable so that he can't leave town.

Once the simulation story has been represented in a way that the computer system can understand and a robust set of adaptation strategies have been identified and created, what is needed is the appropriate set of rules by which the system can operate. For example, one obvious rule is that the first thing for the Experience Manager to do after the participant takes an unexpected action is to check out the consequences of the proposed action. If the storyline can

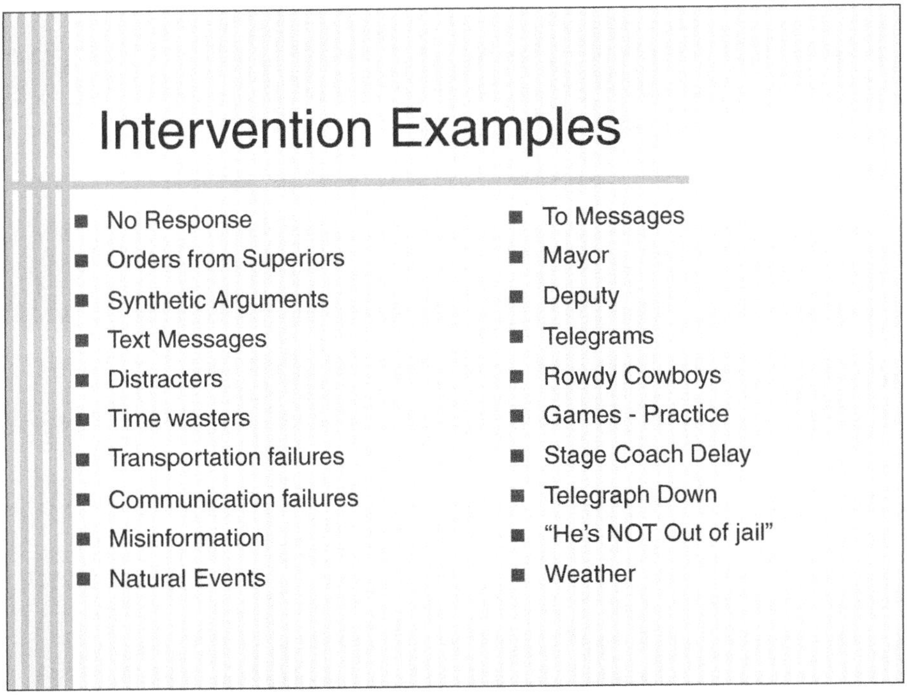

Intervention Examples

- No Response
- Orders from Superiors
- Synthetic Arguments
- Text Messages
- Distracters
- Time wasters
- Transportation failures
- Communication failures
- Misinformation
- Natural Events

- To Messages
- Mayor
- Deputy
- Telegrams
- Rowdy Cowboys
- Games - Practice
- Stage Coach Delay
- Telegraph Down
- "He's NOT Out of jail"
- Weather

Figure 21.5
Examples of adaptation strategies.

continue as written, the dramatic goals met and the action can still be carried out, then that will certainly provide the most rewarding experience for the participant and give the greatest sense of personal control. Other criteria might include whether or not the adaptation strategy has been employed before. If Will Kane, for example, had already run into the young boy who tells him how proud he is of Will's protection, then it is unlikely that the participant will be affected positively by going through the same experience again.

SUMMARY

In this chapter we have talked about Experience Management, a system whereby simulation participants follow the arc of a prescribed story that may have one or two branching paths. As long as they stay on those paths the story stays on track. But when the participants do something that the storywriter did not intend, then it is up to the Experience Management System to get the story back on track. It does this by employing an adaptation response of some kind that either adjusts the story or blocks the participants' new action and forces the story back on track.

The keys to successful implementation of Experience Management are (1) a way to represent the story with metadata so that the computer can understand and manipulate it, and (2) a sophisticated set of general adaptation responses that can be used to block user actions in a way that will not seem too manipulative to the participants, but which will still get the story back on track.

CHAPTER 22

Backstory and Free Play

Nick Iuppa & Terry Borst

The *Grand Theft Auto* (GTA) videogame trilogy *(Liberty City, Vice City, San Andreas)* is arguably the most successful commercial game franchise in history. It has also gained notoriety for its "hidden" sexual content (unlocked via a videogame "mod") and for its nonjudgmental (or amoral) allowance for criminal behavior.

GTA also happens to define one of the most successful storygame models yet developed in the commercial realm. A brief look at some of its techniques and mechanics may inform your approach to a simulation, particularly if you're looking at using the RT3D (real-time 3D-rendered) platform.

GTA is often known as a "sandbox" game. As the tag suggests, players have full freedom to explore the virtual urban environment, for as long as they'd like—an illustration of the pleasures of exploration and navigation. If *GTA* was set in an unpopulated, empty terrain, of course, these pleasures would quickly evaporate. But *GTA* is stuffed with characters, sets, and objects to interact with, and interactivity is nearly always available.

Unauthorized acquisition of vehicles (it *is* called *Grand Theft Auto*, after all) is at the heart of the interactivity. But one simple illustration of the richness of the world is the panoply of radio stations a player can listen to once behind the wheel of a car. The radio station music and chatter further immerses the player in the daily life of *Vice City* or *San Andreas*, and enhances the pleasure of basic navigation, so that even when there is a specific, story-driven task, the execution becomes an exercise in play.

GTA's story is doled out via a combination of cutscenes and missions or quests (combinations of hide-and-seek, solve-the-puzzle, and kill-the-enemy). Ideally, the characters and plot encourage the player to undertake the missions and "learn" the world. The player is amply rewarded (usually with virtual financial

347

remuneration) for successful completion of the missions, and betters himself or herself in a demonstrable way (via the *GTA* virtual economy).

At the same time, players are not forced to complete quests in a certain order; they're allowed enough free will within the game to determine their goals and needs. This encourages players to spend hours of time within the environment, gleaning everything they can from it.

We're not suggesting that your simulation include automobile theft and the underbelly of urban existence, but that you think out your world with the thoroughness that *GTA* has. The little touches do matter. And the more you can encourage your user to explore your world, the more your pedagogical content should be imparted.

Interestingly, *GTA* moved from a purer simulation environment to a much more balanced storygame environment, and consequently became the best-selling game in history. Should there be some question as to the value of story content in a simulation game, the example of *Grand Theft Auto* speaks for itself.

SAN ANDREAS: BACKSTORY, MAIN STORY, AND FREE PLAY

In *San Andreas,* the player avatar, CJ Johnson, grew up in Los Santos (GTA's fictional version of 1990s Los Angeles) and in his teens became a member of the Grove Street Families (GSF, GTA's fictional version of the Bloods, a notorious Los Angeles street gang). The GSF, headed by Ryder, Big Smoke, and CJ's older brother Sweet, were anti-heroin and anti-cocaine. A series of events lead to the death of CJ's younger brother Carl, and because Sweet held CJ responsible for the death, CJ fled the city.

Five years later, the murder of his mother forces CJ to return to Los Santos. He finds the GSF in disarray, having splintered into several gangs and heading toward the drug trade, despite older brother Sweet's best efforts to stay clear of it. These developments force CJ to stick around and help. He soon discovers that Ryder and Big Smoke are in league with corrupt cops and a rival gang. The rival gang ambushes Sweet, setting up Sweet's arrest and incarceration. Corrupt officer Tenpenny kidnaps CJ, who is extorted into carrying out the crooked cop's dirty work.

In the course of these missions, CJ gains new allies, gets involved with Asian gangs, and manages to kill Ryder, the first of the betrayers. One of CJ's new friends is a government agent who eventually helps in freeing CJ's brother, Sweet. Tenpenny, meanwhile, is arrested and tried for his crimes, even as CJ and Sweet are reunited. However, Tenpenny's trial acquittal triggers massive riots in Los Santos. During the chaos, CJ confronts the traitor Smoke and kills him. Tenpenny reappears and nearly kills CJ, while escaping with all of Smoke's cash. Sweet and CJ pursue Tenpenny through the riot-torn streets, and finally achieve a day of reckoning with their nemesis. CJ and Sweet's entire family are reunited as the story ends.

Though the story is extremely linear, every experience of it will tend to feel fresh because of the remarkable freedom that the player has to operate within the world at all times. However, a few narrative devices such as ticking clocks, along with the player's desire to know "what happens next," will tend to keep most players on track in carrying out missions and prodding the story along.

The story compels players to master the pedagogical content (the intent and execution of each mission), while feeling they are part of a very real world with meaning and emotion. Players don't feel burdened by the pedagogy; instead, they feel liberated by the amount of control they have in this world.

VICE CITY: BACKSTORY, MAIN STORY, AND FREE PLAY

In *Vice City* (GTA's fictional version of 1980s Miami), the player avatar, Tommy Vercetti, has recently been released from prison, due to his previous work for the Forelli organized crime family. Attempting to reestablish himself with the family, Tommy is sent to Vice City by Sonny Forelli to oversee an important drug deal.

In the inciting incident of the story, masked gunmen steal the drugs and money and kill almost everyone involved in the deal. Tommy barely escapes with his life. Now, Tommy has one overriding mission: get back the drugs and money and exact vengeance for the ripoff. If he fails, he's just as likely to have Sonny coming after him.

To discover the truth behind the ripoff, Tommy must rise up through the criminal ranks, accumulating wealth and real estate, eventually becoming the city's crime kingpin. Once again, Tommy has the freedom to roam the story space and pursue his own agendas, independent of the story's throughline. However, the desire to know "what happens next" generally propels most users to return to the storyline, but at their own pace, rather than a predetermined story pace.

The story space has self-correcting mechanisms to keep players close to the storyline. For example, too much random stealing of vehicles will trigger intense interest from the local police, and eventually the FBI and the National Guard. At a certain point, the user who has "goofed off" too much will certainly die. The odds for user success increases the more the user works toward mastering the game's pedagogy—the motivation for that is contained in the storyline's addictiveness.

THE SIMS: NOTHING BUT SANDBOX

The Sims videogame franchise (which has gone through several iterations and numerous add-ons over the years) has been referred to by its creator, Will Wright, as a digital dollhouse. The game is completely open-ended, with no goals, objectives, or finish line for the user. This approach may seem like anathema for a pedagogical simulation where specific objectives and endgames are desirable. But since this game may arguably be the best-selling videogame of all time, there are lessons—both illuminating and cautionary—worth noting in its DNA.

The Sims amply illustrates that interactive environments need not be fantastic, noir-ish or scifi-ish to achieve long-term immersive play. Ordinary settings and objects can be immensely absorbing and worth interacting with, when users have nearly total freedom to do so. Although *The Sims* has no built-in narrative, users are almost instantly compelled to begin creating their own storylines out of the sandbox, through their selection and customization of characters and their behavioral interaction with these characters.

Free play is further directed by the "ticking clock" of Sims character lives; as the characters will advance from young adult to adult to elder life stages, the user is under some obligation to help the Sim satisfy his wants and needs.

The Sims uses some of the most advanced character AI yet seen in a commercial videogame environment. Characters have a high degree of autonomy, and may even ignore specific instructions the user gives them, when the instructions clash with current character agendas. Additionally, users can only control their own customized Sims: "visiting" Sims (nonplayer characters) will be fully autonomous, and may interact with the user's own Sims either positively or negatively.

The Sims itself can, potentially, be used as a simulation environment through the deployment of user mods (modifications), which may either disable or expand various game behaviors. The right combination of mods can create a highly customized and specialized world that could focus on very specific workplace or educational endeavors.

One specific drawback, of course, is *The Sims* nonlingual environment. Sims speak "Simlish," a fictional language that is based more on intonation than sophisticated sentence dynamics and construction. Any sort of natural language interface or real-life immersion is, in essence, out of the question. Interaction is purely behaviorally based, rather than drawn from textual or logical pedagogical material. Whether this can deliver sufficient pedagogical content and advancement is highly debatable.

In addition, *The Sims Online* is instructive in terms of massively multiple user behavior in a free play, nondirected environment (some may point to it as a case study of "mob" psychographics). There has been general agreement that the community has degenerated into anti-social behavior (prostitution, extortion, etc.). While a single user will usually carve out a satisfying Sims experience, the presence of numerous, simultaneous users in a completely nondirected environment seems to encourage more extreme selections and interactions. The failure of *The Sims Online* demonstrates that a strong, moderating presence, the man in the loop, becomes more necessary as multi-user autonomy increases.

SUMMARY

A look at some of the most successful videogames in history is useful for seeing ways that backstory and free play are integrated into games. *Grand Theft Auto's* unique combination of these elements has made it a favorite environment for millions of game players, and creates a particularly rich environment. The extreme in nondirected environments, *The Sims*, offers both positive and negative lessons in how users interact within the virtual world.

CHAPTER 23

Stories in State-of-the-Art Serious Games

Nick Iuppa & Terry Borst

Because serious games are developed for a private clientele, rather than the commercial arena, any survey of how story narratives are being used in this field will necessarily be spotty. The Paramount/ICT/Army simulations high-lighted in this book, are all, of course, serious games, and are worthy examples of how story is used in this area.

Several military simulations, *America's Army*, *Full Spectrum Warrior*, *Real War*, and *Close Combat*, have been converted from in-house training games to suc-cessful commercial games. *Close Combat*, for example, hops from engagement to engagement within its series: the Battle of the Bulge; Utah Beach; Beirut, Lebanon during the Marine occupation. All these games are tactical exercises, emphasizing squad-based combat and stealth maneuvers. Story narrative is fairly minimal, although characters do exist and missions do advance progress.

Many serious games hue pretty tightly to tactical simulations, eschewing story, such as:

- *Incident Commander* teaches incident management for terrorist attacks, Columbine-like school shootings, and natural disasters like Hurricane Katrina.
- *Pulse* teaches lifesaving techniques to emergency medical personnel.
- *Interactive Trauma Trainer* is a decision-based surgical training tool.

While story narrative remains fairly minimal in these projects, another Serious Game, *World Hunger: Food Force*, takes a more ambitious approach. A game about world hunger from the United Nations World Food Programme, the story revolves around a political crisis in the Indian Ocean, which triggers food shortages for millions of people. The WFP sends in a new team to step up the program's presence, and via management of planes, ships, and trucks, the user races the clock to get food supplies delivered on time.

DOI: 10.1016/B978-0-240-81343-1.00023-6

Other serious games using real stories include:

- *Insider,* developed for PricewaterhouseCoopers, teaches new auditors to understand derivatives on corporate balance sheets. Set in the future, users join the finance team of intergalactic mining company Gyronortex, where they are required to master the basics of hedging, swaps and options.
- *Objection!,* a game using animated 2D characters, teaches young lawyers in courtroom tactics with a series of civil and criminal trial scenarios.
- *Darwin: Survival of the Fittest,* another animated 2D character game, teaches stock options trading to new hires at a stock trading firm. A scenario involving a new trader trying to move up in the organization unfolds.
- *Catechumen* is a *Half-Life* mod where the user assumes the role of a persecuted Christian in ancient Rome. The Christian warrior-in-training is armed by an angel, with both physical and spiritual weapons, and must battle gladiators, lions, and centurions, in order to survive and help the nascent movement to prosper.

As serious games begin to take full advantage of state-of-the-art game technology (moving from 2D to 3D environments, from turn-based to real-time interactivity), story-driven simulations seem to become more necessary. This probably has much to do with the greater immersion that state-of-the-art media offers. When the pedagogical simulation is only slightly removed from old pen-and-paper training, we don't expect much story narrative. When the simulation looks like a movie or contemporary videogame, we do.

SUMMARY

Serious games have begun to use more story elements to advance the training objectives of the simulation. As serious games become even more immersive, user demands for story are likely to increase, just as they have for entertainment videogames.

SECTION 4
Opening the Doors

CHAPTER 24
Working as a Digital Storyteller

Carolyn Handler Miller

How do you find work as a digital storyteller?

If you've got a great idea for a videogame or other work of interactive entertainment, how do you sell it?

How do you build a career in such a quickly changing field as interactive entertainment?

357

DOI: 10.1016/B978-0-240-81343-1.00024-8

A NEW OCCUPATION

The pioneering individuals that we've met along the way in this book are all practitioners of a new type of creative endeavor, a craft that did not even exist a few decades ago. They are digital storytellers. The work they do spans an assortment of technologies, and the projects they create are a contrast in opposites—everything from talking baby dolls to gritty videogames. Some of these creations appear on the tiny screens of wireless devices, while others play out on huge movie screens. The venues where these works are enjoyed run a gamut of possibilities, too. They may be seen in one's living room, in a theme park, in a schoolroom, in an office—even in the ocean, as with the robotic dolphin, DRU. Yet, despite the great differences among them, the works they create have significant points in common. All of them

- Utilize digital technologies
- Tell a story
- Are perceived as being entertaining
- Engage the users in an interactive experience

Even though being a digital storyteller is a relatively new occupation, it is a type of work that is increasingly in demand. True, you won't find jobs for "digital storytellers" listed in the want ads. That's because the jobs in this arena go by a great variety of titles and call for various kinds of skill sets. As we've seen throughout this book, the people that we would consider to be digital storytellers carry many official titles, including designer, graphic artist, information architect, producer, project manager, writer, and director. The most visionary of the digital storytellers may work across a number of different platforms and media. This chapter will explore ways of finding work and developing a career in the field of digital storytelling.

THE LIFE OF A DIGITAL STORYTELLER

If you were to round up 10 people who could be described as digital storytellers and ask them how they got started, the chances are that they would give you 10 entirely different answers. Many, especially the younger ones, will probably have had some kind of college training in the area, but almost certainly, their career paths will not have been straight ones. Most will have come to their present job by following a dream, by hard work, and by a willingness to take chances.

Kevin Rafferty's career is a perfect illustration of this. Rafferty is a senior concept writer and director for Walt Disney Imagineering, the group at Disney that creates attractions for the theme parks. It's work that Rafferty and other Imagineers refer to as the "dimensional entertainment" side of the storytelling fence. Rafferty was the writer of the kiosk script for the *Discover the Stories Behind the Magic* project. Rafferty's job calls for a mixture of tasks besides writing. He also creates ideas for theme park attractions and helps to take them from concept all the way to completion. In addition, he writes original music, casts and directs voice and camera talent, and directs show programming and figure animation—and that's just a partial list of his responsibilities.

Not surprisingly, Rafferty's dream job at Disney didn't start out on this level. His career path actually started with a humble dishwashing job at Disneyland while he was still in college, where he was an art major. After college, he worked for a while as an advertising copywriter. When he heard that Disney was hiring people to work on the new Epcot theme park, he applied for a job as a writer, figuring he knew a little something about theme parks from his old dishwashing job. He succeeded in getting hired, but not as a writer. Instead, he found himself dusting show models and cutting mats for artwork. But still, he had his foot in the door at Epcot, and he made the most of the opportunity. Working on his own time after hours he created and developed some original ideas and ran them by a friendly vice president, and "after paying a lot of dues and trying to prove my creative worth," Rafferty told me, "I was finally and officially accepted into the creative division."

Thus, a path that began with dishwashing led to an exciting array of assignments at various Disney theme parks. Looking back on his experience, Rafferty quips in classic Disney fashion, "I guess it's true what they say: 'When you DISH upon a star, your dreams come true.' "

Rafferty's career path is typical of many others who have found their way into digital storytelling. A straight, clear-cut route is quite rare. It's not like deciding you want to go into dentistry and knowing that step number one is applying to dental school. In Rafferty's case, his career aspirations evolved over time, and once he knew what he wanted to do—to become a creative part of Disney Imagineering—he focused his efforts and sacrificed his free time to get where he wanted to be.

SOME KEYS TO SUCCESS

Although new media involves cutting-edge technology, two industry pros who were queried on advice for establishing a career in this field mentioned some tried and true old-fashioned values (*GIGnews*, March 2002). In fact, the answers they gave would have worked as well for a stone-age hatchet maker. For example, Stevie Case said the three keys to success were drive, dedication, and the desire to learn, while John Romero named passion, hard work, and an optimistic outlook. And both also stressed the importance of being a finisher—to complete any project you commit yourself to doing.

SELLING AN ORIGINAL IDEA

What if, unlike Rafferty, your dream is not to work within a particular company or hold a particular job, but instead to sell your own original ideas for a game or other type of interactive entertainment? No question, this is an appealing goal, one shared by many hopeful individuals. Sad to say, however, it is not particularly realistic for several reasons.

For one thing, ideas are plentiful, to the point that most companies are flooded with their own internal ideas generated by employees of the company, and thus they are not looking for ideas from the outside. For another thing, as they say in Hollywood, ideas are cheap; execution is everything. Execution is where the real challenge lies, and execution takes experience, talent, time, and often an investment of money. To convince a company that your concept has merit, you'll need more than an idea. You'll want to have something to show them— a concept document, a design document, or, even better, a working prototype. And you'll also need to consider the pitching strategy for your project. Who is the target audience for this product, and why would they like it? What competing projects already exist, and how is yours different and better? And how would your project be a good fit with other offerings in the company's line?

But even if you've done all the necessary groundwork, the companies you are planning to approach are unlikely to give you a warm reception if you are an unknown quantity to them. Developing a game or other work of interactive entertainment is a risky proposition that can cost millions of dollars. If a company is interested at all in hearing pitches from outside vendors, they will be far more likely to be receptive to a known developer with a proven track record than they would be to a stranger.

HELPING HANDS

Despite these discouraging words, if you are convinced that you have a stellar idea and want to have a go at trying to sell it, you can obtain some excellent guidance from a document prepared by the International Game Developers Association (IGDA), the premiere organization of game developers. Called the *Game Submission Guide*, it offers information about the pitching process and includes a checklist of what you will need to include for a professional-looking submission. Although written with videogames in mind, the information pertains equally well to other forms of interactive entertainment. Members can download the guide from the organization's Web site, *www.igda.org*. Although it was written a number of years ago, its points are as relevant as ever.

In addition, the IGDA site also contains a column written by game industry veteran Tom Sloper called *The Games Game* where you can find archived articles about submitting game ideas.

THE DIFFERENT EMPLOYMENT PATHS

If you are interested in finding full-time employment in interactive media, you will be happy to know that a surprisingly wide variety of businesses employ staff members who specialize in this field. The most obvious are the game publishers and game developers. The publishers have deeper pockets than the developers, and they may either develop projects in-house or farm them out to developers, who do the actual creative work, which the publishers then package and market. These publishers and developers do not necessarily restrict themselves to videogames. They may also make games for mobile devices and for the Web, including MMOGs.

In addition to game publishers and developers, another group of entities focuses on interactive media: the design firms that deal with interactive media. Some of them specialize in Web design work, while others pursue cutting-edge projects in iTV and DVDs. Some work in a wide sweep of interactive media. In addition to iTV projects, they do work in kiosks, wireless devices, the Web, and DVDs.

One entire industry that is becoming increasingly involved in interactive media is the Hollywood entertainment business, as we've seen throughout this book. Not only are movie studios making games based on their films, but they are also promoting their films on the Internet and on mobile devices, sometimes using highly creative approaches. Television networks also promote their shows via new media and in some cases enhance their offerings via iTV. Public broadcasters are particularly aggressive in using interactive media to maximize the content of their programming, developing projects for the Web, DVDs, and iTV. Thus, traditional entertainment studios and broadcasters are definitely worth investigating for employment opportunities.

In considering possible employers, do not by any means overlook major corporations. Most of today's large companies have internal divisions that produce content for the Web and other interactive media, work that is often done under the umbrella of the promotion or marketing departments. Other entities that do work in interactive media are toy companies, ad agencies, and PR companies, as well as companies that specialize in interactive training programs. Another group of organizations to consider are cultural institutions—museums, historic sites, aquariums, and so on—all of which may use interactive displays to make their exhibits come to life. And theme park companies employ individuals like Kevin Rafferty to create attractions that take advantage of the latest interactive technologies. In addition, government agencies sometimes produce interactive programming for educational, informational, or training purposes.

361

COMMON ENTRY POINTS

Although, as we've seen from Kevin Rafferty's story, the path to a great job in digital media is not necessarily a straight one, a couple of traditional routes do exist. One is by becoming a beta tester, which is particularly attractive to people who want to work in games. Beta testers are hired to look for bugs in games before they are released to the public, and this type of work is often a stepping stone to a higher level job within the same company. Another proven route is via student internships. Internships offer first-hand exposure to a professional new media work place. Not only are they educational, but such experiences are also good to have on a résumé. And, best of all, they can lead to full-time employment.

Aside from scoring an internship or a job as a beta tester, the pathway into digital storytelling is much like that for any other kind of work. You need to research the field to determine which segment of the industry would offer you the most potential, given your particular talents, interests, and skill set. It is also quite helpful to network and to attend industry events, which we will be discussing in more detail later in the chapter. And before setting out on a job search, you'll want to give serious consideration to creating a portfolio of sample work, which is discussed in detail in Chapter 25.

BREAKING IN: SOME HELPFUL INFORMATION

If you are seriously interested in getting a job in digital media, especially videogames, and want to know how to get into the field, visit the section of the IGDA Web site called *The Games Game*: *http://www.igda.org/games-game-archives*. The site includes an excellent section on major career paths, interviews with professionals in games describing how they broke in, and a list of resources.

In addition, game designer Ernest Adams has a Web page devoted to breaking into the game business: *The Wanna-Be Page: http://www.designersnotebook.com/Wanna-be/wanna-be.htm.*

WORKING AS A FREELANCER

But what if you would prefer to be your own boss rather than to be a full-time employee of an organization—is this an option in new media? The answer is a tentative yes. It depends on your experience, on your specialty, and the tenor of the times. Back in the 1990s, it was quite customary to be hired to work on a specific project and then move on once the project had been completed. Currently, most companies work entirely with full-time staffers. One of the few professional areas that still offers opportunities to freelancers is in writing, my own specialty. The more credits you have, and the more people you know in the industry, the more likely you are to find freelance writing work, though it is more difficult than it used to be.

The work one does as a freelance writer varies tremendously from project to project. Some of the assignments you snag are not much different from doing piece goods work in a factory. You may be expected to churn out hundreds of lines of dialogue, sometimes with little variation between the lines, and the work can be quite tedious. On the other hand, some writing jobs are highly creative. You may have a chance to collaborate on the overall design and content of a project and to develop original characters; you may also be able to help develop what the interactivity will be and how it will work. Each type of interactive medium poses its own challenges. Writing a script for a kiosk will be quite different from writing one for a smart toy, and both will be different again from writing an ARG (Alternate Reality Game) or a serious game.

One of the most stimulating things about being a freelance writer is being able to take on projects that are quite different from each other; your work is always creatively challenging. However, being a freelancer also means dealing with issues that one does not have to worry about as a full-time employee. For example, you might have to chase after a client to get paid or find yourself mired in an unpleasant situation called *project creep*, in which a project grows much bigger than it was originally understood to be. Project creep can cause you to spend many more weeks than you had planned on an assignment but without receiving additional compensation.

Fortunately, freelance writers do not have to go it entirely alone anymore. The IGDA has a SIG (special interest group) for writers, and the Writers Guild of America, West, recently formed the Videogame Writers Caucus, a support and advocacy group for writers in this field. The Writers Guild also offers two special contracts for interactive writing. The first, called the Interactive Program Contract, or IPC, covers writing for most types of interactive media, including videogames and mobile entertainment, while the second, called the Made for Internet Contract, specifically covers original writing done for the Internet. Both contracts are available directly from the Guild's organizing department. Qualified new media writers can even obtain membership in the Guild, which once just included writers of motion pictures and television.

LEGAL CONSIDERATIONS

At some point or other, if you are working in new media, you are bound to run into legal situations. For example, you are quite likely to be faced with issues involving *intellectual property* (IP). Intellectual properties are unique works of human intelligence—images, writings, music, pieces of animation, even game engines or an invention for a toy—that are given certain legal protections, which include copyrights, patents, and trademarks. Intellectual properties can be extremely valuable, and they are fiercely guarded in interactive media with a zeal bordering on paranoia. You may become involved with IP questions when it comes to protecting your own creations; you may also run into IP issues when you want to use the creative work of others in a project.

IP issues can be highly complex, but one thing about them is quite simple: You don't want someone stealing your intellectual property and you don't want to be accused of stealing intellectual property that belongs to someone else. The first situation can result in your losing a significant amount of income; the second can result in a lawsuit. To prevent either situation from occurring, you need to familiarize yourself with the basics of intellectual property law. One place to start is with the archived Web site of entertainment and new media attorney and IP specialist Michael Leventhal (*http://www.mcsquaredlaw.com*). The archived site contains a good primer on IP, called *Intellectual Property 101*, plus a number of links that will take you to more information on the subject.

Another legal matter you will need to be familiar with is a document called a *non-disclosure agreement*, or NDA, often used in high tech circles. You will no doubt become aware of NDAs if you are submitting a project to a company in the hopes of selling it, or if a company is interested in hiring you for a project, but first needs to share with you what has been done with the project to date. Both situations raise the risk of valuable information being seen by strangers who might possibly use it without authorization. To avert such a risk, it is customary for one party to request the other to sign an NDA. When someone signs such a document, he or she promises to keep the information they are receiving confidential (Figure 24.1).

If you are working as a freelancer or are running your own development or design company, you will also need some legal protections in the form of a contract. You will definitely want a contract if you are entering into a new employment relationship; that is, if you or your firm is being hired to do some work for another entity. A contract should specify what your responsibilities will be and what you will be paid at each juncture, often tying payments to the completion of various *milestones* (points when particular parts of the project are due). It should spell out what happens if the work expands beyond what has been assigned, thus avoiding the problem of project creep, discussed earlier. The contract may also include language about the kind of credit you will receive and where the credit will appear, and may note who will hold the copyright to the completed work. If you are inexperienced in negotiating contracts, you would be well advised to seek the help of an attorney. Even if you think you are savvy in such matters, it is always a good idea to have a lawyer look things over before signing.

But even before you reach the contract stage, you need to take some steps to protect yourself against an unscrupulous or inept employer. (Working for a well-intentioned but inexperienced client can be as perilous as working for one who deliberately intends to take advantage of you.) Before going too far in any discussion with a new client, try to learn as much about the company as you can, either by doing some research or by asking the prospective employer a series of focused questions. Asking the right questions about the company and the project will help you determine whether this is something you'll want to pursue—or if it is something you should run from.

EDUCATING YOURSELF

In any case, concerns about contracts and protecting your intellectual property are matters to be dealt with once a career is established. Let's take a few steps back and discuss how one prepares for a career in new media. It usually begins, as you might expect, with the right education. In terms of a formal education, you have a choice of two different paths. Path number one is to get a good foundation in the liberal arts, and then pick up specialized training, if needed, after graduation. Path number two is a more focused route: to enroll in an undergraduate program in computer science or in digital arts. Digital arts programs

NON-DISCLOSURE AGREEMENT

This non-disclosure agreement ("Agreement") is entered into as of _____ ("Effective Date") by and between _____, located at _____ ("Artist"), and _____, located at _____ _____ ("Recipient"). Artist and Recipient are engaged in discussions in contemplation of or in furtherance of a business relationship. In order to induce Artist to disclose its confidential information during such discussions, Recipient agrees to accept such information under the restrictions set forth in this Agreement.

1. Disclosure of Confidential Information. Artist may disclose, either orally or in writing, certain information which Recipient knows or has reason to know is considered confidential by Artist relating to the [NAME] Project ("Artist Confidential Information"). Artist Confidential Information shall include, but not be limited to, creative ideas, story-lines, characters, trade secrets, knowhow, inventions, techniques, processes, algorithms, software programs, schematics, software source documents, contracts, customer lists, financial information, sales and marketing plans and business plans.

2. Confidentiality. Recipient agrees to maintain in confidence Artist Confidential Information. Recipient will use Artist Confidential Information solely to evaluate the commercial potential of a business relationship with Artist. Recipient will not disclose the Artist Confidential Information to any person except its employees or Artist's to whom it is necessary to disclose the Artist Confidential Information for such purposes. Recipient agrees that Artist Confidential Information will be disclosed or made available only to those of its employees or Artist's who have agreed in writing to receive it under terms at least as restrictive as those specified in this Agreement. Recipient will take reasonable measures to maintain the confidentiality of Artist Confidential Information, but not less than the measures it uses for its confidential information of similar type. Recipient will immediately give notice to Artist of any unauthorized use or disclosure of the Artist Confidential Information. Recipient agrees to assist Artist in remedying such unauthorized use or disclosure of the Artist Confidential Information. This obligation will not apply to the extent that Recipient can demonstrate that: (a) the Artist Confidential Information at the time of disclosure is part of the public domain; (b) the Artist Confidential Information became part of the public domain, by publication or otherwise, except by breach of the provisions of this Agreement; (c) the Artist Confidential Information can be established by written evidence to have been in the possession of Recipient at the time of disclosure; (d) the Artist Confidential Information is received from a third party without similar restrictions and without breach of this Agreement; or (e) the Artist Confidential Information is required to be disclosed by a government agency to further the objectives of this Agreement, or by a proper court of competent jurisdiction; provided, however, that Recipient will use its best efforts to minimize the disclosure of such information and will consult with and assist Artist in obtaining a protective order prior to such disclosure.

3. Materials. All materials including, without limitation, documents, drawings, models, apparatus, sketches, designs and lists furnished to Recipient by Artist and any tangible materials embodying Artist Confidential Information created by Recipient shall remain the property of Artist. Recipient shall return to Artist or destroy such materials and all copies thereof upon the termination of this Agreement or upon the written request of Artist.

4. No License. This Agreement does not grant Recipient any license to use Artist Confidential Information except as provided in Article 2.

5. Term.

   (a) This Agreement shall terminate three (3) years after the Effective Date unless terminated earlier by either party. Artist may extend the term of the Agreement by written notice to Recipient. Either party may terminate this Agreement, with or without cause, by giving notice of termination to the other party. The Agreement shall terminate immediately upon receipt of such notice.

365

Figure 24.1
A model NDA (Non-Disclosure Agreement), a document which guarantees that valuable information will be kept confidential. Document courtesy of Michael Leventhal.

(b) Upon termination of this Agreement, Recipient shall cease to use Artist Confidential Information and shall comply with Paragraph 3 within twenty (20) days of the date of termination. Upon the request of Artist, an officer of Recipient shall certify that Recipient has complied with its obligations in this Section.

(c) Notwithstanding the termination of this Agreement, Recipient's obligations in Paragraph 2 shall survive such termination.

6. General Provisions.

(a) This Agreement shall be governed by and construed in accordance with the laws of the United States and of the State of California as applied to transactions entered into and to be performed wholly within California between California residents. In the event of any action, suit, or proceeding arising from or based upon this agreement brought by either party hereto against the other, the prevailing party shall be entitled to recover from the other its reasonable attorneys' fees in connection therewith in addition to the costs of such action, suit, or proceeding.

(b) Any notice provided for or permitted under this Agreement will be treated as having been given when (a) delivered personally, (b) sent by confirmed telefacsimile or telecopy, (c) sent by commercial overnight courier with written verification of receipt, or (d) mailed postage prepaid by certified or registered mail, return receipt requested, to the party to be notified, at the address set forth above, or at such other place of which the other party has been notified in accordance with the provisions of this Section. Such notice will be treated as having been received upon the earlier of actual receipt or five (5) days after posting.

(c) Recipient agrees that the breach of the provisions of this Agreement by Recipient will cause Artist irreparable damage for which recovery of money damages would be inadequate. Artist will, therefore, be entitled to obtain timely injunctive relief to protect Artist's rights under this Agreement in addition to any and all remedies available at law.

(d) This Agreement constitutes the entire agreement between the parties relating to this subject matter and supersedes all prior or simultaneous representations, discussions, negotiations, and agreements, whether written or oral. This Agreement may be amended or supplemented only by a writing that is signed by duly authorized representatives of both parties. Recipient may not assign its rights under this Agreement. No term or provision hereof will be considered waived by either party, and no breach excused by either party, unless such waiver or consent is in writing signed on behalf of the party against whom the waiver is asserted. No consent by either party to, or waiver of, a breach by either party, whether express or implied, will constitute a consent to, waiver of, or excuse of any other, different, or subsequent breach by either party. If any part of this Agreement is found invalid or unenforceable, that part will be amended to achieve as nearly as possible the same economic effect as the original provision and the remainder of this Agreement will remain in full force.

(e) This Agreement may be executed in counterparts and all counterparts so executed by all parties hereto and affixed to this Agreement shall constitute a valid and binding agreement, even though the all of the parties have not signed the same counterpart.

IN WITNESS WHERE OF, the parties have executed this Agreement as of the Effective Date.

RECIPIENT   ARTIST

_____   _____

Typed Name   Typed Name

_____   _____

Title Title

are becoming increasingly common at institutions of higher learning all over the world, both as undergraduate programs and as master degree programs. Specialized programs can give you a good background on theory and invaluable hands-on experience in creating interactive projects; they sometimes offer internship programs and can serve as fairly smooth stepping-stones to a good job.

BUT WHAT IF YOU ARE A LUDDITE?

Not everyone feels that it is good to focus on new media as an undergraduate. For example, designer Greg Roach, introduced in Chapter 11, strongly believes that no matter what position you are angling for in interactive media, you should first have a liberal arts education. He says "a grounding in the classical humanities is critical. Programmer, 3D artist, designer, whatever … I'd much rather hire a traditional painter who's a Luddite [a person who rejects technology] but who understands color theory—and then train her in Maya—than hire a hot-shot 3D modeler whose aesthetic has been shaped exclusively by console games."

If you are already out of college, or if going to college is not an option for you, you might consider a certificate program in new media arts. Such programs are offered by many community colleges and by university extensions. Or your might select just a few courses that prepare you in the direction you wish to go in—classes in Flash animation, for example, or Web design. How much technical know-how you need varies from position to position. It is always helpful to have a general understanding of digital technology and a grasp of basic software programs, but if you want to be a digital storyteller, it is even more important to understand the fundamentals of drama and literature. You would be well advised to take a course that teaches narrative structure, or one in world mythology, and you should definitely take at least one course in dramatic writing.

Not all of your education has to take place in a classroom. If you don't already, spend some time playing games, trying out different genres and different platforms. Include MMOGs, ARGs, mobile, and casual games on your "to play" list so you can see how the experiences differ. Even if you aren't interested in working in games, they can teach you a great deal about design and interactivity. If a particular area of gaming is unfamiliar to you, find someone who plays this kind of game—a relative, a local student, a family friend—and ask them to give you a tour of one or two. Most people are happy to oblige, but you can always make it more attractive by treating your guide to a pizza.

Finally, you can get an excellent free education online by visiting Web sites devoted to various aspects of interactive media. You can also sign up to receive electronic and print trade publications. Each segment of the new media arena has several Web sites devoted to it and usually several electronic publications. Many have been mentioned in this book, and a diligent online search will turn up others.

INDUSTRY EVENTS

Another excellent way to educate yourself is by attending conferences, trade shows, and other industry events. Most of these gatherings are divided into two quite different parts: a conference and an exposition. By strolling around the expo floor, you get a chance to see demonstrations of the latest hardware and software in the field, often given by some of the creators of these very products. And by attending the conference sessions, you will hear talks by industry leaders and learn about the latest developments in the field. Although these trade events can be expensive, many of them offer student discounts and many also have volunteer programs. By working as a volunteer, you can take in as much of the event as you want during your off hours.

Virtually every sector of the interactive arena holds at least one annual event. Two major international conferences are MIPTV featuring Milia, which is held in Cannes, France, and the Tokyo Game Show in Japan. In the United States, the Game Developers Conference (GDC) is well worth attending. It offers excellent presentations on every facet of game design and production, including mobile games, MMOGs, and serious games, and many of the topics are of particular interest to digital storytellers. The Austin Game Conference is another high quality event.

If you are interested in computer graphics, you will definitely want to attend the annual SIGGRAPH conference. It is also one of the few shows where significant attention is paid to VR. For those interested in iTV, the showcases held by AFI's Digital Content Lab offer an excellent opportunity to see demonstrations of cutting-edge iTV programming and other types of interactive media. The training field has its special gatherings, too, with *Training Magazine's* annual conference and expo being just one example. The events mentioned here are just a small sampling of trade shows, conferences, and conventions that involve interactive media; new ones are started every year, and a few older ones sometimes fall by the wayside. The best way to find out about the industry events in your particular area of interest is by subscribing to electronic and print publications that specialize in the field.

THE PEOPLE CONNECTION

Industry events, excellent as they are, only take place at infrequent intervals. To stay more closely involved, and to connect with others who work in new media, you would be well advised to join one of the many professional organizations in this field. Networking with others in the field is one of the best ways to find work and stay on top of developments in the industry, as virtually any career counselor will tell you. It is in even more important in a fast moving field like interactive media. Merely joining and attending an occasional meeting, however, brings limited benefits; you'll reap far greater rewards if you join a SIG (*special interest group*) or a committee within the organization and become an active, contributing member. By participating on a deeper level, you are more likely to form valuable connections that can lead to jobs. Two such organizations are the Academy of Interactive Arts and Sciences (AIAS) and the International Game Developers Association (IGDA).

A number of guilds and other organizations within the Hollywood system now welcome members who specialize in interactive media. Among these mainstream organizations are the Writers Guild, noted earlier, the Producers Guild, and the Academy of Television Arts and Sciences, generally known as the TV Academy. These organizations all have active committees or peer groups made up of new media members and put on special events focusing on interactive entertainment.

Unfortunately, many of the organizations mentioned here only hold meetings in certain geographical regions, and if you live outside these regions, it is difficult to become actively involved. However, you might also look into the possibility of forming a local branch, which can be a great way to meet other members in a less congested setting.

SOME POINTERS FOR A CAREER IN NEW MEDIA

Here are some helpful ideas for establishing and maintaining a career as a digital storyteller:

- Anticipate change. This field does not stay still, so you need to continually educate yourself on digital technologies and new forms of digital entertainment.
- Don't restrict your vision only to this field. Indulge your interests in the world beyond. Not only will this be of value to you in your professional work, but it will also help keep you balanced.
- Educate yourself on narrative techniques. All good storytelling relies on certain basic principles.
- Stay tuned to traditional popular culture—to television, film, and music. To a large extent, new media and traditional media intersect and influence each other.
- If you are angling for a first job or a better job, consider building your own showcase. Not only will it give you a way to display your talents, but you will also learn something in the process. For more on showcases, see the next chapter.
- As one of our experts said in referring to smart toys, sometimes you have to dump all the pieces on the floor and play with them. Playing games and participating in interactive experiences is the single best way to keep your edges sharp.

CHAPTER 25

Creating Your Own Showcase

Carolyn Handler Miller

Is it a good investment of your time to create an original piece of work or a portfolio of samples to show off your talents?

If you do decide to create your own showcase, what should it include, and what is the best way to highlight your strengths?

What sorts of things do not belong in a showcase and can make a negative impression?

SHOWCASING YOUR WORK: IS IT WORTHWHILE?

It is reasonable to wonder, given how much effort it takes to create an original piece of work, if it is ever worth the investment of your time and energy to put together your own showcase. I would answer this question with a resounding yes, based on my own observations of the interactive entertainment industry and also based on the interviews I've done for this book. A little later in this chapter, we will examine some actual situations in which people have successfully showcased their work. Creating your own showcase can benefit you if one of these scenarios fits your personal situation:

1. You have not yet had any professional experience in interactive media but are interested in working in the field.
2. You are already working in digital entertainment but are considering moving into a different area within it or would like to move to a higher level.
3. You are working as an employee in the field but want to work as a freelancer.
4. You are working as a freelancer and want to attract new clients.

Having an original piece of work to show, or a portfolio of work, is of particular importance if you have not yet had any experience in the field. How else will you be able to demonstrate to a prospective employer what you are capable of doing? A well thought out "calling card" of original work illustrates what your special talents are, where your creative leanings lie, and also reveals something about who you are as a person. A showcase of original work also bears a powerful subtext: You are serious enough about working in this field to spend your own time putting together a demonstration of your work. It carries the message that you are energetic, enterprising, and committed.

Producing a showcase project is a strategy used by small companies as well as by individuals. For example, Free Range Graphics undertook *The Meatrix* as a *pro bono* project in part to stimulate new business, a gamble that paid off handsomely.

However, the advice to build a promotional calling card must be given with a serious note of caution. If you do undertake such a significant self-assigned task, you need to go about it in a way that will set off your abilities in the most positive light possible and avoid doing things that can undermine your prospects.

CONSIDERATIONS IN CREATING A PROFESSIONAL SHOWCASE

For some people, putting together a showcase is a relatively easy task because they can use samples of student projects or volunteer work that they've done in the past, or even of professional assignments. But if you don't have any such samples, or the samples you have are not well suited to your current goal, you are faced with the daunting job of creating something original from scratch. You will have a number of things to consider before you actually begin. The following sections will address many questions that will almost certainly cross your mind about making a showcase.

Portfolio or Single-Piece Approach?

A portfolio approach includes several brief examples of work, while a single-piece approach focuses on one well-developed project. Each tactic has its own pros and cons. With the portfolio approach, you can effectively demonstrate your ability to work in a range of styles and on different types of subject matter. However, the portfolio approach also means that you will have to undertake several different projects and build them out to the point that they are solid enough to serve as good samples.

By showcasing a single piece, on the other hand, you can present a more fleshed out and complete project than you'd have in a portfolio, where the samples tend to be short and fairly superficial. But having just one piece of work to showcase can be a little risky because the work you are exhibiting might not be what the prospective employer or client is looking for, and you will have nothing else to illustrate what you are capable of.

So where does this leave you? It's best to make the call based on your own individual situation. If you already have a couple of samples you can use and have some ideas about another one or two you could put together, then you are probably already well down the path toward the portfolio approach. On the other hand, if you feel confident you've got a great concept to showcase and that it would work well as a demo piece, than that's probably the best way for you to proceed. There's no right or wrong answer here.

373

Distribution Method?

You will need to determine what method you will use to make your showcase available to the people you want to see it. The three most obvious choices are the Internet, CD-ROMs, and DVDs. Virtually any prospective employer or client should be able to view your work on any one of these platforms, so ease of viewing is not a factor here. Your work itself, and your own leanings, is really your best guide. It makes sense to distribute your showcase on the medium in which you are most interested in working. But if you want to work in an area that falls outside of the three already mentioned avenues of distribution—if you are interested in iTV, say, or in VR—then pick the medium that you feel would display your material to the best advantage. One final consideration for a multi-project portfolio: It is advisable to package your showcase on a single platform rather than having a jumble of different works that cannot easily be viewed together. If you have both Web and CD-ROM samples, you might want to put your Web pages on the CD-ROM with the other examples, or vice versa. As another possibility, you could embed links to your Web pages in your CD-ROM.

Subject Matter and Approach?

One of the most important questions you will be faced with is what the content of your showcase will be. The honest answer is that no one can tell you what to do here. The best choices are the ones that most closely reflect your own personal interests, talents, and expertise. By picking a subject you really care about, you have the best chance of producing something that will be strong and will stand out from the crowd. The way you decide to construct your showcase should also reflect your personal taste and style—within limits, of course. Coarse humor and disparaging portrayals of any particular ethnic group are never appropriate. Also, you do yourself no favors by employing a sloppy, unprofessional-looking style.

But what if you have tried your best to think of some topics for your showcase and still come up blank? Then you might consider volunteering your services for a nonprofit institution in your community. Possible choices include your church, synagogue, or mosque; the local chamber of commerce or a community service group; or a school sports team or Brownie troop. Another alternative is to create a promotional piece for a business belonging to a friend or relative.

Although on the surface such projects seem to be creatively limiting, you may be inspired to create something quite clever. For instance, you could design an amusing advergame for your brother-in-law's landscaping business, or an interactive adventure tale about Brownies for your niece's Brownie troop. Volunteer projects for nonprofit organizations or for businesses have some solid advantages. They give you hands-on practical experience and also give you a professional sample to include in your showcase, even if the work was done without monetary compensation.

Gaps in Necessary Skills?

Lacking all the skills necessary to put together one's own showcase is a common problem because few people are equipped with the full range of talents necessary for building an effective sample piece. The problem can be solved in two ways: by teaching yourself what you don't already know or by teaming up with someone who is strong where you are weak. Teaching yourself a new skill like Flash animation may seem like an intimidating project, but as we will see from the *Odd Todd* case study later in this chapter, it is manageable. Software is becoming ever easier to use, and books are available that teach animation programs, image manipulation, Web page design, and media authoring. You might also take a community college course to fill in a particular gap.

But if you prefer to team up with a colleague instead, keep in mind you need not even be in the same community. Many collaborations take place in cyberspace, and sometimes they occur between people who have never met in person. Perhaps your strengths are in art, writing, and conceptualizing, while the other person excels at the more technical side of things. If you work together, you can create a project that is more effective than either of you could do alone and also demonstrates your special abilities. This can be a win–win solution for both parties. Of course, you will want to be sure that each person's contribution is made clear in the credits and that no one is claiming solo authorship for the entire project.

ODD TODD: A CASE STUDY

While it is important for a personal showcase to look professional, this does not necessarily mean it needs to follow a conservative, play-by-the-rules approach. If you take a look at the Web site *Odd Todd* (*www.oddtodd.com*), you will find an immensely quirky piece of work that breaks almost all the rules and yet has become a wildly successful endeavor. This is not to say that everyone should build a project as idiosyncratic as this one is, but it does effectively illustrate the power of being fresh and original and of having something meaningful to say. Essentially a one-person operation and done on a tiny budget, *Odd Todd* has thrust its creator, Todd Rosenberg, into the spotlight and changed his life.

The site is named for a fictitious character, Odd Todd, and is loosely based on the experiences of the site's creator, Todd Rosenberg, who lost his job with a dot com company during a radical downsizing. In a series of Flash-animated episodes, we watch Todd as he futilely searches for a new job and gives in to such distractions as fudge-striped cookies, long naps, and fantasies about large-breasted women. The artwork in the cartoons is rough and childlike, and the only human speaking character is Todd, who chronicles his hero's struggles in a voice-over narration (Figure 25.1). The voice he uses is distinctive, marked by a puzzled kind of irony and bewilderment at his predicament, and further made unique by his urban drawl and a particular way of stretching out the end vowels in such words as money (mon-aaay) and cookie (cook-aaay). And though the site is extremely funny, it does have a serious side, touching on the painful issues of being unemployed and serving as a kind of a cyberspace support system for laid off white-collar workers. It even contains a special community feature called *Laidoffland*.

Figure 25.1
Odd Todd is the fictional hero of the *Odd Todd* Web site, an endeavor that has turned its creator's life around. Image courtesy of Todd Rosenberg.

Beginning with just a single animated episode, the site has mushroomed into a full array of features. It includes dozens of cartoons, games, and interactive amusements, all relating to Odd Todd and his life and obsessions. It also includes a variety of daily and weekly specials such as a feature called "What's Happening," a diary-like log of Todd's life, and the Tuesday lunch special-recipe concoctions sent in by fans to nourish other laid-off stay-at-homes.

The Hows and Whys of Odd Todd

Why has a site featuring roughly drawn cartoons about an unshaven, unemployed guy in a blue bathrobe become such a hit? How did Todd Rosenberg set about making this site and how does he keep it going? And as a showcase, what has it done for his career? The real Todd shed some light on these questions during a phone interview and several follow-up emails.

First of all, let's address one burning question right away. No, the real Todd does not sound like the voice he uses on the Web site. That is a made-up voice, and many of the situations depicted in the cartoons are invented as well. But the core conceit—that an unemployed dot comer built the site—is totally true. The authenticity of the character's predicament, the real Todd believes, is an important reason why *Odd Todd* has become so immensely popular. People identify with it, Rosenberg explained. "They see it and say to themselves: 'It's so me!' or 'Someone else is doing exactly what I'm doing!' "

Rosenberg began the site after he was laid off from AtomFilms.com. Thinking he'd only be out of work for a few months, he decided to spend some of it doing something he'd always enjoyed—cartooning—and create something that might possibly help him become employed again. The result was the first episode of *Odd Todd*. The debut episode was a humorous take on what it is like to be newly laid off, with too much time and too little money.

A DO-IT-YOURSELF APPROACH

Although Rosenberg had learned basic HTML at a prior job and had taught himself to draw (by using *Mad Magazine* as a model), he lacked training in almost every other skill he would need in order to build and maintain his new site. When asked what he'd studied in college, the University of Hartford, he confessed: "I never studied in college. I wasn't much of a student." He admitted to filling up his notebooks with cartoons instead of lecture notes. He had no training in screenwriting—he owned books on the subject, he said, but had never read them—and had never acquired experience in acting, either, because he had stage fright.

One of the first things he needed to learn, in order to bring *Odd Todd* to life, was Flash animation. He taught himself how with the help of a book called *Flash 5 Cartooning*. His "studio" was his apartment in New York, and he did everything from there. To lay down the sound track for the cartoons, he used the microphone that came with his computer and did all the voice work himself, including the strange chirps and other sound effects for the site's nonhuman characters. As a result, he managed to keep his start-up costs low, estimating that during his first year he spent under $1000.

Keeping Things Going

Though Rosenberg's cartoons have an unpolished, homemade appearance, he can actually draw much better than the work on his Web site would suggest. In doing the animation for his first cartoon, he made a quick series of drawings, intending to use them as placeholders. But after he refined them, he discovered he much preferred the look of the rough first set and discarded the more polished ones. Even now, with multiple episodes behind him, he still makes five or six versions of each cartoon before he has one that he feels is right. Making the Web site look quickly dashed out and candid is totally in keeping with the fictional Odd Todd character, though accomplishing the right look actually takes a great deal of work.

In the beginning, however, Rosenberg's abilities in many areas truly were less than polished. His Odd Todd character would look different from picture to picture; he had trouble making him consistent. In addition, he didn't know how to synch the sound and the picture properly, or how to make a button to let users replay an episode or game. He kept going back to his books and asking more knowledgeable friends for help before he mastered what he felt he needed to know.

Now that the site has been up and running for a number of years, it still requires regular maintenance and new content. He continues to update it with new cartoons, games, and other features.

A CYBER SUPPORT SYSTEM

Rosenberg has managed to keep his expenses low in part by developing an informal exchange system. For instance, his site is hosted for free by Peak Webhosting, which saves him a great deal of money. In return, he promotes Peak Webhosting on his site, which has brought them business. He has also received significant volunteer assistance from one of his fans, Stacey Kamen, a Web site designer. Rosenberg reciprocates by prominently promoting her design skills and her Web site business on his site. (Kamen and her work will be discussed in more detail later in this chapter.)

Another fan, Geoffrey Noles, volunteers his services to the site by programming the *Odd Todd* games, such as the enormously amusing and popular *Cook-ay Slots*, a wacky slot machine game. Noles, too, receives credit on *Odd Todd*, as well as a link to his site. Rosenberg has never met either of these two important contributors face to face. They communicate by various electronic means, including, in the case of Noles and Rosenberg, by webcam.

Since its launch late in 2001, *Odd Todd* has been visited by millions of unique users and has attracted major media attention. Dozens of articles have been written about the site, and Rosenberg has been featured on a great number of TV and radio shows. Loyal fans have contributed thousands of dollars to *Odd*

Todd's online tip jar, one dollar at a time, and they also support the site by buying a great variety of *Odd Todd* merchandise, from t-shirts to coffee mugs. The site has also spawned a book, *The Odd Todd Handbook: Hard Times, Soft Couch*, which, like the site, was created by Rosenberg.

Over time, however, the life of the fictitious Todd and the real Todd have diverged. While an episode might show a dejected Todd sending out résumés and trying to find work, in actuality Rosenberg is no longer dejected or looking for full-time employment. Instead, he makes enough money from the site and related merchandise, plus freelance work, to keep going. The success of the site, he said, and the creative satisfaction it has brought him, has caused him to lose interest in returning to the 9 to 5 corporate world. Ironically, he's actually making a living by being unemployed.

SOME OTHER APPROACHES TO SHOWCASING

The Internet, especially with the rapid spread of broadband, has proven to be an extremely effective platform for getting one's work seen. Some people, like Rosenberg, have created an entire Web site to promote their work, while others post their creations on sites like YouTube and MySpace. Still others, like Rosenberg's cyber support team, show off their work by collaborating with others.

A Two-Pronged Approach

Stacey Kamen, a Web and graphic designer with a specialty in business imaging (giving businesses a particular image via Web sites, brochures, and other materials), has taken two routes to making her work known. She contributes design work to the *Odd Todd* site and has built a site of her own (*www.StaceyKamen. com*), which is totally different from Rosenberg's.

Interestingly, when she first approached Rosenberg and volunteered her services, she wasn't thinking about how helping him out might boost her own career. She first learned of Rosenberg's Web site when she was working at a dot com company, and it became clear that she was about to lose her job. A friend sent her a link to *Odd Todd*, and she visited it every day. "It made me laugh, and it took away that alone feeling," she told me. "It had a big draw, apart from the humor. You felt you were in good company."

Still, she told me, the site was driving her nuts because the home page was so disorganized and the navigation was so clumsy. She contacted Rosenberg and offered to help, but he wasn't interested, maintaining that the unprofessional look was part of the *Odd Todd* mystique. She persisted anyway, and even sent him a plan of what she had in mind. Finally, the day before Rosenberg was due to make an appearance on CNN, he agreed to let her redesign the home page. She had just one day to do it but managed to tidy things up and add a smoothly functioning, jaunty new navigation bar on the left-hand side of the screen.

That was the beginning of their successful collaboration. Kamen continues to help him out with special tasks, like adding falling snowflakes to the site for Christmas and giving it an appropriate seasonal look for other holidays. In return for her help, Rosenberg makes a point of promoting Kamen throughout his site as "The Official Web Designer of *OddTodd.com*!" As a result, Kamen reports, 90% of the inquires she gets from prospective clients have come to her from the *Odd Todd* site. She's also getting more of her dream clients—companies and individuals from the arts and entertainment world, including musicians.

Looking back on how she first hooked up with Rosenberg and started working with him, Kamen said: "I was coming out of a corporate situation, always working with the same color palette. I was looking for more creative opportunities. It turned out to be the best business move I ever made."

Kamen's own Web site for her freelance design business, which she launched soon after she was laid off from her dot com job, is entirely different from the casual bachelor style of *Odd Todd*. It is crisp, polished, and elegant, laid out in a highly organized way. (See Figure 25.2.) Its design earned it a Golden Web Award from the International Association of Webmasters and Designers.

"My Web site says a lot about me," Kamen said. "For instance, I love nature and earth tones, and I'm organized." She says the site also reflects her skills and style at a glance, without making the visitor sift through mountains of text. She wanted her site to show her creative side and eclectic nature. "A site like everyone else's—standard layout, standard buttons, standard navigation—wouldn't be 'me,' " she asserted. "I created my site with the idea of doing something different, not only its visual structure, but in navigation as well." The samples of her work that are included on the site reveal the diversity of her design approaches. "If you are going to be successful in the design business," she said, "you need to be flexible, and be able to shift gears easily."

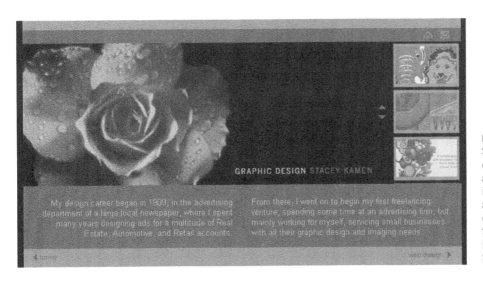

Figure 25.2
Stacey Kamen's elegant style features a bank of scrolling images (far right) and utilizes a quite different approach from *Odd Todd*. Image courtesy of Stacey Kamen.

Lonely No More

LonelyGirl15 is another self-made venture that, like *Odd Todd*, was produced on a shoestring budget and yet thrust its creators into the limelight. Unlike *Odd Todd*, however, this faux video blog was released at first as individual videos on YouTube. (The series now has its own Web site.) The project is the joint effort of Miles Beckett, a young doctor who dropped out of his residency program to do something more creative, and Ramesh Flinders, an aspiring screenwriter.

The two met at a karaoke bar birthday party and discovered they shared a vision of producing a new kind of entertainment specifically geared for the Internet, one that would use the kind of video blogging found on sites like YouTube, to tell a fictional story and that would seem so real that it would pull viewers into the lives of the characters. Together they created *LonelyGirl15*, shooting it in Flinders' bedroom with a cheap webcam, inexpensive props, and unpaid actors. They planned their strategy carefully, giving the episodes a rough-hewn look like other YouTube amateur videos and even having the main character, Bree, refer to recent videos posted on YouTube to make her seem all the more authentic.

STAKING OUT NEW TERRITORY

LonelyGirl15 has been a huge hit, and not even the discovery that Bree was not a real girl has managed to derail it. As of this writing 328 episodes have been released, and Beckett and Flinders are now represented by a major Hollywood talent agency. Interestingly, although they have had meetings with top TV producers, they steadfastly refuse to turn *LonelyGirl15* into just another TV series, preferring instead to stake out uncharted creative territory. As Beckett told a writer from *Wired Magazine* (December, 2006): "The Web isn't just a support system for hit TV shows. It's a new medium. It requires new storytelling techniques. The way the networks look at the Internet now is like the early days of TV, when announcers would just read radio scripts on camera."

An Almighty Hit

Mr. Deity, which made its debut in 2006, is another Web-based video series made on a tiny budget that has given its creator enormous visibility. The *Mr. Deity* of this comedy series is God himself, and he is portrayed as a visionary who is not especially good with the details. The videos are far too quirky to ever find a home on television, but are a great fit for the Web, which loves edgy humor. Though they do not actually mock religion, they do pose some thorny theological questions in a humorous way. For example, why does God allow terrible things to happen to innocent people, and why do so many prayers seem to go unanswered? The series creator, Brian Keith Dalton, it should be noted, is not only an independent filmmaker, but was at one time training to be a missionary and asserts that he has great respect for religious people.

Like *LonelyGirl15*, the first episodes of *Mr. Deity* were released as individual videos on YouTube. They feature a revolving cast of four characters, including God, Jesus, Lucifer, and God's right-hand assistant, the highly efficient Larry. Dalton himself does almost everything: He writes, directs, edits, produces, and stars in the videos and even wrote the theme music. A one-person crew handles both the camera and sound. *Mr. Deity* has not only been a major hit on YouTube but also attracted the attention of Sony Pictures Entertainment, which now features two new episodes a month of *Mr. Deity* on its Web site, Crackle.

Mr. Deity is yet another example of how high originality is more important than a high budget when it comes to creating a showcase for your talent.

GETTING YOUR WORK SEEN

One excellent way to bring attention to your work is to enter it in contests and competitions. A number of new ones have gotten started in recent years, and we can expect to see more of them all the time. It's a good idea to keep your eyes open for them because winning one can bring your work tremendous exposure.

POINTERS FOR MAKING YOUR OWN SHOWCASE

If you are planning to create and build your own professional showcase, the following suggestions are helpful to keep in mind:

1. Don't imitate others; be an original. Let your showcase reflect what you really care about. This is the same advice offered by professionals in every creative field to anyone endeavoring to make something to show off their talents, be it a painting, movie script, novel, or an interactive game.
2. Define your ultimate objectives and mold your showcase accordingly. The material it contains should demonstrate your abilities in the type of work you want to do and be appropriate to the general arena where you hope to find employment.
3. Don't confuse the making of a showcase with the making of a vanity piece. This isn't the place to display cute pet pictures or to brag about your snowboarding trophies. It is, however, appropriate to include your professional credits and contact information.
4. Be sure your showcase actually works. Try to get a friend to beta test it for you. If the piece is for the Web, look at it on different browsers and on both Macs and PCs.
5. If you are lacking in a particular skill, don't let that be a roadblock. Either teach yourself that skill or team up with more skilled colleagues.
6. Humor can be an asset in a showcase, but inappropriate humor can backfire. If you think your piece is comic, run it by other people

to see if they agree. Ideally, seek the opinions of people who are about the same age and at the same professional level as your target audience.

7. If your work includes text, keep it concise and easy to read. Try whenever possible to find a way to do something visually rather than by printed words.

8. Make sure that the interactive elements you include are well integrated into the overall concept, have a legitimate function, and demonstrate that you understand how to use interactivity effectively.

9. If you are taking a portfolio approach instead of showcasing a single piece, select pieces that contain different types of subject matter and display different styles and approaches.

10. Get feedback from others, and be open to what they say. Receiving feedback can be uncomfortable, but it is the only way you will find out how others see your work. Don't become so attached to any one feature that you are unable to discard it, even if it detracts from other aspects of your showcase. As a story editor once said to me: "Sometimes you have to kill your babies."

The process of creating an effective showcase will take time, but be patient. You will probably experience some frustrations and hit some walls. Such setbacks indicate you are stretching yourself, which is a positive thing. If you persist, you will end up knowing more than you did when you began the project, and you are likely to create something of which you can be proud.

CHAPTER 26

Breaking and Entering

Christy Marx

This was the most challenging chapter of the book to write. Although it's difficult to break into any creative field, and difficult enough to break into animation, it was far more challenging for me to come up with cogent, useful advice for breaking into game writing. The advice in this chapter is culled from a large pool of game producers, designers, developers, and writers to supplement my personal experience. Given the rapid pace at which videogames and the videogame market evolves, my advice is subject to change at any time.

There's one especially pesky question that is asked all the time, so let's get it out of the way and move on.

THE $64,000 QUESTION

The question usually comes framed something like this: "I have a great idea for a game! How do I sell it to a game company?"

The short answer is—you don't. Game companies do not buy game ideas from outside people. They don't need to. That's why they have designers working for them, or why designers establish their own companies (for example, Sid Meier, cofounder of Firaxis Games, creator of the *Civilization* game series; and Will Wright, cofounder of Maxis Software, creator of *SimCity*, *The Sims* and *Spore*).

This leaves you with three choices:

- Work your way up from within and try to get the company to do your idea, understanding that you will have to give the company ownership of the idea.

DOI: 10.1016/B978-0-240-81343

- Make it yourself. This would require creating a prototype or demo (demonstration) of your proposed game, which you could then show to game companies or venture capital investors in the hope that they'll fund you to a full game. You would need to have the necessary programmers and artists to carry this out, or be so incredibly talented that you can do it yourself. There is some do-it-yourself game-creation software out there, such as DarkBASIC, if you have the inclination to master it, but this software provides only the programming end of the equation. You would need additional art software to add to it. If you have the courage and energy to go this route, you'll need to find some books or courses on how to make games, which is way beyond the bounds of this book. One more alternative is software from online casual-games company PopCap. They offer free casual-game-creation software via their PopCap Developer Program (*http://sourceforge.net/projects/popcapframework/*). If PopCap is impressed enough with the game you create, they may publish it.
- Develop an intellectual property in some other format (book, comic book, movie, brand name, and so on) that you own so that you can sell the rights to a game company. If you can be the creator and owner of an IP, you will be in a position of power far better than being a designer. A classic example is Marc Ecko, a young hip-hop artist who created a multimillion-dollar line of clothes, shoes, watches, and accessories, then turned his brand-name power into a videogame.

If you come from a teaching or educational background with a good educational résumé, you might have some luck breaking into educational children's games (sometimes referred to as edutainment) as a consultant. Such games are more linear and focused on the teaching elements. It's a rather specialized area of game development, and many of the educational-game companies have teaching experts on staff or as consultants. This is to ensure that the games follow the proper educational guidelines, especially if the company wants to sell them to schools. You should contact the game companies that make educational games, and put yourself forward as a consultant. From that position, you can learn more about creating a game and perhaps eventually move into designing them.

PUBLISHERS AND DEVELOPERS

When sorting out how to break in, it's important to have a grasp on the business structure of game development. Making a game is one thing; having the know-how or resources to handle production, sales, promotion, and distribution is another. In the 1980s, some game companies did everything: created the game; had an art department that created covers, game booklets, ads, posters, fan magazine, and so on; had a production line where the disks were copied, packed into boxes, and shipped; and had sales reps who sold the games to stores. Rarely would a game developer now do all these things, especially the production end. They simply can't afford to.

The business structure has sorted itself out in tiers of publishers and developers. Generally speaking, the development studios create the actual game, and the publisher handles everything else—production, marketing/promotion, sales, distribution, inventory. This may vary according to the type of deal that is worked out between publisher and developer, and it can apply to any kind of game—PC, console, or MMOG.

The tiers look like this:

- Publishers/Platform Owners: Sony, Microsoft, and Nintendo are in a class by themselves because they are not only enormous publishers, they are the companies that invent and sell the hardware platforms on which console games are played—that is, PlayStation, Xbox, and Wii. They license to developer studios the rights to develop games for their platforms. They can control development by funding games to be made solely for their respective platforms.
- Publishers: The big-name publishers are companies such as EA (Electronic Arts) and Ubisoft, plus the games-publishing arms of major entertainment studios such as Buena Vista Games (Disney), Vivendi Universal Games, Warner Bros., and LucasArts. Other substantial publishers include Take-Two Interactive, THQ, Midway Games, and Activision. Overseas publishers include Capcom (Japan), Namco (Japan), NCsoft (South Korea), Webzen (South Korea), Atari/Infogrames Entertainment (France), 1C Company (Russia), SCI Entertainment Group (United Kingdom), and CDV (Germany).
- Internal (in-house) developers: These are usually independent or external development studios that were acquired by a publisher and have become subsidiaries run by the publisher. It's easier to acquire an existing development studio than to build one from scratch. This allows a publisher more control over the development process than going to an external developer.
- External (third-party) developers: These studios either make their own games and make deals with publishers to distribute them, or they're hired to make a game based on some project or property controlled by the publisher.

This publisher/developer structure affects writers in three ways: (*a*) where and how you look for work, (*b*) how much you are paid, and (*c*) whether the project makes it to completion.

One of the unhappy realities of game development is that many games don't make it all the way through the development process to be released. Games can be cancelled for any number of reasons, most commonly because the entity funding the game loses confidence in the project and decides not to keep throwing money at it.

385

Ellen Guon Beeman, a highly experienced game producer with more than a dozen produced games on her credits, summed up the status of game-project development as a food chain. At the bottom of the food chain are those mostly likely to lose out in the event of a budget reduction or game cancellation, moving up the food chain to those least likely to be cut.

The food chain is also cyclical. Historically, game publishers have tended to shift every few years between funding in-house projects and using third-party (external) developers. In-house projects are generally more expensive, but the publisher can maintain more creative control. Third-party developers are often (but not always) less expensive, and the publisher can more easily cancel their projects in the event of a budget cutback.

At the moment, it looks like this in the game industry:

- The top of the food chain is made up of a publisher's internally developed projects. These are the least likely to be cut off if the publisher decides it's necessary to trim budgets—unless the publisher is a publicly traded company that wants to cut personnel to bump up their stock price. (It's always advisable to track your publisher's stock-price fluctuations.)
- Next down are internal producers who manage external projects; meaning a publisher's salaried producer who shepherds an external project to completion. If the publisher needs to cut budgets, guess who is usually going to get hit first?
- Next down are the external developers themselves. See the point above.
- At the bottom are the subcontractors (say, for example, contract writers) who work for the external developers.

Does this mean you should work only for publishers or internal studios rather than independents? Not at all. It does mean that when accepting work, you should be aware of how well established a studio is. Have they been around for a while? Have they produced a number of successful games? If not, do the people in charge have experience and good credentials in the business? Who is their publisher? For what platform(s) will the game be made? For console games in particular, putting out versions of the game for more than one platform is an indication that this game is a big deal, and therefore less likely to be cancelled. If it's made for only one platform, is that because the studio has an exclusive deal with that platform publisher? Don't be afraid to research the studio or company before committing. If anything about the studio seems dubious, you will need to weigh how badly you want the work vs. how sure you are they will be able to pay you for it.

Looking for Work: Freelance or Employee

The first major decision you need to make is whether you want to have a career as a full-time employee at a game company, or as a contract writer (freelance) working for a variety of companies.

THE EMPLOYEE TRACK

As an employee, you will have a steady paycheck while you learn and hone your ability as a game writer and/or narrative designer, but it means dedicating yourself to that one type of writing full time. Once you've built up a track record as a game writer, and have a network of contacts in the business, you'll be in a better position to try going freelance, if that appeals to you.

There aren't many companies that hire a full-time writer or narrative designer to be on staff. Publishers are less likely to make that kind of hire, because they primarily oversee the work done by developers. Consequently, your focus will be on developer studios, and even more precisely, on studios that create the types of games that might call for a full-time writer on staff.

MMOGs require the largest amount of ongoing content creation, so studios that create MMOGs are the best places to start the search. After that, you would need to research studios that create RPGs, FPSs, adventure, action, or other story-driven games.

Because the notion of hiring a full-time writer is fairly new, there are no established rules for the job. For an MMOG, they may post a job for a writer, narrative designer, or story designer because the writer will probably also be involved in creating quests or missions. Consequently, you should familiarize yourself with MMOGs and the other story-driven types of games, so that you have a sense of the design issues. At least one MMOG developer that frequently hires writers requires applicants to create a game writing sample using their proprietary module-creation system. You must be technically prepared to learn, understand, and use their software—which is, of course, based on their game. Unfortunately, learning one piece of proprietary software doesn't mean you can use that precise knowledge anywhere else, because each company's software will be different, but it does show that you are capable of learning such software.

Today, there are more game design courses being offered in colleges, but still very few courses that deal specifically with game writing. A few schools touch upon game writing via game design courses or other media courses.

However, good writing is good writing, so you should have education or training that shows you can write engaging stories with compelling characters. Game writers have debated whether a liberal arts degree is sufficient, whether journalism is valid, and what other forms of writing best prepare a writer to get work in games. There is no consensus.

My recommendation is to study film and TV scriptwriting. These are the forms most closely associated with what you might do for a game company. Get any kind of writing you can under your belt. Write for paper-based RPGs. Write reviews and articles for game magazines or online game sites. Write a good script of any kind (screenplay, teleplay) that can serve as a sample of your work. It's hard to write a useful game writing sample, because each game and each studio can have such different needs or expectations, but any potential employer will know how to read a teleplay, screenplay, or short story. Any type of published/produced work—book, short story, script—will give you credibility.

With more and more games being based on existing properties—such as movies, TV series, and comics—you may also need to be familiar with those properties. One developer that was looking for writers asked the applicants to create a short sample to demonstrate that they could match the tone of the well-known TV property on which the game was based, as well as the manner in which the main characters spoke. The developer was appalled at how many applicants turned in utterly generic samples that completely lacked any flavor of the property, as though all game characters came from some bland cookie-cutter mold. Other applicants were openly scornful of the notion that games needed story or character development!

These are really great ways *not* to get hired as a game writer.

Your résumé should emphasize your education, training, and other writing experience, especially anything you've done that relates to games or multimedia work. Be sure to mention any awards or honors you've gotten for your work.

For the most part when applying for a full-time job, you'll be dealing with someone in the Human Resources (HR) Department. However, you should do the same kind of networking a freelancer would do. Making the right connection inside a company could be the break you need to get in the door. Read the following section to get more details on networking.

THE FREELANCE TRACK

About the only way to establish yourself as a contract writer is to have experience and credits in another area of writing. In other words, you should already be a professional writer. Because contract game writing work is scarce and hard to get, you are best advised to consider it as one of several arenas in which you can work rather than the only one. It is extremely difficult to work full time, or even most of the time, solely as a contract game writer.

Developers that produce MMOGs, RPGs, FPSs, action, adventure, and other story-driven games are the most likely to want the services of a writer. Those that don't want to keep a full-time writer on staff will instead look for contract writers.

Looking for contract work requires having professional credits and solid writing samples. Set up your game writing résumé to emphasize your writing strengths, especially anything that relates to games. If you have game writing credits along with other types of writing, be sure to place the game writing credits first on the résumé to call attention to them.

Note that if you are someone with both game design/narrative design and game writing credits, you need to create two separate résumés—one strictly for finding design work, and one strictly for writing work. Once you're in with a company, you can demonstrate your various talents, but you really want them to be clear on who you are and what specific role they're hiring you for.

However, you will rarely get contract work on the basis of a résumé alone. Most producers don't know where to go to find the kind of writer they need—consequently, they'll go for a known name, whether it's known because of previous work the writer has done (on other games or in other media), known via a personal recommendation from a colleague (very important), or known because the producer is already acquainted with the writer in one way or another. Bob Bates, legendary game designer and writer, put it this way: "Producers are people with problems, and you want to be the solution to their problem." The hard part is making a producer aware that you are an existing solution.

Constant, consistent networking is vital to finding contract work. This requires a variety of approaches, including, but not limited to:

- Be involved in the IGDA (International Game Developers Association) community (consider serving on committees).
- Become a speaker for a lecture, workshop, or seminar for the GDC (Game Developers Conference).
- Take part in email lists with other developers and writers (another benefit of belonging to the IGDA).
- Write articles about writing and game writing for whatever outlet you can (newspapers, magazines, Web sites, e-zines, blogs, and so on).
- Maintain a useful, informative personal Web site or blog that gives your credits, and have samples of your work available on the site. For the Internet search engines, include search tags such as game writer, narrative designer, and story designer.
- Attend every conference and trade show that you can, and schmooze like crazy (more info on conferences and trade shows later in this chapter).
- Speak at other conferences and trade shows (though GDC is always the best).

There are certain methods that are across-the-board *not* recommended, and it's good to know about those as well. At all costs, do not:

- Send out generic email to any and all developers you can track down. They will treat you as spam, with everything that implies. Don't email anyone at a developer studio or publisher unless you have already made contact with them so that they will know who you are and be receptive to your email, or you're answering an online job posting in which you're directed to send email to their HR department.

- Call producers, designers, or other people at the studio or publisher. They are insanely busy most of the time, and the last thing they want is a phone call from an unknown (and therefore unwanted) person looking for work. Call only if you have previously made contact, and they have positively indicated that you can or should call.
- Send out flashy brochures that cost a lot to produce and mail, but can end up tossed into a forgotten file in some Human Resources office. I speak from personal experience here, having once tried this approach. I sent out hundreds of such brochures—which led to exactly no response, except for two postcards with a generic "Thank you for your interest in our company."

Sarah W. Stocker, producer extraordinaire, has worked as a game writer, game designer, and producer at a major independent developer for fourteen years as an executive producer of mobile games, and as a senior producer at Sony. She shares some exceptionally useful tips about searching for game writing.

Sarah points out that the need for writers, plus where and how writers are hired, also depends upon the budget and platform of the project. Here is a summary of her advice on that topic:

- Next-generation console games: Periodically the industry goes through what it calls a "transition year" when the major console makers are in the process of introducing their new, improved, and totally glitzy-awesome versions of their game consoles. The PS3 supersedes the PS2, the Xbox 360 supersedes the Xbox, and so forth. Games made for next-generation consoles are the equivalent of the blockbuster tent-pole summer movie that gets the megamillion budget and the big, big-name stars. The budgets for these games likewise reach into the tens of millions. Consequently, these are "star" games, and the company is going to be very selective about the writer to whom they entrust a megamillion-dollar project. The superior graphics and processing power of next-gen games raises the bar for quality storytelling to match. What producers on these games are looking for is credibility, and they will go for the writer who has the kind of credits that provides them with that credibility.

  The qualities these producers are looking for go beyond raw talent and creativity. They are looking for experience, professionalism, a proven ability to produce, and someone who knows how to work in a collaborative medium. This is where the writer with a name in movies or TV is most likely to be hired, especially if that writer happened to work on the original property on which such a game was based. These producers will be open to a writer with a track record of working on best-selling or critically acclaimed games. A name novelist with credits in the same genre as the game might also be hired to develop the story, though probably not for the more interactive elements of the writing.
- Last-generation console games: There are still plenty of games being made for the previous models of consoles (the ones being replaced by

the next generation), but at lower budgets and with less stress on having to get a top name. Although producers of these games are equally concerned with having excellent content, the budget risk is lower, allowing them to take more risks with talent. These games provide a better chance for a writer to break in.

- MMOGs: As stated elsewhere, they have enormous writing demands, and some of them can have ten to fifteen writers working on them. Producers hiring for an MMOG would likely look for a writer with RPG or game writing background, and would be thrilled if the writer had TV writing on top of it. They might also consider a novelist to do the story.
- PC: Huge numbers of PC games are still being made, so the opportunities for writing are out there. Given the many different genres and types of PC games, you should focus on the types that interest you the most.
- Casual games: This market is exploding. Many of these games are free downloads, and although there isn't a lot of writing in these games at the moment, there is at least some. This could be an easier way for someone without a lot of credits to break in, especially if you're willing to work for less money.
- Mobile games: This is another expanding market, largely powered by huge amounts of iPhone development. Producers of mobile games use writers to create story and take the text that is written in-house by the company and rewrite it. This is short, limited writing (due to the limitations of mobile phones and handheld units), so it's not big money. Once again, though, this might be a way to break into the interactive field.

In contrast to my flashy brochures that didn't work, there is a type of mailed presentation that Sarah Stocker thinks is a good approach. She recommends an excellent, professional-looking presentation package that consists of the following:

- A short, well-written cover letter on letterhead and personalized to the producer (*not* a generic letter)—meaning that you should mention or compliment the producer on his or her latest game, or at least on the company's games. The letter should emphasize your strengths and what type of writing you could best contribute.
- Your résumé.
- *Short* samples of your writing. Note the emphasis on *short* samples. Although producers will appreciate the credibility of a published novel, they won't necessarily have time to read it. That's why sending a script is a better choice. The script could be a spec rather than something that has been produced, but if you have a produced script, so much the better. The producer will be looking for storytelling that shows the writer has a sense of visual direction, character development, and good dialogue. Although animation scripts don't have the same level of credibility as live action,

one thing that an animation script shows is the writer's ability to storyboard a script. It's acceptable to include samples of game writing work if they're in an easy-to-read format, but generally a producer will be more interested in a TV or movie script. A short story would also be acceptable, provided it demonstrates a cinematic sense of storytelling.

Where to Network

Various conferences and trade shows deal with games and electronic entertainment. For writers, it comes down to one that is absolutely vital, the Game Developers Conference (*http://www.gdconf.com*), which is held in March in San Jose, California. GDC describes itself as the official trade event "by game developers for developers" of computer, console, mobile, arcade, online games, and location-based entertainment.

GDC consists of an expo hall and job fair, plus workshops, lectures, and seminars covering all aspects of making games. It is the single most important event to attend in order to network and look for work. Unfortunately, doing the entire conference is highly expensive. As an alternative, go for an expo pass so that you can access the job fair and expo. Most companies have booths with HR people at the job fair. This is most useful if you're looking for an employee situation, not so useful for contract work.

For a contract writer, it's best to send in your résumé and samples ahead of time, then attempt to arrange follow-up meetings with someone at GDC. This gives the producer time to check out your credits and determine whether a meeting would be a good idea. Most people are solidly booked by the time they get to GDC, so spur-of-the-moment meetings just aren't going to happen.

Your strongest position for attending GDC is as a speaker. Each year, GDC invites people to submit proposals for workshops, lectures, and seminars. If your proposal is accepted, you will attend GDC free in exchange for being a speaker, with the extra benefit of a lot of free publicity. The conference lists its requirements for speaker submissions on the GDC Web site sometime in the summer for the conference the following March.

Another route for those on a tight budget to get in free is to volunteer as a conference associate (*http://www.gdconf.com/attend/volunteer.html*). As a CA, you get free entry in exchange for doing such work as guarding doors, monitoring conference sessions, checking badges at meals and special events, stuffing conference bags, and performing data entry.

In previous years, the monster trade show was E^3, which stands for Electronic Entertainment Expo. After the E^3 of 2006, the magnitude and expense of the show was no longer proving as effective as some of the major exhibitors desired, consequently at the time this book went to press, E^3 put out this announcement: "To better address the needs of today's global computer and videogame industry, the 2007 Electronic Entertainment Expo (E3Expo) is evolving into a more intimate event focused on targeted, personalized meetings and activities...."

While E^3 wasn't a great place to go job hunting, it had some usefulness as a place to network, set up meetings (in advance), and get a feel for what was happening in the business. How this "evolution" will affect the use of the show for writers, I can't say, but you'll want to keep an eye on it.

Another version of GDC offers a special two-day Game Writers Summit (*http://www.gdcaustin.com/conference/writers.html*). It's held in September in Austin, Texas, and focuses specifically on game writing and narrative design.

For additional trade-show links and information, look at the GDC Web site and regularly visit *gamasutra.com*.

Timing

To understand *when* to send out your writing-sample package, you should be aware of another reality of game production—many companies aim to have a new game on the shelves no later than Thanksgiving in order to cash in on the all-important Christmas gift-buying season. A PC or console game can take anywhere from eighteen months and up to complete, meaning that it's common for new-game development to ramp up between January and March. This schedule doesn't apply to every game, of course—in fact, it has become more common for games to be released at other times of the year—so consider this only a rough guideline. In addition, companies often suddenly decide they need a writer when the project is halfway or more done, so they could suddenly be looking for a writer at any time of the year.

That said, it is often the case that in the months immediately leading up to Thanksgiving, projects are in crunch mode, with people working frantic overtime to finish a game and get it out the door no later than September in order to go through production and reach the shelves by November. Consequently, the least effective time to send out résumés and sample packages is probably between June and September.

Another time to avoid is immediately prior to and during GDC when producers are distracted by preparing for the conference.

MMOGs could need writers at any time. Development for something as large and complex as an MMOG could cover three to four years before it's ready to launch. And once it goes live (meaning in full operation online with paid subscribers), an MMOG continues to need writers.

How to Find the Right Person

Figuring out the right person to approach when you're looking for game work is one of the most difficult parts of this process. The employee track and the contract-writer track break out quite differently.

THE EMPLOYEE TRACK

You have two options—try to find a job on your own or go through a recruiter. Doing it on your own will take a lot of time and research, and writing jobs are rarely posted. Your search will have to be constant and thorough. This is a very tough way to go. You will need to do the following:

- Contact each company's HR Department to inquire about writing jobs, then send your résumé and samples (if requested).
- Check the company's job listings on their Web site, on the slim chance of a writing job being posted.
- Follow up with HR every couple of months so they won't forget you exist.
- Network and make contacts that might alert you to writing jobs or help you get a foot in the door.

The other option is to go through a recruiter. The difficulty here is that because it's such a rare job, most recruiters don't place writers. Recruiters know exactly how to place a producer, designer, programmer, or artist. They don't usually know what to do with a person who is looking solely for writing work.

Also, be aware that recruiters *cannot* represent you to a company to which you have submitted your résumé in the past twelve months. If you decide to try using a recruiter, you need to take this route first before sending résumés to companies on your own.

Professional Electronic Entertainment Recruiters (PEER) is an organization of game recruiters. Their Web site (*http://www.peer-org.com/members.htm*) lists several reputable recruiters, along with links to the recruiters' Web sites. Be prepared to fill out the recruiters' online forms, and be sure to regularly check the job listings on their Web sites.

A lot of game jobs are listed on *http://www.creativeheads.net*, with a writing job occasionally among them. Once you sign up at their Web site, they will send you emails with job listings.

An important site for job listings is *http://www.gamasutra.com*, which is also a resource for learning about the art and business of making games.

Likewise, *http://www.datascope.co.uk/jobs_by_email.html* will send job listings after you fill out the form on their Web site. They cover both the United Kingdom and the United States.

Other sites to check include the following:

http://www.gamesjobnews.com
http://www.games-match.com
http://www.gignews.com/jobs/index.htm
http://jobs.awn.com (Note: this is the Animation World Network, but has been covering games as well as animation. Writing jobs occasionally show up here, but approach these jobs with caution. They often seem to be of dubious quality or are looking for people who will work for free.)

If you want to try getting in the door via technical writing, there are a few temp agencies that handle technical writers. Recommended ones include Sakson & Taylor (*http://www.sakson.com*), FILTER (*http://www.filtertalent.com*), Excell Data (*http://www.excell.com*), and Volt Services Group (*http://www.volt.com*). However, doing technical writing may require you to live in a particular area to qualify for work, usually West Coast tech centers such as the Bay Area or Seattle.

THE FREELANCE TRACK

There is no quick or easy way to get your résumé to the right person. This is why networking is so vital—much of the time, writing jobs are never posted, and someone is hired long before you might ever hear that a producer was even looking.

The next question is whether to go after producers at the publisher level or the developer level. A producer at a publisher can consider you for more games than can a developer who might work on only one game at a time, but more often it will be the developer that does the hiring. Publishers may be more involved in hiring a contract writer for a high-profile game based on a major entertainment property, but less involved with lower-profile games. The best bet is to go after producers at either tier.

True, you could approach the lead designers, because in most cases they are the ones who have the creative vision for the game and could be crucial in making the recommendation that gets you the job. Usually producers make the decisions about hiring, firing, and budget—and that is why you may do better to focus on producers.

More specifically, first go after a senior producer on a project. If no one has the title of senior producer, go for producer. Avoid contacting executive producers. Executive producers are at such a high level that they tend to be more removed from the day-to-day running of a project, and may have multiple projects to handle at once making them far less likely to read your sample. This will often be true of creative directors as well. A senior producer is more likely to be focused on a particular project, and consequently more aware of when a writer might be needed.

I wish I could tell you there was a simple, easy formula for finding producers, or a nice handy list somewhere. There isn't. This step takes time and research. You will have to look at the credits on games, search out credit listings on the Net, in magazines, and anywhere else you can think of to track down the names of producers. The Internet Movie Database (*http://www.imdb.com*) has some game-credit listings, as does the game-oriented MobyGames (*http://www.mobygames.com*).

Getting hired may involve a number of introductory steps. You might be asked to produce a sample of game work based on their specifications, which could be for free or could be paid work. You might be asked to come to the company and meet the development team, perhaps do some brainstorming, so they can get a feel for how well you work on a collaborative basis.

When you do finally get that meeting, the interviewer(s) will want to hear you talk about story and character. Game people in general have become more savvy about story arcs and character arcs. They'll want to hear what sort of writing or stories grab your enthusiasm. Feel free to gush about your favorite movie or TV series. What they don't want to hear a writer talk about is game design—unless, by some fluke, they are also hiring you to do design such as narrative design. In fact, talking about design could even lose you a job if they worry that you'll try to interfere with design issues rather than being focused on the writing. Understanding and being aware of design issues is a plus; trying to come across like a level or systems designer is a minus.

GETTING PAID

The Employee Track

Game Developer magazine does an annual salary report on what people are making in the games business. Gamasutra posts the results on their site. Unfortunately, "writing" isn't treated as a category by itself, and instead is folded into "design." In the 2003 survey (the most recent one posted at this time), annual salaries in the design category ranged anywhere from $40,000 to $100,000, depending on level of job and level of experience. Because the data collected are provided on an entirely volunteer basis, this survey can be considered a rough guide at best, but it's pretty much all there is, other than what a recruiter might tell you. It also depends on the location of the job. In expensive areas to live, such as the Bay area, California, you can expect to see higher salaries than in a more reasonably priced area such as Austin, Texas.

The Freelance Track

You should aim to be paid a flat fee for your work (one overall amount), which will be broken out into milestone payments. There are no established guidelines for what to charge for a game bible, cinematics, or other writing work. The best you can do is try to estimate how much time the project will take you to complete, and what you feel is adequate compensation for your time.

The amount also depends on various other factors: size of the company, status and budget of the project, type of writing that is needed, and your experience and credits. A big-name writer who is brought in on a high-profile (big-budget) game to create the entire story, lore, and game world from scratch is a higher level of work that might command around $60,000. The pay might be half that if a writer is brought in to polish an existing game bible, or simply to write a script based on existing gameplay. A small developer needing a simple bible might be able to pay only around $15,000 or less.

At the low end, for mobile games, they might pay around $300 to $1,000 to come up with a story for a very short game and a limited script of around thirty to sixty lines.

Some companies will want you to quote an hourly or weekly rate, especially for straightforward writing work such as dialogue, but there are no established rates and no easy sense of what to charge. Depending on the size of the company, the type of writing, and your level of experience, that rate can vary widely, anywhere from $50 an hour to $150 an hour. Rates between $1,500 and $2,500 a week are reasonable.

Note that game scheduling is built around *milestones* (as defined in Chapter 10). Consequently, you will be asked to turn in a certain amount of work (the deliverable) by a certain milestone (a date). As mentioned earlier, most games have a long development cycle—from one and a half years to many years. A contract writer is likely to be involved for only a number of weeks or a few months.

Whether talking about a flat fee or hourly/weekly rate, here are some additional factors to take into account when figuring out what to charge:

- Amount of work: If it's a game bible, get them to specify how many pages they are expecting, how detailed they want it to be, and precisely what it will cover. For cutscenes/cinematics, find out how many they plan to have in the game. Dialogue is much more difficult, but get them to be as specific as possible about how many characters or NPCs are involved, and how many lines for each (be sure to have them define what they mean by "lines," because game companies can view this differently than a TV or film company does). Then you have to do your best guesstimate on how much time you feel you need to create that work. Take into account the ramping-up time to absorb their game design, the time to get a handle on the interface and gameplay, and possibly time to play previous games (if this is a sequel).
- Scheduling: The company may be on a tight schedule with demanding milestones, though most of the time they will work out the milestones with you. You need to do a hard, honest assessment of whether you can meet their milestones, and whether there is any flexibility in the schedule.
- Approvals: Be sure to find out how many people can have notes, input, or right of approval on the work. Ideally, you will work with only one company representative who is the gatekeeper for all such input. Work out how many days the gatekeeper will require to evaluate your work and give you notes. If there are other entities (such as a movie studio) that require approval over scripts, be sure to add extra days in the schedule for that turnaround time. You don't want to have fixed milestones that suddenly become a scheduling nightmare because you had to wait a week to get notes from a third party. In fact, you should aim to include language in your contract to the effect that you must be given one compiled set of *non-conflicting notes* from one person. Notice the emphasis on *non-conflicting notes*. That is to prevent a long list of changes from numerous people who have contradictory notes on what they want you to do. Make them decide what the right direction is before giving you the notes.

- Rewrites: Specify how many rewrites you will do, and how those rewrites will be covered in payment and in the milestones. This is extremely important if you've worked out a flat fee—otherwise you could find yourself doing a lot of free rewrites.
- Additional work: Specify additional writing or work they may want you to do, such as promotional or Web site material, or attending voice-recording sessions. You should be paid separate fees for that work, and the company should cover your expenses for attending voice-recording sessions.
- Travel expenses: It will be common for a game company to ask you to spend some time at their studio or office, particularly at the beginning of the project. They may have software to teach you, aspects of the game to share with you, and people you need to meet and work with over the course of the project. If the company is outside your immediate area, all travel expenses should be covered.

If you happen to be represented by an agent, the agent can handle most of the price negotiation and will handle invoicing and payments.

If no agent is involved, be sure to clarify who should receive the invoice, what the payment period will be (immediately upon receipt of invoice? in fourteen days? twenty days? thirty days?), and keep careful track of your payment schedule. Make sure you specify precisely what deliverables are covered by each invoice.

LOCATION, LOCATION, LOCATION

In the United States, there are some definite hot spots of videogame work. The main clusters are Seattle, the San Francisco Bay Area, Los Angeles, and Austin, Texas. Other major locations include Chicago, San Diego, and various cities on the East Coast. Game companies are popping up across the country, however.

In Canada, the main hot spot is Vancouver, with companies also in Montreal, Toronto, and elsewhere.

There are many companies in the United Kingdom. Scotland especially has been pushing the digital-media and creative industries established there. In 2006, Scotland boasted of an estimated annual sales of $6.1 billion, providing more than 100,000 jobs.

China, South Korea, and Japan are also strong international hot spots for game creation.

The Employee Track

Obviously, you must be ready to move to wherever the game company is located. If you have a definite preference for where you want to live, concentrate on companies in that area. But if you're willing to be flexible, you might find you have a better chance breaking into companies located outside the major game-production cities.

A major issue that has been a hot topic of discussion in the game business for the past few years is quality of life (QoL). Basically, it refers to what sort of working conditions a company provides for its employees.

The reason QoL has become such a significant issue has to do with the nature of the games business itself. Namely, it attracts a great many young and hungry workers who are so enthusiastic about working in games that they accept any kind of working conditions. Unfortunately, too many game companies have happily gone along with this, creating a workplace culture in which employees are expected to put in ten- to twelve-hour days, six to seven days a week. Theoretically, this should be restricted to extremely short time periods (meaning a few days to maybe a week) during crunch time. Crunch time is the all-out, last-minute push to get a game completed so it can ship by a certain date. However, some companies abuse this concept. They'll have extended crunch times, failing to understand that extended crunch times are the result of poor management, poor planning, and a poor grasp of what makes for effective productivity. Productivity actually declines after eight hours of intensive work.

A management that has disdain for QoL issues makes for a miserable place to work. It leads to exhaustion, burnout, and people who are unable to have any kind of life outside the workplace. You are strongly advised to ask questions about the company's attitude toward QoL issues, what sort of working hours are routinely expected, and how frequent or long are their crunch times. If you get the sense they expect endless hours of work just because working on their games is so very special, run away as fast as you can.

The Freelance Track

Although there is less emphasis on being in a specific location to do contract work, it certainly doesn't hurt to be in L.A., Austin, Seattle, or the Bay Area. You should be prepared to travel and spend some time on-site at the game company, especially at the beginning of the project—when you need to meet the team, become familiar with the design, and learn any software tools they may want you to use.

AGENTS

Having an agent to handle game writing work is relevant only to the contract writer. You obviously won't be dealing with an agent if you're seeking full-time employment.

Until recently, there was no such thing as a game agent. For the most part, that remains true, though a couple of enterprising souls in L.A. have attempted to provide a talent pool of writers for whom they more or less work as an agent (though one such person rejected the term "agent," feeling that he was providing more of a production service). As far as I know, none of these people have made significant inroads in representing game writers. One producing entity that deals with game writers is Union Entertainment, a company that has set itself up to concurrently develop properties such as films, videogames, and comic books (and whatever else they can make happen).

The big Hollywood agencies have been adding some agents who deal with game writing to their rosters, but that is primarily as a service to their existing base of Hollywood scriptwriters. So far, there hasn't been enough demand to justify taking on clients who do nothing but write games. I suspect that mostly what that type of agent does is field inquiries that happen to come in from a game producer who is interested in a known Hollywood name.

Note also that it's important to understand that Hollywood agents are licensed and regulated. They can't take more than 10 percent of a writer's income. Other people or firms that set out to represent game writers may not be licensed, because this type of work is so new. If you should happen to find someone who claims to be a game writing agent, check carefully into his background and experience, find out whether he's licensed in the same way as other talent agents, and determine what percentage of your money he wants, or how he intends to make money off you. Finally, have a serious discussion up front about how the agent can realistically find work for you or make contacts that you can't make yourself. Be extremely wary of anyone wanting more than ten or fifteen percent as a commission fee.

In the United Kingdom, there are script agencies or script consultancies, which are game writers who have pooled their resources to provide game scripts to companies as a group service. Joining a script agency isn't easy, but it's worth a try. This idea hasn't caught on in the States as yet, though one or two people are trying to make something work along these lines. The best you can do is keep your eyes and ears open for such agencies.

Is having an agent necessary? That depends. For the next-gen console producer who likes to find big-name writers, you might be considered an amateur if you don't have an agent. On the other hand, some producers and companies are resistant to dealing with agents. This is another one of those gray areas with no easy answer. If you're an established scriptwriter or novelist, you'll already have an agent. Then you can decide whether or not your agent or someone at their agency is qualified to handle repping you for game work.

Otherwise, worry first about getting in the door and getting game work before being concerned with the need for an agent. You may do fine without one.

UNIONS AND ORGANIZATIONS

The WGA (Writers Guild of America) is working hard to represent the interests of game writers. I strongly recommend that you read the information in

Chapter 8 (the animation section of this book) about the protections and benefits the WGA can provide to you as a writer.

Within the WGA, the Videogame Writers Caucus (VWC) deals specifically with games, new and evolving media, and interactive entertainment in any form. Operating under the WGA's Organizing Department, the VWC has drafted two simple contract forms to use for interactive work—one for a single-game project, and one for online games. These contracts are for use as an addition to the basic deal you negotiate and their purpose is to guarantee that you also receive key WGA benefits.

The VWC has also initiated a WGA writing award for game writing. For more information about the Videogame Writers Caucus, the qualifications for membership, how to join, or to download the contracts, visit their Web site (*http:// www.wga.org* and look under the **organize** tab).

If you are a contract writer, you should seriously consider negotiating to have your work covered by the WGA. That way, you will gain pension and health benefits, as well as have a strong organization at your back in case of problems, such as ensuring that you receive a fair credit on the game. Realistically, many companies are uncomfortable negotiating with the WGA. Dealing with a union is unknown territory for them. Ask the company for WGA terms, but decide ahead of time how important that is to you. If a company balks at the notion of paying the additional pension and health benefits, you may be able to restructure the payment so that pension and health benefits come out of the overall fee. This means less in your hands up front, but the benefits can be worth it. That's a personal decision.

However, you will never *lose* a job by asking for WGA coverage. Furthermore, the WGA will bend over backward to help you achieve it in a way that works equally well for both the company and you. One more thing to consider—if a company doesn't think you should be entitled to have health insurance or a pension (via the WGA), then perhaps they don't value you much as a writer either.

The other equally important group to join is the IGDA (International Game Developers Association). According to their mission statement, "The IGDA is committed to advancing the careers and enhancing the lives of game developers by connecting members with their peers, promoting professional development, and advocating on issues that affect the developer community."

The IGDA has numerous SIGs (Special Interest Groups), but the one you want to become involved in is the Game Writers SIG, a great place to network and learn about the business. Go to *http://www.igda.org/writing* for more information.

The IGDA Web site also has white papers about writing for games, as well as a quarterly newsletter that is full of useful interviews and info.

401

Index

Note: Page numbers followed by *b* indicates boxes; *f* indicates figures; *t* indicates tables.

A

Index

Index

409

Index

Models
  definition, 26–27
  TV animation script restrictions,
    49–50
Monsters, game bible, 256
Monsters, Inc., 47
Monteiro, Candace, 127–128
MOO, *see* Multi-User Dungeon
    Object Oriented (MOO)
Motion gags, as comedy devices, 94
Motivation, in interactive media,
    197
MOVE IN, 15, 16*b*
Movie Magic Screenwriter, 50, 271
Mr. Deity, 380
MSWord, for script formatting, 272
MUDs, *see* Multi-User Dungeons
    (MUDs)
Multimedia, *see also* Interactive
    multimedia
  computer-mediated, 210
  definition, 211
Multimedia designer, 277
Multiple personalities, as comedy
    device, 88
Multiple reference, as comedy
    device, 89
Multisensory experience,
    immersiveness, 181
Multi-User Dungeon Object
    Oriented (MOO), and IF, 189
Multi-User Dungeons (MUDs), and
    IF, 189
Murray, Janet H., 187, 188
My Fair Lady, 189
MySpace, 378
Myst, 161, 172, 294
Myths, storytelling lessons, 194–195

N

Naif character type, 68
Name-calling, as comedy device, 91
Nancy Drew games
  character identification, 306–307
  characters, 225, 305
  concept art, 246
  current state of games, 297–298
  example, 201*f*
  exposition, 314–315
  icons, 223
  as interactive narrative, 294
  interface, 218
  as mystery subgenre, 296
  pace, 318–319
  screenshot, 219*f*

script format, 281
  special development documents,
    247
  structure, 313
  text/menus, 223–224
  writer of, 200, 206
  writer's flowchart, 220*f*
Narration, three-column script
    format, 287–289
Narrative
  classical linear elements, 298–302
  definition, 293–294
  elements in interactive media, 234
  story-driven simulations, 326–327
Narrative designer, 146, 147, 387
Narrative proposal, format, 276
Narrative treatment, sample, 276
National Association of Television
    Program Executives
    (NATPE), 109
NATPE, *see* National Association of
    Television Program Executives
    (NATPE)
The Nauticus Shipbuilding Company,
    275, 294
Navigate–move interactivity type, 183
Navigation
  interactive narrative, 273, 308–314
  Odd Todd web site, 378
  storytelling tools, 202–203
Navigation bars, as interactive
    devices, 223
NDA, *see* Non-disclosure agreement
    (NDA)
Negative stereotypes *vs.* classic
    comedy characters, 69–70
NERF, game definitions, 155
Networking
  digital storytelling careers,
    368–369
  for freelancing, 389
  looking for work, 135–136
  publishers/developers, 392–393
  TV animation careers, 118–119
Networks, interactive multimedia,
    212
Newell, Gabe, 310
Nickelodeon, pitching, 126–127
Nickelodeon Productions Writing
    Fellowship Program, 120
NIGHT, script format definitions, 13
Noles, Geoffrey, 377
Non-disclosure agreement (NDA),
    364, 365*f*
Non-game stories, 188–189

Nonhuman characters,
    characteristics, 73–74
Non-linear storyline
  example, 159*f*
  game design, 158–160
  "What if..." questions, 168
Nonplayer character (NPC)
  and AI, 151
  and avatars, 151–152
  character biographies, 255–256
  game definitions, 155
  game dialogue variables, 260
  interactive entertainment, 203
  interactive fiction, 189
  and interfaces, 173–174
  Max Payne example, 161
  player options, 307
  PVE, 156
  PVP, 156
  simulated conversations, 331–332
  spawning, 156
  stats, 157
  triggers, 157
  variables, 169
  waypoints, 157–158
  writing dialogue for, 259–265
Non sequitur, as comedy device, 92
NPCs, *see* Nonplayer character (NPC)

O

Objection!, 354
(O.C.)/OFF CAMERA, 16
Odd Todd website
  character, 375*f*
  cyber support, 377*b*
  maintenance and content,
    377–378
  overview, 375–378
  popularity, 376
O'Meara, Maria, 317
One-of-a-kind character type, 70
Online games, interfaces, 173
On model, definition, 26–27
Opposition
  games as storytelling tools, 192
  in games/drama, 187
The Oregon Trail, 217–218, 223
(O.S.)/OFFSTAGE, 10, 16, 16*b*
OTS (OVER THE SHOULDER), 16,
    16*b*
Our Gang, 95
Outline
  interactive narratives, 272–275
  Prudential Verani web site
    example, 273*b*

413

Index

Index

Index

Printed and bound by CPI Group (UK) Ltd, Croydon, CR0 4YY

21/10/2024

01777093-0007